INTERNATIONAL CLASSIFICATION OF GOODS AND SERVICES

FOR THE PURPOSES
OF THE REGISTRATION OF MARKS

(NICE CLASSIFICATION)

TENTH EDITION

PART I

WITH LIST OF GOODS AND SERVICES
IN ALPHABETICAL ORDER

WIPO
WORLD
INTELLECTUAL PROPERTY
ORGANIZATION

2011

WIPO PUBLICATION
No. 500.1E/10

ISBN 978-92-805-2023-1

CONTENTS

* * *

P R E F A C E

HISTORY AND PURPOSE OF THE NICE CLASSIFICATION

The *International (Nice) Classification of Goods and Services for the Purposes of the Registration of Marks* was established by an Agreement concluded at the Nice Diplomatic Conference, on June 15, 1957, was revised at Stockholm, in 1967, and at Geneva, in 1977, and was amended in 1979.

The countries party to the Nice Agreement constitute a Special Union within the framework of the *Paris Union for the Protection of Industrial Property*. They have adopted and apply the Nice Classification for the purposes of the registration of marks.

Each of the countries party to the Nice Agreement is obliged to apply the Nice Classification in connection with the registration of marks, either as the principal classification or as a subsidiary classification, and has to include in the official documents and publications relating to its registrations of marks the numbers of the classes of the Classification to which the goods or services for which the marks are registered belong.

Use of the Nice Classification is mandatory not only for the national registration of marks in countries party to the Nice Agreement, but also for the international registration of marks effected by the International Bureau of WIPO, under the *Madrid Agreement Concerning the International Registration of Marks* and under the *Protocol Relating to the Madrid Agreement Concerning the International Registration of Marks*, and for the registration of marks by the African Intellectual Property Organization (OAPI), by the African Regional Intellectual Property Organization (ARIPO), by the Benelux Organisation for Intellectual Property (BOIP) and by the European Union Office for Harmonization in the Internal Market (Trade Marks and Designs) (OHIM).

The Nice Classification is also applied in a number of countries not party to the Nice Agreement (see list on page (viii)).

REVISIONS OF THE NICE CLASSIFICATION

The Nice Classification is based on the Classification prepared by the *United International Bureaux for the Protection of Intellectual Property* (BIRPI) - predecessor of WIPO - in 1935. It was that Classification, consisting of a list of 34 classes and an alphabetical list of goods, that was adopted under the Nice Agreement and later expanded to embrace also eleven classes covering services and an alphabetical list of those services.

The Nice Agreement provides for the setting up of a Committee of Experts in which all countries party to the Agreement are represented. The Committee of Experts decides on all changes in the Classification, in particular the transfer of goods and services between various classes, the updating of the alphabetical list and the introduction of necessary explanatory notes.

The Committee of Experts has, since the entry into force of the Nice Agreement, on April 8, 1961, held 21 sessions and has, amongst its most noticeable achievements, undertaken a general review of the Alphabetical List of goods and services from the point of view of form (in the late 1970s); substantially modified the General Remarks, the Class Headings and the Explanatory Notes (in 1982); introduced a "basic number" for each single product or service in the Alphabetical List (in 1990), which number enables the user to find the equivalent product or service in the alphabetical lists of other language versions of the Classification; and revised Class 42 with the creation of Classes 43 to 45 (in 2000).

At its twenty-first session, held in November 2010, the Committee of Experts adopted changes to the ninth edition of the Nice Classification.

EDITIONS OF THE NICE CLASSIFICATION

The first edition of the Nice Classification was published in 1963, the second in 1971, the third in 1981, the fourth in 1983, the fifth in 1987, the sixth in 1992, the seventh in 1996, the eighth in 2001 and the ninth in 2006. This edition (the tenth), published in June 2011, will enter into force on January 1, 2012.

* * *

The authentic versions of the Nice Classification (English and French) are published by WIPO on paper and online. The paper version is published in two parts. Part I (this volume) lists, in alphabetical order, all the goods in one list and all the services in another list. Part II lists, in alphabetical order for each class, the goods or services belonging to that class. There is also a version with a bilingual (English/French) alphabetical list.

The tenth edition of the Nice Classification may be ordered from the World Intellectual Property Organization (WIPO), 34, chemin des Colombettes, P.O. Box 18, CH-1211 Geneva 20 or from the Electronic Bookshop on the website of WIPO at the following address: http://www.wipo.int/ebookshop.

Geneva, June 2011

COUNTRIES PARTY TO THE NICE AGREEMENT

(January 2011)

Albania
Algeria
Argentina
Armenia
Australia
Austria
Azerbaijan
Bahrain
Barbados
Belarus
Belgium
Benin
Bosnia and Herzegovina
Bulgaria
China
Croatia
Cuba
Czech Republic
Democratic People's Republic of Korea
Denmark
Dominica
Egypt
Estonia
Finland
France
Georgia
Germany
Greece
Guinea
Hungary
Iceland
Ireland
Israel
Italy
Jamaica
Japan
Jordan
Kazakhstan
Kyrgyzstan
Latvia
Lebanon
Liechtenstein
Lithuania
Luxembourg
Malawi
Malaysia
Mexico
Monaco
Mongolia
Montenegro
Morocco
Mozambique
Netherlands
Norway
Poland
Portugal
Republic of Korea
Republic of Moldova
Romania
Russian Federation
Saint Kitts and Nevis
Saint Lucia
Serbia
Singapore
Slovakia
Slovenia
Spain
Suriname
Sweden
Switzerland
Syrian Arab Republic
Tajikistan
The former Yugoslav Republic of Macedonia
Trinidad and Tobago
Tunisia
Turkey
Turkmenistan
Ukraine
United Kingdom
United Republic of Tanzania
United States of America
Uruguay
Uzbekistan

(Total: 83 countries)

OTHER COUNTRIES AND ORGANIZATIONS USING THE NICE CLASSIFICATION

(January 2011)

In addition to the 83 countries party to the Nice Agreement, listed on the previous page, the following 66 countries and four organizations also use the Nice Classification:[1] [2]

Angola
Antigua and Barbuda
Bangladesh
Bolivia
Botswana
Brazil
Burundi
Cambodia
Chile
Colombia
Costa Rica
Cyprus
Democratic Republic of the Congo
Djibouti
Ecuador
El Salvador
Ethiopia
Ghana
Guatemala
Guyana
Haiti
Honduras
India
Indonesia
Iran (Islamic Republic of)
Iraq
Kenya
Kuwait
Lesotho
Libya
Madagascar
Malta
Mauritius
Namibia
Nepal
Netherlands Antilles
New Zealand
Nicaragua
Nigeria
Pakistan
Panama
Paraguay
Peru
Philippines
Qatar
Rwanda
Saint Vincent and the Grenadines
Samoa
San Marino
Saudi Arabia
Seychelles
Sierra Leone
Solomon Islands
South Africa
Sri Lanka
Sudan
Swaziland
Thailand
Tonga
Uganda
United Arab Emirates
Venezuela
Viet Nam
Yemen
Zambia
Zimbabwe
African Intellectual Property Organization (OAPI)[1]
African Regional Intellectual Property Organization (ARIPO)[2]
Benelux Organisation for Intellectual Property (BOIP)
Office for Harmonization in the Internal Market (Trade Marks and Designs) (OHIM)

---

1 The following States are members of the African Intellectual Property Organization (OAPI) (January 2011): Benin (also party to the Nice Agreement), Burkina Faso, Cameroon, Central African Republic, Chad, Congo, Côte d'Ivoire, Equatorial Guinea, Gabon, Guinea (also party to the Nice Agreement), Guinea-Bissau, Mali, Mauritania, Niger, Senegal, Togo (16).

2 The following States are members of the African Regional Intellectual Property Organization (ARIPO) (January 2011): Botswana, Gambia, Ghana, Kenya, Lesotho, Liberia, Malawi (also party to the Nice Agreement), Mozambique (also party to the Nice Agreement), Namibia, Sierra Leone, Somalia, Sudan, Swaziland, Tanzania, Uganda, Zambia, Zimbabwe (17).

NICE AGREEMENT

CONCERNING THE INTERNATIONAL CLASSIFICATION OF GOODS AND SERVICES FOR THE PURPOSES OF THE REGISTRATION OF MARKS

of June 15, 1957,
as revised at Stockholm on July 14, 1967, and at Geneva on May 13, 1977,
and as amended at Geneva on September 28, 1979

Article 1

Establishment of a Special Union; Adoption of an International Classification; Definition and Languages of the Classification

(1) The countries to which this Agreement applies constitute a Special Union and adopt a common classification of goods and services for the purposes of the registration of marks (hereinafter designated as "the Classification").

(2) The Classification consists of:

(i) a list of classes, together with, as the case may be, explanatory notes;

(ii) an alphabetical list of goods and services (hereinafter designated as "the alphabetical list") with an indication of the class into which each of the goods or services falls.

(3) The Classification comprises:

(i) the classification published in 1971 by the International Bureau of Intellectual Property (hereinafter designated as "the International Bureau") referred to in the Convention Establishing the World Intellectual Property Organization, it being understood, however, that the explanatory notes to the list of classes included in that publication shall be regarded as provisional and as recommendations until such time as explanatory notes to the list of classes are established by the Committee of Experts referred to in Article 3;

(ii) the amendments and additions which have entered into force, pursuant to Article 4(1) of the Nice Agreement of June 15, 1957, and of the Stockholm Act of July 14, 1967, of that Agreement, prior to the entry into force of the present Act;

(iii) any changes to be made in accordance with Article 3 of this Act and which enter into force pursuant to Article 4(1) of this Act.

(4) The Classification shall be in the English and French languages, both texts being equally authentic.

(5)(a) The classification referred to in paragraph (3)(i), together with those amendments and additions referred to in paragraph (3)(ii) which have entered into force prior to the date this Act is opened for signature, is contained in one authentic copy, in the French language, deposited with the Director General of the World Intellectual Property Organization (hereinafter designated respectively "the Director General" and "the Organization"). Those amendments and additions referred to in paragraph (3)(ii) which enter into force after the date this Act is opened for signature shall also be deposited in one authentic copy, in the French language, with the Director General.

(b) The English version of the texts referred to in subparagraph (a) shall be established by the Committee of Experts referred to in Article 3 promptly after the entry into force of this Act. Its authentic copy shall be deposited with the Director General.

(c) The changes referred to in paragraph (3)(iii) shall be deposited in one authentic copy, in the English and French languages, with the Director General.

(6) Official texts of the Classification, in Arabic, German, Italian, Portuguese, Russian, Spanish and in such other languages as the Assembly referred to in Article 5 may designate, shall be established by the Director General, after consultation with the interested Governments and either on the basis of a translation submitted by those Governments or by any other means which do not entail financial implications for the budget of the Special Union or for the Organization.

(7) The alphabetical list shall mention, opposite each indication of goods or services, a serial number that is specific to the language in which the said list is established, together with:

(i) in the case of the alphabetical list established in English, the serial number mentioned in respect of the same indication in the alphabetical list established in French, and vice versa;

(ii) in the case of any alphabetical list established pursuant to paragraph (6), the serial number mentioned in respect of the same indication in the alphabetical list established in English or in the alphabetical list established in French.

Article 2

Legal Effect and Use of the Classification

(1) Subject to the requirements prescribed by this Agreement, the effect of the Classification shall be that attributed to it by each country of the Special Union. In particular, the Classification shall not bind the countries of the Special Union in respect of either the evaluation of the extent of the protection afforded to any given mark or the recognition of service marks.

(2) Each of the countries of the Special Union reserves the right to use the Classification either as a principal or as a subsidiary system.

(3) The competent Offices of the countries of the Special Union shall include in the official documents and publications relating to registrations of marks the numbers of the classes of the Classification to which the goods or services for which the mark is registered belong.

(4) The fact that a term is included in the alphabetical list in no way affects any rights which might subsist in such a term.

Article 3

Committee of Experts

(1) A Committee of Experts shall be set up in which each country of the Special Union shall be represented.

(2)(a) The Director General may, and, if requested by the Committee of Experts, shall, invite countries outside the Special Union which are members of the Organization or party to the Paris Convention for the Protection of Industrial Property to be represented by observers at meetings of the Committee of Experts.

(b) The Director General shall invite intergovernmental organizations specialized in the field of marks, of which at least one of the member countries is a country of the Special Union, to be represented by observers at meetings of the Committee of Experts.

(c) The Director General may, and, if requested by the Committee of Experts, shall, invite representatives of other intergovernmental organizations and international non-governmental organizations to participate in discussions of interest to them.

(3) The Committee of Experts shall:

(i) decide on changes in the Classification;

(ii) address recommendations to the countries of the Special Union for the purpose of facilitating the use of the Classification and promoting its uniform application;

(iii) take all other measures which, without entailing financial implications for the budget of the Special Union or for the Organization, contribute towards facilitating the application of the Classification by developing countries;

(iv) have the right to establish subcommittees and working groups.

(4) The Committee of Experts shall adopt its own rules of procedure. The latter shall provide for the possibility of participation in meetings of the subcommittees and working groups of the Committee of Experts by those intergovernmental organizations referred to in paragraph (2)(b) which can make a substantial contribution to the development of the Classification.

(5) Proposals for changes in the Classification may be made by the competent Office of any country of the Special Union, the International Bureau, any intergovernmental organization represented in the Committee of Experts pursuant to paragraph (2)(b) and any country or organization specially invited by the Committee of Experts to submit such proposals. The proposals shall be communicated to the International Bureau, which shall submit them to the members of the Committee of Experts and to the observers not later than two months before the session of the Committee of Experts at which the said proposals are to be considered.

(6) Each country of the Special Union shall have one vote.

(7)(a) Subject to subparagraph (b), the decisions of the Committee of Experts shall require a simple majority of the countries of the Special Union represented and voting.

(b) Decisions concerning the adoption of amendments to the Classification shall require a majority of four-fifths of the countries of the Special Union represented and voting. "Amendment" shall mean any transfer of goods or services from one class to another or the creation of any new class.

(c) The rules of procedure referred to in paragraph (4) shall provide that, except in special cases, amendments to the Classification shall be adopted at the end of specified periods; the length of each period shall be determined by the Committee of Experts.

(8) Abstentions shall not be considered as votes.

Article 4

Notification, Entry into Force and Publication of Changes

(1) Changes decided upon by the Committee of Experts and recommendations of the Committee of Experts shall be notified to the competent Offices of the countries of the Special Union by the International Bureau. Amendments shall enter into force six months after the date of dispatch of the notification. Any other change shall enter into force on a date to be specified by the Committee of Experts at the time the change is adopted.

(2) The International Bureau shall incorporate in the Classification the changes which have entered into force. Announcements of those changes shall be published in such periodicals as may be designated by the Assembly referred to in Article 5.

Article 5

Assembly of the Special Union

(1)(a) The Special Union shall have an Assembly consisting of those countries which have ratified or acceded to this Act.

(b) The Government of each country shall be represented by one delegate, who may be assisted by alternate delegates, advisors, and experts.

(c) The expenses of each delegation shall be borne by the Government which has appointed it.

(2)(a) Subject to the provisions of Articles 3 and 4, the Assembly shall:

(i) deal with all matters concerning the maintenance and development of the Special Union and the implementation of this Agreement;

(ii) give directions to the International Bureau concerning the preparation for conferences of revision, due account being taken of any comments made by those countries of the Special Union which have not ratified or acceded to this Act;

(iii) review and approve the reports and activities of the Director General of the Organization (hereinafter designated as “the Director General”) concerning the Special Union, and give him all necessary instructions concerning matters within the competence of the Special Union;

(iv) determine the program and adopt the biennial budget of the Special Union, and approve its final accounts;

(v) adopt the financial regulations of the Special Union;

(vi) establish, in addition to the Committee of Experts referred to in Article 3, such other committees of experts and working groups as it may deem necessary to achieve the objectives of the Special Union;

(vii) determine which countries not members of the Special Union and which intergovernmental and international non-governmental organizations shall be admitted to its meetings as observers;

(viii) adopt amendments to Articles 5 to 8;

(ix) take any other appropriate action designed to further the objectives of the Special Union;

(x) perform such other functions as are appropriate under this Agreement.

(b) With respect to matters which are of interest also to other Unions administered by the Organization, the Assembly shall make its decisions after having heard the advice of the Coordination Committee of the Organization.

(3)(a) Each country member of the Assembly shall have one vote.

(b) One-half of the countries members of the Assembly shall constitute a quorum.

(c) Notwithstanding the provisions of subparagraph (b), if, in any session, the number of countries represented is less than one-half but equal to or more than one-third of the countries members of the Assembly, the Assembly may make decisions but, with the exception of decisions concerning its own procedure, all such decisions shall take effect only if the conditions set forth hereinafter are fulfilled. The International Bureau shall communicate the said decisions to the countries members of the Assembly which were not represented and shall invite them to express in writing their vote or abstention within a period of three months from the date of the communication. If, at the expiration of this period, the number of countries having thus expressed their vote or abstention attains the number of countries which was lacking for attaining the quorum in the session itself, such decisions shall take effect provided that at the same time the required majority still obtains.

(d) Subject to the provisions of Article 8(2), the decisions of the Assembly shall require two-thirds of the votes cast.

(e) Abstentions shall not be considered as votes.

(f) A delegate may represent, and vote in the name of, one country only.

(g) Countries of the Special Union not members of the Assembly shall be admitted to the meetings of the latter as observers.

(4)(a) The Assembly shall meet once in every second calendar year in ordinary session upon convocation by the Director General and, in the absence of exceptional circumstances, during the same period and at the same place as the General Assembly of the Organization.

(b) The Assembly shall meet in extraordinary session upon convocation by the Director General, at the request of one-fourth of the countries members of the Assembly.

(c) The agenda of each session shall be prepared by the Director General.

(5) The Assembly shall adopt its own rules of procedure.

Article 6

International Bureau

(1)(a) Administrative tasks concerning the Special Union shall be performed by the International Bureau.

(b) In particular, the International Bureau shall prepare the meetings and provide the secretariat of the Assembly, the Committee of Experts, and such other committees of experts and working groups as may have been established by the Assembly or the Committee of Experts.

(c) The Director General shall be the chief executive of the Special Union and shall represent the Special Union.

(2) The Director General and any staff member designated by him shall participate, without the right to vote, in all meetings of the Assembly, the Committee of Experts, and such other committees of experts or working groups as may have been established by the Assembly or the Committee of Experts. The Director General, or a staff member designated by him, shall be ex officio secretary of those bodies.

(3)(a) The International Bureau shall, in accordance with the directions of the Assembly, make the preparations for the conferences of revision of the provisions of the Agreement other than Articles 5 to 8.

(b) The International Bureau may consult with intergovernmental and international non-governmental organizations concerning preparations for conferences of revision.

(c) The Director General and persons designated by him shall take part, without the right to vote, in the discussions at those conferences.

(4) The International Bureau shall carry out any other tasks assigned to it.

Article 7

Finances

(1)(a) The Special Union shall have a budget.

(b) The budget of the Special Union shall include the income and expenses proper to the Special Union, its contribution to the budget of expenses common to the Unions, and, where applicable, the sum made available to the budget of the Conference of the Organization.

(c) Expenses not attributable exclusively to the Special Union but also to one or more other Unions administered by the Organization shall be considered as expenses common to the Unions. The share of the Special Union in such common expenses shall be in proportion to the interest the Special Union has in them.

(2) The budget of the Special Union shall be established with due regard to the requirements of coordination with the budgets of the other Unions administered by the Organization.

(3) The budget of the Special Union shall be financed from the following sources:

(i) contributions of the countries of the Special Union;

(ii) fees and charges due for services rendered by the International Bureau in relation to the Special Union;

(iii) sale of, or royalties on, the publications of the International Bureau concerning the Special Union;

(iv) gifts, bequests, and subventions;

(v) rents, interests, and other miscellaneous income.

(4)(a) For the purpose of establishing its contribution referred to in paragraph (3)(i), each country of the Special Union shall belong to the same class as it belongs to in the Paris Union for the Protection of Industrial Property, and shall pay its annual contributions on the basis of the same number of units as is fixed for that class in that Union.

(b) The annual contribution of each country of the Special Union shall be an amount in the same proportion to the total sum to be contributed to the budget of the Special Union by all countries as the number of its units is to the total of the units of all contributing countries.

(c) Contributions shall become due on the first of January of each year.

(d) A country which is in arrears in the payment of its contributions may not exercise its right to vote in any organ of the Special Union if the amount of its arrears equals or exceeds the amount of the contributions due from it for the preceding two full years. However, any organ of the Special Union may allow such a country to continue to exercise its right to vote in that organ if, and as long as, it is satisfied that the delay in payment is due to exceptional and unavoidable circumstances.

(e) If the budget is not adopted before the beginning of a new financial period, it shall be at the same level as the budget of the previous year, as provided in the financial regulations.

(5) The amount of the fees and charges due for services rendered by the International Bureau in relation to the Special Union shall be established, and shall be reported to the Assembly, by the Director General.

(6)(a) The Special Union shall have a working capital fund which shall be constituted by a single payment made by each country of the Special Union. If the fund becomes insufficient, the Assembly shall decide to increase it.

(b) The amount of the initial payment of each country to the said fund or of its participation in the increase thereof shall be a proportion of the contribution of that country for the year in which the fund is established or the decision to increase it is made.

(c) The proportion and the terms of payment shall be fixed by the Assembly on the proposal of the Director General and after it has heard the advice of the Coordination Committee of the Organization.

(7)(a) In the headquarters agreement concluded with the country on the territory of which the Organization has its headquarters, it shall be provided that, whenever the working capital fund is insufficient, such country shall grant advances. The amount of those advances and the conditions on which they are granted shall be the subject of separate agreements, in each case, between such country and the Organization.

(b) The country referred to in subparagraph (a) and the Organization shall each have the right to denounce the obligation to grant advances, by written notification. Denunciation shall take effect three years after the end of the year in which it has been notified.

(8) The auditing of the accounts shall be effected by one or more of the countries of the Special Union or by external auditors, as provided in the financial regulations. They shall be designated, with their agreement, by the Assembly.

Article 8

Amendment of Articles 5 to 8

(1) Proposals for the amendment of Articles 5, 6, 7, and the present Article, may be initiated by any country member of the Assembly, or by the Director General. Such proposals shall be communicated by the Director General to the member countries of the Assembly at least six months in advance of their consideration by the Assembly.

(2) Amendments to the Articles referred to in paragraph (1) shall be adopted by the Assembly. Adoption shall require three-fourths of the votes cast, provided that any amendment to Article 5, and to the present paragraph, shall require four-fifths of the votes cast.

(3) Any amendment to the Articles referred to in paragraph (1) shall enter into force one month after written notifications of acceptance, effected in accordance with their respective constitutional processes, have been received by the Director General from three-fourths of the countries members of the Assembly at the time it adopted the amendment. Any amendment to the said Articles thus accepted shall bind all the countries which are members of the Assembly at the time the amendment enters into force, or which become members thereof at a subsequent date, provided that any amendment increasing the financial obligations of countries of the Special Union shall bind only those countries which have notified their acceptance of such amendment.

Article 9

Ratification and Accession; Entry into Force

(1) Any country of the Special Union which has signed this Act may ratify it, and, if it has not signed it, may accede to it.

(2) Any country outside the Special Union which is party to the Paris Convention for the Protection of Industrial Property may accede to this Act and thereby become a country of the Special Union.

(3) Instruments of ratification and accession shall be deposited with the Director General.

(4)(a) This Act shall enter into force three months after both of the following conditions are fulfilled:

(i) six or more countries have deposited their instruments of ratification or accession;

(ii) at least three of the said countries are countries which, on the date this Act is opened for signature, are countries of the Special Union.

(b) The entry into force referred to in subparagraph (a) shall apply to those countries which, at least three months before the said entry into force, have deposited instruments of ratification or accession.

(c) With respect to any country not covered by subparagraph (b), this Act shall enter into force three months after the date on which its ratification or accession was notified by the Director General, unless a subsequent date has been indicated in the instrument of ratification or accession. In the latter case, this Act shall enter into force with respect to that country on the date thus indicated.

(5) Ratification or accession shall automatically entail acceptance of all the clauses and admission to all the advantages of this Act.

(6) After the entry into force of this Act, no country may ratify or accede to an earlier Act of this Agreement.

Article 10

Duration

This Agreement shall have the same duration as the Paris Convention for the Protection of Industrial Property.

Article 11

Revision

(1) This Agreement may be revised from time to time by a conference of the countries of the Special Union.

(2) The convocation of any revision conference shall be decided upon by the Assembly.

(3) Articles 5 to 8 may be amended either by a revision conference or according to Article 8.

Article 12

Denunciation

(1) Any country may denounce this Act by notification addressed to the Director General. Such denunciation shall constitute also denunciation of the earlier Act or Acts of this Agreement which the country denouncing this Act may have ratified or acceded to, and shall affect only the country making it, the Agreement remaining in full force and effect as regards the other countries of the Special Union.

(2) Denunciation shall take effect one year after the day on which the Director General has received the notification.

(3) The right of denunciation provided by this Article shall not be exercised by any country before the expiration of five years from the date upon which it becomes a country of the Special Union.

Article 13

Reference to Article 24 of the Paris Convention

The provisions of Article 24 of the Stockholm Act of 1967 of the Paris Convention for the Protection of Industrial Property shall apply to this Agreement, provided that, if those provisions are amended in the future, the latest amendment shall apply to this Agreement with respect to those countries of the Special Union which are bound by such amendment.

Article 14

Signature; Languages; Depositary Functions; Notifications

(1)(a) This Act shall be signed in a single original in the English and French languages, both texts being equally authentic, and shall be deposited with the Director General.

(b) Official texts of this Act shall be established by the Director General, after consultation with the interested Governments and within two months from the date of signature of this Act, in the two other languages, Russian and Spanish, in which, together with the languages referred to in subparagraph (a), authentic texts of the Convention Establishing the World Intellectual Property Organization were signed.

(c) Official texts of this Act shall be established by the Director General, after consultation with the interested Governments, in the Arabic, German, Italian and Portuguese languages, and such other languages as the Assembly may designate.

(2) This Act shall remain open for signature until December 31, 1977.

(3)(a) The Director General shall transmit two copies, certified by him, of the signed text of this Act to the Governments of all countries of the Special Union and, on request, to the Government of any other country.

(b) The Director General shall transmit two copies, certified by him, of any amendment to this Act to the Governments of all countries of the Special Union and, on request, to the Government of any other country.

(4) The Director General shall register this Act with the Secretariat of the United Nations.

(5) The Director General shall notify the Governments of all countries party to the Paris Convention for the Protection of Industrial Property of:

(i) signatures under paragraph (1);

(ii) deposits of instruments of ratification or accession under Article 9(3);

(iii) the date of entry into force of this Act under Article 9(4)(a);

(iv) acceptances of amendments to this Act under Article 8(3);

(v) the dates on which such amendments enter into force;

(vi) denunciations received under Article 12.

* * *

MADRID AGREEMENT

CONCERNING THE INTERNATIONAL REGISTRATION OF MARKS[3]

of April 14, 1891,
as revised at Stockholm on July 14, 1967, and as amended at Geneva on September 28, 1979

(extracts)

Article 3

[Contents of Application for International Registration]

(2) The applicant must indicate the goods or services in respect of which protection of the mark is claimed and also, if possible, the corresponding class or classes according to the classification established by the Nice Agreement Concerning the International Classification of Goods and Services for the Purposes of the Registration of Marks. If the applicant does not give such indication, the International Bureau shall classify the goods or services in the appropriate classes of the said classification. The indication of classes given by the applicant shall be subject to control by the International Bureau, which shall exercise the said control in association with the national Office. In the event of disagreement between the national Office and the International Bureau, the opinion of the latter shall prevail.

Article 4

[Effects of International Registration]

(1) From the date of the registration so effected at the International Bureau in accordance with the provisions of Articles 3 and 3*ter*, the protection of the mark in each of the contracting countries concerned shall be the same as if the mark had been filed therein direct. The indication of classes of goods or services provided for in Article 3 shall not bind the contracting countries with regard to the determination of the scope of the protection of the mark.

[3] On January 31, 2011, the following countries were party to this Agreement: Albania, Algeria, Armenia, Austria, Azerbaijan, Belarus, Belgium, Bhutan, Bosnia and Herzegovina, Bulgaria, China, Croatia, Cuba, Cyprus, Czech Republic, Democratic People's Republic of Korea, Egypt, France, Germany, Hungary, Iran (Islamic Republic of), Italy, Kazakhstan, Kenya, Kyrgyzstan, Latvia, Lesotho, Liberia, Liechtenstein, Luxembourg, Monaco, Mongolia, Montenegro, Morocco, Mozambique, Namibia, Netherlands, Poland, Portugal, Republic of Moldova, Romania, Russian Federation, San Marino, Serbia, Sierra Leone, Slovakia, Slovenia, Spain, Sudan, Swaziland, Switzerland, Syrian Arab Republic, Tajikistan, The former Yugoslav Republic of Macedonia, Ukraine, Viet Nam (56).

Article 5

[Refusal by National Offices]

(1) In countries where the legislation so authorizes, Offices notified by the International Bureau of the registration of a mark or of a request for extension of protection made in accordance with Article 3*ter* shall have the right to declare that protection cannot be granted to such mark in their territory. Any such refusal can be based only on the grounds which would apply, under the Paris Convention for the Protection of Industrial Property, in the case of a mark filed for national registration. However, protection may not be refused, even partially, by reason only that national legislation would not permit registration except in a limited number of classes or for a limited number of goods or services.

Article 7

[Renewal of International Registration]

(2) Renewal may not include any change in relation to the previous registration in its latest form.

(3) The first renewal effected under the provisions of the Nice Act of June 15, 1957, or of this Act, shall include an indication of the classes of the International Classification to which the registration relates.

Article 8

[National Fee. International Fee. Division of Excess Receipts, Supplementary Fees, and Complementary Fees]

(2) Registration of a mark at the International Bureau shall be subject to the advance payment of an international fee which shall include:

(a) a basic fee;

(b) a supplementary fee for each class of the International Classification, beyond three, into which the goods or services to which the mark is applied will fall;

(c) a complementary fee for any request for extension of protection under Article 3*ter*.

(3) However, the supplementary fee specified in paragraph (2)(b) may, without prejudice to the date of registration, be paid within a period fixed by the Regulations if the number of classes of goods or services has been fixed or disputed by the International Bureau. If, upon expiration of the said period, the supplementary fee has not been paid or the list of goods or services has not been reduced to the required extent by the applicant, the application for international registration shall be deemed to have been abandoned.

Article 9

[Changes in National Registers also Affecting International Registration. Reduction of List of Goods and Services Mentioned in International Registration. Additions to that List. Substitutions in that List]

(1) The Office of the country of the person in whose name the international registration stands shall likewise notify the International Bureau of all annulments, cancellations, renunciations, transfers, and other changes made in the entry of the mark in the national register, if such changes also affect the international registration.

(2) The Bureau shall record those changes in the International Register, shall notify them in turn to the Offices of the contracting countries, and shall publish them in its journal.

(3) A similar procedure shall be followed when the person in whose name the international registration stands requests a reduction of the list of goods or services to which the registration applies.

(4) Such transactions may be subject to a fee, which shall be fixed by the Regulations.

(5) The subsequent addition of new goods or services to the said list can be obtained only by filing a new application as prescribed in Article 3.

(6) The substitution of one of the goods or services for another shall be treated as an addition.

Article 10

[Assembly of the Special Union]

(2)(a) The Assembly shall:

(iii) modify the Regulations, including the fixation of the amounts of the fees referred to in Article 8(2) and other fees relating to international registration.

* * *

PROTOCOL

RELATING TO THE MADRID AGREEMENT CONCERNING THE INTERNATIONAL REGISTRATION OF MARKS[4]

adopted at Madrid on June 27, 1989

(extracts)

Article 3

International Application

(2) The applicant must indicate the goods and services in respect of which protection of the mark is claimed and also, if possible, the corresponding class or classes according to the classification established by the Nice Agreement Concerning the International Classification of Goods and Services for the Purposes of the Registration of Marks. If the applicant does not give such indication, the International Bureau shall classify the goods and services in the appropriate classes of the said classification. The indication of classes given by the applicant shall be subject to control by the International Bureau, which shall exercise the said control in association with the Office of origin. In the event of disagreement between the said Office and the International Bureau, the opinion of the latter shall prevail.

Article 4

Effects of International Registration

(1)(a) From the date of the registration or recordal effected in accordance with the provisions of Articles 3 and 3*ter*, the protection of the mark in each of the Contracting Parties concerned shall be the same as if the mark had been deposited direct with the Office of that Contracting Party. If no refusal has been notified to the International Bureau in accordance with Article 5(1) and (2) or if a refusal notified in accordance with the said Article has been

4 On January 31, 2011, the following States and intergovernmental organization were party to this Protocol: Albania, Antigua and Barbuda, Armenia, Australia, Austria, Azerbaijan, Bahrain, Belarus, Belgium, Bhutan, Bosnia and Herzegovina, Botswana, Bulgaria, China, Croatia, Cuba, Cyprus, Czech Republic, Democratic People's Republic of Korea, Denmark, Egypt, Estonia, European Union, Finland, France, Georgia, Germany, Ghana, Greece, Hungary, Iceland, Iran (Islamic Republic of), Ireland, Israel, Italy, Japan, Kazakhstan, Kenya, Kyrgyzstan, Latvia, Lesotho, Liberia, Liechtenstein, Lithuania, Luxembourg, Madagascar, Monaco, Mongolia, Montenegro, Morocco, Mozambique, Namibia, Netherlands, Norway, Oman, Poland, Portugal, Republic of Korea, Republic of Moldova, Romania, Russian Federation, San Marino, Sao Tome and Principe, Serbia, Sierra Leone, Singapore, Slovakia, Slovenia, Spain, Sudan, Swaziland, Sweden, Switzerland, Syrian Arab Republic, The former Yugoslav Republic of Macedonia, Turkey, Turkmenistan, Ukraine, United Kingdom, United States of America, Uzbekistan, Viet Nam, Zambia (83).

withdrawn subsequently, the protection of the mark in the Contracting Party concerned shall, as from the said date, be the same as if the mark had been registered by the Office of that Contracting Party.

(b) The indication of classes of goods and services provided for in Article 3 shall not bind the Contracting Parties with regard to the determination of the scope of the protection of the mark.

Article 5

Refusal and Invalidation of Effects of International Registration in Respect of Certain Contracting Parties

(1) Where the applicable legislation so authorizes, any Office of a Contracting Party which has been notified by the International Bureau of an extension to that Contracting Party, under Article 3*ter*(1) or (2), of the protection resulting from the international registration shall have the right to declare in a notification of refusal that protection cannot be granted in the said Contracting Party to the mark which is the subject of such extension. Any such refusal can be based only on the grounds which would apply, under the Paris Convention for the Protection of Industrial Property, in the case of a mark deposited direct with the Office which notifies the refusal. However, protection may not be refused, even partially, by reason only that the applicable legislation would permit registration only in a limited number of classes or for a limited number of goods or services.

Article 8

Fees for International Application and Registration

(2) Registration of a mark at the International Bureau shall be subject to the advance payment of an international fee which shall, subject to the provisions of paragraph (7)(a), include,

(i) a basic fee;

(ii) a supplementary fee for each class of the International Classification, beyond three, into which the goods or services to which the mark is applied will fall;

(iii) a complementary fee for any request for extension of protection under Article 3*ter*.

(3) However, the supplementary fee specified in paragraph (2)(ii) may, without prejudice to the date of the international registration, be paid within the period fixed by the Regulations if the number of classes of goods or services has been fixed or disputed by the International Bureau. If, upon expiry of the said period, the supplementary fee has not been paid or the list of goods or services has not been reduced to the required extent by the applicant, the international application shall be deemed to have been abandoned.

Article 9

Recordal of Change in the Ownership of an International Registration

At the request of the person in whose name the international registration stands, or at the request of an interested Office made ex officio or at the request of an interested person, the International Bureau shall record in the International Register any change in the ownership of that registration, in respect of all or some of the Contracting Parties in whose territories the said registration has effect and in respect of all or some of the goods and services listed in the registration, provided that the new holder is a person who, under Article 2(1), is entitled to file international applications.

* * *

NICE CLASSIFICATION

GUIDANCE FOR THE USER

1. The class headings indicate in a general manner the fields to which the goods and services in principle belong.

2. For ascertaining the correct classification of each individual product or service, the Alphabetical List of goods and services and the Explanatory Notes, relating to the various classes, should be consulted. If a product or service cannot be classified with the aid of the List of Classes, the Explanatory Notes and the Alphabetical List, the General Remarks (see page 3, below) set forth the criteria that should be applied.

3. The Alphabetical List is reproduced in two sets of five columns on each page, which for each product or service indicates:

the first column:	the number of the class to which the product or service belongs;
the second column:	the serial number[5] of the indication of the product or service, in English;
the third column:	the indication of the product or service, in English;
the fourth column:	the serial number[5] of the indication of the product or service, in French;
the fifth column:	the basic number[5] of the indication of the product or service.

4. It should be noted that a given product or service may appear in the Alphabetical List in more than one place, i.e., the product or service is described with different indications, so-called cross-references.

5. The fact that a general term is given in the Alphabetical List in relation to a particular class (covering certain goods or services) does not rule out the possibility of that term appearing also in connection with other classes (covering other goods or services), depending on the way in which the term is qualified. In such cases, the general term (e.g., Clothing, Paints) is marked with an asterisk in the Alphabetical List.

6. In the Alphabetical List, an expression between square brackets is in most cases intended to define more precisely the text preceding the brackets, since the said text is ambiguous or too vague for classification purposes. Sometimes, the square brackets embrace the corresponding American expression of the text preceding the brackets, in most cases of which the expression is followed by "(Am.)".

7. In the Alphabetical List, an expression between round brackets may constitute a different indication of the product or service in question, which in that case also is listed (a so-called cross-reference) in its appropriate place in the Alphabetical List. In other cases, an expression between round brackets may begin with a general term (e.g., apparatus, conducting, machines) under which the product or service cannot be listed in the Alphabetical List. The text preceding the round brackets is considered the most important part of the indication of the product or service in question, and is replaced within the brackets by "–".

[5] While the serial number of a given product or service is specific to each language version of the Classification, its basic number is the same for every language version of the Classification that has been published by, or in collaboration with, WIPO. The basic number enables the user of the Classification to find the equivalent product or service in the alphabetical lists of other language versions of the Classification.

8. For the purposes of the registration of marks, it is highly recommended to use the indications appearing in the Alphabetical List when qualifying goods or services, avoiding using the vague expressions or the general terms, which are not sufficiently qualified.

9. The fact that a product or service indication figures in the Alphabetical List does not in any way prejudge the decisions of national industrial property offices as to the possibility of registering a mark for that product or service (see Article 2(1) of the Nice Agreement).

GENERAL REMARKS

The indications of goods or services appearing in the class headings are general indications relating to the fields to which, in principle, the goods or services belong. The Alphabetical List should therefore be consulted in order to ascertain the exact classification of each individual product or service.

GOODS

If a product cannot be classified with the aid of the List of Classes, the Explanatory Notes and the Alphabetical List, the following remarks set forth the criteria to be applied:

(a) A finished product is in principle classified according to its function or purpose. If the function or purpose of a finished product is not mentioned in any class heading, the finished product is classified by analogy with other comparable finished products, indicated in the Alphabetical List. If none is found, other subsidiary criteria, such as that of the material of which the product is made or its mode of operation, are applied.

(b) A finished product which is a multipurpose composite object (e.g., clocks incorporating radios) may be classified in all classes that correspond to any of its functions or intended purposes. If those functions or purposes are not mentioned in any class heading, other criteria, indicated under (a), above, are to be applied.

(c) Raw materials, unworked or semi-worked, are in principle classified according to the material of which they consist.

(d) Goods intended to form part of another product are in principle classified in the same class as that product only in cases where the same type of goods cannot normally be used for another purpose. In all other cases, the criterion indicated under (a), above, applies.

(e) When a product, whether finished or not, is classified according to the material of which it is made, and it is made of different materials, the product is in principle classified according to the material which predominates.

(f) Cases adapted to the product they are intended to contain are in principle classified in the same class as the product.

SERVICES

If a service cannot be classified with the aid of the List of Classes, the Explanatory Notes and the Alphabetical List, the following remarks set forth the criteria to be applied:

(a) Services are in principle classified according to the branches of activities specified in the headings of the service classes and in their Explanatory Notes or, if not specified, by analogy with other comparable services indicated in the Alphabetical List.

(b) Rental services are in principle classified in the same classes as the services provided by means of the rented objects (e.g., Rental of telephones, covered by Class 38). Leasing services are analogous to rental services and therefore should be classified in the same way. However, hire- or lease-purchase financing is classified in Class 36 as a financial service.

(c) Services that provide advice, information or consultation are in principle classified in the same classes as the services that correspond to the subject matter of the advice, information or consultation, e.g., transportation consultancy (Cl. 39), business management consultancy (Cl. 35), financial consultancy (Cl. 36), beauty consultancy (Cl. 44). The rendering of the advice, information or consultancy by electronic means (e.g., telephone, computer) does not affect the classification of these services.

(d) Services rendered in the framework of franchising are in principle classified in the same class as the particular services provided by the franchisor (e.g., business advice relating to franchising (Class 35), financing services relating to franchising (Class 36), legal services relating to franchising (Class 45)).

CLASS HEADINGS

GOODS

Class 1 Chemicals used in industry, science and photography, as well as in agriculture, horticulture and forestry; unprocessed artificial resins, unprocessed plastics; manures; fire extinguishing compositions; tempering and soldering preparations; chemical substances for preserving foodstuffs; tanning substances; adhesives used in industry

Class 2 Paints, varnishes, lacquers; preservatives against rust and against deterioration of wood; colorants; mordants; raw natural resins; metals in foil and powder form for painters, decorators, printers and artists

Class 3 Bleaching preparations and other substances for laundry use; cleaning, polishing, scouring and abrasive preparations; soaps; perfumery, essential oils, cosmetics, hair lotions; dentifrices

Class 4 Industrial oils and greases; lubricants; dust absorbing, wetting and binding compositions; fuels (including motor spirit) and illuminants; candles and wicks for lighting

Class 5 Pharmaceutical and veterinary preparations; sanitary preparations for medical purposes; dietetic food and substances adapted for medical or veterinary use, food for babies; dietary supplements for humans and animals; plasters, materials for dressings; material for stopping teeth, dental wax; disinfectants; preparations for destroying vermin; fungicides, herbicides

Class 6 Common metals and their alloys; metal building materials; transportable buildings of metal; materials of metal for railway tracks; non-electric cables and wires of common metal; ironmongery, small items of metal hardware; pipes and tubes of metal; safes; goods of common metal not included in other classes; ores

Class 7 Machines and machine tools; motors and engines (except for land vehicles); machine coupling and transmission components (except for land vehicles); agricultural implements other than hand-operated; incubators for eggs; automatic vending machines

Class 8 Hand tools and implements (hand-operated); cutlery; side arms; razors

Class 9 Scientific, nautical, surveying, photographic, cinematographic, optical, weighing, measuring, signalling, checking (supervision), life-saving and teaching apparatus and instruments; apparatus and instruments for conducting, switching, transforming, accumulating, regulating or controlling electricity; apparatus for recording, transmission or reproduction of sound or images; magnetic data carriers, recording discs; compact discs, DVDs and other digital recording media; mechanisms for coin-operated apparatus; cash registers, calculating machines, data processing equipment, computers; computer software; fire-extinguishing apparatus

Class 10 Surgical, medical, dental and veterinary apparatus and instruments, artificial limbs, eyes and teeth; orthopedic articles; suture materials

Class 11 Apparatus for lighting, heating, steam generating, cooking, refrigerating, drying, ventilating, water supply and sanitary purposes

Class 12 Vehicles; apparatus for locomotion by land, air or water

Class 13 Firearms; ammunition and projectiles; explosives; fireworks

Class 14 Precious metals and their alloys and goods in precious metals or coated therewith, not included in other classes; jewellery, precious stones; horological and chronometric instruments

Class 15 Musical instruments

Class 16 Paper, cardboard and goods made from these materials, not included in other classes; printed matter; bookbinding material; photographs; stationery; adhesives for stationery or household purposes; artists' materials; paint brushes; typewriters and office requisites (except furniture); instructional and teaching material (except apparatus); plastic materials for packaging (not included in other classes); printers' type; printing blocks

Class 17 Rubber, gutta-percha, gum, asbestos, mica and goods made from these materials and not included in other classes; plastics in extruded form for use in manufacture; packing, stopping and insulating materials; flexible pipes, not of metal

Class 18 Leather and imitations of leather, and goods made of these materials and not included in other classes; animal skins, hides; trunks and travelling bags; umbrellas and parasols; walking sticks; whips, harness and saddlery

Class 19 Building materials (non-metallic); non-metallic rigid pipes for building; asphalt, pitch and bitumen; non-metallic transportable buildings; monuments, not of metal

Class 20 Furniture, mirrors, picture frames; goods (not included in other classes) of wood, cork, reed, cane, wicker, horn, bone, ivory, whalebone, shell, amber, mother-of-pearl, meerschaum and substitutes for all these materials, or of plastics

Class 21 Household or kitchen utensils and containers; combs and sponges; brushes (except paint brushes); brush-making materials; articles for cleaning purposes; steelwool; unworked or semi-worked glass (except glass used in building); glassware, porcelain and earthenware not included in other classes

Class 22 Ropes, string, nets, tents, awnings, tarpaulins, sails, sacks and bags (not included in other classes); padding and stuffing materials (except of rubber or plastics); raw fibrous textile materials

Class 23 Yarns and threads, for textile use

Class 24 Textiles and textile goods, not included in other classes; bed covers; table covers

Class 25 Clothing, footwear, headgear

Class 26 Lace and embroidery, ribbons and braid; buttons, hooks and eyes, pins and needles; artificial flowers

Class 27 Carpets, rugs, mats and matting, linoleum and other materials for covering existing floors; wall hangings (non-textile)

Class 28 Games and playthings; gymnastic and sporting articles not included in other classes; decorations for Christmas trees

Class 29 Meat, fish, poultry and game; meat extracts; preserved, frozen, dried and cooked fruits and vegetables; jellies, jams, compotes; eggs; milk and milk products; edible oils and fats

Class 30	Coffee, tea, cocoa and artificial coffee; rice; tapioca and sago; flour and preparations made from cereals; bread, pastry and confectionery; ices; sugar, honey, treacle; yeast, baking-powder; salt; mustard; vinegar, sauces (condiments); spices; ice
Class 31	Grains and agricultural, horticultural and forestry products not included in other classes; live animals; fresh fruits and vegetables; seeds; natural plants and flowers; foodstuffs for animals; malt
Class 32	Beers; mineral and aerated waters and other non-alcoholic beverages; fruit beverages and fruit juices; syrups and other preparations for making beverages
Class 33	Alcoholic beverages (except beers)
Class 34	Tobacco; smokers' articles; matches

SERVICES

Class 35	Advertising; business management; business administration; office functions
Class 36	Insurance; financial affairs; monetary affairs; real estate affairs
Class 37	Building construction; repair; installation services
Class 38	Telecommunications
Class 39	Transport; packaging and storage of goods; travel arrangement
Class 40	Treatment of materials
Class 41	Education; providing of training; entertainment; sporting and cultural activities
Class 42	Scientific and technological services and research and design relating thereto; industrial analysis and research services; design and development of computer hardware and software
Class 43	Services for providing food and drink; temporary accomodation
Class 44	Medical services; veterinary services; hygienic and beauty care for human beings or animals; agriculture, horticulture and forestry services
Class 45	Legal services; security services for the protection of property and individuals; personal and social services rendered by others to meet the needs of individuals

LIST OF CLASSES, WITH EXPLANATORY NOTES

GOODS

CLASS 1

Chemicals used in industry, science and photography, as well as in agriculture, horticulture and forestry;

unprocessed artificial resins, unprocessed plastics;

manures;

fire extinguishing compositions;

tempering and soldering preparations;

chemical substances for preserving foodstuffs;

tanning substances;

adhesives used in industry.

Explanatory Note

Class 1 includes mainly chemical products used in industry, science and agriculture, including those which go to the making of products belonging to other classes.

This Class includes, in particular:

- compost;
- salt for preserving other than for foodstuffs;
- certain additives for the food industry (consult the Alphabetical List of Goods).

This Class does not include, in particular:

- raw natural resins (Cl. 2);
- chemical products for use in medical science (Cl. 5);
- fungicides, herbicides and preparations for destroying vermin (Cl. 5);
- adhesives for stationery or household purposes (Cl. 16);
- salt for preserving foodstuffs (Cl. 30);
- straw mulch (Cl. 31).

CLASS 2

Paints, varnishes, lacquers;

preservatives against rust and against deterioration of wood;

colorants;

mordants;

raw natural resins;

metals in foil and powder form for painters, decorators, printers and artists.

Explanatory Note

Class 2 includes mainly paints, colorants and preparations used for the protection against corrosion.

This Class includes, in particular:

- paints, varnishes and lacquers for industry, handicrafts and arts;
- dyestuffs for clothing;
- colorants for foodstuffs and beverages.

This Class does not include, in particular:

- unprocessed artificial resins (Cl. 1);
- laundry blueing (Cl. 3);
- cosmetic dyes (Cl. 3);
- paint boxes (articles for use in school) (Cl. l6);
- insulating paints and varnishes (Cl. l7).

CLASS 3

Bleaching preparations and other substances for laundry use;

cleaning, polishing, scouring and abrasive preparations;

soaps;

perfumery, essential oils, cosmetics, hair lotions;

dentifrices.

Explanatory Note

Class 3 includes mainly cleaning preparations and toilet preparations.

This Class includes, in particular:

- deodorants for human beings or for animals;
- room fragrancing preparations;
- sanitary preparations being toiletries.

This Class does not include, in particular:

- chemical chimney cleaners (Cl. 1);
- degreasing preparations for use in manufacturing processes (Cl. 1);
- deodorants other than for human beings or for animals (Cl. 5);
- sharpening stones and grindstones (hand tools) (Cl. 8).

CLASS 4

Industrial oils and greases;

lubricants;

dust absorbing, wetting and binding compositions;

fuels (including motor spirit) and illuminants;

candles and wicks for lighting.

Explanatory Note

Class 4 includes mainly industrial oils and greases, fuels and illuminants.

This Class does not include, in particular:

- certain special industrial oils and greases (consult the Alphabetical List of Goods).

CLASS 5

Pharmaceutical and veterinary preparations;

sanitary preparations for medical purposes;

dietetic food and substances adapted for medical or veterinary use, food for babies;

dietary supplements for humans and animals;

plasters, materials for dressings;

material for stopping teeth, dental wax;

disinfectants;

preparations for destroying vermin;

fungicides, herbicides.

Explanatory Note

Class 5 includes mainly pharmaceuticals and other preparations for medical or veterinary purposes.

This Class includes, in particular:

- sanitary preparations for personal hygiene, other than toiletries;
- deodorants other than for human beings or for animals;
- dietary supplements, intended to supplement a normal diet or to have health benefits;

- meal replacements, dietetic food and beverages, adapted for medical or veterinary use;
- cigarettes without tobacco, for medical purposes.

This Class does not include, in particular:

- sanitary preparations being toiletries (Cl. 3);
- deodorants for human beings or for animals (Cl. 3);
- supportive bandages (Cl. 10);
- meal replacements, dietetic food and beverages not for medical or veterinary purposes (Cl. 29, 30, 31, 32 or 33).

CLASS 6

Common metals and their alloys;

metal building materials;

transportable buildings of metal;

materials of metal for railway tracks;

non-electric cables and wires of common metal;

ironmongery, small items of metal hardware;

pipes and tubes of metal;

safes;

goods of common metal not included in other classes;

ores.

Explanatory Note

Class 6 includes mainly unwrought and partly wrought common metals as well as simple products made of them.

This Class does not include, in particular:

- bauxite (Cl. 1);
- mercury, antimony, alkaline and alkaline-earth metals (Cl. 1);
- metals in foil and powder form for painters, decorators, printers and artists (Cl. 2).

CLASS 7

Machines and machine tools;

motors and engines (except for land vehicles);

machine coupling and transmission components (except for land vehicles);

agricultural implements other than hand-operated;

incubators for eggs;

automatic vending machines.

Explanatory Note

Class 7 includes mainly machines, machine tools, motors and engines.

This Class includes, in particular:

- parts of motors and engines (of all kinds);
- electric cleaning machines and apparatus.

This Class does not include, in particular:

- certain special machines and machine tools (consult the Alphabetical List of Goods);
- hand tools and implements, hand-operated (Cl. 8);
- motors and engines for land vehicles (Cl. 12).

CLASS 8

Hand tools and implements (hand-operated);

cutlery;

side arms;

razors.

Explanatory Note

Class 8 includes mainly hand-operated implements used as tools in the respective professions.

This Class includes, in particular:

- cutlery of precious metals;
- electric razors and clippers (hand instruments).

This Class does not include, in particular:

- certain special instruments (consult the Alphabetical List of Goods);
- machine tools and implements driven by a motor (Cl. 7);
- surgical cutlery (Cl. I0);
- side arms being firearms (Cl. 13);
- paper knives (Cl. 16);
- fencing weapons (Cl. 28).

CLASS 9

Scientific, nautical, surveying, photographic, cinematographic, optical, weighing, measuring, signalling, checking (supervision), life-saving and teaching apparatus and instruments; apparatus and instruments for conducting, switching, transforming, accumulating, regulating or controlling electricity;

apparatus for recording, transmission or reproduction of sound or images;

magnetic data carriers, recording discs;

compact discs, DVDs and other digital recording media;

mechanisms for coin-operated apparatus;

cash registers, calculating machines, data processing equipment, computers;

computer software;

fire-extinguishing apparatus.

Explanatory Note

This Class includes, in particular:

- apparatus and instruments for scientific research in laboratories;
- apparatus and instruments for controlling ships, such as apparatus and instruments for measuring and for transmitting orders;
- protractors;
- punched card office machines;
- all computer programs and software regardless of recording media or means of dissemination, that is, software recorded on magnetic media or downloaded from a remote computer network.

This Class does not include, in particular:

- the following electrical apparatus and instruments:
  - (a) electromechanical apparatus for the kitchen (grinders and mixers for foodstuffs, fruit presses, electrical coffee mills, etc.), and certain other apparatus and instruments driven by an electrical motor, all coming under Class 7;
  - (b) apparatus for pumping or dispensing fuels (Cl. 7);
  - (c) electric razors, clippers (hand instruments) and flat irons (Cl. 8);
  - (d) electrical apparatus for space heating or for the heating of liquids, for cooking, ventilating, etc. (Cl. 11);
  - (e) electric toothbrushes and combs (Cl. 21);
- clocks and watches and other chronometric instruments (Cl. 14);
- control clocks (Cl. 14);
- amusement and game apparatus adapted for use with an external display screen or monitor (Cl. 28).

CLASS 10

Surgical, medical, dental and veterinary apparatus and instruments, artificial limbs, eyes and teeth;

orthopedic articles;

suture materials.

Explanatory Note

Class 10 includes mainly medical apparatus, instruments and articles.

This Class includes, in particular:

- special furniture for medical use;
- hygienic rubber articles (consult the Alphabetical List of Goods);
- supportive bandages.

CLASS 11

Apparatus for lighting, heating, steam generating, cooking, refrigerating, drying, ventilating, water supply and sanitary purposes.

Explanatory Note

This Class includes, in particular:

- air conditioning apparatus;
- bedwarmers, hot water bottles, warming pans, electric or non-electric;
- electrically heated cushions (pads) and blankets, not for medical purposes;
- electric kettles;
- electric cooking utensils.

This Class does not include, in particular:

- steam producing apparatus (parts of machines) (Cl. 7);
- electrically heated clothing (Cl. 9).

CLASS 12

Vehicles;

apparatus for locomotion by land, air or water.

Explanatory Note

This Class includes, in particular:

- motors and engines for land vehicles;
- couplings and transmission components for land vehicles;
- air cushion vehicles.

This Class does not include, in particular:

- certain parts of vehicles (consult the Alphabetical List of Goods);
- railway material of metal (Cl. 6);
- motors, engines, couplings and transmission components other than for land vehicles (Cl. 7);
- parts of motors and engines (of all kinds) (Cl. 7).

CLASS 13

Firearms;

ammunition and projectiles;

explosives;

fireworks.

Explanatory Note

Class 13 includes mainly firearms and pyrotechnical products.

This Class does not include, in particular:

- matches (Cl. 34).

CLASS 14

Precious metals and their alloys and goods in precious metals or coated therewith, not included in other classes;

jewellery, precious stones;

horological and chronometric instruments.

Explanatory Note

Class 14 includes mainly precious metals, goods in precious metals not included in other classes and, in general jewellery, clocks and watches.

This Class includes, in particular:

- jewellery (i.e., imitation jewellery and jewellery of precious metal and stones);
- cuff links, tie pins.

This Class does not include, in particular:

- goods in precious metals classified according to their function or purpose, for example, metals in foil and powder form for painters, decorators, printers and artists (Cl. 2), amalgam of gold for dentists (Cl. 5), cutlery (Cl. 8), electric contacts (Cl. 9), pen nibs of gold (Cl. 16), teapots (Cl. 21), gold and silver embroidery (Cl. 26), cigar boxes (Cl. 34);
- objects of art not of precious metals (classified according to the material of which they consist).

CLASS 15

Musical instruments.

Explanatory Note

This Class includes, in particular:

- mechanical pianos and their accessories;
- musical boxes;
- electrical and electronic musical instruments.

This Class does not include, in particular:

- apparatus for the recording, transmission, amplification and reproduction of sound (Cl. 9).

CLASS 16

Paper, cardboard and goods made from these materials, not included in other classes;
printed matter;
bookbinding material;
photographs;
stationery;
adhesives for stationery or household purposes;
artists' materials;
paint brushes;
typewriters and office requisites (except furniture);
instructional and teaching material (except apparatus);
plastic materials for packaging (not included in other classes);
printers' type;
printing blocks.

Explanatory Note

Class 16 includes mainly paper, goods made from that material and office requisites.

This Class includes, in particular:

- paper knives;
- duplicators;
- plastic sheets, sacks and bags for wrapping and packaging.

This Class does not include, in particular:

- certain goods made of paper and cardboard (consult the Alphabetical List of Goods);
- colours (Cl. 2);
- hand tools for artists (for example, spatulas, sculptors' chisels) (Cl. 8).

CLASS 17

Rubber, gutta-percha, gum, asbestos, mica and goods made from these materials and not included in other classes;

plastics in extruded form for use in manufacture;

packing, stopping and insulating materials;

flexible pipes, not of metal.

Explanatory Note

Class 17 includes mainly electrical, thermal and acoustic insulating materials and plastics, being for use in manufacture in the form of sheets, blocks and rods.

This Class includes, in particular:

- rubber material for recapping tyres;
- padding and stuffing materials of rubber or plastics;
- floating anti-pollution barriers.

CLASS 18

Leather and imitations of leather, and goods made of these materials and not included in other classes;

animal skins, hides;

trunks and travelling bags;

umbrellas and parasols;

walking sticks;

whips, harness and saddlery.

Explanatory Note

Class 18 includes mainly leather, leather imitations, travel goods not included in other classes and saddlery.

This Class does not include, in particular:

- clothing, footwear, headgear (consult the Alphabetical List of Goods).

CLASS 19

Building materials (non-metallic);

non-metallic rigid pipes for building;

asphalt, pitch and bitumen;

non-metallic transportable buildings;

monuments, not of metal.

Explanatory Note

Class 19 includes mainly non-metallic building materials.

This Class includes, in particular:

- semi-worked woods (for example, beams, planks, panels);
- veneers;
- building glass (for example, floor slabs, glass tiles);
- glass granules for marking out roads;
- letter boxes of masonry.

This Class does not include, in particular:

- cement preservatives and cement-waterproofing preparations (Cl. 1);
- fireproofing preparations (Cl. 1).

CLASS 20

Furniture, mirrors, picture frames;

goods (not included in other classes) of wood, cork, reed, cane, wicker, horn, bone, ivory, whalebone, shell, amber, mother-of-pearl, meerschaum and substitutes for all these materials, or of plastics.

Explanatory Note

Class 20 includes mainly furniture and its parts and plastic goods, not included in other classes.

This Class includes, in particular:

- metal furniture and furniture for camping;
- bedding (for example, mattresses, spring mattresses, pillows);
- looking glasses and furnishing or toilet mirrors;
- registration number plates not of metal;
- letter boxes not of metal or masonry.

This Class does not include, in particular:

- certain special types of mirrors, classified according to their function or purpose (consult the Alphabetical List of Goods);
- special furniture for laboratories (Cl. 9);
- special furniture for medical use (Cl. 10);
- bedding linen (Cl. 24);
- eiderdowns (Cl. 24).

CLASS 21

Household or kitchen utensils and containers;

combs and sponges;

brushes (except paint brushes);

brush-making materials;

articles for cleaning purposes;

steelwool;

unworked or semi-worked glass (except glass used in building);

glassware, porcelain and earthenware not included in other classes.

Explanatory Note

Class 21 includes mainly small, hand-operated utensils and apparatus for household and kitchen use as well as toilet utensils, glassware and articles in porcelain.

This Class includes, in particular:

- utensils and containers for household and kitchen use, for example, kitchen utensils, pails, pans of iron, of aluminium, of plastics or of other materials, small hand-operated apparatus for mincing, grinding, pressing, etc.;
- electric combs;
- electric toothbrushes;
- dish stands and decanter stands.

This Class does not include, in particular:

- certain goods made of glass, porcelain and earthenware (consult the Alphabetical List of Goods);
- cleaning preparations, soaps, etc. (Cl. 3);
- small apparatus for mincing, grinding, pressing, etc., driven by electricity (Cl. 7);
- razors and shaving apparatus, clippers (hand instruments), metal implements and utensils for manicure and pedicure (Cl. 8);
- cooking utensils, electric (Cl. 11);
- toilet mirrors (Cl. 20).

CLASS 22

Ropes, string, nets, tents, awnings, tarpaulins, sails, sacks and bags (not included in other classes);

padding and stuffing materials (except of rubber or plastics);

raw fibrous textile materials.

Explanatory Note

Class 22 includes mainly rope and sail manufacture products, padding and stuffing materials and raw fibrous textile materials.

This Class includes, in particular:

- cords and twines in natural or artificial textile fibres, paper or plastics.

This Class does not include, in particular:

- certain nets, sacks and bags (consult the Alphabetical List of Goods);
- strings for musical instruments (Cl. 15).

CLASS 23

Yarns and threads, for textile use.

CLASS 24

Textiles and textile goods, not included in other classes;

bed covers;

table covers.

Explanatory Note

Class 24 includes mainly textiles (piece goods) and textile covers for household use.

This Class includes, in particular:

- bedding linen of paper.

This Class does not include, in particular:

- certain special textiles (consult the Alphabetical List of Goods);
- electrically heated blankets, for medical purposes (Cl. 10) and not for medical purposes (Cl. 11);
- table linen of paper (Cl. l6);
- horse blankets (Cl. 18).

CLASS 25

Clothing, footwear, headgear.

Explanatory Note

This Class does not include, in particular:

- certain clothing and footwear for special use (consult the Alphabetical List of Goods).

CLASS 26

Lace and embroidery, ribbons and braid;

buttons, hooks and eyes, pins and needles;

artificial flowers.

Explanatory Note

Class 26 includes mainly dressmakers' articles.

This Class includes, in particular:

- slide fasteners.

This Class does not include, in particular:

- certain special types of hooks (consult the Alphabetical List of Goods);
- certain special types of needles (consult the Alphabetical List of Goods);
- yarns and threads for textile use (Cl. 23).

CLASS 27

Carpets, rugs, mats and matting, linoleum and other materials for covering existing floors;

wall hangings (non-textile).

Explanatory Note

Class 27 includes mainly products intended to be added as furnishings to previously constructed floors and walls.

This Class does not include, in particular:

- wooden flooring (Cl. 19).

CLASS 28

Games and playthings;

gymnastic and sporting articles not included in other classes;

decorations for Christmas trees.

Explanatory Note

This Class includes, in particular:

- amusement and game apparatus adapted for use with an external display screen or monitor;
- fishing tackle;
- equipment for various sports and games.

This Class does not include, in particular:

- Christmas tree candles (Cl. 4);
- diving equipment (Cl. 9);
- electrical lamps (garlands) for Christmas trees (Cl. 11);
- fishing nets (Cl. 22);
- clothing for gymnastics and sports (Cl. 25);
- confectionery and chocolate decorations for Christmas trees (Cl. 30).

CLASS 29

Meat, fish, poultry and game;

meat extracts;

preserved, frozen, dried and cooked fruits and vegetables;

jellies, jams, compotes;

eggs;

milk and milk products;

edible oils and fats.

Explanatory Note

Class 29 includes mainly foodstuffs of animal origin as well as vegetables and other horticultural comestible products which are prepared for consumption or conservation.

This Class includes, in particular:

- milk beverages (milk predominating).

This Class does not include, in particular:

- certain foodstuffs of plant origin (consult the Alphabetical List of Goods);
- baby food (Cl. 5);
- dietetic food and substances adapted for medical use (Cl. 5);
- dietary supplements (Cl. 5);
- salad dressings (Cl. 30);
- fertilised eggs for hatching (Cl. 31);
- foodstuffs for animals (Cl. 31);
- live animals (Cl. 31).

CLASS 30

Coffee, tea, cocoa and artificial coffee;

rice;

tapioca and sago;

flour and preparations made from cereals;

bread, pastry and confectionery;

ices;

sugar, honey, treacle;

yeast, baking-powder;

salt;

mustard;

vinegar, sauces (condiments);

spices;

ice.

Explanatory Note

Class 30 includes mainly foodstuffs of plant origin prepared for consumption or conservation as well as auxiliaries intended for the improvement of the flavour of food.

This Class includes, in particular:

- beverages with coffee, cocoa, chocolate or tea base;
- cereals prepared for human consumption (for example, oat flakes and those made of other cereals).

This Class does not include, in particular:

- certain foodstuffs of plant origin (consult the Alphabetical List of Goods);
- salt for preserving other than for foodstuffs (Cl. 1);
- medicinal teas and dietetic food and substances adapted for medical use (Cl. 5);
- baby food (Cl. 5);
- dietary supplements (Cl. 5);
- raw cereals (Cl. 31);
- foodstuffs for animals (Cl. 31).

CLASS 31

Grains and agricultural, horticultural and forestry products not included in other classes;

live animals;

fresh fruits and vegetables;

seeds;

natural plants and flowers;

foodstuffs for animals;

malt.

Explanatory Note

Class 31 includes mainly land products not having been subjected to any form of preparation for consumption, live animals and plants as well as foodstuffs for animals.

This Class includes, in particular:

- raw woods;
- raw cereals;
- fertilised eggs for hatching;
- mollusca and crustacea (live).

This Class does not include, in particular:

- cultures of micro-organisms and leeches for medical purposes (Cl. 5);
- dietary supplements for animals (Cl. 5);
- semi-worked woods (Cl. 19);
- artificial fishing bait (Cl. 28);
- rice (Cl. 30);
- tobacco (Cl. 34).

CLASS 32

Beers;

mineral and aerated waters and other non-alcoholic beverages;

fruit beverages and fruit juices;

syrups and other preparations for making beverages.

Explanatory Note

Class 32 includes mainly non-alcoholic beverages, as well as beer.

This Class includes, in particular:

- de-alcoholised beverages.

This Class does not include, in particular:

- beverages for medical purposes (Cl. 5);
- milk beverages (milk predominating) (Cl. 29);
- beverages with coffee, cocoa or chocolate base (Cl. 30).

CLASS 33

Alcoholic beverages (except beers).

Explanatory Note

This Class does not include, in particular:

- medicinal beverages (Cl. 5);
- de-alcoholised beverages (Cl. 32).

CLASS 34

Tobacco;

smokers' articles;

matches.

Explanatory Note

This Class includes, in particular:

- tobacco substitutes (not for medical purposes).

This Class does not include, in particular:

- cigarettes without tobacco, for medical purposes (Cl. 5).

S E R V I C E S

CLASS 35

Advertising;

business management;

business administration;

office functions.

Explanatory Note

Class 35 includes mainly services rendered by persons or organizations principally with the object of:

(1) help in the working or management of a commercial undertaking, or

(2) help in the management of the business affairs or commercial functions of an industrial or commercial enterprise,

as well as services rendered by advertising establishments primarily undertaking communications to the public, declarations or announcements by all means of diffusion and concerning all kinds of goods or services.

This Class includes, in particular:

- the bringing together, for the benefit of others, of a variety of goods (excluding the transport thereof), enabling customers to conveniently view and purchase those goods; such services may be provided by retail stores, wholesale outlets, through mail order catalogues or by means of electronic media, for example, through web sites or television shopping programmes;
- services consisting of the registration, transcription, composition, compilation or systematization of written communications and registrations, and also the compilation of mathematical or statistical data;
- services of advertising agencies and services such as the distribution of prospectuses, directly or through the post, or the distribution of samples. This Class may refer to advertising in connection with other services, such as those concerning bank loans or advertising by radio.

This Class does not include, in particular:

- services such as evaluations and reports of engineers which do not directly refer to the working or management of affairs in a commercial or industrial enterprise (consult the Alphabetical List of Services).

CLASS 36

Insurance;

financial affairs;

monetary affairs;

real estate affairs.

Explanatory Note

Class 36 includes mainly services rendered in financial and monetary affairs and services rendered in relation to insurance contracts of all kinds.

This Class includes, in particular:

- services relating to financial or monetary affairs comprise the following:
  - (a) services of all the banking establishments, or institutions connected with them such as exchange brokers or clearing services;
  - (b) services of credit institutions other than banks such as co-operative credit associations, individual financial companies, lenders, etc.;
  - (c) services of "investment trusts," of holding companies;
  - (d) services of brokers dealing in shares and property;
  - (e) services connected with monetary affairs vouched for by trustees;
  - (f) services rendered in connection with the issue of travellers' cheques and letters of credit;
- hire- or lease-purchase financing;
- services of realty administrators of buildings, i.e., services of letting or valuation, or financing;
- services dealing with insurance such as services rendered by agents or brokers engaged in insurance, services rendered to insured, and insurance underwriting services.

CLASS 37

Building construction;

repair;

installation services.

Explanatory Note

Class 37 includes mainly services rendered by contractors or subcontractors in the construction or making of permanent buildings, as well as services rendered by persons or organizations engaged in the restoration of objects to their original condition or in their preservation without altering their physical or chemical properties.

This Class includes, in particular:

- services relating to the construction of buildings, roads, bridges, dams or transmission lines and services of undertakings specializing in the field of construction such as those of painters, plumbers, heating installers or roofers;
- services auxiliary to construction services like inspections of construction plans;
- services of shipbuilding;
- services consisting of hiring of tools or building materials;
- repair services, i.e., services which undertake to put any object into good condition after wear, damage, deterioration or partial destruction (restoration of an existing building or another object that has become imperfect and is to be restored to its original condition);
- various repair services such as those in the fields of electricity, furniture, instruments, tools, etc.;
- services of maintenance for preserving an object in its original condition without changing any of its properties (for the difference between this Class and Class 40 see the Explanatory Note of Class 40).

This Class does not include, in particular:

- services consisting of storage of goods such as clothes or vehicles (Cl. 39);
- services connected with dyeing of cloth or clothes (Cl. 40).

CLASS 38

Telecommunications.

Explanatory Note

Class 38 includes mainly services allowing at least one person to communicate with another by a sensory means. Such services include those which:

(1) allow one person to talk to another,

(2) transmit messages from one person to another, and

(3) place a person in oral or visual communication with another (radio and television).

This Class includes, in particular:

- services which consist essentially of the diffusion of radio or television programmes.

This Class does not include, in particular:

- radio advertising services (Cl. 35);
- telephone marketing (telemarketing) services (Cl. 35).

CLASS 39

Transport;

packaging and storage of goods;

travel arrangement.

Explanatory Note

Class 39 includes mainly services rendered in transporting people or goods from one place to another (by rail, road, water, air or pipeline) and services necessarily connected with such transport, as well as services relating to the storing of goods in a warehouse or other building for their preservation or guarding.

This Class includes, in particular:

- services rendered by companies exploiting stations, bridges, rail-road ferries, etc., used by the transporter;
- services connected with the hiring of transport vehicles;
- services connected with maritime tugs, unloading, the functioning of ports and docks and the salvaging of wrecked ships and their cargoes;
- services connected with the packaging and parcelling of goods before dispatch;
- services consisting of information about journeys or the transport of goods by brokers and tourist agencies, information relating to tariffs, timetables and methods of transport;
- services relating to the inspection of vehicles or goods before transport.

This Class does not include, in particular:

- services relating to advertising transport undertakings such as the distribution of prospectuses or advertising on the radio (Cl. 35);
- services relating to the issuing of travellers' cheques or letters of credit by brokers or travel agents (Cl. 36);
- services relating to insurances (commercial, fire or life) during the transport of persons or goods (Cl. 36);
- services rendered by the maintenance and repair of vehicles, nor the maintenance or repair of objects connected with the transport of persons or goods (Cl. 37);
- services relating to reservation of rooms in a hotel by travel agents or brokers (Cl. 43).

CLASS 40

Treatment of materials.

Explanatory Note

Class 40 includes mainly services not included in other classes, rendered by the mechanical or chemical processing or transformation of objects or inorganic or organic substances.

For the purposes of classification, the mark is considered a service mark only in cases where processing or transformation is effected for the account of another person. A mark is considered a trade mark in all cases where the substance or object is marketed by the person who processed or transformed it.

This Class includes, in particular:

- services relating to transformation of an object or substance and any process involving a change in its essential properties (for example, dyeing a garment); consequently, a maintenance service, although usually in Class 37, is included in Class 40 if it entails such a change (for example, the chroming of motor vehicle bumpers);
- services of material treatment which may be present during the production of any substance or object other than a building; for example, services which involve cutting, shaping, polishing by abrasion or metal coating.

This Class does not include, in particular:

- repair services (Cl. 37).

CLASS 41

Education;

providing of training;

entertainment;

sporting and cultural activities.

Explanatory Note

Class 41 covers mainly services rendered by persons or institutions in the development of the mental faculties of persons or animals, as well as services intended to entertain or to engage the attention.

This Class includes, in particular:

- services consisting of all forms of education of persons or training of animals;
- services having the basic aim of the entertainment, amusement or recreation of people;
- presentation of works of visual art or literature to the public for cultural or educational purposes.

CLASS 42

Scientific and technological services and research and design relating thereto;

industrial analysis and research services;

design and development of computer hardware and software.

Explanatory Note

Class 42 includes mainly services provided by persons, individually or collectively, in relation to the theoretical and practical aspects of complex fields of activities; such services are provided by members of professions such as chemists, physicists, engineers, computer programmers, etc.

This Class includes, in particular:

- the services of engineers who undertake evaluations, estimates, research and reports in the scientific and technological fields;
- scientific research services for medical purposes.

This Class does not include, in particular:

- business research and evaluations (Cl. 35);
- word processing and computer file management services (Cl. 35);
- financial and fiscal evaluations (Cl. 36);
- mining and oil extraction (Cl. 37);
- computer (hardware) installation and repair services (Cl. 37);
- services provided by the members of professions such as medical doctors, veterinary surgeons, psychoanalysts (Cl. 44);
- medical treatment services (Cl. 44);
- garden design (Cl. 44);
- legal services (Cl. 45).

CLASS 43

Services for providing food and drink;

temporary accommodation.

Explanatory Note

Class 43 includes mainly services provided by persons or establishments whose aim is to prepare food and drink for consumption and services provided to obtain bed and board in hotels, boarding houses or other establishments providing temporary accommodation.

This Class includes, in particular:

- reservation services for travellers' accommodation, particularly through travel agencies or brokers;
- boarding for animals.

This Class does not include, in particular:

- rental services for real estate such as houses, flats, etc., for permanent use (Cl. 36);
- arranging travel by tourist agencies (Cl. 39);
- preservation services for food and drink (Cl. 40);
- discotheque services (Cl. 41);
- boarding schools (Cl. 41);
- rest and convalescent homes (Cl. 44).

CLASS 44

Medical services;

veterinary services;

hygienic and beauty care for human beings or animals;

agriculture, horticulture and forestry services.

Explanatory Note

Class 44 includes mainly medical care, hygienic and beauty care given by persons or establishments to human beings and animals; it also includes services relating to the fields of agriculture, horticulture and forestry.

This Class includes, in particular:

- medical analysis services relating to the treatment of persons (such as x-ray examinations and taking of blood samples);
- artificial insemination services;
- pharmacy advice;
- animal breeding;
- services relating to the growing of plants such as gardening;
- services relating to floral art such as floral compositions as well as garden design.

This Class does not include, in particular:

- vermin exterminating (other than for agriculture, horticulture and forestry) (Cl. 37);
- installation and repair services for irrigation systems (Cl. 37);
- ambulance transport (Cl. 39);
- animal slaughtering services and taxidermy (Cl. 40);
- timber felling and processing (Cl. 40);
- animal training services (Cl. 41);
- health clubs for physical exercise (Cl. 41);
- scientific research services for medical purposes (Cl. 42);
- boarding for animals (Cl. 43);
- retirement homes (Cl. 43).

CLASS 45

Legal services; security services for the protection of property and individuals; personal and social services rendered by others to meet the needs of individuals.

Explanatory Note

This Class includes, in particular:

- services rendered by lawyers to individuals, groups of individuals, organizations and enterprises;
- investigation and surveillance services relating to the safety of persons and entities;
- services provided to individuals in relation with social events, such as social escort services, matrimonial agencies, funeral services.

This Class does not include, in particular:

- professional services giving direct aid in the operations or functions of a commercial undertaking (Cl. 35);
- services relating to financial or monetary affairs and services dealing with insurance (Cl. 36);
- escorting of travellers (Cl. 39);
- security transport (Cl. 39);
- services consisting of all forms of education of persons (Cl. 41);
- performances of singers or dancers (Cl. 41);
- computer services for the protection of software (Cl. 42);
- services provided by others to give medical, hygienic or beauty care for human beings or animals (Cl. 44);
- certain rental services (consult the Alphabetical List of Services and General Remark (b) relating to the classification of services).

*   *   *

ALPHABETICAL LIST

OF GOODS

Cl.	SERIAL No. (E)	INDICATION OF GOODS	SERIAL No. (F)	BASIC No.
09	A 0001	Abacuses	B 0730	090627
10	A 0002	Abdominal belts	A 0004	100001
10	A 0003	Abdominal corsets	C 1327	100003
10	A 0004	Abdominal pads	P 0308	100098
08	A 0005	Abrading instruments [hand instruments]	A 0008	080002
03	A 0006	Abrasive cloth	T 0321	030160
21	A 0007	Abrasive pads for kitchen purposes	T 0086	210259
03	A 0008	Abrasive paper	P 0123	030166
21	A 0009	Abrasive sponges for scrubbing the skin	E 0399	210331
03	A 0010	Abrasives *	A 0009	030165
01	A 0011	Abrasives (Auxiliary fluids for use with —)	F 0317	010004
05	A 0012	Abrasives (Dental —)	A 0010	050001
05	A 0013	Absorbent cotton	H 0203	050176
34	A 0014	Absorbent paper for tobacco pipes	P 0080	340011
16	A 0015	Absorbent sheets of paper or plastic for foodstuff packaging	F 0126	160355
05	A 0016	Absorbent wadding	H 0203	050176
01	A 0017	Absorbing oil (Synthetic materials for —)	A 0015	010620
05	A 0018	Acaricides	A 0016	050387
01	A 0019	Accelerators (Vulcanisation —)	A 0018	010005
15	A 0020	Accordions	A 0023	150001
09	A 0021	Accounting machines	C 0096	090135
09	A 0022	Accumulator boxes	C 0097	090009
09	A 0023	Accumulator jars	B 0007	090008
01	A 0024	Accumulators (Acidulated water for recharging —)	E 0002	010251
09	A 0025	Accumulators, electric	A 0035	090361
09	A 0026	Accumulators, electric, for vehicles	A 0040	090007
11	A 0027	Accumulators (Heat —)	A 0032	110002
11	A 0028	Accumulators (Steam —)	A 0033	110242
01	A 0029	Acetate (Aluminium —) *	A 0043	010565
17	A 0030	Acetate (Cellulose —), semi-processed	A 0045	170001
01	A 0031	Acetate of cellulose, unprocessed	A 0044	010008
01	A 0032	Acetates [chemicals] *	A 0047	010007
05	A 0033	Acetates for pharmaceutical purposes	A 0046	050291
01	A 0034	Acetic anhydride	A 0049	010010
01	A 0035	Acetification (Bacteriological preparations for —)	B 0019	010009
01	A 0036	Acetone	A 0050	010011
01	A 0037	Acetylene	A 0051	010012
11	A 0038	Acetylene burners	B 0292	110003
07	A 0039	Acetylene cleaning apparatus	P 1051	070002
11	A 0040	Acetylene flares	A 0056	110005
11	A 0041	Acetylene generators	G 0161	110004
01	A 0042	Acetylene tetrachloride	A 0057	010013
13	A 0043	Acetyl-nitrocellulose	A 0058	130001
09	A 0044	Acid hydrometers	P 0348	090387
01	A 0045	Acid proof chemical compositions	A 0062	010016
09	A 0046	Acidimeters for batteries	A 0041	090010
01	A 0047	Acids *	A 0060	010014
05	A 0048	Acids for pharmaceutical purposes	A 0061	050292
01	A 0049	Acidulated water for recharging accumulators	E 0002	010251
01	A 0050	Acidulated water for recharging batteries	E 0002	010251
05	A 0051	Aconitine	A 0081	050002
09	A 0052	Acoustic conduits	C 1160	090015
09	A 0053	Acoustic couplers	C 1403	090593
09	A 0054	Acoustic [sound] alarms	A 0863	090014
17	A 0055	Acrylic resins [semi-finished products]	A 0091	170002
01	A 0056	Acrylic resins, unprocessed	A 0090	010461
01	A 0057	Actinium	A 0093	010018
09	A 0058	Actinometers	A 0094	090018
01	A 0059	Activated carbons	C 0506	010025
10	A 0060	Acupuncture needles	A 0196	100199
09	A 0061	Adding machines	A 0101	090019
01	A 0062	Additives (Chemical —) for oils	A 0098	010654
01	A 0063	Additives, chemical, to drilling muds	A 0096	010019
01	A 0064	Additives, chemical, to fungicides	F 0342	010309
01	A 0065	Additives, chemical, to insecticides	I 0094	010308
01	A 0066	Additives, chemical, to motor fuel	A 0097	010020
01	A 0067	Additives (Detergent —) to gasoline [petrol]	A 0099	010021
04	A 0068	Additives, non-chemical, to motor-fuel	A 0100	040085
16	A 0069	Address plates for addressing machines	P 0596	160268
16	A 0070	Address stamps	C 0941	160004
16	A 0071	Addressing machines	A 0124	160005
05	A 0072	Adhesive bands for medical purposes	B 0149	050294
07	A 0073	Adhesive bands for pulleys	B 0126	070314
16	A 0074	Adhesive bands for stationery or household purposes	B 0150	160267
17	A 0075	Adhesive bands other than stationery and not for medical or household purposes	B 0148	170085
24	A 0076	Adhesive fabric for application by heat	T 0297	240001
05	A 0077	Adhesive plaster	S 0481	050019
01	A 0078	Adhesive preparations for surgical bandages	A 0106	010022
07	A 0079	Adhesive tape dispensers [machines]	D 0259	070004
16	A 0080	Adhesive tape dispensers [office requisites]	D 0258	160003
05	A 0081	Adhesive tapes for medical purposes	B 0149	050294
16	A 0082	Adhesive tapes for stationery or household purposes	R 0428	160266
17	A 0083	Adhesive tapes other than stationery and not for medical or household purposes	B 0148	170085
05	A 0084	Adhesives (Fly catching —)	G 0234	050217

Cl.	SERIAL No. (E)	INDICATION OF GOODS	SERIAL No. (F)	BASIC No.
03	A 0085	Adhesives for affixing false hair	A 0108	030001
01	A 0086	Adhesives for billposting	C 1033	010028
03	A 0087	Adhesives for cosmetic purposes	A 0103	030199
05	A 0088	Adhesives for dentures	A 0109	050003
01	A 0089	Adhesives for industrial purposes	A 0105	010002
01	A 0090	Adhesives for paperhanging	C 1036	010203
01	A 0091	Adhesives for wall tiles	A 0107	010573
16	A 0092	Adhesives [glues] for stationery or household purposes	A 0104	160265
05	A 0093	Adjuvants for medical purposes	A 0117	050396
16	A 0094	Advertisement boards of paper or cardboard	A 0154	160008
19	A 0095	Advertisement columns, not of metal	C 1048	190001
06	A 0096	Advertisement columns of metal	C 1047	060411
08	A 0097	Adzes [tools]	H 0070	080141
07	A 0098	Aerated beverage-making machines	B 0579	070056
32	A 0099	Aerated water	E 0052	320035
07	A 0100	Aerated water making apparatus	E 0053	070163
32	A 0101	Aerated water (Preparations for making —)	E 0054	320013
07	A 0102	Aerating pumps for aquaria	P 0775	070005
07	A 0103	Aerators	G 0134	070432
12	A 0104	Aerial conveyors	A 0131	120004
09	A 0105	Aerials	A 0568	090045
07	A 0106	Aerocondensers	A 0133	070006
09	A 0107	Aerometers	A 0135	090020
12	A 0108	Aeronautical apparatus, machines and appliances	A 0136	120203
24	A 0109	Aeronautical balloons (Fabric impervious to gases for —)	B 0116	240002
07	A 0110	Aeronautical engines	A 0137	070386
07	A 0111	Aeroplane engines	A 0873	070029
12	A 0112	Aeroplanes	A 0872	120027
10	A 0113	Aerosol dispensers for medical purposes	A 0139	100160
21	A 0114	Aerosol dispensers, not for medical purposes	A 0140	210233
01	A 0115	Aerosols (Gas propellents for —)	G 0124	010026
03	A 0116	After-shave lotions	L 0370	030200
01	A 0117	Agar-agar	A 0164	010029
14	A 0118	Agates	A 0165	140001
09	A 0119	Agendas (Electronic —)	A 0166	090628
01	A 0120	Agglutinants for concrete	A 0170	010030
02	A 0121	Agglutinants for paints	L 0234	020087
07	A 0122	Agitators	A 0172	070007
01	A 0123	Agricultural chemicals, except fungicides, weedkillers, herbicides, insecticides and parasiticides	A 0186	010031
07	A 0124	Agricultural elevators	A 0184	070009
08	A 0125	Agricultural implements, hand-operated	A 0181	080200

Cl.	SERIAL No. (E)	INDICATION OF GOODS	SERIAL No. (F)	BASIC No.
07	A 0126	Agricultural implements other than hand-operated	A 0182	070388
07	A 0127	Agricultural machines	A 0183	070008
01	A 0128	Agriculture (Manure for —)	E 0326	010271
09	A 0129	Air analysis apparatus	A 0225	090025
12	A 0130	Air bags [safety devices for automobiles]	C 1450	120247
12	A 0131	Air balloons	B 0115	120006
07	A 0132	Air brushes for applying colour	B 0864	070514
03	A 0133	Air (Canned pressurized —) for cleaning and dusting purposes	A 0254	030209
07	A 0134	Air condensers	A 0237	070011
11	A 0135	Air conditioners for vehicles	C 0947	110079
11	A 0136	Air conditioning apparatus	C 0944	110099
11	A 0137	Air conditioning installations	A 0243	110014
06	A 0138	Air conditioning installations (Ducts of metal for ventilating and —)	C 1162	060415
11	A 0139	Air cooling apparatus	A 0241	110010
07	A 0140	Air cushion devices for moving loads	C 1449	070129
12	A 0141	Air cushion vehicles	A 0134	120237
07	A 0142	Air cushion vehicles (Engines for —)	V 0046	070380
10	A 0143	Air cushions for medical purposes	C 1444	100162
20	A 0144	Air cushions, not for medical purposes	C 1445	200201
11	A 0145	Air deodorising apparatus	A 0224	110009
05	A 0146	Air deodorising preparations	D 0132	050401
11	A 0147	Air driers [dryers]	S 0162	110013
11	A 0148	Air filtering installations	A 0245	110015
03	A 0149	Air fragrancing preparations	P 0163	030215
10	A 0150	Air mattresses, for medical purposes	M 0211	100163
20	A 0151	Air mattresses, not for medical purposes	M 0212	200202
11	A 0152	Air or water (Ionization apparatus for the treatment of —)	A 0251	110174
10	A 0153	Air pillows for medical purposes	O 0101	100161
20	A 0154	Air pillows, not for medical purposes	O 0102	200158
28	A 0155	Air pistols [toys]	A 0253	280117
13	A 0156	Air pistols [weapons]	A 0252	130059
07	A 0157	Air pumps [garage installations]	P 0767	070310
12	A 0158	Air pumps [vehicle accessories]	P 0765	120009
11	A 0159	Air purifying apparatus and machines	P 1052	110207
05	A 0160	Air purifying preparations	A 0255	050005
11	A 0161	Air reheaters	R 0137	110012
11	A 0162	Air sterilisers	A 0258	110245
07	A 0163	Air suction machines	A 0795	070398
11	A 0164	Air valves for steam heating installations	P 1050	110205
12	A 0165	Air vehicles	A 0132	120005
11	A 0166	Air vehicles (Lighting installations for —)	A 0130	110007
12	A 0167	Aircraft	A 0138	120184

Cl.	SERIAL No. (E)	INDICATION OF GOODS	SERIAL No. (F)	BASIC No.
12	A 0168	Airplanes (Amphibious —)	A 0474	120012
12	A 0169	Airships	B 0119	120030
29	A 0170	Ajvar [preserved peppers]	A 0261	290165
19	A 0171	Alabaster	A 0268	190003
19	A 0172	Alabaster glass	V 0135	190002
09	A 0173	Alarm bells, electric	T 0268	090071
14	A 0174	Alarm clocks	R 0285	140082
09	A 0175	Alarms *	A 0267	090026
09	A 0176	Alarms (Fire —)	A 0868	090068
29	A 0177	Albumen for culinary purposes	A 0269	290001
01	A 0178	Albumen (Iodised —)	A 0273	010034
01	A 0179	Albumen (Malt —)	A 0272	010035
01	A 0180	Albumin [animal or vegetable, raw material]	A 0271	010033
05	A 0181	Albumin dietary supplements	C 1101	050420
29	A 0182	Albumin milk	L 0042	290174
01	A 0183	Albuminized paper	P 0081	010036
05	A 0184	Albuminous foodstuffs for medical purposes	A 0270	050006
05	A 0185	Albuminous preparations for medical purposes	A 0275	050007
16	A 0186	Albums	A 0277	160013
01	A 0187	Alcohol *	A 0289	010040
11	A 0188	Alcohol burners	B 0293	110247
01	A 0189	Alcohol (Ethyl —)	A 0297	010041
05	A 0190	Alcohol for pharmaceutical purposes	A 0304	050008
04	A 0191	Alcohol [fuel]	A 0300	040003
33	A 0192	Alcohol (Rice —)	A 0296	330032
33	A 0193	Alcoholic beverages containing fruit	B 0568	330031
33	A 0194	Alcoholic beverages, except beer	B 0567	330026
33	A 0195	Alcoholic essences	E 0448	330024
33	A 0196	Alcoholic extracts	E 0567	330025
09	A 0197	Alcoholmeters	A 0305	090027
01	A 0198	Aldehydes *	A 0306	010042
05	A 0199	Aldehydes for pharmaceutical purposes	A 0307	050009
31	A 0200	Algae for human or animal consumption	A 0325	310003
31	A 0201	Algarovilla for animal consumption	A 0314	310124
05	A 0202	Algicides	A 0315	050312
05	A 0203	Alginate dietary supplements	A 0319	050432
29	A 0204	Alginates for culinary purposes	A 0316	290116
01	A 0205	Alginates for industrial purposes	A 0317	010564
05	A 0206	Alginates for pharmaceutical purposes	A 0318	050433
01	A 0207	Alginates for the food industry	A 0320	010669
09	A 0208	Alidades	A 0326	090028
02	A 0209	Alizarine dyes	A 0348	020006
03	A 0210	Alkali (Volatile —) [ammonia] [detergent]	A 0458	030167
01	A 0211	Alkali (Volatile —) [ammonia] for industrial purposes	A 0279	010558
01	A 0212	Alkalies	A 0286	010037
01	A 0213	Alkaline iodides for industrial purposes	A 0282	010559

Cl.	SERIAL No. (E)	INDICATION OF GOODS	SERIAL No. (F)	BASIC No.
05	A 0214	Alkaline iodides for pharmaceutical purposes	A 0283	050348
01	A 0215	Alkaline metals	M 0301	010560
01	A 0216	Alkaline metals (Salts of —)	A 0285	010561
01	A 0217	Alkaline-earth metals	M 0300	010039
01	A 0218	Alkaloids *	A 0287	010562
05	A 0219	Alkaloids for medical purposes	A 0288	050296
01	A 0220	Alloying of metals (Chemical preparations for facilitating the —)	A 0351	010045
06	A 0221	Alloys of common metal	A 0352	060269
14	A 0222	Alloys of precious metal	A 0354	140104
05	A 0223	Alloys of precious metals for dental purposes	A 0355	050010
30	A 0224	Allspice	Q 0008	300056
16	A 0225	Almanacs	A 0377	160269
30	A 0226	Almond confectionery	A 0404	300138
03	A 0227	Almond milk for cosmetic purposes	L 0048	030169
03	A 0228	Almond oil	H 0130	030006
30	A 0229	Almond paste	P 0191	300004
03	A 0230	Almond soap	A 0412	030007
31	A 0231	Almonds [fruits]	A 0405	310125
29	A 0232	Almonds, ground	A 0411	290117
32	A 0233	Almonds (Milk of —) [beverage]	L 0050	320032
05	A 0234	Almonds (Milk of —) for pharmaceutical purposes	L 0049	050300
32	A 0235	Aloe vera drinks, non-alcoholic	B 0590	320051
31	A 0236	Aloe vera plants	A 0378	310148
03	A 0237	Aloe vera preparations for cosmetic purposes	A 0379	030219
05	A 0238	Aloe vera preparations for pharmaceutical purposes	A 0380	050409
29	A 0239	Aloe vera prepared for human consumption	A 0381	290172
18	A 0240	Alpenstocks	A 0382	180001
07	A 0241	Alternators	A 0384	070018
09	A 0242	Altimeters	A 0385	090033
01	A 0243	Alum	A 0399	010052
03	A 0244	Alum stones [astringents]	P 0460	030168
01	A 0245	Alumina	A 0386	010046
06	A 0246	Aluminium	A 0392	060017
01	A 0247	Aluminium acetate *	A 0043	010565
05	A 0248	Aluminium acetate for pharmaceutical purposes	A 0388	050299
01	A 0249	Aluminium alum	A 0389	010047
01	A 0250	Aluminium chloride	A 0393	010050
06	A 0251	Aluminium foil *	A 0394	060270
01	A 0252	Aluminium hydrate	A 0390	010048
01	A 0253	Aluminium iodide	A 0396	010051
02	A 0254	Aluminium paints	A 0397	020007
02	A 0255	Aluminium powder for painting	P 0908	020008
01	A 0256	Aluminium silicate	A 0391	010049
06	A 0257	Aluminium wire	A 0395	060019
05	A 0258	Amalgams (Dental —)	A 0403	050012
03	A 0259	Amber [perfume]	A 0421	030008
20	A 0260	Amber (Yellow —)	A 0418	200005
20	A 0261	Ambroid bars	A 0422	200203
20	A 0262	Ambroid plates	A 0424	200204

Cl.	SERIAL No. (E)	INDICATION OF GOODS	SERIAL No. (F)	BASIC No.
10	A 0263	Ambulance stretchers	B 0791	100037
12	A 0264	Ambulances	A 0425	120233
01	A 0265	Americium	A 0427	010054
05	A 0266	Amino acids for medical purposes	A 0451	050376
05	A 0267	Amino acids for veterinary purposes	A 0452	050377
09	A 0268	Ammeters	A 0473	090036
01	A 0269	Ammonia *	A 0456	010061
01	A 0270	Ammonia alum	A 0460	010063
03	A 0271	Ammonia [volatile alkali] [detergent]	A 0458	030167
01	A 0272	Ammonia [volatile alkali] for industrial purposes	A 0279	010558
01	A 0273	Ammoniacal salts	A 0455	010060
01	A 0274	Ammonium aldehyde	A 0459	010062
13	A 0275	Ammonium nitrate explosives	N 0072	130005
01	A 0276	Ammonium salts	A 0462	010567
13	A 0277	Ammunition	M 0565	130027
12	A 0278	Amphibious airplanes	A 0474	120012
09	A 0279	Amplifiers	A 0475	090037
09	A 0280	Amplifying tubes	T 0558	090038
09	A 0281	Amplifying valves	T 0558	090038
14	A 0282	Amulets [jewellery, jewelry (Am.)]	A 0484	140006
28	A 0283	Amusement machines, automatic and coin-operated	J 0037	280189
01	A 0284	Amyl acetate	A 0485	010064
01	A 0285	Amyl alcohol	A 0486	010065
10	A 0286	Anaesthetic apparatus	A 0498	100057
10	A 0287	Anaesthetic masks	M 0180	100112
05	A 0288	Anaesthetics	A 0499	050017
05	A 0289	Analgesics	A 0487	050124
01	A 0290	Analyses in laboratories (Chemical preparations for—), other than for medical or veterinary purposes	A 0491	010181
10	A 0291	Analysis (Apparatus for use in medical—)	A 0488	100180
06	A 0292	Anchor plates	A 0494	060020
06	A 0293	Anchors *	A 0495	060273
14	A 0294	Anchors [clock and watch making]	A 0496	140106
29	A 0295	Anchovy	A 0493	290006
09	A 0296	Anemometers	A 0497	090039
06	A 0297	Angle irons	C 1301	060345
19	A 0298	Angle irons, not of metal	C 1302	190067
05	A 0299	Angostura bark for medical purposes	A 0502	050020
01	A 0300	Anhydrides	A 0507	010067
01	A 0301	Anhydrous ammonia	A 0504	010066
02	A 0302	Aniline dyes	A 0508	020052
01	A 0303	Animal albumen [raw material]	A 0512	010069
01	A 0304	Animal carbon	C 0507	010568
01	A 0305	Animal carbon preparations	C 0508	010165
01	A 0306	Animal charcoal	N 0083	010068
31	A 0307	Animal fattening preparations	E 0327	310052
31	A 0308	Animal foodstuffs	A 0343	310007
31	A 0309	Animal forage (Lime for—)	C 0666	310028
22	A 0310	Animal hair	C 1559	220065
20	A 0311	Animal hooves	S 0008	200179
20	A 0312	Animal horns	C 1290	200035
31	A 0313	Animal litter (Products for—)	L 0338	310080
29	A 0314	Animal marrow for food	M 0440	290081
18	A 0315	Animal skins	P 0244	180002
05	A 0316	Animal washes	A 0540	050189
31	A 0317	Animals (Edible chews for—)	A 0535	310141
31	A 0318	Animals (Live—)	A 0545	310006
31	A 0319	Animals (Menagerie—)	A 0523	310005
06	A 0320	Animals (Metal cages for wild—)	C 0089	060433
20	A 0321	Animals (Stuffed—)	A 0531	200006
06	A 0322	Animals (Traps for wild—)*	P 0444	060025
09	A 0323	Animated cartoons	D 0145	090176
33	A 0324	Anise [liqueur]	A 0548	330004
30	A 0325	Aniseed	A 0547	300006
33	A 0326	Anisette [liqueur]	A 0549	330005
02	A 0327	Annatto [dyestuff]	R 0356	020098
02	A 0328	Annotto [dyestuff]	R 0356	020098
16	A 0329	Announcement cards [stationery]	F 0004	160284
08	A 0330	Annular screw plates	A 0565	080020
09	A 0331	Anode batteries	B 0261	090044
09	A 0332	Anodes	A 0566	090043
09	A 0333	Answering machines	R 0235	090629
09	A 0334	Antennas	A 0568	090045
05	A 0335	Anthelmintics	V 0127	050154
04	A 0336	Anthracite	A 0569	040008
05	A 0337	Antibiotics	A 0572	050388
01	A 0338	Anti-boil preparations for engine coolants	E 0070	010645
09	A 0339	Anticathodes	A 0574	090507
02	A 0340	Anti-corrosive bands	B 0170	020021
02	A 0341	Anti-corrosive preparations	C 1316	020010
05	A 0342	Anticryptogamic preparations	A 0576	050135
11	A 0343	Anti-dazzle devices for automobiles [lamp fittings]	A 0851	110030
12	A 0344	Anti-dazzle devices for vehicles *	A 0586	120204
17	A 0345	Anti-dazzle films for windows [tinted films]	F 0127	170115
09	A 0346	Anti-dazzle shades	V 0266	090047
02	A 0347	Anti-fouling paints	P 0287	020122
01	A 0348	Antifreeze	A 0592	010072
07	A 0349	Anti-friction bearings for machines	A 0588	070396
06	A 0350	Anti-friction metal	A 0589	060027
07	A 0351	Anti-friction pads for machines	A 0588	070396
01	A 0352	Anti-frothing solutions for accumulators	A 0042	010006
01	A 0353	Anti-frothing solutions for batteries	A 0042	010006
12	A 0354	Anti-glare devices for vehicles *	A 0586	120204
11	A 0355	Anti-glare devices for vehicles [lamp fittings]	A 0587	110249
09	A 0356	Anti-glare glasses	A 0584	090046
09	A 0357	Anti-glare visors	V 0266	090047
01	A 0358	Anti-incrustants	A 0596	010073
09	A 0359	Anti-interference devices [electricity]	A 0606	090048

Cl.	SERIAL No. (E)	INDICATION OF GOODS	SERIAL No. (F)	BASIC No.
01	A 0360	Anti-knock substances for internal combustion engines	A 0582	010071
01	A 0361	Antimony	A 0600	010074
01	A 0362	Antimony oxide	O 0163	010075
01	A 0363	Antimony sulphide	A 0602	010076
05	A 0364	Antioxidant pills	A 0603	050418
05	A 0365	Antiparasitic collars for animals	C 1038	050087
05	A 0366	Antiparasitic preparations	A 0605	050029
03	A 0367	Antiperspirant soap	S 0116	030163
03	A 0368	Antiperspirants [toiletries]	T 0477	030162
17	A 0369	Anti-pollution barriers (Floating —)	B 0200	170108
07	A 0370	Anti-pollution devices for motors and engines	A 0608	070273
05	A 0371	Anti-rheumatism bracelets	B 0780	050015
05	A 0372	Anti-rheumatism rings	A 0551	050016
02	A 0373	Anti-rust greases	G 0315	020079
02	A 0374	Anti-rust oils	H 0147	020083
02	A 0375	Anti-rust preparations for preservation	P 0947	020107
05	A 0376	Antiseptic cotton	A 0613	050031
05	A 0377	Antiseptics	A 0614	050030
12	A 0378	Anti-skid chains	C 0425	120014
11	A 0379	Anti-splash tap nozzles	B 0832	110055
01	A 0380	Anti-sprouting preparations for vegetables	G 0185	010571
03	A 0381	Antistatic preparations for household purposes	E 0187	030083
01	A 0382	Antistatic preparations, other than for household purposes	E 0188	010260
01	A 0383	Anti-tarnishing chemicals for windows	V 0281	010523
02	A 0384	Anti-tarnishing preparations for metals	T 0203	020093
12	A 0385	Anti-theft alarms for vehicles	A 0866	120211
12	A 0386	Anti-theft devices for vehicles	A 0619	120200
09	A 0387	Anti-theft warning apparatus	A 0865	090511
05	A 0388	Anti-uric preparations	A 0617	050032
20	A 0389	Antlers (Stag —)	R 0069	200049
01	A 0390	Antranilic acid	A 0570	010070
06	A 0391	Anvils	E 0291	060097
06	A 0392	Anvils [portable]	T 0140	060248
33	A 0393	Aperitifs *	A 0620	330006
32	A 0394	Aperitifs, non-alcoholic	A 0621	320042
09	A 0395	Apertometers [optics]	A 0622	090050
05	A 0396	Appetite suppressant pills	C 1388	050415
05	A 0397	Appetite suppressants for medical purposes	C 1387	050389
29	A 0398	Apple purée	C 1112	290155
25	A 0399	Aprons [clothing]	T 0050	250096
07	A 0400	Aprons [parts of machines]	T 0049	070360
16	A 0401	Aquarelles	A 0633	160020
07	A 0402	Aquaria (Aerating pumps for —)	P 0775	070005
21	A 0403	Aquaria (Indoor —)	A 0635	210336
19	A 0404	Aquaria [structures]	A 0634	190190
11	A 0405	Aquarium filtration apparatus	F 0254	110307
19	A 0406	Aquarium gravel	G 0336	190233
11	A 0407	Aquarium heaters	C 0604	110308
21	A 0408	Aquarium hoods	C 1472	210337
11	A 0409	Aquarium lights	L 0101	110309
19	A 0410	Aquarium sand	S 0005	190234
33	A 0411	Arak [arrack]	A 0648	330007
19	A 0412	Arbours [structures not of metal]	T 0401	190175
06	A 0413	Arbours [structures of metal]	T 0400	060436
11	A 0414	Arc lamps	L 0088	110023
28	A 0415	Arcade video game machines	M 0011	280216
10	A 0416	Arch supports for footwear	R 0281	100040
28	A 0417	Archery implements	A 0672	280008
16	A 0418	Architects' models	M 0136	160021
01	A 0419	Argon	A 0714	010082
16	A 0420	Arithmetical tables	T 0033	160027
26	A 0421	Arm bands [clothing accessories]	B 0799	260024
09	A 0422	Armatures [electricity]	I 0079	090305
20	A 0423	Armchairs	F 0027	200063
10	A 0424	Armchairs for medical or dental purposes	F 0028	100088
06	A 0425	Armour plate	C 1616	060107
06	A 0426	Armour plating	B 0493	060047
04	A 0427	Arms [weapons] (Grease for —)	A 0739	040011
30	A 0428	Aromatic preparations for food	A 0750	300011
31	A 0429	Aromatic sand for pets [litter]	S 0003	310147
03	A 0430	Aromatics [essential oils]	A 0748	030172
33	A 0431	Arrack [arak]	A 0648	330007
01	A 0432	Arsenate (Lead —)	A 0767	010083
01	A 0433	Arsenic	A 0768	010084
01	A 0434	Arsenious acid	A 0769	010085
20	A 0435	Art (Works of —) of wood, wax, plaster or plastic	A 0770	200205
10	A 0436	Arterial blood pressure measuring apparatus	S 0495	100129
10	A 0437	Artificial breasts	S 0182	100141
30	A 0438	Artificial coffee	S 0559	300152
10	A 0439	Artificial eyes	Y 0005	100159
26	A 0440	Artificial flowers	F 0293	260059
26	A 0441	Artificial fruit	F 0452	260061
26	A 0442	Artificial garlands	G 0378	260065
20	A 0443	Artificial honeycombs	C 0886	200039
10	A 0444	Artificial jaws	M 0017	100111
10	A 0445	Artificial limbs	P 1017	100117
17	A 0446	Artificial resins [semi-finished products]	R 0268	170075
01	A 0447	Artificial resins, unprocessed	R 0263	010462
10	A 0448	Artificial respiration (Apparatus for —)	R 0273	100139
10	A 0449	Artificial skin for surgical purposes	P 0234	100125
19	A 0450	Artificial stone	P 0449	190142
01	A 0451	Artificial sweeteners [chemical preparations]	E 0165	010607
10	A 0452	Artificial teeth	D 0093	100052
10	A 0453	Artificial teeth (Sets of —)	D 0087	100076
27	A 0454	Artificial turf	G 0142	270003
13	A 0455	Artillery guns [cannons]	P 0431	130014
16	A 0456	Artists' watercolor [watercolour] saucers	G 0257	160166
17	A 0457	Asbestos	A 0431	170091

Cl.	SERIAL No. (E)	INDICATION OF GOODS	SERIAL No. (F)	BASIC No.
19	A 0458	Asbestos cement	C 0852	190004
17	A 0459	Asbestos cloth	T 0323	170080
09	A 0460	Asbestos clothing for protection against fire	A 0438	090035
17	A 0461	Asbestos coverings	R 0292	170078
17	A 0462	Asbestos fabrics	T 0300	170079
17	A 0463	Asbestos felt	F 0138	170044
17	A 0464	Asbestos fibers [fibres]	F 0179	170088
09	A 0465	Asbestos gloves for protection against accidents	A 0433	090034
17	A 0466	Asbestos mill boards	C 0309	170087
19	A 0467	Asbestos mortar	A 0434	190005
17	A 0468	Asbestos packing	T 0505	170081
02	A 0469	Asbestos paints	A 0435	020009
17	A 0470	Asbestos paper	P 0124	170071
17	A 0471	Asbestos safety curtains	R 0319	170003
09	A 0472	Asbestos screens for firemen	P 0144	090689
17	A 0473	Asbestos sheets	D 0308	170035
17	A 0474	Asbestos slate	A 0682	170005
17	A 0475	Asbestos soles	S 0220	170027
28	A 0476	Ascenders [mountaineering equipment]	A 0784	280201
25	A 0477	Ascots	L 0160	250157
05	A 0478	Aseptic cotton	A 0787	050034
11	A 0479	Ash boxes (Furnace —)	C 0388	110154
11	A 0480	Ash conveyor installations, automatic	C 0384	110231
11	A 0481	Ash pits for furnaces	C 0388	110154
01	A 0482	Ash (Soda —)	S 0415	010100
03	A 0483	Ash (Volcanic —) for cleaning	C 0387	030038
34	A 0484	Ashtrays for smokers	C 0389	340036
19	A 0485	Asphalt	A 0788	190013
19	A 0486	Asphalt paving	A 0789	190014
01	A 0487	Astatine	A 0802	010086
05	A 0488	Asthmatic tea	A 0571	050022
03	A 0489	Astringents for cosmetic purposes	A 0804	030191
09	A 0490	Astronomy (Apparatus and instruments for —)	A 0805	090384
09	A 0491	Astrophotography (Lenses for —)	A 0806	090059
16	A 0492	Atlases	A 0807	160034
14	A 0493	Atomic clocks	H 0088	140042
11	A 0494	Atomic piles	R 0122	110253
01	A 0495	Atomic piles (Fuel for —)	C 1077	010087
07	A 0496	Atomisers [machines]	P 1039	070214
08	A 0497	Atomizers (Insecticide —) [hand tools]	P 1041	080144
18	A 0498	Attaché cases	M 0059	180073
21	A 0499	Attracting and killing insects (Electric devices for —)	A 0820	210345
09	A 0500	Audiovisual teaching apparatus	A 0823	090061
08	A 0501	Augers [hand tools]	T 0133	080194
02	A 0502	Auramine	A 0827	020018
11	A 0503	Autoclaves [electric pressure cookers]	M 0153	110254
21	A 0504	Autoclaves [pressure cookers], non-electric	A 0839	210236
09	A 0505	Automated teller machines [ATM]	G 0368	090686
13	A 0506	Automatic firearm ammunition belts	B 0174	130075
07	A 0507	Automatic grapnels for marine purposes	G 0328	070073
12	A 0508	Automobile bodies	A 0848	120207
01	A 0509	Automobile body fillers	M 0200	010649
27	A 0510	Automobile carpets	T 0120	270010
12	A 0511	Automobile chains	A 0849	120024
12	A 0512	Automobile chassis	A 0850	120025
12	A 0513	Automobile hoods	A 0847	120023
11	A 0514	Automobile lights	A 0852	110256
12	A 0515	Automobile tires [tyres]	A 0846	120206
12	A 0516	Automobiles	A 0843	120205
11	A 0517	Automobiles (Anti-dazzle devices for —) [lamp fittings]	A 0851	110030
12	A 0518	Automobiles (Sun-blinds adapted for —)	S 0548	120245
01	A 0519	Auxiliary fluids for use with abrasives	F 0317	010004
19	A 0520	Aviaries, not of metal [structures]	V 0322	190184
06	A 0521	Aviaries of metal [structures]	V 0321	060263
09	A 0522	Aviators (Protective suits for —)	C 1067	090070
08	A 0523	Awls	A 0308	080008
22	A 0524	Awnings	T 0195	220071
22	A 0525	Awnings of synthetic materials	M 0167	220102
22	A 0526	Awnings of textile	M 0168	220058
08	A 0527	Axes	H 0009	080069
12	A 0528	Axle journals	F 0506	120120
07	A 0529	Axles for machines	A 0653	070020
12	A 0530	Axles for vehicles	E 0455	120119
09	A 0531	Azimuth instruments	A 0884	090512

Cl.	SERIAL No. (E)	INDICATION OF GOODS	SERIAL No. (F)	BASIC No.
10	B 0001	Babies' bottles	B 0360	100028
05	B 0002	Babies' napkin-pants [diaper-pants]	C 1360	050413
10	B 0003	Babies' pacifiers [teats]	S 0560	100145
25	B 0004	Babies' pants [clothing]	C 1649	250058
21	B 0005	Baby baths, portable	B 0055	210301
12	B 0006	Baby carriages	V 0299	120163
12	B 0007	Baby carriages (Covers for —)	B 0003	120164
20	B 0008	Baby changing mats	T 0114	200279
20	B 0009	Baby changing platforms	T 0032	200278
28	B 0010	Backgammon games	T 0521	280114
18	B 0011	Backpacks	S 0023	180058
29	B 0012	Bacon	L 0144	290076
05	B 0013	Bacterial poisons	B 0015	050038
05	B 0014	Bacterial preparations for medical and veterinary use	B 0013	050039
01	B 0015	Bacterial preparations other than for medical and veterinary use	B 0014	010594
02	B 0016	Bactericidal paints	P 0288	020019
01	B 0017	Bactericides (Oenological —) [chemical preparations used in wine making]	B 0012	010096
05	B 0018	Bacteriological cultures (Bouillons for —)	B 0718	050036
05	B 0019	Bacteriological cultures (Media for —)	B 0718	050036
01	B 0020	Bacteriological preparations for acetification	B 0019	010009
05	B 0021	Bacteriological preparations for medical and veterinary use	B 0017	050037
01	B 0022	Bacteriological preparations other than for medical and veterinary use	B 0018	010595
26	B 0023	Badges [buttons] (Ornamental novelty —)	B 0020	260113
26	B 0024	Badges for wear, not of precious metal	I 0101	260101
06	B 0025	Badges of metal for vehicles	E 0162	060155
14	B 0026	Badges of precious metal	I 0100	140152
03	B 0027	Badian essence	B 0021	030015
02	B 0028	Badigeon	B 0023	020020
19	B 0029	Bagasses of cane (Agglomerated —) [building material]	A 0169	190231
31	B 0030	Bagasses of cane [raw material]	B 0025	310131
15	B 0031	Bagpipes	M 0574	150051
16	B 0032	Bags (Conical paper —)	C 1295	160102
18	B 0033	Bags [envelopes, pouches] of leather, for packaging	S 0040	180079
16	B 0034	Bags [envelopes, pouches] of paper or plastics, for packaging	S 0019	160246
17	B 0035	Bags [envelopes, pouches] of rubber, for packaging	S 0016	170077
22	B 0036	Bags [envelopes, pouches] of textile, for packaging	S 0041	220069
28	B 0037	Bags especially designed for skis and surfboards	H 0121	280166
18	B 0038	Bags for campers	S 0030	180075
18	B 0039	Bags for climbers	S 0029	180074
16	B 0040	Bags for microwave cooking	S 0020	160323
18	B 0041	Bags for sports*	S 0036	180118
22	B 0042	Bags for washing hosiery	S 0034	220106
18	B 0043	Bags (Game —) [hunting accessories]	G 0187	180019
16	B 0044	Bags (Garbage —) of paper or of plastics	S 0026	160292
18	B 0045	Bags (Garment —) for travel	S 0052	180111
22	B 0046	Bags (Mail —)	S 0048	220104
18	B 0047	Bags (Net —) for shopping	F 0192	180114
18	B 0048	Bags (Nose —) [feed bags]	M 0575	180050
22	B 0049	Bags [sacks] for the transport and storage of materials in bulk	S 0051	220068
20	B 0050	Bags (Sleeping —) for camping	S 0032	200234
07	B 0051	Bags (Vacuum cleaner —)	S 0049	070521
26	B 0052	Bags (Zip fasteners for —)	S 0043	260087
28	B 0053	Bait (Artificial fishing —)	A 0464	280002
31	B 0054	Bait (Fishing —), live	A 0623	310132
20	B 0055	Bakers' bread baskets	P 0057	200163
11	B 0056	Bakers' ovens	B 0721	110053
30	B 0057	Baking powder	P 0907	300199
30	B 0058	Baking soda [bicarbonate of soda for cooking purposes]	B 0371	300200
12	B 0059	Balance weights for vehicle wheels	P 0652	120116
09	B 0060	Balances (Precision —)	T 0491	090489
09	B 0061	Balances [steelyards]	R 0358	090433
09	B 0062	Balancing apparatus	E 0418	090237
17	B 0063	Balata	B 0101	170010
07	B 0064	Ball rings for bearings	B 0027	070339
07	B 0065	Ball-bearings	R 0404	070049
10	B 0066	Balling guns	P 0486	100127
13	B 0067	Ballistic missiles	E 0323	130015
13	B 0068	Ballistic weapons	E 0323	130015
12	B 0069	Balloons (Air —)	B 0115	120006
12	B 0070	Balloons (Dirigible —)	B 0119	120030
24	B 0071	Balloons (Fabric impervious to gases for aeronautical —)	B 0116	240002
09	B 0072	Balloons (Meteorological —)	B 0121	090075
28	B 0073	Balloons (Play —)	B 0117	280012
16	B 0074	Balls for ball-point pens	B 0431	160253
28	B 0075	Balls for games	B 0113	280011
06	B 0076	Balls of steel	B 0427	060265
01	B 0077	Balm of gurjun [gurjon, gurjan] for making varnish	B 0275	010343
05	B 0078	Balms for medical purposes	B 0277	050050
03	B 0079	Balms other than for medical purposes	B 0278	030222
02	B 0080	Balsam (Canada —)	B 0276	020022
05	B 0081	Balsamic preparations for medical purposes	B 0122	050046
19	B 0082	Balustrading	B 0123	190016
20	B 0083	Bamboo	B 0124	200019
20	B 0084	Bamboo curtains	R 0316	200255
15	B 0085	Bamboo flutes	F 0325	150082
01	B 0086	Bandages (Adhesive preparations for surgical —)	A 0106	010022
10	B 0087	Bandages, elastic	B 0133	100022

Cl.	SERIAL No. (E)	INDICATION OF GOODS	SERIAL No. (F)	BASIC No.
05	B 0088	Bandages for dressings	B 0169	050049
10	B 0089	Bandages for joints, anatomical	B 0135	100020
05	B 0090	Bandages (Hygienic —)	B 0160	050047
10	B 0091	Bandages (Knee —), orthopedic	G 0167	100193
05	B 0092	Bandages (Menstruation —)	B 0167	050233
10	B 0093	Bandages (Supportive —)	B 0135	100020
10	B 0094	Bandages (Suspensory —)	S 0615	100148
25	B 0095	Bandanas [neckerchiefs]	B 0138	250148
18	B 0096	Bandoliers	B 0176	180096
13	B 0097	Bandoliers for weapons	B 0177	130063
15	B 0098	Bandonions	B 0175	150011
05	B 0099	Bands (Adhesive —), for medical purposes	B 0149	050294
07	B 0100	Bands (Adhesive —) for pulleys	B 0126	070314
17	B 0101	Bands (Adhesive —) other than stationery and not for medical or household purposes	B 0148	170085
02	B 0102	Bands (Anti-corrosive —)	B 0170	020021
26	B 0103	Bands (Expanding —) for holding sleeves	B 0788	260023
12	B 0104	Bands for wheel hubs	F 0433	120127
26	B 0105	Bands (Hair —)	B 0143	260013
22	B 0106	Bands (Hemp —)	S 0077	220015
22	B 0107	Bands, not of metal, for wrapping or binding	B 0147	220078
18	B 0108	Bands of leather	S 0078	180080
06	B 0109	Bands of metal for tying-up purposes	B 0146	060285
17	B 0110	Bands of rubber for unscrewing jar lids	B 0511	170012
24	B 0111	Banners	B 0178	240006
09	B 0112	Bar code readers	L 0179	090581
11	B 0113	Barbecue grills (Lava rocks for use in —)	P 0462	110326
11	B 0114	Barbecues	B 0189	110265
06	B 0115	Barbed wire	B 0190	060041
28	B 0116	Bar-bells	H 0019	280075
12	B 0117	Barges	C 0445	120063
01	B 0118	Barium	B 0213	010101
01	B 0119	Barium compounds	B 0214	010104
01	B 0120	Barium sulphate	B 0215	010574
17	B 0121	Bark coverings for sound insulation	E 0118	170037
03	B 0122	Bark (Quillaia —) for washing	E 0115	030093
05	B 0123	Barks for pharmaceutical purposes	E 0116	050132
31	B 0124	Barks (Raw —)	E 0117	310139
31	B 0125	Barley *	O 0113	310095
30	B 0126	Barley (Crushed —)	O 0114	300105
30	B 0127	Barley (Husked —)	O 0116	300100
30	B 0128	Barley meal	O 0115	300061
09	B 0129	Barometers	B 0199	090079
20	B 0130	Barrel hoops, not of metal	C 0404	200211
06	B 0131	Barrel hoops of metal	C 0403	060288
15	B 0132	Barrel organs	B 0182	150012
14	B 0133	Barrels [clock and watch making]	B 0194	140014
13	B 0134	Barrels (Gun —)	C 0184	130021
20	B 0135	Barrels, not of metal	B 0198	200210
06	B 0136	Barrels of metal	T 0396	060287

Cl.	SERIAL No. (E)	INDICATION OF GOODS	SERIAL No. (F)	BASIC No.
13	B 0137	Barrels (Rifle —)	C 0184	130021
26	B 0138	Barrettes [hair-slides]	B 0208	260040
06	B 0139	Barriers (Crash —) of metal for roads	G 0229	060397
17	B 0140	Barriers (Floating anti-pollution —)	B 0200	170108
08	B 0141	Bars (Cutting —)	B 0204	080027
06	B 0142	Bars for metal railings	B 0201	060042
06	B 0143	Bars (Latch —) of metal	C 0937	060022
12	B 0144	Bars (Torsion —) for vehicles	B 0205	120034
01	B 0145	Baryta	B 0211	010102
01	B 0146	Baryta paper	P 0085	010103
01	B 0147	Barytes	S 0485	010495
28	B 0148	Baseball gloves	G 0047	280141
01	B 0149	Bases [chemical preparations]	B 0225	010106
01	B 0150	Basic gallate of bismuth	G 0022	010126
21	B 0151	Basins [bowls]	B 0631	210039
10	B 0152	Basins for medical purposes	B 0229	100026
21	B 0153	Basins [receptacles]	B 0234	210025
07	B 0154	Basket presses	P 0967	070533
12	B 0155	Baskets adapted for cycles	P 0061	120248
20	B 0156	Baskets (Fishing —)	P 0058	200021
21	B 0157	Baskets for domestic use	C 1252	210266
20	B 0158	Baskets, not of metal	P 0060	200243
06	B 0159	Baskets of metal	C 1253	060199
15	B 0160	Basses [musical instruments]	B 0227	150013
20	B 0161	Bassinettes	B 0321	200023
21	B 0162	Basting spoons, for kitchen use	L 0375	210156
01	B 0163	Bate for dressing skins	C 1173	010208
11	B 0164	Bath fittings	B 0074	110037
11	B 0165	Bath fittings (Hot air —)	B 0077	110017
11	B 0166	Bath installations	B 0063	110039
11	B 0167	Bath installations (Sauna —)	S 0108	110297
24	B 0168	Bath linen, except clothing	L 0287	240005
11	B 0169	Bath linings	G 0069	110034
27	B 0170	Bath mats	D 0119	270001
11	B 0171	Bath plumbing fixtures	B 0063	110039
05	B 0172	Bath preparations, medicated	B 0084	050041
25	B 0173	Bath robes	B 0066	250127
05	B 0174	Bath salts for medical purposes	S 0215	050302
03	B 0175	Bath salts, not for medical purposes	S 0216	030175
25	B 0176	Bath sandals	B 0069	250004
25	B 0177	Bath slippers	B 0072	250005
05	B 0178	Bath (Therapeutic preparations for the —)	B 0068	050045
11	B 0179	Bath tubs	B 0050	110033
11	B 0180	Bath tubs for sitz baths	B 0056	110035
25	B 0181	Bathing caps	B 0057	250124
25	B 0182	Bathing drawers	C 0125	250125
25	B 0183	Bathing suits	B 0065	250126
25	B 0184	Bathing trunks	C 0125	250125
21	B 0185	Baths (Baby —), portable	B 0055	210301
06	B 0186	Baths (Bird —) [structures of metal]	B 0052	060280
03	B 0187	Baths (Cosmetic preparations for —)	B 0067	030016
01	B 0188	Baths (Fixing —) [photography]	B 0078	010097
01	B 0189	Baths for galvanizing	B 0079	010098

Cl.	SERIAL No. (E)	INDICATION OF GOODS	SERIAL No. (F)	BASIC No.
11	B 0190	Baths (Heaters for—)	C 0609	110038
05	B 0191	Baths (Oxygen—)	B 0083	050043
05	B 0192	Baths (Salts for mineral water—)	B 0082	050042
11	B 0193	Baths (Spa—) [vessels]	B 0073	110291
01	B 0194	Baths (Toning—) [photography]	B 0081	010099
15	B 0195	Batons (Conductors'—)	B 0044	150009
28	B 0196	Bats for games	R 0075	280081
01	B 0197	Batteries (Acidulated water for recharging—)	E 0002	010251
01	B 0198	Batteries (Anti-frothing solutions for—)	A 0042	010006
09	B 0199	Batteries, electric	P 0479	090360
09	B 0200	Batteries, electric, for vehicles	A 0040	090007
09	B 0201	Batteries for lighting	B 0260	090031
01	B 0202	Batteries (Liquids for removing sulphates from—)	A 0038	010500
01	B 0203	Batteries (Salts for galvanic—)	S 0214	010261
09	B 0204	Battery boxes	C 0097	090009
09	B 0205	Battery chargers	C 0532	090266
09	B 0206	Battery jars	B 0007	090008
28	B 0207	Batting gloves [accessories for games]	B 0267	280015
01	B 0208	Bauxite	B 0279	010108
08	B 0209	Bayonets	B 0088	080025
18	B 0210	Beach bags	S 0035	180076
25	B 0211	Beach clothes	P 0556	250104
25	B 0212	Beach shoes	C 0639	250105
09	B 0213	Beacons, luminous	B 0107	090513
19	B 0214	Beacons, not of metal, non-luminous	B 0109	190195
06	B 0215	Beacons of metal, non-luminous	B 0108	060282
20	B 0216	Bead curtains for decoration	R 0318	200167
14	B 0217	Beads for making jewelry	P 0337	140167
26	B 0218	Beads other than for making jewelry	P 0335	260123
06	B 0219	Beak-irons [bick-irons]	B 0411	060045
19	B 0220	Beams, not of metal	P 0938	190083
30	B 0221	Bean meal	F 0147	300058
31	B 0222	Beans, fresh	F 0148	310054
31	B 0223	Beans (Locust—)	C 0271	310022
29	B 0224	Beans, preserved	F 0146	290123
08	B 0225	Beard clippers	C 1382	080026
03	B 0226	Beard dyes	B 0186	030176
26	B 0227	Beards (False—)	B 0191	260014
07	B 0228	Bearing brackets for machines	C 0439	070091
07	B 0229	Bearings (Ball rings for—)	B 0027	070339
07	B 0230	Bearings for transmission shafts	P 0044	070290
07	B 0231	Bearings [parts of machines]	C 1439	070130
21	B 0232	Beaters (Carpet—), not being machines	T 0105	210008
07	B 0233	Beaters, electric	B 0266	070403
21	B 0234	Beaters, non-electric	B 0268	210238
07	B 0235	Beating machines	B 0271	070044
03	B 0236	Beauty masks	M 0181	030020
24	B 0237	Bed blankets	C 1478	240114
20	B 0238	Bed casters, not of metal	L 0350	200139

Cl.	SERIAL No. (E)	INDICATION OF GOODS	SERIAL No. (F)	BASIC No.
06	B 0239	Bed casters of metal	L 0349	060166
24	B 0240	Bed clothes	L 0327	240099
24	B 0241	Bed covers	C 1490	240029
24	B 0242	Bed covers of paper	C 1479	240032
20	B 0243	Bed fittings, not of metal	G 0081	200124
24	B 0244	Bed linen	L 0288	240068
10	B 0245	Bed pans	B 0230	100025
10	B 0246	Bed vibrators	V 0231	100157
20	B 0247	Bedding, except linen	L 0326	200077
22	B 0248	Bedding (Feathers for—)	P 0669	220057
20	B 0249	Beds *	L 0339	200102
06	B 0250	Beds (Fittings of metal for—)	G 0080	060393
20	B 0251	Beds for household pets	C 1361	200007
20	B 0252	Beds (Hospital—)	L 0344	200138
10	B 0253	Beds (Hydrostatic [water]—) for medical purposes	L 0347	100096
20	B 0254	Beds (Hydrostatic [water]—), not for medical purposes	L 0348	200230
10	B 0255	Beds, specially made for medical purposes	L 0341	100173
24	B 0256	Bedspreads	C 1490	240029
20	B 0257	Bedsteads of wood	B 0533	200026
11	B 0258	Bedwarmers	C 0614	110304
30	B 0259	Bee glue*	P 0988	300166
20	B 0260	Beehives	R 0449	200001
20	B 0261	Beehives (Comb foundations for—)	R 0109	200004
20	B 0262	Beehives (Sections of wood for—)	C 0066	200040
32	B 0263	Beer	B 0410	320002
07	B 0264	Beer (Apparatus for drawing up - under pressure)	B 0402	070012
02	B 0265	Beer (Colorants for—)	B 0404	020024
21	B 0266	Beer mugs	C 0796	210032
01	B 0267	Beer preserving agents	C 1182	010619
07	B 0268	Beer pumps	P 0768	070390
30	B 0269	Beer vinegar	B 0409	300148
32	B 0270	Beer wort	B 0406	320005
01	B 0271	Beer-clarifying and preserving agents	B 0408	010121
04	B 0272	Beeswax	A 0006	040001
31	B 0273	Beet	B 0350	310015
08	B 0274	Bellows (Fireplace—) [hand tools]	S 0441	080255
15	B 0275	Bellows for musical instruments	S 0437	150064
07	B 0276	Bellows [machines]	S 0434	070350
06	B 0277	Bells *	S 0401	060241
09	B 0278	Bells (Alarm—), electric	T 0268	090071
06	B 0279	Bells for animals	S 0398	060240
12	B 0280	Bells for bicycles, cycles	S 0402	120098
28	B 0281	Bells for Christmas trees	C 0957	280039
09	B 0282	Bells (Signal—)	C 0954	090127
09	B 0283	Bells [warning devices]	S 0400	090402
26	B 0284	Belt clasps	F 0082	260031
07	B 0285	Belt conveyors	C 1418	070037
06	B 0286	Belt stretchers of metal	T 0183	060101
04	B 0287	Belting wax	C 0888	040028
13	B 0288	Belts adapted for ammunition	C 0366	130074
25	B 0289	Belts [clothing]	C 0359	250031
07	B 0290	Belts (Dynamo—)	C 1422	070126

Cl.	SERIAL No. (E)	INDICATION OF GOODS	SERIAL No. (F)	BASIC No.
10	B 0291	Belts, electric, for medical purposes	C 0361	100175
07	B 0292	Belts for conveyors	C 1427	070036
07	B 0293	Belts for machines	C 1424	070074
10	B 0294	Belts for medical purposes	C 0360	100045
07	B 0295	Belts for motors and engines	C 1432	070343
05	B 0296	Belts for sanitary napkins [towels]	C 0365	050071
04	B 0297	Belts (Grease for—)	C 1431	040033
18	B 0298	Belts (Leather shoulder—)	B 0176	180096
25	B 0299	Belts (Money—) [clothing]	C 0363	250160
04	B 0300	Belts (Non-slipping preparations for—)	A 0581	040009
22	B 0301	Belts, not of metal, for handling loads	S 0081	220082
06	B 0302	Belts of metal for handling loads	S 0080	060305
10	B 0303	Belts (Orthopaedic [orthopedic]—)	C 0362	100047
08	B 0304	Belts (Tool—) [holders]	C 0364	080247
28	B 0305	Belts (Weight lifting—) [sports articles]	C 0357	280176
20	B 0306	Benches [furniture]	B 0125	200020
20	B 0307	Benches (Vice—) not of metal	E 0491	200209
06	B 0308	Benches (Vice—) of metal	E 0490	060283
20	B 0309	Benches (Work—)	E 0474	200106
07	B 0310	Bending machines	C 0869	070104
13	B 0311	Bengal lights	F 0142	130017
01	B 0312	Bentonite	B 0308	010109
04	B 0313	Benzene	B 0309	040082
01	B 0314	Benzene derivatives	B 0311	010111
01	B 0315	Benzene (Methyl—)	B 0312	010577
01	B 0316	Benzene-based acids	B 0310	010110
04	B 0317	Benzine	E 0449	040043
01	B 0318	Benzoic acid	B 0314	010112
01	B 0319	Benzoic sulphinide	S 0579	010113
04	B 0320	Benzol	B 0316	040083
01	B 0321	Benzol (Methyl—)	B 0317	010576
25	B 0322	Berets	B 0322	250009
03	B 0323	Bergamot oil	B 0323	030021
01	B 0324	Berkelium	B 0324	010115
31	B 0325	Berries, fresh fruits	B 0049	310013
12	B 0326	Berths (Sleeping—) for vehicles	C 1362	120081
06	B 0327	Beryllium [glucinium]	B 0325	060043
09	B 0328	Betatrons	B 0337	090085
11	B 0329	Beverage cooling apparatus	B 0571	110119
07	B 0330	Beverage preparation machines, electromechanical	B 0570	070315
33	B 0331	Beverages (Alcoholic—), except beer	B 0567	330026
30	B 0332	Beverages (Chocolate-based—)	B 0563	300151
30	B 0333	Beverages (Cocoa-based—)	B 0561	300150
30	B 0334	Beverages (Coffee-based—)	B 0562	300149
33	B 0335	Beverages (Distilled—)	B 0577	330008
03	B 0336	Beverages (Flavorings [flavourings] for—) [essential oils]	B 0573	030173
30	B 0337	Beverages (Flavorings [flavourings], other than essential oils, for—)	B 0572	300141
31	B 0338	Beverages for pets	A 0518	310142
21	B 0339	Beverages (Heat insulated containers for—)	B 0587	210035
32	B 0340	Beverages (Non-alcoholic—)	B 0588	320031
32	B 0341	Beverages (Preparations for making—)	B 0586	320008
30	B 0342	Beverages (Tea-based—)	B 0565	300187
32	B 0343	Beverages (Whey—)	B 0564	320007
25	B 0344	Bibs, not of paper	B 0283	250128
16	B 0345	Bibs of paper	B 0282	160276
01	B 0346	Bicarbonate of soda for chemical purposes	B 0369	010578
30	B 0347	Bicarbonate of soda for cooking purposes [baking soda]	B 0371	300200
05	B 0348	Bicarbonate of soda for pharmaceutical purposes	B 0370	050304
01	B 0349	Bichloride of tin	B 0373	010118
01	B 0350	Bichromate of potassium	B 0374	010119
01	B 0351	Bichromate of soda	B 0375	010120
07	B 0352	Bicycle assembling machines	B 0393	070512
12	B 0353	Bicycle bells	S 0402	120098
12	B 0354	Bicycle brakes	B 0387	120086
12	B 0355	Bicycle chains	C 0430	120061
07	B 0356	Bicycle dynamos	B 0382	070047
12	B 0357	Bicycle frames	C 0061	120221
12	B 0358	Bicycle handle bars	G 0371	120080
11	B 0359	Bicycle lights	B 0383	110045
19	B 0360	Bicycle parking installations, not of metal	B 0391	190199
06	B 0361	Bicycle parking installations of metal	B 0390	060293
12	B 0362	Bicycle pumps	B 0394	120093
12	B 0363	Bicycle rims	B 0392	120088
12	B 0364	Bicycle saddles	B 0396	120096
12	B 0365	Bicycle spokes	B 0395	120094
12	B 0366	Bicycle stands	B 0379	120046
12	B 0367	Bicycle tires [tyres]	B 0378	120084
12	B 0368	Bicycles	B 0377	120044
28	B 0369	Bicycles (Stationary exercise—)	B 0385	280017
11	B 0370	Bidets	B 0398	110046
08	B 0371	Bill-hooks	S 0240	080188
28	B 0372	Billiard balls	B 0428	280019
24	B 0373	Billiard cloth	T 0113	240007
28	B 0374	Billiard cue tips	P 0976	280122
28	B 0375	Billiard cues	Q 0011	280121
28	B 0376	Billiard markers	B 0424	280021
28	B 0377	Billiard table cushions	B 0153	280013
28	B 0378	Billiard tables	T 0034	280123
28	B 0379	Billiard tables (Coin-operated—)	T 0035	280124
01	B 0380	Billposting (Adhesives for—)	C 1033	010028
16	B 0381	Binders (Loose-leaf—)	B 0368	160035
30	B 0382	Binding agents for ice cream [edible ices]	L 0230	300074
19	B 0383	Binding agents for making briquettes	L 0232	190040
07	B 0384	Binding apparatus for hay	B 0660	070058
26	B 0385	Binding needles	A 0190	260006

Cl.	SERIAL No. (E)	INDICATION OF GOODS	SERIAL No. (F)	BASIC No.
02	B 0386	Binding preparations for paints	L 0234	020087
20	B 0387	Binding screws, not of metal, for cables	S 0244	200224
06	B 0388	Binding screws of metal for cables	S 0243	060314
16	B 0389	Binding strips [bookbinding]	O 0069	160205
01	B 0390	Binding substances (Foundry—)	L 0231	010306
22	B 0391	Binding thread, not of metal, for agricultural purposes	L 0245	220086
06	B 0392	Binding thread of metal for agricultural purposes	L 0243	060319
06	B 0393	Bindings of metal	L 0242	060363
28	B 0394	Bingo cards	C 0289	280178
09	B 0395	Binoculars	J 0064	090475
21	B 0396	Bins (Dust—)	P 0905	210194
20	B 0397	Bins, not of metal	C 0104	200207
06	B 0398	Bins of metal	C 0997	060398
20	B 0399	Bins of wood or plastic	C 0098	200228
01	B 0400	Biochemical catalysts	B 0438	010122
05	B 0401	Biocides	B 0439	050052
05	B 0402	Biological preparations for medical purposes	B 0440	050305
05	B 0403	Biological preparations for veterinary purposes	B 0441	050361
01	B 0404	Biological preparations, other than for medical or veterinary purposes	B 0442	010579
16	B 0405	Biological samples for use in microscopy [teaching materials]	C 1396	160039
05	B 0406	Biological tissue cultures for medical purposes	C 1657	050405
05	B 0407	Biological tissue cultures for veterinary purposes	C 1658	050406
01	B 0408	Biological tissue cultures other than for medical or veterinary purposes	C 1659	010658
21	B 0409	Bird baths *	B 0051	210019
19	B 0410	Bird baths [structures, not of metal]	B 0053	190194
06	B 0411	Bird baths [structures of metal]	B 0052	060280
31	B 0412	Bird food	O 0034	310035
21	B 0413	Birdcages	V 0320	210059
01	B 0414	Birdlime	G 0233	010334
06	B 0415	Bird-repelling devices made of metal (Wind-driven—)	O 0040	060432
26	B 0416	Birds' feathers [clothing accessories]	O 0042	260074
20	B 0417	Birds (Stuffed—)	O 0041	200156
30	B 0418	Biscuits	B 0448	300016
31	B 0419	Biscuits (Dog—)	B 0449	310031
01	B 0420	Bismuth	B 0450	010125
01	B 0421	Bismuth (Basic gallate of—)	G 0022	010126
01	B 0422	Bismuth nitrite for chemical purposes	B 0453	010494
05	B 0423	Bismuth preparations for pharmaceutical purposes	B 0452	050053
05	B 0424	Bismuth subnitrate for pharmaceutical purposes	B 0454	050263
28	B 0425	Bite indicators [fishing tackle]	B 0680	280154
28	B 0426	Bite sensors [fishing tackle]	D 0165	280155
18	B 0427	Bits for animals [harness]	M 0476	180017
08	B 0428	Bits [hand tools]	T 0500	080197
08	B 0429	Bits [parts of hand tools]	M 0246	080016
33	B 0430	Bitters	A 0428	330003
19	B 0431	Bitumen	B 0456	190017
07	B 0432	Bitumen making machines	B 0458	070050
02	B 0433	Bitumen varnish	B 0459	020025
19	B 0434	Bituminous coatings for roofing	T 0363	190082
19	B 0435	Bituminous products for building	B 0460	190025
02	B 0436	Black japan	A 0790	020017
01	B 0437	Black (Lamp—) for industrial purposes	N 0086	010316
29	B 0438	Black pudding	B 0690	290013
16	B 0439	Blackboards	T 0028	160201
02	B 0440	Blacks [colorants or paints]	N 0088	020051
28	B 0441	Bladders of balls for games	C 0459	280001
07	B 0442	Blade holders [parts of machines]	P 0817	070227
08	B 0443	Blade sharpening instruments	L 0080	080093
07	B 0444	Blade sharpening [stropping] machines	L 0081	070225
07	B 0445	Blades (Chaff cutter—)	L 0073	070223
08	B 0446	Blades for planes	F 0112	080119
08	B 0447	Blades [hand tools]	L 0082	080149
07	B 0448	Blades [parts of machines]	F 0115	070189
08	B 0449	Blades [weapons]	L 0071	080150
24	B 0450	Blankets (Bed—)	C 1478	240114
10	B 0451	Blankets, electric, for medical purposes	C 1474	100191
11	B 0452	Blankets, electric, not for medical purposes	C 1475	110305
19	B 0453	Blast furnaces (Cement for—)	H 0046	190093
01	B 0454	Bleaching chemicals (Fat-—)	G 0320	010339
01	B 0455	Bleaching chemicals (Oil-—)	H 0168	010353
01	B 0456	Bleaching chemicals (Organic-—)	B 0479	010129
01	B 0457	Bleaching chemicals (Wax-—)	C 0898	010128
03	B 0458	Bleaching (Leather—) preparations	C 1611	030025
03	B 0459	Bleaching preparations [decolorants] for cosmetic purposes	D 0032	030192
01	B 0460	Bleaching preparations [decolorants] for industrial purposes	D 0033	010580
03	B 0461	Bleaching preparations [laundry]	L 0205	030124
03	B 0462	Bleaching salts	S 0212	030026
03	B 0463	Bleaching soda	S 0417	030027
07	B 0464	Blenders, electric, for household purposes	E 0274	070444
21	B 0465	Blenders, non-electric, for household purposes	E 0275	210096
18	B 0466	Blinders [harness]	O 0012	180056
20	B 0467	Blinds (Indoor window—) [shades] [furniture]	S 0545	200272

Cl.	SERIAL No. (E)	INDICATION OF GOODS	SERIAL No. (F)	BASIC No.
22	B 0468	Blinds (Ladder tapes or webbing for venetian —)	R 0431	220045
19	B 0469	Blinds [outdoor], not of metal and not of textile	S 0543	190107
20	B 0470	Blinds (Slatted indoor —)	S 0544	200136
18	B 0471	Blinkers [harness]	O 0012	180056
09	B 0472	Blinkers [signalling lights]	C 0943	090126
28	B 0473	Blocks (Building —) [toys]	B 0495	280025
01	B 0474	Blood charcoal	C 0513	010168
05	B 0475	Blood for medical purposes	S 0074	050265
05	B 0476	Blood plasma	P 0618	050248
29	B 0477	Blood sausage	B 0690	290013
10	B 0478	Blood testing apparatus	A 0490	100087
06	B 0479	Blooms [metallurgy]	L 0376	060168
16	B 0480	Blotters	B 0918	160051
26	B 0481	Blouse fasteners	C 1323	260048
07	B 0482	Blowing engines	S 0434	070350
07	B 0483	Blowing machines	S 0435	070534
07	B 0484	Blowing machines for the compression, exhaustion and transport of gases	S 0439	070199
07	B 0485	Blowing machines for the compression, sucking and carrying of grain	S 0440	070203
08	B 0486	Bludgeons	M 0230	080130
03	B 0487	Blueing for laundry	B 0491	030014
03	B 0488	Blueing (Laundry —)	C 1056	030059
09	B 0489	Blueprint apparatus	P 0384	090106
01	B 0490	Blueprint cloth	T 0294	010434
01	B 0491	Blueprint paper	P 0114	010432
16	B 0492	Blueprints	P 0585	160223
03	B 0493	Bluing for laundry	B 0491	030014
28	B 0494	Board games	J 0041	280156
20	B 0495	Boarding stairs, not of metal, mobile, for passengers	E 0093	200093
06	B 0496	Boarding stairs of metal, mobile, for passengers	E 0092	060362
20	B 0497	Boards (Display —)	T 0022	200002
19	B 0498	Boards (Floor —)	B 0559	190035
21	B 0499	Boards (Ironing —)	P 0569	210179
06	B 0500	Boards of metal (Building —)	P 0065	060381
25	B 0501	Boas [necklets]	B 0500	250011
12	B 0502	Boat hooks	C 1568	120036
12	B 0503	Boats	B 0236	120021
07	B 0504	Boats (Engines for —)	B 0241	070401
09	B 0505	Boats (Fire —)	B 0247	090601
12	B 0506	Boats (Masts for —)	M 0236	120259
07	B 0507	Boats (Motors for —)	B 0243	070402
26	B 0508	Bobbins for retaining embroidery floss or wool [not parts of machines]	B 0506	260124
07	B 0509	Bobbins for weaving looms	B 0502	070054
28	B 0510	Bob-sleighs	B 0509	280026
25	B 0511	Bodices [lingerie]	C 0149	250025
12	B 0512	Bodies for vehicles	C 0279	120222
26	B 0513	Bodkins	P 0177	260090
22	B 0514	Body bags	S 0047	220107
28	B 0515	Body boards	B 0513	280177
10	B 0516	Body cavities (Appliances for washing —)	C 0352	100044
28	B 0517	Body-building apparatus	C 1660	280044
28	B 0518	Body-training apparatus	C 1660	280044
12	B 0519	Bogies for railway cars	B 0515	120047
17	B 0520	Boiler composition to prevent the radiation of heat	C 0592	170026
09	B 0521	Boiler control instruments	C 0591	090120
11	B 0522	Boiler pipes [tubes] for heating installations	T 0560	110078
07	B 0523	Boiler scale collectors (Machine —)	C 1029	070110
07	B 0524	Boiler tubes [parts of machines]	T 0561	070471
11	B 0525	Boilers, other than parts of machines	C 0580	110047
20	B 0526	Bolsters	T 0490	200195
24	B 0527	Bolting cloth	E 0484	240009
20	B 0528	Bolts (Door —) not of metal	V 0180	200280
06	B 0529	Bolts (Door —) of metal	V 0179	060220
06	B 0530	Bolts, flat	T 0131	060247
06	B 0531	Bolts (Lock —)	P 0312	060204
20	B 0532	Bolts, not of metal	B 0732	200218
06	B 0533	Bolts of metal	B 0731	060049
28	B 0534	Bonbons (Explosive —) [Christmas crackers]	B 0636	280027
05	B 0535	Bone cement for surgical and orthopaedic purposes	C 0854	050385
01	B 0536	Bone charcoal	C 0515	010167
29	B 0537	Bone oil, edible	O 0131	290092
04	B 0538	Bone oil for industrial purposes	O 0132	040067
20	B 0539	Book rests [furniture]	P 0818	200270
07	B 0540	Bookbinding apparatus and machines for industrial purposes	R 0203	070327
16	B 0541	Bookbinding apparatus and machines [office equipment]	R 0205	160330
16	B 0542	Bookbinding cloth	T 0326	160238
16	B 0543	Bookbinding cords	F 0242	160239
16	B 0544	Bookbinding material	R 0207	160236
16	B 0545	Bookbindings	R 0206	160237
16	B 0546	Bookends	S 0247	160018
16	B 0547	Booklets	L 0357	160189
16	B 0548	Bookmarkers	S 0319	160249
16	B 0549	Books	L 0353	160095
34	B 0550	Books of cigarette papers	C 0093	340010
03	B 0551	Boot cream	C 1540	030039
21	B 0552	Boot jacks	T 0278	210041
03	B 0553	Boot polish	C 1540	030039
21	B 0554	Boot trees [stretchers]	C 0646	210120
25	B 0555	Boot uppers	T 0261	250040
25	B 0556	Boots *	B 0661	250014
10	B 0557	Boots for medical purposes	B 0662	100031
25	B 0558	Boots for sports *	C 0642	250141
04	B 0559	Boots (Grease for —)	G 0317	040026
28	B 0560	Boots (Skating —) with skates attached	B 0666	280028
25	B 0561	Boots (Ski —)	C 0641	250145
01	B 0562	Borax	B 0647	010134
08	B 0563	Border shears	F 0023	080112
08	B 0564	Borers	P 0327	080067
07	B 0565	Borers (Mine —)	T 0132	070264

Cl.	SERIAL No. (E)	INDICATION OF GOODS	SERIAL No. (F)	BASIC No.
01	B 0566	Boric acid for industrial purposes	B 0653	010135
07	B 0567	Bottle capping machines	C 0210	070411
20	B 0568	Bottle caps, not of metal	C 0215	200219
06	B 0569	Bottle caps of metal	C 0214	060299
20	B 0570	Bottle casings of wood	E 0236	200238
20	B 0571	Bottle closures, not of metal	F 0075	200220
06	B 0572	Bottle closures of metal	F 0074	060300
16	B 0573	Bottle envelopes of cardboard or paper	E 0361	160282
22	B 0574	Bottle envelopes of straw	E 0239	220080
06	B 0575	Bottle fasteners of metal	F 0074	060300
07	B 0576	Bottle filling machines	R 0221	070064
21	B 0577	Bottle gourds	B 0399	210144
21	B 0578	Bottle openers	O 0157	210048
20	B 0579	Bottle racks	B 0745	200031
07	B 0580	Bottle sealing machines	B 0755	070412
07	B 0581	Bottle stoppering machines	B 0753	070410
07	B 0582	Bottle washing machines	R 0328	070065
16	B 0583	Bottle wrappers of cardboard or paper	E 0237	160304
21	B 0584	Bottles	B 0741	210045
20	B 0585	Bottles (Corks for—)	B 0674	200029
06	B 0586	Bottles [metal containers] for compressed gas or liquid air	B 0758	060050
21	B 0587	Bottles (Refrigerating—)	B 0759	210047
22	B 0588	Bottles (Straw wrappers for—)	E 0239	220080
10	B 0589	Bougies [surgery]	B 0704	100033
29	B 0590	Bouillon	B 0717	290014
29	B 0591	Bouillon concentrates	C 1127	290023
29	B 0592	Bouillon (Preparations for making—)	B 0719	290015
05	B 0593	Bouillons for bacteriological cultures	B 0718	050036
15	B 0594	Bow nuts for musical instruments	H 0042	150005
08	B 0595	Bow saws	S 0138	080021
28	B 0596	Bowling apparatus and machinery	J 0034	280031
21	B 0597	Bowls [basins]	B 0631	210039
21	B 0598	Bowls (Glass—)	B 0728	210044
28	B 0599	Bows for archery	A 0679	280007
15	B 0600	Bows for musical instruments	A 0676	150004
26	B 0601	Bows for the hair	N 0082	260114
16	B 0602	Bows (Paper—)	N 0081	160351
06	B 0603	Box fasteners of metal	F 0073	060048
07	B 0604	Boxes for matrices [printing]	C 0336	070081
26	B 0605	Boxes for needles	C 0333	260092
16	B 0606	Boxes for pens	P 0671	160133
21	B 0607	Boxes for sweetmeats	B 0634	210244
20	B 0608	Boxes (Nesting—)	N 0065	200109
16	B 0609	Boxes of cardboard or paper	B 0619	160280
06	B 0610	Boxes of common metal	B 0623	060295
21	B 0611	Boxes of glass	B 0625	210243
18	B 0612	Boxes of leather (Hat—)	B 0594	180023
18	B 0613	Boxes of leather or leather board	B 0620	180089
21	B 0614	Boxes of metal, for dispensing paper towels	B 0622	210036
14	B 0615	Boxes of precious metal	B 0624	140113
18	B 0616	Boxes of vulcanised fibre	B 0621	180098
20	B 0617	Boxes of wood or plastic	C 0098	200228
06	B 0618	Boxes (Safety cash—)	C 0335	060066
26	B 0619	Boxes (Sewing—)	B 0600	260049
21	B 0620	Boxes (Soap—)	B 0606	210037
28	B 0621	Boxing gloves	G 0048	280032
09	B 0622	Bracelets (Encoded identification—), magnetic	B 0785	090692
05	B 0623	Bracelets for medical purposes	B 0779	050060
20	B 0624	Bracelets (Identification—), not of metal, for hospital purposes	B 0784	200221
14	B 0625	Bracelets [jewellery, jewelry (Am.)]	B 0781	140015
06	B 0626	Bracelets of metal (Identification—) for hospitals	B 0783	060051
26	B 0627	Braces (Fastenings for—)	B 0805	260026
25	B 0628	Braces for clothing [suspenders]	B 0804	250018
22	B 0629	Braces, not of metal, for handling loads	B 0807	220081
06	B 0630	Braces of metal for handling loads	B 0806	060026
07	B 0631	Brackets (Bearing—) for machines	C 0439	070091
11	B 0632	Brackets for gas burners	A 0625	110251
06	B 0633	Brackets of metal for building	E 0415	060123
20	B 0634	Brackets (Picture frame—)	L 0325	200226
06	B 0635	Brads	P 0715	060086
08	B 0636	Braiders [hand tools]	M 0448	080161
07	B 0637	Braiding machines	T 0503	070372
26	B 0638	Braids	L 0007	260062
01	B 0639	Brake fluid	L 0316	010315
17	B 0640	Brake lining materials, partly processed	F 0426	170048
12	B 0641	Brake linings for vehicles	G 0078	120215
07	B 0642	Brake linings other than for vehicles	G 0076	070405
12	B 0643	Brake pads for automobiles	P 0616	120263
07	B 0644	Brake pads other than for vehicles	P 0615	070524
12	B 0645	Brake segments for vehicles	S 0176	120236
07	B 0646	Brake segments other than for vehicles	S 0175	070407
12	B 0647	Brake shoes for vehicles	S 0011	120216
07	B 0648	Brake shoes other than for vehicles	S 0010	070406
12	B 0649	Brakes for bicycles, cycles	B 0387	120086
12	B 0650	Brakes for vehicles	F 0422	120126
31	B 0651	Bran	S 0389	310016
31	B 0652	Bran mash for animal consumption	C 1171	310039
09	B 0653	Branch boxes [electricity]	B 0613	090094
19	B 0654	Branching pipes, not of metal	E 0251	190080
06	B 0655	Branching pipes of metal	E 0250	060366
08	B 0656	Branding irons	F 0103	080122
33	B 0657	Brandy	E 0065	330019
06	B 0658	Brass, unwrought or semi-wrought	L 0065	060157
26	B 0659	Brassards	B 0799	260024

Cl.	SERIAL No. (E)	INDICATION OF GOODS	SERIAL No. (F)	BASIC No.
25	B 0660	Brassieres	S 0477	250114
22	B 0661	Brattice cloth (Tarred —)	C 0959	220001
06	B 0662	Brazing alloys	B 0801	060053
01	B 0663	Brazing fluxes	F 0333	010583
01	B 0664	Brazing preparations	B 0798	010137
06	B 0665	Brazing (Rods of metal for —)	B 0796	060302
30	B 0666	Bread	P 0020	300093
11	B 0667	Bread baking machines	P 0025	110329
20	B 0668	Bread baskets (Bakers' —)	P 0057	200163
21	B 0669	Bread baskets, domestic	P 0021	210017
21	B 0670	Bread bins	B 0605	210310
21	B 0671	Bread boards	P 0568	210169
07	B 0672	Bread cutting machines	P 0024	070288
05	B 0673	Bread (Diabetic —) adapted for medical use	P 0027	050121
30	B 0674	Bread (Ginger —)	P 0022	300055
30	B 0675	Bread rolls	P 0360	300110
11	B 0676	Bread toasters	G 0348	110171
30	B 0677	Breadcrumbs	C 0505	300189
11	B 0678	Bread-making machines	M 0008	110332
08	B 0679	Breast drills	V 0241	080199
10	B 0680	Breast pumps	T 0282	100107
05	B 0681	Breast-nursing pads	C 1438	050378
10	B 0682	Breasts (Artificial —)	S 0182	100141
03	B 0683	Breath freshening sprays	A 0142	030204
03	B 0684	Breath freshening strips	B 0145	030216
09	B 0685	Breathing apparatus, except for artificial respiration	R 0272	090431
09	B 0686	Breathing apparatus for underwater swimming	N 0002	090355
31	B 0687	Bred stock	E 0210	310050
25	B 0688	Breeches for wear	C 1646	250063
13	B 0689	Breeches of firearms	C 1643	130031
07	B 0690	Brewing machines	B 0800	070066
19	B 0691	Bricks	B 0820	190038
19	B 0692	Bricks (Earth for —)	T 0208	190039
01	B 0693	Brickwork preservatives, except paints and oils	B 0821	010381
15	B 0694	Bridges for musical instruments	C 0711	150054
07	B 0695	Bridges (Roller —)	P 0788	070313
18	B 0696	Bridles [harness]	B 0813	180112
18	B 0697	Bridoons	B 0815	180011
18	B 0698	Briefcases	S 0273	180083
03	B 0699	Brightening chemicals (Color- [colour-] —) for household purposes [laundry]	A 0875	030174
01	B 0700	Brightening chemicals (Color- [colour-] —) for industrial purposes	A 0876	010570
04	B 0701	Briquettes (Combustible —)	B 0827	040019
04	B 0702	Briquettes (Wood —)	B 0828	040018
21	B 0703	Bristles (Animal —) [brushware]	S 0369	210010
24	B 0704	Brocades	B 0833	240011
01	B 0705	Bromine for chemical purposes	B 0850	010585
05	B 0706	Bromine for pharmaceutical purposes	B 0851	050306
05	B 0707	Bronchodilating preparations	B 0852	050390
06	B 0708	Bronze	B 0855	060018
02	B 0709	Bronze powder	B 0856	020032

Cl.	SERIAL No. (E)	INDICATION OF GOODS	SERIAL No. (F)	BASIC No.
06	B 0710	Bronzes for tombstones	B 0858	060055
06	B 0711	Bronzes [works of art]	B 0859	060056
02	B 0712	Bronzing lacquers	B 0854	020031
26	B 0713	Brooches [clothing accessories]	B 0834	260027
14	B 0714	Brooches [jewellery, jewelry (Am.)]	B 0835	140019
20	B 0715	Broom handles, not of metal	M 0076	200208
06	B 0716	Broom handles of metal	M 0075	060281
21	B 0717	Brooms	B 0091	210020
29	B 0718	Broth	B 0717	290014
29	B 0719	Broth concentrates	C 1127	290023
21	B 0720	Brush goods	B 0861	210053
20	B 0721	Brush mountings	M 0469	200033
21	B 0722	Brushes *	B 0863	210014
21	B 0723	Brushes (Dishwashing —)	B 0872	210304
07	B 0724	Brushes (Dynamo —)	B 0094	070033
21	B 0725	Brushes (Electric —), except parts of machines	B 0867	210251
07	B 0726	Brushes, electrically operated	B 0868	070413
10	B 0727	Brushes for cleaning body cavities	E 0123	100178
21	B 0728	Brushes for cleaning tanks and containers	E 0124	210278
21	B 0729	Brushes for footwear	C 0630	210071
07	B 0730	Brushes [parts of machines]	B 0870	070068
21	B 0731	Brush-making (Material for —)	B 0862	210054
16	B 0732	Bubble packs (Plastic —) for wrapping or packaging	F 0128	160285
15	B 0733	Buccins [trumpets]	B 0892	150016
21	B 0734	Buckets	S 0154	210023
26	B 0735	Buckles [clothing accessories]	B 0685	260097
06	B 0736	Buckles of common metal [hardware]	B 0688	060298
26	B 0737	Buckles (Shoe —)	B 0686	260088
24	B 0738	Buckram	B 0711	240010
21	B 0739	Buckskin for cleaning	P 0245	210263
08	B 0740	Budding knives	E 0160	080099
12	B 0741	Buffers for railway rolling stock	T 0090	120078
17	B 0742	Buffers of rubber (Shock-absorbing —)	T 0087	170021
28	B 0743	Building blocks [toys]	B 0495	280025
06	B 0744	Building boards of metal	P 0065	060381
19	B 0745	Building cardboard [asphalted]	C 0300	190046
19	B 0746	Building (Framework for —), not of metal	C 0546	190050
06	B 0747	Building (Framework of metal for —)	C 0545	060328
28	B 0748	Building games	C 1202	280041
19	B 0749	Building glass	V 0140	190063
19	B 0750	Building materials, not of metal	M 0218	190197
06	B 0751	Building materials of metal	M 0217	060291
06	B 0752	Building or furniture fittings of nickel-silver	A 0313	060015
19	B 0753	Building panels, not of metal	P 0066	190223
06	B 0754	Building panels of metal	P 0065	060381
19	B 0755	Building paper	P 0092	190062
06	B 0756	Building (Reinforcing materials of metal for —)	A 0723	060276
19	B 0757	Building stone	P 0456	190141
19	B 0758	Building timber	B 0530	190027

Cl.	SERIAL No. (E)	INDICATION OF GOODS	SERIAL No. (F)	BASIC No.
06	B 0759	Buildings (Fittings of metal for—)	F 0094	060140
19	B 0760	Buildings, not of metal	C 1206	190061
06	B 0761	Buildings of metal	C 1205	060339
19	B 0762	Buildings, transportable, not of metal	C 1208	190119
06	B 0763	Buildings, transportable, of metal	C 1207	060170
31	B 0764	Bulbs	O 0030	310091
07	B 0765	Bulldozers	B 0762	070069
09	B 0766	Bullet-proof waistcoats [vests (Am.)]	G 0193	090582
12	B 0767	Bumpers for automobiles	A 0853	120209
12	B 0768	Bumpers (Vehicle—)	P 0154	120077
20	B 0769	Bungs, not of metal	B 0639	200213
06	B 0770	Bungs of metal	B 0638	060296
05	B 0771	Bunion pads	C 1441	050391
30	B 0772	Buns	B 0819	300023
24	B 0773	Bunting	E 0483	240043
09	B 0774	Buoys (Marking—)	B 0697	090583
20	B 0775	Buoys (Mooring—) not of metal	B 0696	200251
06	B 0776	Buoys (Mooring—) of metal	B 0695	060412
09	B 0777	Buoys (Signalling—)	B 0699	090518
11	B 0778	Burners	B 0883	110060
11	B 0779	Burners (Acetylene—)	B 0292	110003
11	B 0780	Burners for lamps	B 0298	110044
11	B 0781	Burners (Gas—)	B 0296	110161
11	B 0782	Burners (Germicidal—)	B 0885	110061
11	B 0783	Burners (Incandescent—)	B 0294	110043
11	B 0784	Burners (Laboratory—)	B 0884	110058
21	B 0785	Burners (Perfume—)	B 0882	210056
05	B 0786	Burns (Preparations for the treatment of—)	B 0888	050061
10	B 0787	Burs (Dental—)	F 0417	100072
12	B 0788	Buses (Motor—)	A 0831	120018
31	B 0789	Bushes	A 0667	310011
08	B 0790	Bushhammers	B 0669	080036
26	B 0791	Busks (Corset—)	B 0105	260012
21	B 0792	Busts of china, terra-cotta or glass	B 0913	210252
06	B 0793	Busts of common metal	B 0910	060307
14	B 0794	Busts of precious metal	B 0911	140123
19	B 0795	Busts of stone, concrete or marble	B 0912	190202
20	B 0796	Busts of wood, wax, plaster or plastic	B 0909	200223
29	B 0797	Butter	B 0351	290008
29	B 0798	Butter (Chocolate nut—)	B 0356	290009
29	B 0799	Butter (Cocoa—)	B 0356	290009
29	B 0800	Butter (Coconut—)	B 0357	290010
02	B 0801	Butter (Colorants for—)	B 0353	020023
21	B 0802	Butter dishes	B 0359	210030
07	B 0803	Butter machines	B 0358	070046
29	B 0804	Butter (Peanut—)	B 0355	290007
29	B 0805	Buttercream	B 0354	290011
21	B 0806	Butter-dish covers	C 0952	210031
28	B 0807	Butterfly nets	F 0191	280165
21	B 0808	Buttonhooks	T 0280	210223
26	B 0809	Buttons *	B 0764	260021
18	B 0810	Butts [parts of hides]	C 1582	180038
09	B 0811	Buzzers	R 0365	090522
31	B 0812	By-products of the processing of cereals, for animal consumption	R 0260	310129
05	B 0813	By-products of the processing of cereals for dietetic or medical purposes	R 0258	050321
01	B 0814	By-products of the processing of cereals for industrial purposes	R 0259	010460

Cl.	SERIAL No. (E)	INDICATION OF GOODS	SERIAL No. (F)	BASIC No.
19	C 0001	Cabanas not of metal	C 0004	190203
06	C 0002	Cabanas of metal	C 0003	060308
21	C 0003	Cabarets [trays]	C 0001	210058
20	C 0004	Cabinet work	E 0067	200088
09	C 0005	Cabinets for loudspeakers	B 0629	090087
16	C 0006	Cabinets for stationery [office requisites]	C 1006	160289
20	C 0007	Cabinets (Index—) [furniture]	F 0171	200043
20	C 0008	Cabinets (Medicine—)	A 0744	200015
12	C 0009	Cable cars	T 0162	120190
20	C 0010	Cable clips, not of metal	S 0244	200224
06	C 0011	Cable joints of metal, non-electric	R 0009	060059
20	C 0012	Cable or pipe clips of plastics	P 0225	200016
12	C 0013	Cable transport apparatus and installations	T 0480	120188
06	C 0014	Cables and pipes (Clips of metal for—)	P 0226	060313
09	C 0015	Cables (Coaxial—)	C 0016	090665
09	C 0016	Cables, electric	C 0020	090215
09	C 0017	Cables (Fibre [fiber (Am.)] optic—)	C 0014	090666
17	C 0018	Cables (Insulators for—)	C 0023	170094
09	C 0019	Cables (Junction sleeves for electric—)	M 0088	090626
22	C 0020	Cables, not of metal	C 0025	220084
06	C 0021	Cables of metal, non-electric	C 0024	060311
05	C 0022	Cachets for pharmaceutical purposes	C 0047	050243
05	C 0023	Cachou for pharmaceutical purposes	C 0053	050062
06	C 0024	Cadmium	C 0055	060061
01	C 0025	Caesium	C 0423	010163
21	C 0026	Cages for household pets	C 0090	210302
06	C 0027	Cages (Metal—) for wild animals	C 0089	060433
19	C 0028	Caissons for construction work under water	C 0106	190042
12	C 0029	Caissons [vehicles]	C 0107	120052
03	C 0030	Cake flavourings [essential oils]	G 0095	030107
21	C 0031	Cake molds [moulds]	G 0096	210142
31	C 0032	Cake (Oil—)	T 0440	310026
30	C 0033	Cake paste	P 0198	300072
31	C 0034	Cake (Peanut—) for animals	A 0647	310128
30	C 0035	Cake powder	P 0910	300071
31	C 0036	Cake (Rape—) for cattle	C 1063	310036
30	C 0037	Cakes	G 0093	300029
30	C 0038	Cakes (Flavorings [flavourings], other than essential oils, for—)	G 0094	300070
03	C 0039	Cakes of toilet soap	S 0114	030152
30	C 0040	Cakes (Rice—)	C 0108	300178
19	C 0041	Calcareous marl	M 0156	190211
19	C 0042	Calcareous stone	C 0115	190043
01	C 0043	Calcined soda	S 0413	010488
01	C 0044	Calcium carbide	C 0117	010152
01	C 0045	Calcium cyanamide [fertilizer]	C 1678	010141
01	C 0046	Calcium salts	C 0118	010510
09	C 0047	Calculating disks	D 0230	090101
09	C 0048	Calculating machines	C 0123	090103
16	C 0049	Calculating tables	T 0033	160027

Cl.	SERIAL No. (E)	INDICATION OF GOODS	SERIAL No. (F)	BASIC No.
16	C 0050	Calendars	C 0126	160270
07	C 0051	Calenders	C 0113	070292
09	C 0052	Calibrating rings	A 0550	090040
24	C 0053	Calico	C 0131	240095
24	C 0054	Calico cloth (Printed—)	I 0075	240061
01	C 0055	Californium	C 0132	010142
09	C 0056	Calipers	C 0130	090066
05	C 0057	Callouses (Preparations for—)	C 0133	050063
05	C 0058	Calomel	C 0135	050064
09	C 0059	Camcorders	C 0145	090630
22	C 0060	Camel hair	C 0468	220012
09	C 0061	Cameras (Cinematographic—)	C 0144	090107
09	C 0062	Cameras [photography]	P 0398	090184
25	C 0063	Camisoles	C 0036	250022
22	C 0064	Camouflage (Covers for—)	C 0151	220085
22	C 0065	Camouflage (Nets for—)	C 0153	220009
28	C 0066	Camouflage screens [sports articles]	E 0125	280195
01	C 0067	Camphor, for industrial purposes	C 0155	010638
05	C 0068	Camphor for medical purposes	C 0156	050309
05	C 0069	Camphor oil for medical purposes	H 0129	050308
12	C 0070	Camping cars	A 0832	120249
07	C 0071	Can openers, electric	O 0155	070287
08	C 0072	Can openers, non-electric	O 0156	080169
02	C 0073	Canada balsam	B 0276	020022
21	C 0074	Candelabra [candlesticks]	C 0480	210245
21	C 0075	Candle extinguishers	E 0492	210295
28	C 0076	Candle holders for Christmas trees	B 0709	280029
21	C 0077	Candle rings	B 0501	210242
04	C 0078	Candles	B 0707	040015
04	C 0079	Candles (Christmas tree—)	B 0710	040010
04	C 0080	Candles (Perfumed—)	B 0708	040105
21	C 0081	Candlesticks	C 0480	210245
30	C 0082	Candy*	S 0563	300153
21	C 0083	Candy boxes	B 0634	210244
05	C 0084	Candy for medical purposes	S 0564	050310
05	C 0085	Candy, medicated	B 0637	050057
18	C 0086	Canes	C 0171	180015
03	C 0087	Canned pressurized air for cleaning and dusting purposes	A 0254	030209
13	C 0088	Cannons	C 0182	130020
10	C 0089	Cannulae	C 0189	100042
05	C 0090	Cantharides (Powder of—)	C 0188	050065
16	C 0091	Canvas for painting	T 0336	160216
24	C 0092	Canvas for tapestry or embroidery	C 0166	240015
17	C 0093	Canvas hose pipes	L 0284	170065
25	C 0094	Cap peaks	V 0267	250030
09	C 0095	Capacitors	C 1130	090140
17	C 0096	Capacitors (Paper for electrical—)	P 0111	170029
30	C 0097	Capers	C 0209	300031
09	C 0098	Capillary tubes	T 0559	090109
06	C 0099	Caps (Bottle—) of metal	C 0214	060299
28	C 0100	Caps for pistols [toys]	A 0468	280003

Cl.	SERIAL No. (E)	INDICATION OF GOODS	SERIAL No. (F)	BASIC No.
12	C 0101	Caps for vehicle petrol [gas] tanks	B 0683	120241
25	C 0102	Caps [headwear]	B 0643	250012
20	C 0103	Caps, not of metal (Bottle —)	C 0215	200219
20	C 0104	Caps, not of metal (Sealing —)	C 0213	200214
25	C 0105	Caps (Shower —)	B 0645	250158
07	C 0106	Capstans	C 0002	070072
05	C 0107	Capsules for medicines	C 0218	050068
05	C 0108	Capsules for pharmaceutical purposes	C 0047	050243
06	C 0109	Capsules of metal for bottles	C 0214	060299
01	C 0110	Car body fillers	M 0200	010649
22	C 0111	Car towing ropes	V 0065	220103
02	C 0112	Caramel [food colorant]	C 0232	020034
30	C 0113	Caramels [candy]	C 0231	300032
12	C 0114	Caravans	C 0233	120056
01	C 0115	Carbide	C 0252	010151
03	C 0116	Carbides of metal [abrasives]	C 0253	030035
13	C 0117	Carbines	C 0223	130022
01	C 0118	Carbolineum for the protection of plants	C 0243	010586
05	C 0119	Carbolineum [parasiticide]	C 0241	050311
01	C 0120	Carbon	C 0235	010148
01	C 0121	Carbon black for industrial purposes	N 0084	010597
02	C 0122	Carbon black [pigment]	N 0085	020039
07	C 0123	Carbon brushes [electricity]	B 0093	070093
22	C 0124	Carbon fibers [fibres] for textile use	F 0151	220087
17	C 0125	Carbon fibers [fibres], other than for textile use	F 0152	170096
11	C 0126	Carbon for arc lamps	C 0519	110072
01	C 0127	Carbon for filters	C 0518	010166
16	C 0128	Carbon paper	P 0087	160066
01	C 0129	Carbon preparations (Animal —)	C 0508	010165
01	C 0130	Carbon sulphide	C 0238	010149
01	C 0131	Carbon tetrachloride	C 0239	010528
01	C 0132	Carbonates	C 0234	010146
01	C 0133	Carbonic acid	C 0240	010150
01	C 0134	Carbonic hydrates	C 0236	010357
01	C 0135	Carbons (Activated —)	C 0506	010025
02	C 0136	Carbonyl [wood preservative]	C 0242	020113
21	C 0137	Carboys	D 0008	210040
04	C 0138	Carburants	C 0245	040081
07	C 0139	Carburetter feeders	A 0335	070015
07	C 0140	Carburetters	C 0250	070078
18	C 0141	Card cases [notecases]	P 0802	180021
07	C 0142	Card clothing [parts of carding machines]	C 0258	070079
16	C 0143	Cardboard *	C 0299	160075
16	C 0144	Cardboard articles	C 0307	160079
19	C 0145	Cardboard (Building —)	C 0304	190045
16	C 0146	Cardboard tubes	T 0563	160078
22	C 0147	Carded wool	L 0025	220051
07	C 0148	Carding machines	C 0259	070364
16	C 0149	Cards *	C 0285	160070
28	C 0150	Cards (Bingo —)	C 0289	280178
09	C 0151	Cards (Encoded magnetic —)	C 0295	090599

Cl.	SERIAL No. (E)	INDICATION OF GOODS	SERIAL No. (F)	BASIC No.
20	C 0152	Cards (Plastic key —), not encoded	C 0298	200260
28	C 0153	Cards (Playing —)	C 0287	280191
15	C 0154	Carillons [musical instruments]	C 0261	150017
02	C 0155	Carmine (Cochineal —)	C 0262	020045
04	C 0156	Carnauba wax	C 0264	040021
08	C 0157	Carpenters' augers	E 0454	080104
09	C 0158	Carpenters' rules	R 0185	090343
21	C 0159	Carpet beaters [hand instruments]	T 0105	210008
07	C 0160	Carpet shampooing (Machines and apparatus for —), electric	S 0289	070481
21	C 0161	Carpet sweepers	B 0097	210021
27	C 0162	Carpet underlay	S 0473	270015
27	C 0163	Carpets	T 0109	270011
11	C 0164	Carpets (Electrically heated —)	T 0111	110310
27	C 0165	Carpets for automobiles	T 0120	270010
07	C 0166	Carriage aprons	T 0049	070360
07	C 0167	Carriages for knitting machines	C 0542	070097
12	C 0168	Carriages [railways]	W 0003	120140
12	C 0169	Carrier tricycles	T 0529	120162
09	C 0170	Carriers for dark plates [photography]	I 0113	090309
12	C 0171	Carriers (Luggage —) for vehicles	P 0799	120029
12	C 0172	Cars	V 0298	120199
12	C 0173	Cars for cable transport installations	C 0006	120051
09	C 0174	Cartoons (Animated —)	D 0145	090176
13	C 0175	Cartridge belts (Apparatus for filling —)	C 0318	130016
13	C 0176	Cartridge cases	D 0292	130019
13	C 0177	Cartridge loading apparatus	C 0313	130024
13	C 0178	Cartridge pouches	C 0317	130025
13	C 0179	Cartridges	C 0312	130023
07	C 0180	Cartridges for filtering machines	C 0316	070424
12	C 0181	Carts	C 0548	120219
20	C 0182	Carts for computers [furniture]	D 0139	200266
05	C 0183	Casein dietary supplements	C 0321	050434
01	C 0184	Casein for industrial purposes	C 0320	010591
01	C 0185	Casein for the food industry	C 0322	010677
19	C 0186	Casement windows, not of metal	V 0044	190179
06	C 0187	Casement windows of metal	V 0043	060260
13	C 0188	Cases (Cartridge —)	D 0292	130019
34	C 0189	Cases (Cigar —)	E 0526	340015
34	C 0190	Cases (Cigarette —)	E 0527	340016
21	C 0191	Cases (Comb —)	E 0534	210128
09	C 0192	Cases especially made for photographic apparatus and instruments	E 0538	090246
09	C 0193	Cases (Eyeglass —)	E 0535	090248
10	C 0194	Cases fitted for medical instruments	M 0060	100116
10	C 0195	Cases fitted for use by surgeons and doctors	T 0541	100152
09	C 0196	Cases fitted with dissecting instruments [microscopy]	T 0542	090563
14	C 0197	Cases for clock- and watchmaking	E 0532	140039

Cl.	SERIAL No. (E)	INDICATION OF GOODS	SERIAL No. (F)	BASIC No.
15	C 0198	Cases for musical instruments	E 0531	150035
16	C 0199	Cases for stamps [seals]	C 1003	160259
14	C 0200	Cases for watches [presentation]	E 0140	140145
13	C 0201	Cases (Gun —)	E 0530	130033
26	C 0202	Cases (Needle —)	A 0209	260091
18	C 0203	Cases, of leather or leatherboard	C 0099	180091
20	C 0204	Cases of wood or plastic	C 0098	200228
09	C 0205	Cases (Pince-nez —)	E 0535	090248
08	C 0206	Cases (Razor —)	E 0536	080107
13	C 0207	Cases (Rifle —)	E 0530	130033
09	C 0208	Cash registers	C 0102	090525
06	C 0209	Cashboxes of metal	C 0334	060029
12	C 0210	Casings for pneumatic tires [tyres]	E 0365	120114
18	C 0211	Casings, of leather, for springs	G 0012	180052
06	C 0212	Casings of metal for oilwells	C 0991	060337
20	C 0213	Casings of wood (Bottle —)	E 0236	200238
20	C 0214	Cask hoops, not of metal	C 0404	200211
20	C 0215	Cask stands, not of metal	C 0486	200120
06	C 0216	Cask stands of metal	C 0485	060391
19	C 0217	Cask wood	M 0289	190125
20	C 0218	Casks, not of metal	T 0397	200119
06	C 0219	Casks of metal	B 0209	060289
20	C 0220	Casks of wood for decanting wine	F 0529	200017
20	C 0221	Casks (Taps for —), not of metal	R 0350	200042
06	C 0222	Casks (Taps for —), of metal	R 0349	060402
09	C 0223	Cassette players	L 0178	090631
01	C 0224	Cassiopium [lutetium]	C 0338	010153
06	C 0225	Cast iron, unwrought or semi-wrought	F 0344	060133
06	C 0226	Cast steel	A 0071	060005
15	C 0227	Castanets	C 0339	150018
12	C 0228	Casters for trolleys [vehicles] [carts (Am.)]	R 0412	120250
20	C 0229	Casters, not of metal (Furniture —)	R 0410	200149
06	C 0230	Casters of metal (Furniture —)	R 0409	060187
12	C 0231	Casting carriages	C 0536	120067
12	C 0232	Casting cars	C 0536	120067
05	C 0233	Castor oil for medical purposes	H 0134	050344
04	C 0234	Castor oil for technical purposes	H 0135	040089
10	C 0235	Castrating pincers	T 0182	100049
18	C 0236	Cat o' nine tails	M 0177	180061
16	C 0237	Catalogues	C 0340	160080
01	C 0238	Catalysts	C 0341	010154
07	C 0239	Catalytic converters	C 1228	070482
01	C 0240	Catechu	C 0052	010139
10	C 0241	Catgut	C 0343	100035
15	C 0242	Catgut for musical instruments	B 0776	150015
10	C 0243	Catheters	C 0344	100015
09	C 0244	Cathodes	C 0345	090543
09	C 0245	Cathodic anti-corrosion apparatus	R 0393	090412
31	C 0246	Cattle cake	T 0440	310026
06	C 0247	Cattle chains	B 0329	060044
31	C 0248	Cattle food	F 0399	310060
08	C 0249	Cattle marking tools	B 0330	080031
10	C 0250	Cattle (Obstetric apparatus for —)	B 0328	100027
08	C 0251	Cattle shearers	B 0336	080033
18	C 0252	Cattle skins	B 0672	180088
08	C 0253	Cattle stunning appliances	B 0333	080032
05	C 0254	Cattle washes	B 0331	050051
21	C 0255	Cauldrons	C 0594	210070
08	C 0256	Caulking irons	C 0127	080045
17	C 0257	Caulking materials	E 0517	170040
01	C 0258	Caustic alkali	A 0278	010038
05	C 0259	Caustic pencils	C 1516	050102
01	C 0260	Caustic soda for industrial purposes	S 0414	010490
01	C 0261	Caustics for industrial purposes	C 0346	010489
05	C 0262	Caustics for pharmaceutical purposes	C 0347	050319
29	C 0263	Caviar	C 0351	290016
05	C 0264	Cedar wood for use as an insect repellent	B 0529	050379
03	C 0265	Cedarwood (Essential oils of —)	C 0353	030037
11	C 0266	Ceiling lights	P 0554	110136
19	C 0267	Ceilings, not of metal	P 0553	190148
06	C 0268	Ceilings of metal	P 0552	060209
30	C 0269	Celery salt	C 0367	300123
09	C 0270	Cell phone straps	C 1270	090703
09	C 0271	Cell switches [electricity]	R 0161	090168
01	C 0272	Cellulose	C 0372	010155
01	C 0273	Cellulose (Acetate of —), unprocessed	A 0044	010008
17	C 0274	Cellulose acetate, semi-processed	A 0045	170001
01	C 0275	Cellulose derivatives [chemicals]	C 0375	010592
01	C 0276	Cellulose esters for industrial purposes	C 0376	010590
05	C 0277	Cellulose esters for pharmaceutical purposes	C 0377	050318
01	C 0278	Cellulose ethers for industrial purposes	C 0378	010593
05	C 0279	Cellulose ethers for pharmaceutical purposes	C 0379	050320
17	C 0280	Cellulose (Foil of regenerated —) other than for packing	C 0380	170053
06	C 0281	Celtium [hafnium]	C 0382	060067
19	C 0282	Cement *	C 0850	190036
19	C 0283	Cement coatings (Fireproof —)	E 0310	190056
05	C 0284	Cement for animal hooves	C 0859	050083
01	C 0285	Cement for footwear	M 0206	010170
01	C 0286	Cement for mending broken articles	C 0863	010194
01	C 0287	Cement for pneumatic tires [tyres]	M 0209	010193
01	C 0288	Cement [metallurgy]	C 0383	010158
01	C 0289	Cement (Oil —) [putty]	M 0198	010655
19	C 0290	Cement posts	C 0857	190058
01	C 0291	Cement preservatives, except paints and oils	C 0861	010196

Cl.	SERIAL No. (E)	INDICATION OF GOODS	SERIAL No. (F)	BASIC No.
19	C 0292	Cement slabs	C 0856	190057
01	C 0293	Cement-waterproofing preparations, except paints	C 0860	010195
09	C 0294	Centering apparatus for photographic transparencies	D 0197	090183
06	C 0295	Central heating installations (Ducts and pipes of metal for —)	C 1161	060076
11	C 0296	Central heating radiators	C 0601	110083
09	C 0297	Central processing units [processors]	P 0977	090619
07	C 0298	Central vacuum cleaning installations	N 0055	070483
08	C 0299	Centre punches [hand tools]	P 0712	080175
07	C 0300	Centrifugal machines	C 0393	070086
07	C 0301	Centrifugal mills	C 0390	070087
07	C 0302	Centrifugal pumps	P 0774	070088
07	C 0303	Centrifuges [machines]	C 0393	070086
01	C 0304	Ceramic compositions for sintering [granules and powders]	C 1107	010646
01	C 0305	Ceramic glazings	G 0225	010160
01	C 0306	Ceramic materials in particulate form, for use as filtering media	C 0399	010621
02	C 0307	Ceramic paints	C 0395	020037
01	C 0308	Ceramics (Compositions for the manufacture of technical —)	C 0398	010631
21	C 0309	Ceramics for household purposes	C 0400	210068
30	C 0310	Cereal preparations	C 0411	300034
31	C 0311	Cereal seeds, unprocessed	C 0409	310023
30	C 0312	Cereal-based snack food	E 0283	300195
01	C 0313	Cereals (By-products of the processing of —) for industrial purposes	R 0259	010460
31	C 0314	Cereals (Residual products of —) for animal consumption	R 0260	310129
04	C 0315	Ceresine	C 0416	040022
01	C 0316	Cerium	C 0420	010161
06	C 0317	Cermets	C 0421	060401
07	C 0318	Chaff cutter blades	L 0073	070223
07	C 0319	Chaff cutters	H 0008	070210
18	C 0320	Chain mesh purses	B 0739	180090
07	C 0321	Chain saws	S 0139	070484
12	C 0322	Chains (Anti-skid —)	C 0425	120014
12	C 0323	Chains (Cycle —)	C 0430	120061
07	C 0324	Chains (Driving —) other than for land vehicles	C 0428	070425
09	C 0325	Chains (Eyeglass —)	C 0438	090115
12	C 0326	Chains for bicycles, cycles	C 0430	120061
14	C 0327	Chains [jewellery, jewelry (Am.)]	C 0426	140024
06	C 0328	Chains of metal *	C 0434	060068
14	C 0329	Chains (Watch —)	C 0431	140025
12	C 0330	Chairlifts	T 0175	120180
10	C 0331	Chairs (Commode —)	C 0442	100210
20	C 0332	Chairs [seats]	C 0444	200050
03	C 0333	Chalk (Cleaning —)	C 1502	030067
28	C 0334	Chalk for billiard cues	C 1503	280020
16	C 0335	Chalk for lithography	C 1501	160110
16	C 0336	Chalk holders	P 0809	160112
16	C 0337	Chalk (Marking —)	C 1497	160193
19	C 0338	Chalk (Raw —)	C 1499	190072
21	C 0339	Chamber pots	P 0901	210192
11	C 0340	Chambers (Clean —) [sanitary installations]	C 0463	110325
21	C 0341	Chamois leather for cleaning	P 0245	210263
18	C 0342	Chamois leather, other than for cleaning purposes	P 0242	180094
11	C 0343	Chandeliers	L 0397	110133
16	C 0344	Chaplets	C 0503	160083
01	C 0345	Charcoal (Animal —)	N 0083	010068
01	C 0346	Charcoal (Blood —)	C 0513	010168
01	C 0347	Charcoal (Bone —)	C 0515	010167
05	C 0348	Charcoal for pharmaceutical purposes	C 0511	050056
04	C 0349	Charcoal [fuel]	C 0512	040014
16	C 0350	Charcoal pencils	F 0504	160160
29	C 0351	Charcuterie	C 0521	290018
09	C 0352	Chargers for electric batteries	A 0036	090083
14	C 0353	Charms [jewellery, jewelry (Am.)]	B 0803	140018
16	C 0354	Chart pointers, non-electronic	B 0046	160350
16	C 0355	Charts	C 0285	160070
12	C 0356	Chassis (Automobile —)	A 0850	120025
02	C 0357	Chassis of vehicles (Undercoating for —)	R 0297	020040
02	C 0358	Chassis of vehicles (Undersealing for —)	R 0297	020040
12	C 0359	Chassis (Vehicle —)	C 0573	120069
25	C 0360	Chasubles	C 0576	250035
16	C 0361	Checkbooks [cheque books] (Holders for —)	P 0804	160333
28	C 0362	Checkerboards	D 0009	280057
28	C 0363	Checkers [games]	D 0006	280049
29	C 0364	Cheese	F 0449	290034
24	C 0365	Cheese cloth	T 0329	240053
08	C 0366	Cheese slicers, non-electric	T 0463	080248
30	C 0367	Cheeseburgers [sandwiches]	C 0668	300208
21	C 0368	Cheese-dish covers	C 0953	210265
01	C 0369	Chemical additives for oils	A 0098	010654
05	C 0370	Chemical conductors for electrocardiograph electrodes	C 1142	050091
01	C 0371	Chemical elements (Fissionable —)	C 0762	010180
01	C 0372	Chemical intensifiers for paper	R 0224	010639
01	C 0373	Chemical intensifiers for rubber	R 0223	010640
01	C 0374	Chemical preparations for facilitating the alloying of metals	A 0351	010045
05	C 0375	Chemical preparations for medical purposes	C 0763	050362
05	C 0376	Chemical preparations for pharmaceutical purposes	C 0764	050323
01	C 0377	Chemical preparations for scientific purposes, other than for medical or veterinary use	C 0765	010177
05	C 0378	Chemical preparations for veterinary purposes	C 0766	050363

Cl.	SERIAL No. (E)	INDICATION OF GOODS	SERIAL No. (F)	BASIC No.
05	C 0379	Chemical reagents for medical or veterinary purposes	R 0125	050364
01	C 0380	Chemical reagents, other than for medical or veterinary purposes	R 0126	010178
01	C 0381	Chemical substances for analyses in laboratories, other than for medical or veterinary purposes	A 0491	010181
01	C 0382	Chemicals (Agricultural —), except fungicides, weedkillers, herbicides, insecticides and parasiticides	A 0186	010031
01	C 0383	Chemicals for forestry, except fungicides, herbicides, insecticides and parasiticides	S 0618	010505
01	C 0384	Chemicals (Industrial —)	C 0770	010176
05	C 0385	Chemico-pharmaceutical preparations	C 0759	050077
09	C 0386	Chemistry apparatus and instruments	C 0760	090549
24	C 0387	Chenille fabric	T 0293	240111
26	C 0388	Chenille [passementerie]	C 0706	260037
23	C 0389	Chenille yarn	C 0705	230031
28	C 0390	Chess games	E 0087	280055
28	C 0391	Chessboards	E 0095	280056
28	C 0392	Chest expanders [exercisers]	E 0553	280051
31	C 0393	Chestnuts, fresh	C 0577	310027
20	C 0394	Chests for toys	C 0994	200256
20	C 0395	Chests, not of metal	C 0104	200207
20	C 0396	Chests of drawers	C 1090	200066
06	C 0397	Chests of metal	C 0997	060398
06	C 0398	Chests of metal for food	G 0067	060392
24	C 0399	Cheviots [cloth]	C 0742	240023
30	C 0400	Chewing gum*	G 0269	300035
05	C 0401	Chewing gum for medical purposes	G 0270	050198
34	C 0402	Chewing tobacco	C 0776	340012
31	C 0403	Chews for animals (Edible —)	A 0535	310141
19	C 0404	Chicken-houses, not of metal	P 0916	190156
06	C 0405	Chicken-houses, of metal	P 0915	060425
30	C 0406	Chicory [coffee substitute]	C 0747	300036
31	C 0407	Chicory roots	C 0745	310029
31	C 0408	Chicory [salad]	C 0746	310030
05	C 0409	Chilblain preparations	E 0322	050103
10	C 0410	Childbirth mattresses	M 0214	100004
06	C 0411	Chill-molds [foundry]	C 1248	060096
06	C 0412	Chill-moulds [foundry]	C 1248	060096
20	C 0413	Chimes (Wind —) [decoration]	M 0424	200268
11	C 0414	Chimney blowers	T 0286	110094
01	C 0415	Chimney cleaners, chemical	C 0681	010174
19	C 0416	Chimney cowls, not of metal	C 0221	190212
06	C 0417	Chimney cowls of metal	C 0220	060318
11	C 0418	Chimney flues	C 0268	110093
19	C 0419	Chimney pots, not of metal	M 0421	190216
06	C 0420	Chimney pots of metal	M 0420	060331
19	C 0421	Chimney shafts, not of metal	T 0589	190218
06	C 0422	Chimney shafts of metal	C 0685	060414
11	C 0423	Chimneys (Lamp —)	T 0562	110092
19	C 0424	Chimneys, not of metal	C 0680	190055

Cl.	SERIAL No. (E)	INDICATION OF GOODS	SERIAL No. (F)	BASIC No.
06	C 0425	Chimneys of metal	C 0677	060413
15	C 0426	Chin rests for violins	M 0280	150050
18	C 0427	Chin straps, of leather	M 0279	180062
21	C 0428	China ornaments	C 0773	210078
01	C 0429	China slip	K 0003	010370
11	C 0430	Chinese lanterns	L 0115	110185
05	C 0431	Chinoline for medical purposes	Q 0021	050257
30	C 0432	Chips [cereal products]	F 0305	300161
09	C 0433	Chips (DNA —)	P 1030	090684
28	C 0434	Chips for gambling	J 0029	280206
29	C 0435	Chips (Fruit —)	T 0460	290131
09	C 0436	Chips [integrated circuits]	P 1031	090540
29	C 0437	Chips (Potato —)	P 0756	290019
08	C 0438	Chisels	M 0229	080159
07	C 0439	Chisels for machines	C 0907	070107
01	C 0440	Chlorates	C 0785	010182
01	C 0441	Chlorides	C 0791	010554
01	C 0442	Chlorine	C 0787	010183
05	C 0443	Chloroform	C 0790	050080
30	C 0444	Chocolate	C 0793	300038
30	C 0445	Chocolate beverages with milk	L 0047	300085
29	C 0446	Chocolate nut butter	B 0356	290009
30	C 0447	Chocolate-based beverages	B 0563	300151
09	C 0448	Choking coils [impedance]	S 0192	090441
01	C 0449	Cholic acid	C 0795	010186
08	C 0450	Choppers [knives]	H 0013	080138
20	C 0451	Chopping blocks [tables]	H 0014	200126
21	C 0452	Chopsticks	B 0041	210311
30	C 0453	Chow-chow [condiment]	C 0799	300162
04	C 0454	Christmas tree candles	B 0710	040010
28	C 0455	Christmas tree stands	A 0660	280120
31	C 0456	Christmas trees	A 0654	310009
30	C 0457	Christmas trees (Confectionery for decorating —)	S 0569	300008
11	C 0458	Christmas trees (Electric lights for —)	L 0104	110195
28	C 0459	Christmas trees of synthetic material	A 0657	280006
28	C 0460	Christmas trees (Ornaments for —), except illumination articles and confectionery	D 0038	280119
01	C 0461	Chromates	C 0800	010187
11	C 0462	Chromatography apparatus for industrial purposes	C 0801	110292
09	C 0463	Chromatography apparatus for laboratory use	C 0802	090585
01	C 0464	Chrome alum	C 0804	010188
06	C 0465	Chrome iron	F 0084	060080
06	C 0466	Chrome ores	C 0805	060081
01	C 0467	Chrome salts	C 0807	010190
01	C 0468	Chromic acid	C 0808	010191
01	C 0469	Chromic salts	C 0809	010477
06	C 0470	Chromium	C 0803	060079
01	C 0471	Chromium oxide	O 0164	010189
16	C 0472	Chromolithographs [chromos]	C 0810	160090
16	C 0473	Chromos	C 0810	160090
09	C 0474	Chronographs [time recording apparatus]	C 0812	090586
14	C 0475	Chronographs [watches]	C 0813	140027

Cl.	SERIAL No. (E)	INDICATION OF GOODS	SERIAL No. (F)	BASIC No.
14	C 0476	Chronometers	C 0814	140028
14	C 0477	Chronometrical instruments	C 0816	140030
14	C 0478	Chronoscopes	C 0817	140029
07	C 0479	Chucks [parts of machines]	M 0097	070194
07	C 0480	Churns	B 0181	070038
30	C 0481	Chutneys [condiments]	C 0819	300182
33	C 0482	Cider	C 0822	330009
32	C 0483	Cider, non-alcoholic	J 0069	320047
16	C 0484	Cigar bands	C 0827	160016
34	C 0485	Cigar cases	E 0526	340015
34	C 0486	Cigar cutters	C 1384	340014
34	C 0487	Cigar holders	F 0478	340017
12	C 0488	Cigar lighters for automobiles	A 0369	120266
34	C 0489	Cigar lighters (Gas containers for—)	R 0250	340008
34	C 0490	Cigarette cases	E 0527	340016
34	C 0491	Cigarette filters	F 0266	340006
34	C 0492	Cigarette holders	F 0479	340022
34	C 0493	Cigarette holders (Mouthpieces for—)	B 0773	340023
07	C 0494	Cigarette machines for industrial purposes	C 0841	070103
34	C 0495	Cigarette paper	P 0076	340024
34	C 0496	Cigarette papers (Books of—)	C 0093	340010
34	C 0497	Cigarette tips	B 0772	340005
34	C 0498	Cigarettes	C 0834	340020
34	C 0499	Cigarettes containing tobacco substitutes, not for medical purposes	C 0838	340019
34	C 0500	Cigarettes (Pocket machines for rolling—)	C 0835	340021
05	C 0501	Cigarettes (Tobacco-free—) for medical purposes	C 0844	050081
34	C 0502	Cigarillos	C 0845	340025
34	C 0503	Cigars	C 0825	340013
05	C 0504	Cinchona for medical purposes	Q 0022	050255
21	C 0505	Cinder sifters [household utensils]	T 0084	210067
07	C 0506	Cinder sifters [machines]	T 0083	070082
09	C 0507	Cinematographic cameras	C 0144	090107
09	C 0508	Cinematographic film (Apparatus for editing—)	F 0206	090124
09	C 0509	Cinematographic film, exposed	C 0866	090550
01	C 0510	Cinematographic film, sensitized but not exposed	C 0867	010598
30	C 0511	Cinnamon [spice]	C 0169	300030
09	C 0512	Circuit breakers	D 0225	090191
09	C 0513	Circuit closers	C 1177	090143
01	C 0514	Citric acid for industrial purposes	C 0911	010199
03	C 0515	Citron (Essential oils of—)	C 0913	030056
31	C 0516	Citrus fruit	A 0187	310002
17	C 0517	Clack valves of rubber	C 0924	170019
07	C 0518	Clack valves [parts of machines]	C 0920	070108
19	C 0519	Cladding, not of metal, for building	R 0291	190150
06	C 0520	Cladding of metal for construction and building	R 0290	060211

Cl.	SERIAL No. (E)	INDICATION OF GOODS	SERIAL No. (F)	BASIC No.
08	C 0521	Clamps for carpenters or coopers	S 0246	080147
29	C 0522	Clams [not live]	P 0054	290132
01	C 0523	Clarification preparations	C 0925	010254
15	C 0524	Clarionets	C 0926	150023
15	C 0525	Clarions	C 0915	150071
26	C 0526	Clasp (Belt—)	F 0082	260031
20	C 0527	Claws (Animal—)	A 0533	200010
19	C 0528	Clay *	A 0710	190096
01	C 0529	Clay (China—)	K 0003	010370
01	C 0530	Clay (Expanded-—) for hydroponic plant growing [substrate]	A 0713	010652
28	C 0531	Clay pigeon traps	T 0287	280080
28	C 0532	Clay pigeons [targets]	P 0475	280101
19	C 0533	Clay (Potters'—) [raw material]	C 0397	190047
11	C 0534	Clean chambers [sanitary installations]	C 0463	110325
01	C 0535	Cleaners, chemical (Chimney—)	C 0681	010174
07	C 0536	Cleaning apparatus (Acetylene—)	P 1051	070002
09	C 0537	Cleaning apparatus for phonograph records	D 0233	090230
09	C 0538	Cleaning apparatus for sound recording discs	D 0233	090230
07	C 0539	Cleaning appliances utilizing steam	N 0048	070485
13	C 0540	Cleaning brushes for firearms	E 0122	130010
03	C 0541	Cleaning chalk	C 1502	030067
03	C 0542	Cleaning dentures (Preparations for—)	N 0051	030194
21	C 0543	Cleaning instruments, hand-operated	N 0056	210104
07	C 0544	Cleaning (Machines and apparatus for—), electric	N 0057	070281
03	C 0545	Cleaning preparations	N 0058	030104
05	C 0546	Cleaning preparations (Contact lens—)	N 0052	050365
21	C 0547	Cleaning (Rags [cloth] for—)	T 0404	210077
21	C 0548	Cleaning tow	E 0516	210312
12	C 0549	Cleaning trolleys	C 0538	120251
03	C 0550	Cleansing milk for toilet purposes	L 0066	030123
12	C 0551	Cleats [nautical]	T 0126	120179
08	C 0552	Cleavers	C 1394	080077
28	C 0553	Climbers' harness	B 0272	280142
19	C 0554	Clinker ballast	B 0111	190105
19	C 0555	Clinker stone	P 0463	190143
09	C 0556	Clinometers	I 0068	090299
16	C 0557	Clipboards	P 0581	160349
07	C 0558	Clippers [machines]	T 0388	070122
20	C 0559	Clips (Cable and pipe—) of plastics	P 0225	200016
09	C 0560	Clips for divers and swimmers (Nose—)	P 0510	090655
16	C 0561	Clips for offices	A 0175	160010
16	C 0562	Clips (Money—)	P 0500	160353
06	C 0563	Clips of metal for cables and pipes	P 0226	060313

Cl.	SERIAL No. (E)	INDICATION OF GOODS	SERIAL No. (F)	BASIC No.
12	C 0564	Clips (Spoke —) for wheels	T 0186	120169
10	C 0565	Clips, surgical	A 0174	100007
14	C 0566	Clips (Tie —)	F 0280	140033
14	C 0567	Clock cases	C 0012	140044
14	C 0568	Clock hands [clock and watch making]	A 0204	140002
14	C 0569	Clocks	H 0087	140011
14	C 0570	Clocks and watches, electric	H 0090	140032
09	C 0571	Clocks (Time —) [time recording devices]	P 0717	090649
14	C 0572	Clockworks	C 0058	140023
14	C 0573	Cloisonné jewellery [jewelry (Am.)]	B 0415	140165
20	C 0574	Closets (Towel —) [furniture]	P 0860	200276
20	C 0575	Closures (Bottle —), not of metal	F 0075	200220
21	C 0576	Closures for pot lids	F 0078	210091
20	C 0577	Closures, not of metal, for containers	F 0077	200112
06	C 0578	Closures of metal for containers	F 0076	060395
24	C 0579	Cloth *	T 0318	240013
17	C 0580	Cloth (Asbestos —)	T 0323	170080
01	C 0581	Cloth (Blueprint —)	T 0294	010434
16	C 0582	Cloth for bookbinding	T 0326	160238
21	C 0583	Cloth for washing floors	S 0242	210303
22	C 0584	Cloth (Tarred brattice —)	C 0959	220001
20	C 0585	Clothes hooks, not of metal	P 0201	200166
06	C 0586	Clothes hooks of metal	P 0200	060202
21	C 0587	Clothes racks, for drying	S 0165	210205
21	C 0588	Clothes-pegs	P 0505	210313
21	C 0589	Clothes-pins	P 0505	210313
25	C 0590	Clothing *	V 0187	250045
05	C 0591	Clothing (Deodorants for —) and textiles	D 0133	050400
26	C 0592	Clothing (Edgings for —)	B 0652	260018
10	C 0593	Clothing especially for operating rooms	V 0213	100200
09	C 0594	Clothing especially made for laboratories	V 0212	090691
26	C 0595	Clothing (Eyelets for —)	O 0014	260073
26	C 0596	Clothing (Fastenings for —)	F 0080	260010
25	C 0597	Clothing for gymnastics	V 0192	250149
18	C 0598	Clothing for pets	H 0006	180054
09	C 0599	Clothing for protection against accidents, irradiation and fire	V 0194	090005
09	C 0600	Clothing for protection against fire	H 0003	090288
25	C 0601	Clothing of imitations of leather	V 0197	250150
25	C 0602	Clothing of leather	V 0196	250151
26	C 0603	Clothing (Shoulder pads for —)	E 0381	260118
21	C 0604	Clothing stretchers	T 0187	210221
21	C 0605	Cloths for cleaning	T 0404	210077
03	C 0606	Cloths impregnated with a detergent for cleaning	T 0405	030211
30	C 0607	Cloves [spice]	C 0967	300040
28	C 0608	Clubs (Golf —)	C 1577	280034
17	C 0609	Clutch linings	G 0086	170039
12	C 0610	Clutches for land vehicles	E 0256	120111
07	C 0611	Clutches other than for land vehicles	E 0254	070174
04	C 0612	Coal	C 0510	040023
04	C 0613	Coal briquettes	B 0729	040016
04	C 0614	Coal dust [fuel]	P 0930	040072
04	C 0615	Coal naphtha	H 0103	040054
01	C 0616	Coal saving preparations	C 0520	010169
19	C 0617	Coal tar	H 0102	190097
04	C 0618	Coal tar oil	G 0283	040053
07	C 0619	Coalcutting machines	H 0049	070094
21	C 0620	Coasters, not of paper and other than table linen	D 0148	210258
16	C 0621	Coasters of paper	D 0146	160283
24	C 0622	Coasters [table linen]	D 0147	240096
20	C 0623	Coat hangers	C 0868	200059
20	C 0624	Coathooks, not of metal	C 1571	200080
19	C 0625	Coatings [building materials]	E 0312	190129
02	C 0626	Coatings for roofing felt [paints]	C 0301	020036
02	C 0627	Coatings [paints]	E 0313	020070
25	C 0628	Coats	M 0120	250086
25	C 0629	Coats (Top —)	P 0150	250115
20	C 0630	Coatstands	P 0821	200144
09	C 0631	Coaxial cables	C 0016	090665
02	C 0632	Cobalt oxide [colorant]	C 0973	020044
01	C 0633	Cobalt oxide for industrial purposes	O 0165	010599
06	C 0634	Cobalt, raw	C 0971	060088
03	C 0635	Cobblers' wax	P 0735	030050
05	C 0636	Cocaine	C 0974	050086
02	C 0637	Cochineal carmine	C 0262	020045
21	C 0638	Cocktail stirrers	B 0253	210314
33	C 0639	Cocktails *	C 0977	330010
32	C 0640	Cocktails, non-alcoholic	C 0978	320043
30	C 0641	Cocoa	C 0030	300024
31	C 0642	Cocoa beans, raw	F 0145	310020
30	C 0643	Cocoa beverages with milk	L 0044	300083
29	C 0644	Cocoa butter	B 0356	290009
30	C 0645	Cocoa products	C 0034	300025
30	C 0646	Cocoa-based beverages	B 0561	300150
29	C 0647	Coconut butter	B 0357	290010
29	C 0648	Coconut, desiccated	N 0094	290021
29	C 0649	Coconut fat	G 0308	290121
22	C 0650	Coconut fiber [fibre]	C 0981	220018
29	C 0651	Coconut oil	C 0984	290122
31	C 0652	Coconut shell	C 1242	310033
31	C 0653	Coconuts	N 0092	310034
22	C 0654	Cocoons	C 0987	220019
05	C 0655	Cod liver oil	H 0132	050150
30	C 0656	Coffee	C 0070	300026
30	C 0657	Coffee (Artificial —)	S 0559	300152
30	C 0658	Coffee beverages with milk	L 0045	300084
11	C 0659	Coffee filters, electric	F 0258	110260
21	C 0660	Coffee filters, non-electric	F 0260	210256
16	C 0661	Coffee filters (Paper —)	F 0259	160324
30	C 0662	Coffee flavorings [flavourings]	C 0071	300010
21	C 0663	Coffee grinders, hand-operated	C 0077	210254
07	C 0664	Coffee grinders, other than hand-operated	C 0078	070415
11	C 0665	Coffee machines, electric	C 0085	110262
11	C 0666	Coffee percolators, electric	P 0328	110261
21	C 0667	Coffee percolators, non-electric	P 0329	210257
11	C 0668	Coffee roasters	C 0083	110066

Cl.	SERIAL No. (E)	INDICATION OF GOODS	SERIAL No. (F)	BASIC No.
21	C 0669	Coffee services [tableware]	C 0082	210255
30	C 0670	Coffee substitutes (Vegetal preparations for use as—)	C 0081	300028
30	C 0671	Coffee (Unroasted—)	C 0084	300027
30	C 0672	Coffee-based beverages	B 0562	300149
21	C 0673	Coffeepots, non-electric	C 0086	210287
20	C 0674	Coffin fittings, not of metal	G 0071	200048
20	C 0675	Coffins	C 0405	200047
06	C 0676	Coffins (Fittings of metal for—)	G 0070	060324
09	C 0677	Coils (Choking—) [impedance]	S 0192	090441
09	C 0678	Coils, electric	B 0503	090001
09	C 0679	Coils (Electromagnetic—)	A 0221	090024
09	C 0680	Coils (Holders for electric—)	B 0504	090514
11	C 0681	Coils [parts of distilling, heating or cooling installations]	S 0239	110224
09	C 0682	Coin-operated apparatus (Mechanisms for—)	P 0943	090063
28	C 0683	Coin-operated billiard tables	T 0035	280124
09	C 0684	Coin-operated mechanisms for television sets	T 0177	090340
07	C 0685	Coin-operated washing machines	L 0166	070236
14	C 0686	Coins	M 0457	140034
23	C 0687	Coir thread and yarn	C 0982	230006
04	C 0688	Coke	C 1013	040031
31	C 0689	Cola nuts	N 0095	310074
21	C 0690	Coldboxes (Non-electric portable—)	G 0222	210261
25	C 0691	Collar protectors	C 0035	250021
26	C 0692	Collar supports	B 0045	260046
25	C 0693	Collars [clothing]	C 1059	250020
18	C 0694	Collars for animals	C 1041	180030
05	C 0695	Collars for animals (Antiparasitic—)	C 1038	050087
06	C 0696	Collars of metal for fastening pipes	C 1040	060312
09	C 0697	Collectors, electric	C 1030	090129
07	C 0698	Collectors (Machine boiler scale—)	C 1029	070110
01	C 0699	Collodion *	C 1042	010206
05	C 0700	Collodion for pharmaceutical purposes	C 1043	050324
05	C 0701	Collyrium	C 1044	050088
02	C 0702	Colophony	C 1050	020046
02	C 0703	Colorants *	C 1054	020047
02	C 0704	Colorants (Food—)	C 1055	020005
02	C 0705	Colorants for beer	B 0404	020024
02	C 0706	Colorants for beverages	B 0574	020004
02	C 0707	Colorants for butter	B 0353	020023
02	C 0708	Colorants for liqueurs	L 0311	020088
03	C 0709	Colorants for toilet purposes	C 1057	030060
02	C 0710	Colorants (Malt—)	M 0071	020048
03	C 0711	Color-brightening chemicals for household purposes [laundry]	A 0875	030174
01	C 0712	Color-brightening chemicals for industrial purposes	A 0876	010570
01	C 0713	Coloring metal (Salts for—)	S 0213	010207
03	C 0714	Color-removing preparations	T 0152	030087
07	C 0715	Colour (Air brushes for applying—)	B 0864	070514
03	C 0716	Colour-brightening chemicals for household purposes [laundry]	A 0875	030174
01	C 0717	Colour-brightening chemicals for industrial purposes	A 0876	010570
01	C 0718	Colouring metal (Salts for—)	S 0213	010207
03	C 0719	Colour-removing preparations	T 0152	030087
07	C 0720	Colour-washing machines	B 0022	070030
19	C 0721	Columns (Advertisement—), not of metal	C 1048	190001
06	C 0722	Columns (Advertisement—) of metal	C 1047	060411
29	C 0723	Colza oil for food	C 1062	290022
21	C 0724	Comb cases	E 0534	210128
20	C 0725	Comb foundations for beehives	C 0886	200039
22	C 0726	Combed wool	L 0038	220052
25	C 0727	Combinations [clothing]	C 1068	250053
21	C 0728	Combs	P 0264	210076
21	C 0729	Combs (Electric—)	P 0266	210176
21	C 0730	Combs for animals	A 0537	210075
21	C 0731	Combs for the hair (Large-toothed—)	D 0067	210110
04	C 0732	Combustible oil	H 0145	040084
01	C 0733	Combusting preparations [chemical additives to motor fuel]	C 1069	010001
16	C 0734	Comic books	B 0156	160331
10	C 0735	Commode chairs	C 0442	100210
06	C 0736	Common metals, unwrought or semi-wrought	M 0304	060182
09	C 0737	Commutation (Electric apparatus for—)	C 1092	090163
09	C 0738	Commutators	C 1091	090132
09	C 0739	Compact disc players	L 0180	090632
09	C 0740	Compact discs [audio-video]	D 0236	090587
09	C 0741	Compact discs [read-only memory]	D 0239	090588
09	C 0742	Comparators	C 1097	090067
09	C 0743	Compasses (Directional—)	B 0740	090523
16	C 0744	Compasses for drawing	C 1099	160096
09	C 0745	Compasses [measuring instruments]	C 1100	090200
26	C 0746	Competitors' numbers	D 0284	260112
16	C 0747	Composing frames [printing]	C 0060	160084
16	C 0748	Composing sticks	C 1110	160098
01	C 0749	Compositions for the manufacture of phonograph records	C 1108	010603
01	C 0750	Compost	C 1109	010622
07	C 0751	Compressed air engines	A 0235	070391
07	C 0752	Compressed air guns for the extrusion of mastics	P 0532	070456
07	C 0753	Compressed air machines	A 0234	070392
17	C 0754	Compressed air pipe fittings, not of metal	A 0233	170086
07	C 0755	Compressed air pumps	P 0766	070393
05	C 0756	Compresses	C 1113	050089
10	C 0757	Compresses (Thermo-electric—) [surgery]	C 1114	100059
07	C 0758	Compressors for refrigerators	C 1117	070437

Cl.	SERIAL No. (E)	INDICATION OF GOODS	SERIAL No. (F)	BASIC No.
07	C 0759	Compressors [machines]	C 1116	070113
10	C 0760	Compressors [surgical]	C 1115	100060
09	C 0761	Computer game programs	L 0362	090670
09	C 0762	Computer keyboards	C 0931	090537
09	C 0763	Computer memory devices	M 0267	090342
09	C 0764	Computer operating programs, recorded	P 0981	090589
09	C 0765	Computer peripheral devices	P 0333	090590
16	C 0766	Computer printers (Inking ribbons for—)	R 0438	160326
16	C 0767	Computer programmes (Paper tapes and cards for the recordal of—)	P 0978	160231
09	C 0768	Computer programmes [programs], recorded	P 0979	090373
09	C 0769	Computer programs [downloadable software]	P 0980	090658
09	C 0770	Computer software, recorded	L 0363	090591
09	C 0771	Computers	O 0091	090372
09	C 0772	Computers (Printers for use with—)	I 0028	090618
29	C 0773	Concentrates (Bouillon—)	C 1127	290023
29	C 0774	Concentrates (Broth—)	C 1127	290023
15	C 0775	Concertinas	C 1128	150026
19	C 0776	Concrete	B 0339	190023
01	C 0777	Concrete (Agglutinants for—)	A 0170	010030
19	C 0778	Concrete building elements	B 0344	190024
07	C 0779	Concrete mixers [machines]	B 0349	070045
12	C 0780	Concrete mixing vehicles	B 0348	120213
01	C 0781	Concrete preservatives, except paints and oils	B 0347	010117
19	C 0782	Concrete (Shuttering, not of metal, for—)	C 0993	190198
01	C 0783	Concrete-aeration chemicals	B 0346	010116
01	C 0784	Condensation preparations (Chemical—)	C 1134	010015
01	C 0785	Condensation-preventing chemicals	B 0893	010138
09	C 0786	Condensers [capacitors]	C 1130	090140
11	C 0787	Condensers (Gas—), other than parts of machines	C 1135	110294
09	C 0788	Condensers (Optical—)	C 1132	090592
07	C 0789	Condensers [steam] [parts of machines]	C 1136	070115
07	C 0790	Condensing installations	C 1133	070116
30	C 0791	Condiments	C 1137	300041
11	C 0792	Conditioning air (Installations for—)	A 0243	110014
10	C 0793	Condoms	P 0946	100128
15	C 0794	Conductors' batons	B 0044	150009
05	C 0795	Conductors (Chemical—) for electrocardiograph electrodes	C 1142	050091
09	C 0796	Conductors, electric	C 1143	090141
09	C 0797	Conductors (Lightning—)	P 0143	090381
09	C 0798	Conduits (Acoustic—)	C 1160	090015
09	C 0799	Conduits (Electricity—)	C 1154	090142
05	C 0800	Condurango bark for medical purposes	C 1165	050092
31	C 0801	Cones (Hop—)	C 1166	310038
31	C 0802	Cones (Pine—)	P 0759	310105
21	C 0803	Confectioners' decorating bags [pastry bags]	P 0685	210315
30	C 0804	Confectionery	C 1170	300042
30	C 0805	Confectionery for decorating Christmas trees	S 0569	300008
05	C 0806	Confectionery, medicated	B 0637	050057
28	C 0807	Confetti	C 1169	280192
28	C 0808	Conjuring apparatus	P 0969	280105
17	C 0809	Connecting hose for vehicle radiators	T 0595	170074
12	C 0810	Connecting rods for land vehicles, other than parts of motors and engines	B 0401	120242
07	C 0811	Connecting rods for machines, motors and engines	B 0400	070048
09	C 0812	Connections, electric	R 0004	090220
09	C 0813	Connections for electric lines	R 0006	090219
09	C 0814	Connectors [electricity]	C 1178	090144
05	C 0815	Constipation (Medicines for alleviating—)	C 1200	050093
19	C 0816	Construction materials, not of metal	M 0218	190197
05	C 0817	Contact lens cleaning preparations	N 0052	050365
09	C 0818	Contact lenses	L 0195	090554
09	C 0819	Contact lenses (Containers for—)	E 0537	090555
05	C 0820	Contact lenses (Solutions for use with—)	V 0171	050094
09	C 0821	Contacts, electric	C 1211	090148
20	C 0822	Containers (Closures, not of metal, for—)	F 0077	200112
10	C 0823	Containers especially made for medical waste	R 0154	100216
09	C 0824	Containers for contact lenses	E 0537	090555
21	C 0825	Containers for household or kitchen use	R 0153	210199
09	C 0826	Containers for microscope slides	C 1007	090128
20	C 0827	Containers, not of metal, for liquid fuel	R 0151	200065
20	C 0828	Containers, not of metal [storage, transport]	C 1215	200068
06	C 0829	Containers of metal for compressed gas or liquid air	R 0150	060112
06	C 0830	Containers of metal for liquid fuel	R 0149	060338
06	C 0831	Containers of metal for storing acids	R 0148	060065
06	C 0832	Containers of metal [storage, transport]	C 1214	060094
20	C 0833	Containers of plastic (Packaging—)	R 0142	200100
11	C 0834	Containers (Refrigerating—)	R 0147	110157
05	C 0835	Contraceptives (Chemical—)	C 1216	050095
10	C 0836	Contraceptives, non-chemical	C 1217	100184
07	C 0837	Control cables for machines, engines or motors	C 0018	070434
14	C 0838	Control clocks [master clocks]	C 1226	140043
07	C 0839	Control mechanisms for machines, engines or motors	C 1083	070435

Cl.	SERIAL No. (E)	INDICATION OF GOODS	SERIAL No. (F)	BASIC No.
09	C 0840	Control panels [electricity]	T 0024	090217
07	C 0841	Controls (Hydraulic —) for machines, motors and engines	C 1088	070472
07	C 0842	Controls (Pneumatic —) for machines, motors and engines	C 1089	070473
07	C 0843	Conversion apparatus (Fuel —) for internal combustion engines	C 1230	070463
09	C 0844	Converters, electric	C 1233	090153
07	C 0845	Converters for steel works	C 1229	070003
12	C 0846	Converters (Torque —) for land vehicles	C 1232	120227
12	C 0847	Conveyors (Aerial —)	A 0131	120004
07	C 0848	Conveyors [machines]	T 0485	070371
11	C 0849	Cookers	C 1630	110108
21	C 0850	Cookery molds [moulds]	M 0526	210103
21	C 0851	Cookie [biscuit] cutters	E 0272	210316
21	C 0852	Cookie jars	B 0592	210317
30	C 0853	Cookies	B 0447	300018
11	C 0854	Cooking apparatus and installations	C 1632	110109
21	C 0855	Cooking pot sets	B 0262	210026
21	C 0856	Cooking pots	M 0152	210101
01	C 0857	Cooking (Preparations for stimulating —) for industrial purposes	C 1635	010557
11	C 0858	Cooking rings	R 0136	110210
30	C 0859	Cooking salt	S 0184	300049
21	C 0860	Cooking skewers, of metal	B 0837	210049
11	C 0861	Cooking utensils, electric	U 0020	110107
21	C 0862	Cooking utensils, non-electric	U 0021	210274
01	C 0863	Coolants (Anti-boil preparations for engine —)	E 0070	010645
01	C 0864	Coolants for vehicle engines	R 0177	010647
11	C 0865	Coolers for furnaces	B 0010	110032
21	C 0866	Coolers [ice pails]	G 0210	210196
21	C 0867	Coolers (Non-electric portable —) (Am.)	G 0222	210261
11	C 0868	Cooling appliances and installations	R 0176	110214
21	C 0869	Cooling devices (Food —) containing heat exchange fluids, for household purposes	R 0175	210293
11	C 0870	Cooling installations and machines	R 0050	110209
11	C 0871	Cooling installations for liquids	R 0178	110188
11	C 0872	Cooling installations for tobacco	T 0004	110227
11	C 0873	Cooling installations for water	E 0043	110125
05	C 0874	Cooling sprays for medical purposes	S 0509	050407
02	C 0875	Copal	C 1234	020050
02	C 0876	Copal varnish	C 1235	020114
06	C 0877	Copper rings	C 1638	060110
01	C 0878	Copper sulphate [vitriol]	V 0288	010225
14	C 0879	Copper tokens	J 0027	140049
06	C 0880	Copper, unwrought or semi-wrought	C 1639	060109
09	C 0881	Copper wire, insulated	C 1640	090558
06	C 0882	Copper wire, not insulated	C 1641	060353
31	C 0883	Copra	C 1239	310040
16	C 0884	Copying paper [stationery]	P 0077	160332
20	C 0885	Coral	C 1249	200071
07	C 0886	Cord making machines	C 1269	070119
16	C 0887	Cords for bookbinding	F 0242	160239
26	C 0888	Cords for clothing	C 1260	260047
22	C 0889	Cords for hanging pictures, etc.	C 1277	220089
26	C 0890	Cords for rimming, for clothing	C 1274	260096
17	C 0891	Cords of rubber	C 1267	170031
22	C 0892	Cords (Sash —)	C 1275	220088
20	C 0893	Cork bands	C 1280	200073
19	C 0894	Cork [compressed]	L 0239	190111
31	C 0895	Cork (Rough —)	L 0241	310078
20	C 0896	Corks	B 0675	200030
20	C 0897	Corks for bottles	B 0674	200029
21	C 0898	Corkscrews	T 0279	210043
30	C 0899	Corn flakes	F 0307	300043
30	C 0900	Corn flour	M 0040	300059
07	C 0901	Corn husking machines	D 0039	070089
10	C 0902	Corn knives	C 1386	100062
30	C 0903	Corn meal	M 0040	300059
30	C 0904	Corn, milled	M 0045	300091
29	C 0905	Corn oil	M 0044	290058
30	C 0906	Corn (Pop —)	M 0043	300044
05	C 0907	Corn remedies	C 1320	050098
05	C 0908	Corn rings for the feet	A 0561	050040
30	C 0909	Corn, roasted	M 0042	300092
15	C 0910	Cornets [musical instruments]	C 1292	150031
19	C 0911	Cornices, not of metal	C 1299	190064
06	C 0912	Cornices of metal	C 1296	060343
20	C 0913	Corozo	C 1305	200076
16	C 0914	Correcting fluids [office requisites]	C 1312	160103
16	C 0915	Correcting ink [heliography]	E 0299	160104
09	C 0916	Correcting lenses [optics]	V 0167	090159
16	C 0917	Correcting tapes [office requisites]	R 0429	160357
01	C 0918	Corrosive preparations	C 1315	010214
25	C 0919	Corselets	C 1324	250055
26	C 0920	Corset busks	B 0105	260012
10	C 0921	Corsets (Abdominal —)	C 1327	100003
10	C 0922	Corsets for medical purposes	G 0010	100183
26	C 0923	Corsets (Hooks for —)	C 1328	260098
25	C 0924	Corsets [underclothing]	C 1326	250078
03	C 0925	Corundum [abrasive]	C 1284	030062
28	C 0926	Cosaques [toy fireworks]	B 0636	280027
21	C 0927	Cosies (Tea —)	C 1341	210343
03	C 0928	Cosmetic kits	N 0033	030064
03	C 0929	Cosmetic preparations for slimming purposes	C 1334	030177
21	C 0930	Cosmetic utensils	C 1335	210087
03	C 0931	Cosmetics	C 1332	030065
03	C 0932	Cosmetics for animals	C 1333	030063
09	C 0933	Cosmographic instruments	C 1336	090161
20	C 0934	Costume stands	B 0914	200038
25	C 0935	Costumes (Masquerade —)	C 1339	250153
20	C 0936	Cots	B 0321	200023
06	C 0937	Cotter pins of metal	C 0929	060082

Cl.	SERIAL No. (E)	INDICATION OF GOODS	SERIAL No. (F)	BASIC No.
24	C 0938	Cotton fabrics	C 1353	240028
05	C 0939	Cotton for medical purposes	C 1344	050099
13	C 0940	Cotton (Gun—)	C 1354	130030
22	C 0941	Cotton (Raw—)	C 1345	220025
03	C 0942	Cotton sticks for cosmetic purposes	B 0252	030019
23	C 0943	Cotton thread and yarn	C 1350	230002
22	C 0944	Cotton tow	C 1348	220026
22	C 0945	Cotton waste [flock] for padding and stuffing	D 0022	220090
21	C 0946	Cotton waste for cleaning	C 1347	210268
03	C 0947	Cotton wool for cosmetic purposes	O 0137	030066
17	C 0948	Cotton wool for packing [caulking]	C 1343	170032
30	C 0949	Coulis (Fruit—) [sauces]	C 1378	300206
09	C 0950	Counterfeit [false] coin detectors	D 0163	090173
09	C 0951	Counter-operated apparatus (Mechanisms for—)	J 0026	090064
09	C 0952	Counters	C 1124	090138
28	C 0953	Counters [discs] for games	J 0028	280040
20	C 0954	Counters [tables]	C 1125	200067
09	C 0955	Couplers (Acoustic—)	C 1403	090593
09	C 0956	Couplers [data processing equipment]	C 1404	090594
09	C 0957	Couplings, electric	R 0004	090220
12	C 0958	Couplings for land vehicles	A 0029	120003
06	C 0959	Couplings of metal for chains	R 0010	060073
07	C 0960	Couplings other than for land vehicles	A 0026	070385
12	C 0961	Couplings (Railway—)	A 0815	120002
05	C 0962	Court plaster	S 0481	050019
30	C 0963	Couscous [semolina]	C 1435	300163
27	C 0964	Coverings (Floor—)	R 0296	270002
28	C 0965	Coverings for skis (Sole—)	R 0298	280109
18	C 0966	Coverings (Furniture—) of leather	R 0293	180116
24	C 0967	Coverings (Furniture—) of textile	R 0295	240117
19	C 0968	Coverings, not of metal, for building	R 0291	190150
24	C 0969	Coverings of plastic for furniture	R 0294	240075
18	C 0970	Coverings of skins [furs]	C 1484	180037
24	C 0971	Coverlets [bedspreads]	C 1490	240029
24	C 0972	Covers (Fitted toilet lid—) of fabric	H 0114	240118
18	C 0973	Covers for animals	H 0006	180054
12	C 0974	Covers for baby carriages	B 0003	120164
20	C 0975	Covers for clothing [wardrobe]	H 0108	200129
24	C 0976	Covers for cushions	C 1451	240115
21	C 0977	Covers for dishes	C 1468	210269
09	C 0978	Covers for electric outlets	C 0039	090667
18	C 0979	Covers for horse-saddles	H 0111	180097
12	C 0980	Covers for vehicle steering wheels	H 0120	120260
20	C 0981	Covers (Garment—) [storage]	H 0119	200252
24	C 0982	Covers [loose] for furniture	H 0109	240059
21	C 0983	Covers, not of paper, for flower pots	C 0038	210253
16	C 0984	Covers of paper for flower pots	C 0037	160229
12	C 0985	Covers (Seat—) for vehicles	H 0118	120132
16	C 0986	Covers [stationery]	C 1485	160108
18	C 0987	Covers (Umbrella—)	F 0400	180051
07	C 0988	Cowlings [parts of machines]	C 0208	070075
30	C 0989	Crackers	C 1495	300174
20	C 0990	Cradles	B 0321	200023
06	C 0991	Crampons [climbing irons]	C 1505	060149
06	C 0992	Crampons of metal [cramps]	C 1507	060102
06	C 0993	Cramps of metal [crampons]	C 1507	060102
29	C 0994	Cranberry sauce [compote]	C 1111	290156
07	C 0995	Cranes [lifting and hoisting apparatus]	G 0363	070453
07	C 0996	Crank shafts	A 0651	070021
12	C 0997	Crankcases for land vehicle components, other than for engines	C 0284	120058
07	C 0998	Crankcases for machines, motors and engines	C 0283	070474
12	C 0999	Cranks for cycles	M 0113	120089
07	C 1000	Cranks [parts of machines]	M 0114	070230
19	C 1001	Crash barriers, not of metal, for roads	G 0230	190227
06	C 1002	Crash barriers of metal for roads	G 0229	060397
09	C 1003	Crash test dummies	M 0116	090697
20	C 1004	Crates	H 0026	200128
31	C 1005	Crayfish, live	E 0138	310133
29	C 1006	Crayfish, not live	E 0137	290040
16	C 1007	Cream containers of paper	C 1542	160115
29	C 1008	Cream [dairy products]	C 1535	290033
30	C 1009	Cream (Ice—)	C 1539	300046
01	C 1010	Cream of tartar for chemical purposes	C 1527	010219
30	C 1011	Cream of tartar for cooking purposes	C 1531	300211
30	C 1012	Cream of tartar for culinary purposes	C 1528	300215
01	C 1013	Cream of tartar for industrial purposes	C 1529	010668
05	C 1014	Cream of tartar for pharmaceutical purposes	C 1530	050325
01	C 1015	Cream of tartar for the food industry	C 1532	010667
29	C 1016	Cream (Whipped—)	C 1533	290141
07	C 1017	Cream/milk separators	E 0136	070083
03	C 1018	Creams (Cosmetic—)	C 1538	030071
03	C 1019	Creams for leather	C 1541	030074
03	C 1020	Creams (Skin whitening—)	P 0235	030023
16	C 1021	Credit card imprinters, non-electric	P 0953	160345
28	C 1022	Creels [fishing traps]	N 0010	280094
01	C 1023	Creosote for chemical purposes	C 1544	010602
05	C 1024	Creosote for pharmaceutical purposes	C 1545	050326
02	C 1025	Creosote for wood preservation	C 1546	020056
24	C 1026	Crepe [fabric]	C 1547	240035
24	C 1027	Crepon	C 1549	240036
28	C 1028	Cricket bags	S 0033	280047
08	C 1029	Crimping irons	F 0110	080121

Cl.	SERIAL No. (E)	INDICATION OF GOODS	SERIAL No. (F)	BASIC No.
29	C 1030	Crisps (Potato—)	P 0756	290019
26	C 1031	Crochet hooks (Embroidering—)	C 1566	260051
21	C 1032	Crockery	F 0003	210129
29	C 1033	Croquettes	C 1576	290036
05	C 1034	Croton bark	C 1580	050105
01	C 1035	Crotonic aldehyde	C 1581	010220
08	C 1036	Crow bars	B 0202	080250
09	C 1037	Crucibles [laboratory]	C 1550	090170
21	C 1038	Cruet stands for oil and vinegar	H 0170	210292
21	C 1039	Cruets	B 0906	210057
21	C 1040	Crumb trays	R 0062	210160
07	C 1041	Crushers/grinders, electric (Domestic—)	B 0879	070256
07	C 1042	Crushing machines	B 0878	070263
31	C 1043	Crustaceans, live	C 1586	310134
29	C 1044	Crustaceans, not live	C 1585	290037
10	C 1045	Crutches	B 0320	100168
10	C 1046	Crutches for invalids (Tips for—)	E 0248	100126
01	C 1047	Cryogenic preparations	C 1587	010221
21	C 1048	Crystal [glassware]	C 1565	210098
29	C 1049	Crystallized fruits	C 1172	290035
11	C 1050	Cubicles [enclosures (Am.)] (Shower—)	C 0005	110298
31	C 1051	Cucumbers, fresh	C 1129	310037
28	C 1052	Cue tips (Billiard—)	P 0976	280122
28	C 1053	Cues (Billiard—)	Q 0011	280121
14	C 1054	Cuff links	B 0765	140122
25	C 1055	Cuffs	M 0086	250095
07	C 1056	Cultivators [machines]	C 1650	070138
07	C 1057	Cultivators (Motorized—)	M 0502	070513
05	C 1058	Cultures of microorganisms for medical and veterinary use	C 1655	050213
01	C 1059	Cultures of microorganisms other than for medical and veterinary use	C 1656	010596
20	C 1060	Cupboards	A 0743	200014
09	C 1061	Cupels [laboratory]	C 1550	090170
10	C 1062	Cupping glasses	V 0122	100155
21	C 1063	Cups	T 0141	210220
21	C 1064	Cups (Egg—)	C 1243	210165
28	C 1065	Cups for dice	G 0256	280074
21	C 1066	Cups (Fruit—)	C 1395	210089
21	C 1067	Cups of paper or plastic	G 0255	210318
33	C 1068	Curacao	C 1661	330011
05	C 1069	Curare	C 1662	050106
29	C 1070	Curd	L 0046	290161
01	C 1071	Curium	C 1670	010226
08	C 1072	Curlers (Eyelash—)	P 0511	080252
11	C 1073	Curling lamps	L 0090	110158
08	C 1074	Curling tongs	F 0100	080058
07	C 1075	Current generators	C 1408	070124
09	C 1076	Current rectifiers	R 0160	090167
18	C 1077	Curried skins	C 1319	180032
30	C 1078	Curry [spice]	C 1671	300033
21	C 1079	Currycombs	E 0523	210028
01	C 1080	Currying preparations for leather	C 1317	010215
01	C 1081	Currying preparations for skins	P 0248	010216
07	C 1082	Curtain drawing devices, electrically operated	R 0320	070331
26	C 1083	Curtain headings (Tapes for—)	R 0439	260120
20	C 1084	Curtain holders, not of textile material	E 0253	200101
24	C 1085	Curtain holders of textile material	E 0252	240047
20	C 1086	Curtain hooks	C 1572	200176
20	C 1087	Curtain rails	R 0058	200171
20	C 1088	Curtain rings	A 0554	200011
20	C 1089	Curtain rods	T 0524	200175
20	C 1090	Curtain rollers	G 0021	200121
20	C 1091	Curtain tie-backs	P 0202	200177
20	C 1092	Curtains (Bamboo—)	R 0316	200255
20	C 1093	Curtains (Bead—) for decoration	R 0318	200167
17	C 1094	Curtains of asbestos (Safety—)	R 0319	170003
24	C 1095	Curtains of textile or plastic	R 0321	240085
20	C 1096	Cushions	C 1443	200078
24	C 1097	Cushions (Covers for—)	C 1451	240115
10	C 1098	Cushions for medical purposes	C 1446	100064
10	C 1099	Cushions (Heating—), electric, for medical purposes	C 1447	100050
26	C 1100	Cushions (Needle—)	P 0306	260078
11	C 1101	Cushions [pads] (Heating—), electric, not for medical purposes	C 1448	110296
20	C 1102	Cushions (Pet—)	C 1452	200271
26	C 1103	Cushions (Pin—)	P 0307	260055
30	C 1104	Custard	C 1526	300175
08	C 1105	Cuticle nippers	P 0503	080101
08	C 1106	Cuticle tweezers	P 0503	080101
08	C 1107	Cutlery *	C 1460	080078
10	C 1108	Cutlery [surgical]	C 1461	100065
08	C 1109	Cutter bars	A 0309	080009
08	C 1110	Cutters *	C 1405	080076
34	C 1111	Cutters (Cigar—)	C 1384	340014
07	C 1112	Cutters [machines]	C 1399	070123
16	C 1113	Cutters (Paper—) [office requisites]	C 1391	160291
08	C 1114	Cutters (Pizza—), non-electric	C 1393	080249
07	C 1115	Cutting apparatus (Electric arc—)	A 0670	070531
08	C 1116	Cutting bars	B 0204	080027
07	C 1117	Cutting blow pipes, gas-operated	C 0452	070486
21	C 1118	Cutting boards for the kitchen	P 0564	210108
04	C 1119	Cutting fluids	H 0131	040101
07	C 1120	Cutting machines	D 0042	070146
08	C 1121	Cutting tools [hand tools]	D 0043	080230
31	C 1122	Cuttle bone for birds	O 0130	310097
01	C 1123	Cyanides [prussiates]	C 1680	010228
01	C 1124	Cyanotyping (Solutions for—)	C 1679	010227
12	C 1125	Cycle bells	S 0402	120098
12	C 1126	Cycle brakes	B 0387	120086
12	C 1127	Cycle cars	C 1681	120099
12	C 1128	Cycle chains	C 0430	120061
12	C 1129	Cycle frames	C 0061	120221

Cl.	SERIAL No. (E)	INDICATION OF GOODS	SERIAL No. (F)	BASIC No.
12	C 1130	Cycle handle bars	G 0371	120080
12	C 1131	Cycle hubs	C 1697	120091
11	C 1132	Cycle lights	C 1690	110110
12	C 1133	Cycle mudguards	C 1692	120087
12	C 1134	Cycle pumps	B 0394	120093
12	C 1135	Cycle rims	B 0392	120088
12	C 1136	Cycle saddles	B 0396	120096
12	C 1137	Cycle spokes	B 0395	120094
12	C 1138	Cycle stands	B 0318	120097
12	C 1139	Cycle tires [tyres]	B 0378	120084
12	C 1140	Cycles	B 0377	120044
25	C 1141	Cyclists' clothing	C 1705	250065
26	C 1142	Cyclists (Trouser clips for—)	P 0509	260119
09	C 1143	Cyclotrons	C 1707	090172
07	C 1144	Cylinder heads for engines	C 1644	070137
17	C 1145	Cylinder jointings	C 1712	170033
07	C 1146	Cylinders for machines	C 1708	070139
07	C 1147	Cylinders for motors and engines	C 1710	070446
07	C 1148	Cylinders (Pistons for—)	C 1713	070197
15	C 1149	Cymbals	C 1714	150032
01	C 1150	Cymene	C 1715	010230

Cl.	SERIAL No. (E)	INDICATION OF GOODS	SERIAL No. (F)	BASIC No.
08	D 0001	Daggers	P 0698	080246
07	D 0002	Dairy machines	L 0061	070222
24	D 0003	Damask	D 0005	240037
01	D 0004	Damp proofing preparations, except paints, for masonry	H 0180	010617
15	D 0005	Dampers for musical instruments	S 0465	150065
11	D 0006	Dampers [heating]	R 0179	110215
05	D 0007	Dandruff (Pharmaceutical preparations for treating —)	P 0304	050241
09	D 0008	Darkroom lamps [photography]	L 0111	090318
09	D 0009	Darkrooms [photography]	C 0467	090117
26	D 0010	Darning lasts	B 0724	260020
07	D 0011	Darning machines	R 0243	070329
26	D 0012	Darning needles	A 0191	260007
23	D 0013	Darning thread and yarn	R 0242	230015
28	D 0014	Darts	F 0288	280067
07	D 0015	Dashpot plungers [parts of machines]	A 0470	070395
09	D 0016	Data media (Magnetic —)	S 0592	090607
09	D 0017	Data media (Optical —)	S 0593	090616
09	D 0018	Data processing apparatus	I 0083	090306
29	D 0019	Dates	D 0010	290038
12	D 0020	Davits for boats	B 0659	120048
07	D 0021	De-aerators for feedwater	D 0116	070147
10	D 0022	Deafness (Apparatus for the treatment of —)	S 0600	100147
16	D 0023	Decalcomanias	D 0015	160119
21	D 0024	Decanters	C 0226	210063
08	D 0025	Decanting liquids (Implements for —) [hand tools]	S 0478	080191
01	D 0026	Decarbonising engines (Chemical preparations for —)	D 0014	010089
20	D 0027	Deck chairs	T 0465	200194
05	D 0028	Decoctions for pharmaceutical purposes	D 0028	050109
01	D 0029	Decolorants for industrial purposes	D 0033	010580
09	D 0030	Decompression chambers	C 0105	090595
26	D 0031	Decoration of textile articles (Heat adhesive patches for —) [haberdashery]	P 0429	260111
20	D 0032	Decorations of plastic for foodstuffs	D 0037	200003
28	D 0033	Decoys for hunting or fishing	L 0216	280082
11	D 0034	Deep fryers, electric	F 0444	110266
21	D 0035	Deep fryers, non-electric	F 0445	210260
10	D 0036	Defibrillators	D 0047	100211
01	D 0037	Defoliants	D 0048	010236
11	D 0038	Defrosters for vehicles	D 0052	110112
11	D 0039	Defrosting windows of vehicles (Heating apparatus for —)	V 0071	110250
07	D 0040	Degreasers [machines]	D 0055	070149
03	D 0041	Degreasers other than for use in manufacturing processes	D 0053	030077
01	D 0042	Degreasing preparations for use in manufacturing processes	D 0054	010231
01	D 0043	Degumming preparations	D 0044	010234
11	D 0044	Dehydrating (Apparatus for —) foodstuff organic materials	D 0123	110321
01	D 0045	Dehydrating preparations for industrial purposes	D 0122	010239
12	D 0046	Delivery tricycles	T 0529	120162
09	D 0047	Demagnetizing apparatus for magnetic tapes	D 0059	090076
21	D 0048	Demijohns	D 0008	210040
09	D 0049	Densimeters	D 0072	090175
09	D 0050	Densitometers	D 0073	090532
05	D 0051	Dental abrasives	A 0010	050001
05	D 0052	Dental amalgams	A 0403	050012
10	D 0053	Dental apparatus	D 0077	100073
10	D 0054	Dental apparatus, electric	D 0076	100179
03	D 0055	Dental bleaching gels	G 0159	030210
05	D 0056	Dental cements	C 0862	050082
05	D 0057	Dental impression materials	E 0273	050111
05	D 0058	Dental lacquer	L 0138	050112
05	D 0059	Dental mastics	M 0203	050113
11	D 0060	Dental ovens	F 0410	110311
03	D 0061	Dentifrices	D 0088	030079
10	D 0062	Dentists' armchairs	D 0089	100048
03	D 0063	Denture polishes	P 1022	030198
10	D 0064	Dentures	D 0087	100076
05	D 0065	Dentures (Adhesives for —)	A 0109	050003
03	D 0066	Dentures (Preparations for cleaning —)	N 0051	030194
03	D 0067	Deodorant soap	S 0119	030149
05	D 0068	Deodorants for clothing and textiles	D 0133	050400
03	D 0069	deodorants for human beings or for animals	D 0099	030180
03	D 0070	Deodorants for pets	D 0100	030217
05	D 0071	Deodorants, other than for human beings or for animals	D 0131	050119
21	D 0072	Deodorising apparatus for personal use	D 0135	210277
11	D 0073	Deodorising apparatus, not for personal use	D 0136	110275
08	D 0074	Depilation appliances, electric and non-electric	E 0388	080242
03	D 0075	Depilatories	D 0102	030096
03	D 0076	Depilatory preparations	D 0102	030096
05	D 0077	Depuratives	D 0111	050117
07	D 0078	Derricks	M 0233	070251
11	D 0079	Desalination plants	D 0137	110116
11	D 0080	Desiccating apparatus	D 0140	110117
20	D 0081	Desks	B 0905	200036
20	D 0082	Desks (Standing —)	P 1044	200152
08	D 0083	Destructing apparatus for plant parasites	P 0140	080088
25	D 0084	Detachable collars	F 0037	250050
09	D 0085	Detectors	D 0162	090180
09	D 0086	Detectors (Metal —) for industrial or military purposes	D 0166	090178
09	D 0087	Detectors (Smoke —)	D 0164	090623
01	D 0088	Detergent additives to petrol [gasoline]	A 0099	010021
05	D 0089	Detergents for medical purposes	D 0170	050108

Cl.	SERIAL No. (E)	INDICATION OF GOODS	SERIAL No. (F)	BASIC No.
01	D 0090	Detergents for use in manufacturing processes	D 0172	010241
03	D 0091	Detergents other than for use in manufacturing operations and for medical purposes	D 0171	030075
13	D 0092	Detonating caps other than toys	A 0466	130066
28	D 0093	Detonating caps [toys]	A 0467	280118
13	D 0094	Detonating fuses for explosives	C 1259	130062
13	D 0095	Detonating plugs	B 0678	130018
13	D 0096	Detonators	D 0173	130006
01	D 0097	Developers (Photographic—)	R 0286	010435
01	D 0098	Dextrine size	D 0180	010242
05	D 0099	Diabetic bread adapted for medical use	P 0027	050121
05	D 0100	Diagnosis of pregnancy (Chemical preparations for the—)	G 0359	050166
10	D 0101	Diagnostic apparatus for medical purposes	D 0183	100201
09	D 0102	Diagnostic apparatus, not for medical purposes	D 0184	090633
05	D 0103	Diagnostic preparations for medical purposes	D 0186	050330
01	D 0104	Diagnostic preparations, other than for medical or veterinary purposes	D 0185	010243
16	D 0105	Diagrams	D 0187	160126
14	D 0106	Dials [clock and watch making]	C 0056	140021
14	D 0107	Dials (Sun—)	C 0057	140022
10	D 0108	Dialyzers	D 0188	100212
03	D 0109	Diamantine [abrasive]	D 0189	030082
14	D 0110	Diamonds	D 0190	140035
08	D 0111	Diamonds (Glaziers'—) [parts of hand tools]	D 0192	080089
24	D 0112	Diapered linen	L 0297	240069
05	D 0113	Diaper-pants (Babies'—)	C 1360	050413
05	D 0114	Diapers [babies' napkins]	C 1359	050412
09	D 0115	Diaphragms [acoustics]	D 0194	090182
09	D 0116	Diaphragms for scientific apparatus	S 0136	090439
09	D 0117	Diaphragms [photography]	D 0195	090562
07	D 0118	Diaphragms (Pump—)	M 0265	070257
01	D 0119	Diastase for industrial purposes	D 0200	010244
05	D 0120	Diastase for medical purposes	D 0201	050366
01	D 0121	Diatomaceous earth	T 0209	010632
01	D 0122	Diazo paper	P 0095	010245
28	D 0123	Dice	D 0115	280050
28	D 0124	Dice (Cups for—)	G 0256	280074
09	D 0125	Dictating machines	D 0205	090188
07	D 0126	Die-cutting and tapping machines	T 0128	070167
17	D 0127	Dielectrics [insulators]	D 0206	170034
08	D 0128	Dies [hand tools]	F 0203	080066
04	D 0129	Diesel oil	G 0091	040048
07	D 0130	Die-stamping machines	E 0469	070181
05	D 0131	Dietary supplements for animals	C 1102	050419
05	D 0132	Dietetic beverages adapted for medical purposes	B 0576	050307
05	D 0133	Dietetic foods adapted for medical purposes	A 0342	050297
05	D 0134	Dietetic substances adapted for medical use	D 0210	050350
09	D 0135	Diffraction apparatus [microscopy]	D 0211	090189
11	D 0136	Diffusers (Light—)	D 0213	110118
33	D 0137	Digesters [liqueurs and spirits]	D 0215	330012
05	D 0138	Digestives for pharmaceutical purposes	D 0214	050122
08	D 0139	Diggers [hand tools]	A 0755	080204
07	D 0140	Diggers [machines]	A 0754	070397
05	D 0141	Digitalin	D 0216	050123
05	D 0142	Dill oil for medical purposes	E 0444	050018
24	D 0143	Dimity	B 0226	240054
09	D 0144	Dimmers [regulators] (Light—), electric	V 0036	090606
12	D 0145	Dining cars	W 0009	120172
12	D 0146	Dining cars [carriages]	B 0896	120220
12	D 0147	Dinner wagons [carriages]	B 0896	120220
20	D 0148	Dinner wagons [furniture]	B 0895	200222
01	D 0149	Dioxalate (Potassium—)	B 0443	010123
01	D 0150	Dioxide of hydrogen	E 0036	010414
01	D 0151	Dioxide (Titanium—) for industrial purposes	A 0505	010536
02	D 0152	Dioxide (Titanium—) [pigment]	A 0506	020106
12	D 0153	Direction indicators for bicycles	B 0389	120045
12	D 0154	Direction signals for vehicles	I 0066	120228
12	D 0155	Dirigible balloons [airships]	B 0119	120030
11	D 0156	Discharge tubes, electric, for lighting	T 0556	110111
09	D 0157	Discharge tubes, electric, other than for lighting	T 0555	090559
09	D 0158	Discs (Compact—) [audio-video]	D 0236	090587
09	D 0159	Discs (Compact—) [read-only memory]	D 0239	090588
09	D 0160	Discs (Optical—)	D 0238	090617
28	D 0161	Discuses for sports	D 0240	280052
12	D 0162	Disengaging gear for boats	B 0240	120038
21	D 0163	Dish covers	C 1468	210269
21	D 0164	Dishes	P 0637	210208
21	D 0165	Dishes (Butter—)	B 0359	210030
21	D 0166	Dishes for soap	P 0856	210191
07	D 0167	Dishwashers	V 0007	070231
21	D 0168	Dishwashing brushes	B 0872	210304
01	D 0169	Disincrustants	D 0124	010240
11	D 0170	Disinfectant apparatus	D 0129	110115
11	D 0171	Disinfectant dispensers for toilets	D 0256	110114
11	D 0172	Disinfectant distributors for toilets	D 0256	110114
03	D 0173	Disinfectant soap	S 0118	030080
05	D 0174	Disinfectants for chemical toilets	D 0127	050380
05	D 0175	Disinfectants for hygiene purposes	D 0125	050118
07	D 0176	Disintegrators	D 0130	070153
09	D 0177	Disk drives for computers	M 0241	090634
09	D 0178	Disks, magnetic	D 0237	090533

Cl.	SERIAL No. (E)	INDICATION OF GOODS	SERIAL No. (F)	BASIC No.
16	D 0179	Dispensers (Adhesive tape—) [office requisites]	D 0258	160003
21	D 0180	Dispensers (Soap—)	D 0260	210117
20	D 0181	Dispensers (Towel—), not of metal, fixed	D 0262	200084
21	D 0182	Dispensing paper towels (Metal boxes for—)	B 0622	210036
01	D 0183	Dispersants (Oil—)	H 0144	010352
01	D 0184	Dispersants (Petroleum—)	P 0363	010351
01	D 0185	Dispersions of plastics	D 0226	010605
20	D 0186	Display boards	T 0022	200002
11	D 0187	Display cabinets (Refrigerating—) [display cases]	V 0286	110330
20	D 0188	Display stands	P 0945	200057
11	D 0189	Disposable sterilization pouches	P 0687	110324
21	D 0190	Disposable table plates	A 0800	210333
07	D 0191	Disposals (Garbage [waste]—)	B 0877	070414
09	D 0192	Distance measuring apparatus	M 0295	090187
09	D 0193	Distance recording apparatus	E 0332	090194
02	D 0194	Distempers	D 0174	020062
11	D 0195	Distillation apparatus	D 0248	110120
09	D 0196	Distillation apparatus for scientific purposes	D 0249	090564
11	D 0197	Distillation columns	C 1046	110101
33	D 0198	Distilled beverages	B 0577	330008
01	D 0199	Distilled water	E 0027	010247
31	D 0200	Distillery waste for animal consumption	R 0257	310048
09	D 0201	Distribution boards [electricity]	T 0026	090197
09	D 0202	Distribution boxes [electricity]	A 0745	090054
09	D 0203	Distribution consoles [electricity]	P 1046	090198
07	D 0204	Distribution machines, automatic	D 0253	070537
08	D 0205	Ditchers [hand tools]	F 0372	080234
07	D 0206	Ditchers [ploughs]	F 0371	070458
20	D 0207	Divans	D 0269	200085
09	D 0208	Divers' masks	M 0183	090597
07	D 0209	Dividing machines	D 0270	070448
19	D 0210	Diving boards, not of metal	P 0660	190152
06	D 0211	Diving boards of metal	P 0659	060215
11	D 0212	Diving lights	P 0982	110322
09	D 0213	Diving suits	C 1064	090162
28	D 0214	Divot repair tools [golf accessories]	O 0148	280179
09	D 0215	DNA chips	P 1030	090684
19	D 0216	Docks, not of metal, for mooring boats (Floating—)	Q 0002	190188
06	D 0217	Docks of metal for mooring boats (Floating—)	Q 0001	060272
16	D 0218	Document files [stationery]	D 0285	160022
16	D 0219	Document holders [stationery]	P 0690	160361
16	D 0220	Document laminators for office use	D 0271	160346
31	D 0221	Dog biscuits	B 0449	310031
20	D 0222	Dog kennels	C 0751	200058
05	D 0223	Dog lotions	C 0750	050322
05	D 0224	Dog washes	C 0752	050075

Cl.	SERIAL No. (E)	INDICATION OF GOODS	SERIAL No. (F)	BASIC No.
09	D 0225	Dog whistles	S 0305	090508
05	D 0226	Dogs (Repellents for—)	R 0248	050076
28	D 0227	Dolls	P 0921	280088
28	D 0228	Dolls' beds	L 0343	280085
28	D 0229	Dolls' clothes	V 0193	280103
28	D 0230	Dolls' feeding bottles	B 0363	280016
28	D 0231	Dolls' houses	M 0050	280086
28	D 0232	Dolls' rooms	C 0464	280104
01	D 0233	Dolomite for industrial purposes	D 0277	010248
21	D 0234	Domestic grinders, non-electric	B 0880	210158
28	D 0235	Dominoes	D 0278	280054
06	D 0236	Door bells, non-electric	P 0855	060121
06	D 0237	Door cases of metal	C 0568	060329
19	D 0238	Door casings, not of metal	C 0569	190209
07	D 0239	Door closers, electric	F 0069	070538
06	D 0240	Door closers, non-electric	F 0070	060135
24	D 0241	Door curtains	P 0864	240082
20	D 0242	Door fittings, not of metal	G 0085	200125
06	D 0243	Door fittings, of metal	G 0084	060394
19	D 0244	Door frames, not of metal	C 0569	190209
06	D 0245	Door frames of metal	C 0568	060329
20	D 0246	Door handles, not of metal	P 0702	200273
06	D 0247	Door handles of metal	P 0701	060216
06	D 0248	Door knockers	M 0171	060180
27	D 0249	Door mats	G 0330	270008
07	D 0250	Door openers and closers (Hydraulic—) [parts of machines]	P 0840	070515
07	D 0251	Door openers and closers (Pneumatic—) [parts of machines]	P 0842	070520
07	D 0252	Door openers, electric	P 0839	070539
06	D 0253	Door openers, non-electric	P 0841	060320
19	D 0254	Door panels, not of metal	P 0852	190154
06	D 0255	Door panels of metal	P 0851	060219
06	D 0256	Door scrapers	D 0045	060113
06	D 0257	Door springs, non-electric	F 0070	060135
06	D 0258	Door stops of metal	A 0757	060036
20	D 0259	Doors for furniture	P 0837	200170
12	D 0260	Doors for vehicles	P 0838	120160
19	D 0261	Doors, not of metal *	P 0850	190069
06	D 0262	Doors of metal *	P 0849	060100
09	D 0263	Dosage dispensers	D 0283	090565
09	D 0264	Dosimeters	D 0283	090565
15	D 0265	Double basses	C 1219	150027
10	D 0266	Douche bags	P 0688	100218
05	D 0267	Douching preparations for medical purposes	L 0158	050402
03	D 0268	Douching preparations for personal sanitary or deodorant purposes [toiletries]	L 0156	030218
20	D 0269	Dowels, not of metal	C 0740	200217
22	D 0270	Down [feathers]	D 0319	220028
09	D 0271	Downloadable image files	F 0170	090696
09	D 0272	Downloadable music files	F 0169	090695
09	D 0273	Downloadable ring tones for mobile phones	T 0384	090694
31	D 0274	Draff	D 0310	310049
07	D 0275	Drain cocks	E 0044	070439
19	D 0276	Drain pipes, not of metal	T 0594	190220

Cl.	SERIAL No. (E)	INDICATION OF GOODS	SERIAL No. (F)	BASIC No.
06	D 0277	Drain pipes of metal	D 0300	060114
19	D 0278	Drain traps [valves], not of metal or plastic	C 0923	190221
06	D 0279	Drain traps [valves] of metal	C 0922	060335
20	D 0280	Drain traps [valves] of plastic	C 0921	200231
07	D 0281	Drainage machines	D 0299	070158
10	D 0282	Drainage tubes for medical purposes	D 0302	100081
09	D 0283	Drainers for use in photography	E 0173	090212
17	D 0284	Draught excluder strips	B 0734	170013
28	D 0285	Draughtboards	D 0009	280057
20	D 0286	Draughtman's tables	T 0031	200083
28	D 0287	Draughts [games]	D 0006	280049
08	D 0288	Draw wires [hand tools]	R 0434	080258
16	D 0289	Drawer liners of paper, perfumed or not	P 0091	160344
25	D 0290	Drawers [clothing]	C 0124	250023
16	D 0291	Drawing boards	P 0565	160123
16	D 0292	Drawing instruments	D 0142	160125
08	D 0293	Drawing knives	P 0583	080049
16	D 0294	Drawing materials	D 0141	160124
16	D 0295	Drawing pads	B 0494	160041
16	D 0296	Drawing pens	T 0283	160185
16	D 0297	Drawing pins	P 1042	160048
16	D 0298	Drawing sets	T 0540	160151
16	D 0299	Drawing squares	E 0414	160297
16	D 0300	Drawing T-squares	T 0218	160298
10	D 0301	Draw-sheets for sick beds	A 0263	100013
12	D 0302	Dredgers [boats]	D 0295	120105
26	D 0303	Dress body fasteners	C 1323	260048
26	D 0304	Dress fastenings	F 0080	260010
12	D 0305	Dress guards for bicycles, cycles	F 0201	120122
25	D 0306	Dress shields	D 0154	250017
25	D 0307	Dresses	R 0343	250109
01	D 0308	Dressing and finishing preparations for textiles	A 0627	010077
07	D 0309	Dressing (Apparatus for —)	D 0311	070159
01	D 0310	Dressing chemicals (Leather- —)	C 1622	010223
01	D 0311	Dressing, except oils, for skins	C 1173	010208
25	D 0312	Dressing gowns	P 0269	250033
20	D 0313	Dressing tables	T 0038	200189
30	D 0314	Dressings for salad	S 0099	300188
05	D 0315	Dressings, medical	P 0068	050114
05	D 0316	Dressings (Surgical —)	E 0511	050140
20	D 0317	Dressmakers' dummies	M 0115	200064
09	D 0318	Dressmakers' measures	C 1466	090169
11	D 0319	Driers (Air —)	S 0162	110013
11	D 0320	Driers (Hair —)	S 0159	110095
07	D 0321	Drill chucks [parts of machines]	P 0816	070428
08	D 0322	Drill holders [hand tools]	P 0815	080218
07	D 0323	Drilling bits [parts of machines]	C 1413	070449
07	D 0324	Drilling heads [parts of machines]	C 1414	070125
07	D 0325	Drilling machines	F 0358	070299
01	D 0326	Drilling muds	B 0702	010136
01	D 0327	Drilling muds (Chemical additives to —)	A 0096	010019
07	D 0328	Drilling rigs, floating or non-floating	T 0436	070462
08	D 0329	Drills	D 0312	080094
07	D 0330	Drills (Electric hand —)	P 0321	070300
21	D 0331	Drinking flasks for travellers	B 0399	210144
21	D 0332	Drinking glasses	V 0166	210319
21	D 0333	Drinking straws	P 0013	210342
21	D 0334	Drinking troughs	A 0014	210001
21	D 0335	Drinking vessels	R 0140	210034
11	D 0336	Drinking water (Filters for —)	E 0038	110147
05	D 0337	Drinks (Medicinal —)	P 0895	050332
11	D 0338	Drip irrigation emitters [irrigation fittings]	D 0212	110323
09	D 0339	Drives (Disk —) for computers	M 0241	090634
07	D 0340	Drives (Pedal —) for sewing machines	C 1087	070111
12	D 0341	Driving chains for land vehicles	C 0429	120225
07	D 0342	Driving chains other than for land vehicles	C 0428	070425
12	D 0343	Driving motors for land vehicles	M 0509	120139
07	D 0344	Driving motors other than for land vehicles	M 0508	070241
10	D 0345	Dropper bottles for medical purposes	F 0282	100089
10	D 0346	Droppers for medical purposes	C 1121	100061
24	D 0347	Drugget	D 0314	240044
05	D 0348	Drugs for medical purposes	D 0313	050125
15	D 0349	Drumheads	P 0247	150059
15	D 0350	Drums [musical instruments]	T 0078	150066
07	D 0351	Drums [parts of machines]	T 0077	070039
15	D 0352	Drumsticks	B 0039	150010
01	D 0353	Dry ice [carbon dioxide]	G 0211	010333
05	D 0354	Dry rot fungus (Preparations for destroying —)	A 0597	050026
03	D 0355	Dry shampoos	S 0288	030223
03	D 0356	Dry-cleaning preparations	N 0046	030205
11	D 0357	Dryers (Air —)	S 0162	110013
11	D 0358	Dryers (Hair —)	S 0159	110095
03	D 0359	Drying agents for dishwashing machines	S 0157	030214
11	D 0360	Drying apparatus	S 0166	110097
11	D 0361	Drying apparatus and installations	S 0158	110222
11	D 0362	Drying apparatus for fodder and forage	F 0394	110141
09	D 0363	Drying apparatus for photographic prints	E 0408	090282
21	D 0364	Drying racks for washing	E 0493	210126
09	D 0365	Drying racks [photography]	S 0164	090122
19	D 0366	Duckboards, not of metal	C 0095	190241
06	D 0367	Duckboards of metal	C 0094	060317
09	D 0368	Ducts [electricity]	C 0159	090216
19	D 0369	Ducts, not of metal, for ventilating and air-conditioning installations	C 1163	190235
06	D 0370	Ducts of metal, for central heating installations	C 1161	060076
06	D 0371	Ducts of metal for ventilating and air conditioning installations	C 1162	060415

Cl.	SERIAL No. (E)	INDICATION OF GOODS	SERIAL No. (F)	BASIC No.
28	D 0372	Dumb-bells	H 0019	280075
10	D 0373	Dummies [teats] for babies	S 0560	100145
16	D 0374	Duplicators	D 0316	160128
16	D 0375	Duplicators (Inking sheets for —)	T 0332	160199
04	D 0376	Dust binding compositions for sweeping	B 0102	040012
07	D 0377	Dust exhausting installations for cleaning purposes	A 0796	070487
04	D 0378	Dust laying compositions	A 0168	040079
07	D 0379	Dust removing installations for cleaning purposes	D 0108	070488
04	D 0380	Dust removing preparations	D 0109	040038
21	D 0381	Dustbins	P 0905	210194
21	D 0382	Dusters (Furniture —)	E 0463	210125
21	D 0383	Dusting apparatus, non-electric	D 0110	210111
21	D 0384	Dusting cloths [rags]	E 0405	210282
09	D 0385	DVD players	L 0181	090685
07	D 0386	Dyeing machines	T 0148	070362
02	D 0387	Dyes *	T 0149	020058
03	D 0388	Dyes (Cosmetic —)	T 0151	030156
02	D 0389	Dyes (Food —)	C 1055	020005
02	D 0390	Dyestuffs	C 1054	020047
02	D 0391	Dyestuffs (Wood —)	B 0525	020112
02	D 0392	Dyewood	B 0524	020111
02	D 0393	Dyewood extracts	B 0525	020112
13	D 0394	Dynamite	D 0320	130032
07	D 0395	Dynamo belts	C 1422	070126
07	D 0396	Dynamo brushes	B 0094	070033
09	D 0397	Dynamometers	D 0323	090203
07	D 0398	Dynamos	D 0324	070160
01	D 0399	Dysprosium	D 0325	010250

Cl.	SERIAL No. (E)	INDICATION OF GOODS	SERIAL No. (F)	BASIC No.

Cl.	SERIAL No. (E)	INDICATION OF GOODS	SERIAL No. (F)	BASIC No.
25	E 0001	Ear muffs [clothing]	C 1491	250059
10	E 0002	Ear picks	C 1668	100071
10	E 0003	Ear plugs [ear protection devices]	O 0107	100224
09	E 0004	Ear plugs for divers	T 0091	090401
10	E 0005	Ear trumpets	C 1293	100006
08	E 0006	Ear-piercing apparatus	P 0320	080241
14	E 0007	Earrings	B 0687	140118
01	E 0008	Earth (Diatomaceous —)	T 0209	010632
19	E 0009	Earth for bricks	T 0208	190039
01	E 0010	Earth for growing	T 0213	010524
07	E 0011	Earth moving machines	T 0207	070417
08	E 0012	Earth rammers [hand tools]	D 0007	080083
02	E 0013	Earth (Sienna —)	T 0212	020029
21	E 0014	Earthenware	F 0003	210129
01	E 0015	Earths (Metal —)	M 0323	010392
01	E 0016	Earths (Rare —)	T 0216	010526
16	E 0017	Easels (Painters' —)	C 0712	160087
02	E 0018	Easter eggs (Paper for dyeing —)	P 0116	020096
20	E 0019	Easy chairs	C 0441	200051
03	E 0020	Eau de Cologne	E 0018	030058
17	E 0021	Ebonite [vulcanite]	C 0194	170036
17	E 0022	Ebonite [vulcanite] molds [moulds]	M 0527	170100
11	E 0023	Economizers (Fuel —) *	E 0114	110102
08	E 0024	Edge tools [hand tools]	T 0061	080192
28	E 0025	Edges of skis	A 0687	280009
26	E 0026	Edgings for clothing	B 0652	260018
26	E 0027	Edgings (Lace for —)	B 0649	260019
20	E 0028	Edgings of plastic for furniture	M 0340	200173
29	E 0029	Edible birds' nests	N 0067	290143
29	E 0030	Edible fats	G 0313	290005
30	E 0031	Edible ices	G 0214	300136
29	E 0032	Edible oils	H 0146	290032
07	E 0033	Edible pastes (Machines for making —)	P 0205	070296
09	E 0034	Editing appliances for cinematographic films	F 0206	090124
32	E 0035	Effervescing beverages (Pastilles for —)	P 0188	320033
32	E 0036	Effervescing beverages (Powders for —)	B 0581	320034
21	E 0037	Egg cups	C 1243	210165
31	E 0038	Egg laying poultry (Preparations for —)	P 0785	310111
29	E 0039	Egg nog (Non-alcoholic —)	L 0053	290168
08	E 0040	Egg slicers, non-electric	T 0464	080251
09	E 0041	Egg timers [sandglasses]	S 0006	090683
09	E 0042	Egg-candlers	M 0407	090241
29	E 0043	Eggs *	O 0018	290086
31	E 0044	Eggs for hatching, fertilised	O 0019	310045
29	E 0045	Eggs (Powdered —)	O 0025	290087
29	E 0046	Eggs (Snail —) for consumption	O 0024	290139
22	E 0047	Eiderdown	E 0163	220029
24	E 0048	Eiderdowns [down coverlets]	E 0164	240045
12	E 0049	Ejector seats for aircraft	S 0301	120223
07	E 0050	Ejectors	E 0176	070170
16	E 0051	Elastic bands for offices	E 0178	160275

Cl.	SERIAL No. (E)	INDICATION OF GOODS	SERIAL No. (F)	BASIC No.
26	E 0052	Elastic ribbons	R 0435	260095
10	E 0053	Elastic stockings for surgical purposes	B 0217	100165
23	E 0054	Elastic thread and yarn for textile use	F 0230	230019
17	E 0055	Elastic threads, not for use in textiles	F 0231	170038
24	E 0056	Elastic woven material	T 0301	240046
17	E 0057	Elastic yarns, not for use in textiles	F 0231	170038
28	E 0058	Elbow guards [sports articles]	P 1009	280143
06	E 0059	Elbows of metal for pipes	C 1363	060099
10	E 0060	Electric acupuncture instruments	A 0095	100202
11	E 0061	Electric appliances for making yogurt	Y 0004	110312
07	E 0062	Electric arc cutting apparatus	A 0670	070531
07	E 0063	Electric arc welding apparatus	A 0668	070530
09	E 0064	Electric door bells	S 0403	090566
07	E 0065	Electric hammers	M 0172	070489
09	E 0066	Electric installations for the remote control of industrial operations	C 1079	090130
11	E 0067	Electric lamps	L 0102	110024
09	E 0068	Electric loss indicators	I 0069	090213
17	E 0069	Electric mains (Insulators for —)	C 1155	170098
12	E 0070	Electric vehicles	V 0072	120110
07	E 0071	Electric welding apparatus	S 0433	070526
04	E 0072	Electrical energy	E 0314	040106
11	E 0073	Electrically heated carpets	T 0111	110310
09	E 0074	Electricity conduits	C 1154	090142
09	E 0075	Electricity mains (Materials for —) [wires, cables]	E 0186	090553
09	E 0076	Electrified fences	C 0962	090669
09	E 0077	Electrified rails for mounting spot lights	R 0055	090635
05	E 0078	Electrocardiograph electrodes (Chemical conductors for —)	C 1142	050091
16	E 0079	Electrocardiograph paper	P 0112	160140
10	E 0080	Electrocardiographs	E 0202	100084
05	E 0081	Electrodes (Chemical conductors for electrocardiograph —)	C 1142	050091
10	E 0082	Electrodes for medical use	E 0204	100174
07	E 0083	Electrodes for welding machines	E 0206	070525
09	E 0084	Electro-dynamic apparatus for the remote control of railway points	A 0198	090022
09	E 0085	Electro-dynamic apparatus for the remote control of signals	S 0313	090447
09	E 0086	Electrolysers	E 0207	090226
09	E 0087	Electromagnetic coils	A 0221	090024
07	E 0088	Electromechanical machines for chemical industry	I 0080	070490
15	E 0089	Electronic musical instruments	I 0108	150044
09	E 0090	Electronic notice boards	T 0023	090643
09	E 0091	Electronic pens [visual display units]	C 1518	090598
09	E 0092	Electronic pocket translators	T 0446	090636

Cl.	SERIAL No. (E)	INDICATION OF GOODS	SERIAL No. (F)	BASIC No.
09	E 0093	Electronic publications, downloadable	P 1028	090657
09	E 0094	Electronic tags for goods	E 0505	090637
28	E 0095	Electronic targets	C 0821	280193
01	E 0096	Electrophoresis gels, other than for medical or veterinary purposes	G 0158	010650
07	E 0097	Electroplating machines	G 0039	070535
16	E 0098	Electrotypes	G 0040	160163
11	E 0099	Elements (Heating —)	C 1309	110085
07	E 0100	Elevating apparatus	E 0216	070172
12	E 0101	Elevating tailgates (Am.) [parts of land vehicles]	H 0051	120243
07	E 0102	Elevator belts	C 1429	070127
07	E 0103	Elevator chains [parts of machines]	E 0212	070491
07	E 0104	Elevator operating apparatus	A 0786	070540
07	E 0105	Elevators [lifts]	E 0211	070024
05	E 0106	Elixirs [pharmaceutical preparations]	E 0219	050133
08	E 0107	Embossers [hand tools]	E 0468	080105
07	E 0108	Embossing machines	G 0101	070206
26	E 0109	Embroidering crochet hooks	C 1566	260051
26	E 0110	Embroidery	B 0849	260028
16	E 0111	Embroidery designs [patterns]	M 0434	160047
20	E 0112	Embroidery frames	M 0328	200032
23	E 0113	Embroidery thread and yarn	B 0843	230003
23	E 0114	Embroidery (Thread of metal for —)	C 0180	230032
24	E 0115	Embroidery (Traced cloth for —)	T 0309	240049
07	E 0116	Emergency power generators	G 0360	070492
03	E 0117	Emery	E 0257	030094
03	E 0118	Emery cloth	T 0324	030086
08	E 0119	Emery files	L 0265	080257
08	E 0120	Emery grinding wheels	E 0258	080226
03	E 0121	Emery paper	P 0096	030084
01	E 0122	Emollients for industrial purposes	E 0263	010609
01	E 0123	Emulsifiers	E 0276	010268
01	E 0124	Emulsions (Photographic —)	E 0279	010267
02	E 0125	Emulsions (Silver —) [pigments]	E 0278	020015
01	E 0126	Enamel (Chemical preparations, except pigments, for the manufacture of —)	E 0223	010107
01	E 0127	Enamel (Opacifiers for —)	E 0220	010262
21	E 0128	Enamelled glass	V 0141	210119
02	E 0129	Enamels for painting	E 0222	020065
02	E 0130	Enamels [varnishes]	E 0225	020064
01	E 0131	Enamel-staining chemicals	E 0224	010265
06	E 0132	Enclosures of metal for tombs	E 0281	060367
19	E 0133	Enclosures (Tomb or grave —), not of metal	E 0282	190081
09	E 0134	Encoded identification bracelets, magnetic	B 0785	090692
09	E 0135	Encoded magnetic cards	C 0295	090599
09	E 0136	Encoders (Magnetic —)	E 0292	090608
10	E 0137	Enema apparatus for medical purposes	I 0130	100104
04	E 0138	Energy (Electrical —)	E 0314	040106

Cl.	SERIAL No. (E)	INDICATION OF GOODS	SERIAL No. (F)	BASIC No.
01	E 0139	Engine coolants (Anti-boil preparations for —)	E 0070	010645
01	E 0140	Engine-decarbonising chemicals	D 0014	010089
01	E 0141	Engines (Coolants for vehicle —)	R 0177	010647
07	E 0142	Engines for boats	B 0241	070401
12	E 0143	Engines for land vehicles	M 0497	120130
07	E 0144	Engines, other than for land vehicles	M 0489	070433
12	E 0145	Engines (Traction —)	L 0359	120137
02	E 0146	Engraving ink	G 0338	020080
07	E 0147	Engraving machines	G 0333	070207
08	E 0148	Engraving needles	G 0337	080131
16	E 0149	Engraving plates	P 0566	160170
16	E 0150	Engravings	G 0339	160028
09	E 0151	Enlarging apparatus [photography]	A 0180	090021
16	E 0152	Envelope sealing machines, for offices	E 0363	160146
22	E 0153	Envelopes (Bottle —) of straw	E 0239	220080
18	E 0154	Envelopes, of leather, for packaging	S 0040	180079
16	E 0155	Envelopes [stationery]	E 0364	160127
05	E 0156	Enzyme dietary supplements	E 0374	050429
01	E 0157	Enzyme preparations for industrial purposes	E 0367	010272
05	E 0158	Enzyme preparations for medical purposes	E 0368	050370
01	E 0159	Enzyme preparations for the food industry	E 0370	010660
05	E 0160	Enzyme preparations for veterinary purposes	E 0369	050371
01	E 0161	Enzymes for industrial purposes	E 0371	010273
05	E 0162	Enzymes for medical purposes	E 0372	050368
01	E 0163	Enzymes for the food industry	E 0375	010661
05	E 0164	Enzymes for veterinary purposes	E 0373	050369
21	E 0165	Epergnes	S 0608	210219
09	E 0166	Epidiascopes	E 0387	090235
01	E 0167	Epoxy resins, unprocessed	E 0406	010274
16	E 0168	Erasers (Writing board —)	E 0170	160348
16	E 0169	Erasing products	E 0169	160135
16	E 0170	Erasing shields	G 0002	160138
01	E 0171	Erbium	E 0419	010276
09	E 0172	Ergometers	E 0420	090239
05	E 0173	Ergot for pharmaceutical purposes	S 0180	050269
07	E 0174	Escalators	E 0426	070178
24	E 0175	Esparto fabric	S 0484	240090
22	E 0176	Esparto grass	S 0483	220070
25	E 0177	Esparto shoes or sandals	E 0433	250073
03	E 0178	Essences (Ethereal —)	E 0450	030099
30	E 0179	Essences for foodstuffs, except etheric essences and essential oils	E 0452	300048
32	E 0180	Essences for making beverages	E 0451	320009
03	E 0181	Essential oils	H 0153	030100

Cl.	SERIAL No. (E)	INDICATION OF GOODS	SERIAL No. (F)	BASIC No.
01	E 0182	Esters *	E 0470	010279
05	E 0183	Esters for pharmaceutical purposes	E 0471	050138
10	E 0184	Esthetic massage apparatus	M 0192	100063
16	E 0185	Etching needles	E 0096	160309
16	E 0186	Etchings	E 0066	160129
01	E 0187	Ethane	E 0494	010280
04	E 0188	Ethanol [fuel]	E 0495	040107
04	E 0189	Ether (Petroleum —)	E 0496	040044
03	E 0190	Ethereal essences	E 0450	030099
03	E 0191	Ethereal oils	H 0153	030100
01	E 0192	Ethers *	E 0498	010281
05	E 0193	Ethers for pharmaceutical purposes	E 0499	050139
01	E 0194	Ethyl alcohol	A 0297	010041
01	E 0195	Ethyl ether	E 0501	010282
05	E 0196	Eucalyptol for pharmaceutical purposes	E 0540	050141
05	E 0197	Eucalyptus for pharmaceutical purposes	E 0541	050142
01	E 0198	Europium	E 0542	010287
05	E 0199	Evacuants	P 1048	050143
11	E 0200	Evaporators	E 0545	110142
07	E 0201	Excavators	E 0550	070184
01	E 0202	Exchangers (Ion —) [chemicals]	E 0078	010255
28	E 0203	Exercise bicycles (Rollers for stationary —)	R 0401	280059
28	E 0204	Exercise bicycles (Stationary —)	B 0385	280017
28	E 0205	Exercisers [expanders]	E 0553	280051
07	E 0206	Exhausts for motors and engines	P 0902	070451
01	E 0207	Expanded-clay for hydroponic plant growing [substrate]	A 0713	010652
08	E 0208	Expanders [hand tools]	M 0096	080090
26	E 0209	Expanding bands for holding sleeves	B 0788	260023
17	E 0210	Expansion joint fillers	J 0047	170041
11	E 0211	Expansion tanks for central heating installations	V 0042	110313
07	E 0212	Expansion tanks [parts of machines]	V 0041	070493
28	E 0213	Explosive bonbons [Christmas crackers]	B 0636	280027
13	E 0214	Explosive cartridges	E 0558	130003
13	E 0215	Explosive powders	P 0913	130051
13	E 0216	Explosives	E 0555	130034
09	E 0217	Exposure meters [light meters]	E 0560	090251
08	E 0218	Extension pieces for braces for screwtaps	A 0357	080012
09	E 0219	Extinguishers	E 0564	090041
01	E 0220	Extinguishing compositions (Fire —)	E 0565	010288
11	E 0221	Extractor hoods for kitchens	H 0094	110314
07	E 0222	Extractors for mines	E 0566	070185
08	E 0223	Extractors (Nail —)	A 0753	080023
03	E 0224	Extracts of flowers [perfumes]	E 0568	030101
06	E 0225	Eye bolts	T 0281	060143
21	E 0226	Eyebrow brushes	S 0462	210215
03	E 0227	Eyebrow cosmetics	S 0463	030131
03	E 0228	Eyebrow pencils	S 0464	030154
09	E 0229	Eyeglass cases	E 0535	090248
09	E 0230	Eyeglass chains	C 0438	090115
09	E 0231	Eyeglass cords	C 1276	090156
09	E 0232	Eyeglass frames	M 0470	090364
09	E 0233	Eyeglasses	P 0493	090397
08	E 0234	Eyelash curlers	P 0511	080252
03	E 0235	Eyelashes (Adhesives for affixing false —)	C 0849	030178
03	E 0236	Eyelashes (Cosmetic preparations for —)	C 0846	030043
03	E 0237	Eyelashes (False —)	C 0848	030042
26	E 0238	Eyelets for clothing	O 0014	260073
26	E 0239	Eyelets (Shoe —)	O 0013	260036
05	E 0240	Eyepatches for medical purposes	C 0040	050398
09	E 0241	Eyepieces	O 0010	090134
09	E 0242	Eyepieces (Instruments containing —)	L 0392	090332
10	E 0243	Eyes (Artificial —)	Y 0005	100159
05	E 0244	Eye-washes	L 0159	050414

Cl.	SERIAL No. (E)	INDICATION OF GOODS	SERIAL No. (F)	BASIC No.
24	F 0001	Fabric *	T 0295	240008
24	F 0002	Fabric for footwear	T 0308	240021
24	F 0003	Fabric, impervious to gases, for aeronautical balloons	B 0116	240002
24	F 0004	Fabric of imitation animal skins	T 0305	240003
03	F 0005	Fabric softeners for laundry use	A 0801	030193
17	F 0006	Fabrics (Asbestos —)	T 0300	170079
21	F 0007	Fabrics (Buckets made of woven —)	E 0509	210127
17	F 0008	Fabrics (Fiberglass [fibreglass] —), for insulation	T 0303	170104
16	F 0009	Fabrics for bookbinding	E 0512	160150
24	F 0010	Fabrics for textile use	T 0296	240116
17	F 0011	Fabrics (Insulating —)	T 0306	170056
01	F 0012	Fabrics (Stain-preventing chemicals for use on —)	T 0053	010286
16	F 0013	Face towels of paper	S 0265	160307
24	F 0014	Face towels of textile	S 0264	240087
09	F 0015	Face-shields (Workmen's protective —)	E 0131	090210
19	F 0016	Facings, not of metal, for building	R 0291	190150
09	F 0017	Facsimile machines	T 0154	090600
19	F 0018	Fair huts	F 0331	190020
28	F 0019	Fairground ride apparatus	M 0098	280157
11	F 0020	Fairy lights for festive decoration	L 0115	110185
26	F 0021	False beards	B 0191	260014
09	F 0022	False coin detectors	D 0163	090173
03	F 0023	False eyelashes	C 0848	030042
26	F 0024	False hair	C 0732	260043
03	F 0025	False hair (Adhesives for affixing —)	A 0108	030001
26	F 0026	False hems	F 0034	260056
26	F 0027	False moustaches	M 0550	260072
03	F 0028	False nails	O 0066	030136
07	F 0029	Fan belts for motors and engines	C 1428	070441
26	F 0030	Fancy goods [embroidery]	B 0849	260028
11	F 0031	Fans [air-conditioning]	V 0115	110065
11	F 0032	Fans (Electric —) for personal use	V 0117	110315
07	F 0033	Fans for motors and engines	V 0118	070381
20	F 0034	Fans for personal use, non-electric	E 0546	200110
07	F 0035	Fans for the compression, sucking and carrying of grain	S 0440	070203
11	F 0036	Fans [parts of air-conditioning installations]	S 0438	110225
30	F 0037	Farinaceous food pastes	P 0204	300003
30	F 0038	Farinaceous foods	M 0334	300064
08	F 0039	Farriers' knives	R 0357	080132
26	F 0040	Fasteners (Shoe —)	A 0178	260001
26	F 0041	Fasteners (Slide —) [zippers]	F 0071	260053
06	F 0042	Fastening pipes (Collars of metal for —)	C 1040	060312
26	F 0043	Fastenings for clothing	F 0080	260010
18	F 0044	Fastenings for saddles	A 0813	180006
26	F 0045	Fastenings for suspenders	B 0805	260026
29	F 0046	Fat (Coconut —)	G 0308	290121
01	F 0047	Fat-bleaching chemicals	G 0320	010339
29	F 0048	Fat-containing mixtures for bread slices	M 0260	290054
31	F 0049	Fattening preparations (Animal —)	E 0327	310052
01	F 0050	Fatty acids	G 0329	010340
29	F 0051	Fatty substances for the manufacture of edible fats	G 0314	290053
11	F 0052	Faucets for pipes (Am.)	R 0348	110068
21	F 0053	Feather-dusters	P 0662	210281
26	F 0054	Feathers [clothing accessories]	P 0666	260082
22	F 0055	Feathers for bedding	P 0669	220057
22	F 0056	Feathers for stuffing upholstery	P 0670	220064
05	F 0057	Febrifuges	F 0039	050146
07	F 0058	Feeders (Mechanized livestock —)	A 0339	070517
07	F 0059	Feeders [parts of machines]	E 0356	070176
07	F 0060	Feeding apparatus for engine boilers	A 0334	070430
11	F 0061	Feeding apparatus for heating boilers	A 0333	110273
10	F 0062	Feeding bottle teats	T 0220	100170
10	F 0063	Feeding bottle valves	F 0072	100169
10	F 0064	Feeding bottles	B 0360	100028
28	F 0065	Feeding bottles (Dolls' —)	B 0363	280016
11	F 0066	Feeding bottles (Heaters, electric, for —)	C 0610	110257
21	F 0067	Feeding bottles (Heaters for —), non-electric	C 0611	210239
21	F 0068	Feeding troughs	A 0824	210002
07	F 0069	Feedwater regulators	R 0195	070161
24	F 0070	Felt *	F 0137	240027
17	F 0071	Felt (Asbestos —)	F 0138	170044
19	F 0072	Felt for building	F 0139	190090
17	F 0073	Felt (Insulating —)	F 0140	170045
09	F 0074	Fences (Electrified —)	C 0962	090669
19	F 0075	Fences, not of metal	C 0964	190135
06	F 0076	Fences of metal	C 0963	060368
28	F 0077	Fencing gauntlets	G 0056	280132
28	F 0078	Fencing masks	M 0186	280131
28	F 0079	Fencing weapons	A 0738	280130
12	F 0080	Fenders for ships	D 0046	120252
05	F 0081	Fennel for medical purposes	F 0053	050147
09	F 0082	Fermentation (Apparatus for —) [laboratory apparatus]	F 0062	090253
29	F 0083	Fermented vegetable foods [kimchi]	A 0336	290162
01	F 0084	Fermenting wine (Chemicals used in —)	B 0012	010096
01	F 0085	Ferments for chemical purposes	F 0063	010291
30	F 0086	Ferments for pastes	F 0068	300066
05	F 0087	Ferments for pharmaceutical purposes	F 0064	050333
01	F 0088	Ferments (Milk —) for chemical purposes	L 0016	010374
29	F 0089	Ferments (Milk —) for culinary purposes	F 0065	290178
01	F 0090	Ferments (Milk —) for industrial purposes	F 0066	010676

Cl.	SERIAL No. (E)	INDICATION OF GOODS	SERIAL No. (F)	BASIC No.
05	F 0091	Ferments (Milk —) for pharmaceutical purposes	L 0017	050187
01	F 0092	Ferments (Milk —) for the food industry	F 0067	010675
01	F 0093	Fermium	F 0081	010159
01	F 0094	Ferrocyanides	F 0085	010229
06	F 0095	Ferrotitanium	F 0088	060138
01	F 0096	Ferrotype plates [photography]	F 0090	010292
06	F 0097	Ferrules of metal	V 0255	060262
06	F 0098	Ferrules of metal for handles	M 0084	060172
06	F 0099	Ferrules of metal for walking sticks	E 0249	060064
12	F 0100	Ferry boats	B 0006	120028
01	F 0101	Fertilizers	E 0326	010271
01	F 0102	Fertilizing preparations	F 0117	010293
26	F 0103	Festoons [embroidery]	F 0118	260057
22	F 0104	Fiber (Coconut —)	C 0981	220018
05	F 0105	Fiber (Dietary —)	F 0150	050367
17	F 0106	Fiber (Vulcanized —)	F 0149	170046
17	F 0107	Fiberglass fabrics for insulation	T 0303	170104
24	F 0108	Fiberglass fabrics, for textile use	T 0302	240104
17	F 0109	Fiberglass for insulation	F 0157	170103
21	F 0110	Fiberglass other than for insulation or textile use	F 0156	210284
23	F 0111	Fiberglass thread for textile use	F 0227	230017
21	F 0112	Fiberglass thread, not for textile use	F 0228	210286
17	F 0113	Fibers (Asbestos —)	F 0179	170088
17	F 0114	Fibers (Glass —), for insulation	F 0157	170103
17	F 0115	Fibers (Plastic —), not for use in textiles	F 0161	170102
22	F 0116	Fibers (Textile —)	F 0164	220076
22	F 0117	Fibre (Coconut —)	C 0981	220018
05	F 0118	Fibre (Dietary —)	F 0150	050367
09	F 0119	Fibre [fiber (Am.)] optic cables	C 0014	090666
17	F 0120	Fibre (Vulcanized —)	F 0149	170046
17	F 0121	Fibreglass fabrics for insulation	T 0303	170104
24	F 0122	Fibreglass fabrics for textile use	T 0302	240104
17	F 0123	Fibreglass for insulation	F 0157	170103
21	F 0124	Fibreglass other than for insulation or textile use	F 0156	210284
23	F 0125	Fibreglass thread for textile use	F 0227	230017
21	F 0126	Fibreglass thread, not for textile use	F 0228	210286
17	F 0127	Fibres (Asbestos —)	F 0179	170088
17	F 0128	Fibres (Glass —), for insulation	F 0157	170103
17	F 0129	Fibres (Plastic —), not for use in textiles	F 0161	170102
22	F 0130	Fibres (Textile —)	F 0164	220076
06	F 0131	Figurines [statuettes] of common metal	F 0173	060382
16	F 0132	Figurines [statuettes] of papier mâché	F 0175	160155
21	F 0133	Figurines [statuettes] of porcelain, ceramic, earthenware or glass	F 0177	210285
14	F 0134	Figurines [statuettes] of precious metal	F 0174	140146
19	F 0135	Figurines [statuettes] of stone, concrete or marble	F 0176	190224
20	F 0136	Figurines [statuettes] of wood, wax, plaster or plastic	F 0172	200239
11	F 0137	Filaments, electric (Heating —)	F 0181	110293
11	F 0138	Filaments for electric lamps	F 0180	110145
11	F 0139	Filaments (Magnesium —) for lighting	F 0225	110190
16	F 0140	Files [office requisites]	C 0927	160092
08	F 0141	Files [tools]	L 0263	080227
20	F 0142	Filing cabinets	C 0323	200044
06	F 0143	Filings of metal	L 0262	060161
17	F 0144	Fillers (Expansion joint —)	J 0047	170041
01	F 0145	Fillers for automobile bodies	M 0200	010649
01	F 0146	Fillers for car bodies	M 0200	010649
01	F 0147	Fillers (Tree cavity —) [forestry]	M 0201	010080
29	F 0148	Fillets (Fish —)	F 0196	290041
07	F 0149	Filling machines	S 0479	070353
09	F 0150	Film (Cinematographic —), exposed	C 0866	090550
09	F 0151	Film cutting apparatus	F 0205	090262
17	F 0152	Film (Plastic —), not for wrapping	P 0301	170072
16	F 0153	Film (Plastic cling —) extensible, for palletization	P 0300	160325
17	F 0154	Films (Anti-dazzle —) for windows [tinted films]	F 0127	170115
01	F 0155	Films (Cinematographic —), sensitized but not exposed	C 0867	010598
09	F 0156	Films (Editing appliances for cinematographic —)	F 0206	090124
09	F 0157	Films, exposed	F 0209	090515
01	F 0158	Films (Sensitized —), unexposed	F 0213	010581
09	F 0159	Films (X-ray —), exposed	F 0211	090573
01	F 0160	Films (X-ray —), sensitized but not exposed	R 0035	010464
16	F 0161	Filter paper	P 0121	160156
07	F 0162	Filter presses	F 0272	070109
07	F 0163	Filtering machines	F 0257	070192
01	F 0164	Filtering materials [chemical preparations]	F 0251	010611
01	F 0165	Filtering materials [mineral substances]	F 0252	010612
24	F 0166	Filtering materials of textile	F 0249	240105
16	F 0167	Filtering materials [paper]	F 0250	160157
17	F 0168	Filtering materials [semi-processed foams or films of plastic]	F 0248	170106
01	F 0169	Filtering materials [unprocessed plastics]	F 0247	010610
01	F 0170	Filtering materials [vegetable substances]	F 0253	010613
01	F 0171	Filtering media (Ceramic materials in particulate form, for use as —)	C 0399	010621
01	F 0172	Filtering preparations for the beverages industry	B 0566	010296
34	F 0173	Filters (Cigarette —)	F 0266	340006
11	F 0174	Filters (Coffee —), electric	F 0258	110260

Cl.	SERIAL No. (E)	INDICATION OF GOODS	SERIAL No. (F)	BASIC No.
11	F 0175	Filters for air conditioning	A 0242	110011
07	F 0176	Filters for cleaning cooling air, for engines	A 0240	070010
11	F 0177	Filters for drinking water	E 0038	110147
09	F 0178	Filters for respiratory masks	F 0269	090263
10	F 0179	Filters for ultraviolet rays, for medical purposes	F 0270	100181
09	F 0180	Filters for ultraviolet rays, for photography	F 0271	090574
16	F 0181	Filters (Paper coffee—)	F 0259	160324
11	F 0182	Filters [parts of household or industrial installations]	F 0265	110146
07	F 0183	Filters [parts of machines or engines]	F 0264	070457
09	F 0184	Filters [photography]	F 0267	090264
10	F 0185	Finger guards for medical purposes	D 0274	100079
08	F 0186	Fingernail polishers, electric or non-electric	P 0747	080214
16	F 0187	Finger-stalls [office requisites]	D 0275	160064
01	F 0188	Fining preparation (Must-—)	C 1017	010200
01	F 0189	Finings (Wine—)	C 1024	010205
07	F 0190	Finishing machines	F 0273	070193
01	F 0191	Finishing preparations for use in the manufacture of steel	A 0075	010017
09	F 0192	Fire alarms	A 0868	090068
11	F 0193	Fire bars	G 0350	110152
09	F 0194	Fire beaters	B 0265	090082
09	F 0195	Fire blankets	C 1476	090638
09	F 0196	Fire boats	B 0247	090601
19	F 0197	Fire burrs	P 0470	190012
09	F 0198	Fire (Clothing for protection against—)	H 0003	090288
09	F 0199	Fire engines	P 0770	090298
09	F 0200	Fire escapes	E 0089	090205
09	F 0201	Fire extinguishing apparatus	E 0564	090041
01	F 0202	Fire extinguishing compositions	E 0565	010288
09	F 0203	Fire hose	T 0585	090708
09	F 0204	Fire hose nozzles	L 0122	090296
08	F 0205	Fire irons	R 0331	080181
20	F 0206	Fire screens, domestic	E 0126	200046
13	F 0207	Firearm sights	M 0408	130011
13	F 0208	Firearms	A 0726	130009
13	F 0209	Firearms (Ammunition for—)	A 0733	130042
13	F 0210	Firearms (Cleaning brushes for—)	E 0122	130010
19	F 0211	Fireclay	C 0471	190048
13	F 0212	Firecrackers	P 0355	130072
06	F 0213	Firedogs [andirons]	C 0704	060431
20	F 0214	Fireguards	E 0126	200046
04	F 0215	Firelighters	A 0370	040007
09	F 0216	Firemen (Asbestos screens for—)	P 0144	090689
08	F 0217	Fireplace bellows [hand tools]	S 0441	080255
11	F 0218	Fireplaces, domestic	C 0672	110267
19	F 0219	Fireproof cement coatings	E 0310	190056
02	F 0220	Fireproof paints	P 0290	020085
01	F 0221	Fireproofing preparations	I 0012	010294
34	F 0222	Firestones	P 0458	340027
04	F 0223	Firewood	B 0517	040013
13	F 0224	Fireworks	F 0141	130013
13	F 0225	Firing lanyards for explosives	C 1259	130062
13	F 0226	Firing platforms	T 0509	130057
05	F 0227	First-aid boxes, filled	P 0375	050244
29	F 0228	Fish fillets	F 0196	290041
29	F 0229	Fish (Food products made from—)	M 0335	290125
28	F 0230	Fish hooks	H 0023	280076
31	F 0231	Fish, live	P 0729	310103
01	F 0232	Fish meal fertilizers	F 0116	010659
31	F 0233	Fish meal for animal consumption	F 0013	310143
29	F 0234	Fish meal for human consumption	F 0014	290145
05	F 0235	Fish meal for pharmaceutical purposes	F 0012	050381
29	F 0236	Fish, not live	P 0724	290047
04	F 0237	Fish oil, not edible	P 0726	040057
06	F 0238	Fish plates [rails]	E 0109	060116
29	F 0239	Fish, preserved	P 0725	290136
29	F 0240	Fish (Salted—)	P 0727	290149
31	F 0241	Fish spawn	O 0022	310089
29	F 0242	Fish spawn (Processed—)	O 0021	290170
08	F 0243	Fish tapes [hand tools]	R 0434	080258
29	F 0244	Fish, tinned [canned (Am.)]	C 1197	290144
31	F 0245	Fishing bait, live	A 0623	310132
20	F 0246	Fishing baskets	P 0058	200021
08	F 0247	Fishing (Harpoons for—)	P 0252	080170
22	F 0248	Fishing nets	F 0194	220011
28	F 0249	Fishing tackle	P 0250	280083
25	F 0250	Fishing vests	V 0186	250159
01	F 0251	Fissionable chemical elements	C 0762	010180
01	F 0252	Fissionable material for nuclear energy	F 0274	010297
24	F 0253	Fitted toilet lid covers of fabric	H 0114	240118
11	F 0254	Fittings (Bath—)	B 0074	110037
17	F 0255	Fittings (Compressed air pipe—), not of metal	A 0233	170086
07	F 0256	Fittings for engine boilers	G 0072	070101
18	F 0257	Fittings (Harness—)	G 0079	180120
20	F 0258	Fittings, not of metal (Bed—)	G 0081	200124
20	F 0259	Fittings, not of metal (Coffin—)	G 0071	200048
20	F 0260	Fittings, not of metal (Door—)	G 0085	200125
20	F 0261	Fittings, not of metal (Furniture—)	G 0083	200113
20	F 0262	Fittings, not of metal (Window—)	G 0075	200123
06	F 0263	Fittings of metal for beds	G 0080	060393
06	F 0264	Fittings of metal for building	F 0094	060140
06	F 0265	Fittings of metal for coffins	G 0070	060324
06	F 0266	Fittings of metal for compressed air ducts	A 0232	060267
25	F 0267	Fittings of metal for footwear	F 0091	250048
06	F 0268	Fittings of metal for furniture	G 0082	060380
06	F 0269	Fittings of metal for windows	G 0074	060130
11	F 0270	Fittings, shaped, for furnaces	G 0089	110151
11	F 0271	Fittings, shaped, for ovens	G 0089	110151
02	F 0272	Fixatives for watercolors [watercolours]	A 0632	020011

Cl.	SERIAL No. (E)	INDICATION OF GOODS	SERIAL No. (F)	BASIC No.
02	F 0273	Fixatives [varnishes]	F 0277	020072
01	F 0274	Fixing baths [photography]	B 0078	010097
01	F 0275	Fixing solutions [photography]	F 0276	010298
20	F 0276	Flagpoles	H 0024	200127
24	F 0277	Flags, not of paper	D 0305	240042
16	F 0278	Flags of paper	D 0304	160286
30	F 0279	Flakes (Corn —)	F 0307	300043
30	F 0280	Flakes (Maize —)	F 0307	300043
30	F 0281	Flakes (Oat —)	F 0304	300145
29	F 0282	Flakes (Potato —)	F 0308	290154
12	F 0283	Flanges for railway wheel tires [tyres]	B 0691	120033
06	F 0284	Flanges of metal [collars]	B 0811	060054
24	F 0285	Flannel [fabric]	F 0285	240050
24	F 0286	Flannel (Sanitary —)	F 0284	240051
11	F 0287	Flare stacks for use in the oil industry	T 0597	110059
11	F 0288	Flares	F 0283	110148
09	F 0289	Flash-bulbs [photography]	F 0286	090206
09	F 0290	Flashing lights [luminous signals]	C 0943	090126
19	F 0291	Flashing, not of metal, for building	N 0103	190131
06	F 0292	Flashing of metal, for building	N 0102	060195
01	F 0293	Flashlight preparations	F 0287	010256
09	F 0294	Flashlights [photography]	A 0478	090639
11	F 0295	Flashlights [torches]	T 0403	110202
21	F 0296	Flasks	F 0281	210289
21	F 0297	Flasks for travellers (Drinking —)	B 0399	210144
10	F 0298	Flat feet (Supports for —)	P 0439	100146
08	F 0299	Flat irons	R 0229	080224
21	F 0300	Flat-iron stands	F 0107	210112
03	F 0301	Flavorings for beverages [essential oils]	B 0573	030173
30	F 0302	Flavorings, other than essential oils	A 0747	300140
30	F 0303	Flavorings, other than essential oils, for beverages	B 0572	300141
30	F 0304	Flavorings, other than essential oils, for cakes	G 0094	300070
03	F 0305	Flavourings for beverages [essential oils]	B 0573	030173
03	F 0306	Flavourings for cakes [essential oils]	G 0095	030107
30	F 0307	Flavourings, other than essential oils	A 0747	300140
30	F 0308	Flavourings, other than essential oils, for beverages	B 0572	300141
30	F 0309	Flavourings, other than essential oils, for cakes	G 0094	300070
31	F 0310	Flax meal [fodder]	F 0011	310079
05	F 0311	Flaxseed dietary supplements	L 0273	050421
31	F 0312	Flaxseed for animal consumption	L 0280	310150
30	F 0313	Flaxseed for human consumption	L 0281	300212
05	F 0314	Flaxseed for pharmaceutical purposes	G 0293	050162
31	F 0315	Flaxseed meal for animal consumption	L 0277	310151
05	F 0316	Flaxseed meal for pharmaceutical purposes	F 0010	050190
05	F 0317	Flaxseed oil dietary supplements	L 0274	050422
29	F 0318	Flaxseed oil for culinary purposes	L 0282	290175
10	F 0319	Fleams	L 0125	100077
22	F 0320	Fleece wool	T 0356	220072
08	F 0321	Fleshing knives [hand tools]	H 0012	080236
07	F 0322	Fleshing machines	E 0083	070166
17	F 0323	Flexible tubes, not of metal	T 0604	170022
28	F 0324	Flippers for swimming	P 0052	280093
20	F 0325	Floating containers, not of metal	C 1213	200069
06	F 0326	Floating containers of metal	C 1212	060340
19	F 0327	Floating docks, not of metal, for mooring boats	Q 0002	190188
06	F 0328	Floating docks of metal for mooring boats	Q 0001	060272
28	F 0329	Floats for bathing and swimming	F 0313	280211
28	F 0330	Floats for fishing	F 0314	280069
01	F 0331	Flocculants	F 0309	010587
22	F 0332	Flock (Silk —)	F 0292	220040
22	F 0333	Flock [stuffing]	B 0736	220007
22	F 0334	Flock (Wool —)	F 0306	220041
19	F 0335	Floor boards (Parquet —)	L 0076	190106
27	F 0336	Floor coverings	R 0296	270002
19	F 0337	Floor tiles, not of metal	C 0277	190214
06	F 0338	Floor tiles, of metal	D 0002	060040
03	F 0339	Floor wax	C 0881	030053
03	F 0340	Floor wax removers [scouring preparations]	D 0018	030206
19	F 0341	Flooring (Parquet —)	P 0170	190112
03	F 0342	Floors (Non-slipping liquids for —)	L 0314	030208
03	F 0343	Floors (Non-slipping wax for —)	C 0884	030207
19	F 0344	Floors, not of metal	P 0562	190147
06	F 0345	Floors of metal	P 0561	060210
09	F 0346	Floppy disks	D 0244	090534
21	F 0347	Floss for dental purposes	F 0178	210320
26	F 0348	Flounces (Skirt —)	V 0311	260084
30	F 0349	Flour*	F 0017	300057
01	F 0350	Flour for industrial purposes	F 0018	010289
05	F 0351	Flour for pharmaceutical purposes	F 0019	050144
07	F 0352	Flour mill machines	M 0404	070266
30	F 0353	Flour-milling products	M 0405	300099
17	F 0354	Flower arrangements (Foam supports for —) [semi-finished products]	P 0522	170112
31	F 0355	Flower bulbs	O 0030	310091
03	F 0356	Flower perfumes (Bases for —)	F 0295	030105
21	F 0357	Flower pots	P 0897	210133
01	F 0358	Flower preservatives	F 0301	010209
21	F 0359	Flower-pot covers, not of paper	C 0038	210253
16	F 0360	Flower-pot covers of paper	C 0037	160229
20	F 0361	Flower-pot pedestals	P 0433	200116

Cl.	SERIAL No. (E)	INDICATION OF GOODS	SERIAL No. (F)	BASIC No.
26	F 0362	Flowers (Artificial—)	F 0293	260059
31	F 0363	Flowers, dried, for decoration	F 0302	310056
03	F 0364	Flowers (Extracts of—) [perfumes]	E 0568	030101
31	F 0365	Flowers, natural	F 0297	310055
01	F 0366	Flowers of sulphur for chemical purposes	F 0290	010299
05	F 0367	Flowers of sulphur for pharmaceutical purposes	F 0291	050334
26	F 0368	Flowers (Wreaths of artificial—)	C 1415	260099
31	F 0369	Flowers (Wreaths of natural—)	C 1416	310044
20	F 0370	Flower-stands [furniture]	J 0015	200115
11	F 0371	Flues (Chimney—)	C 0268	110093
07	F 0372	Flues for engine boilers	C 0267	070416
11	F 0373	Flues for heating boilers	C 0266	110264
01	F 0374	Fluid (Power steering—)	F 0318	010643
01	F 0375	Fluid (Transmission—)	F 0319	010644
01	F 0376	Fluids (Brake—)	L 0316	010315
04	F 0377	Fluids (Cutting—)	H 0131	040101
01	F 0378	Fluids for hydraulic circuits	L 0315	010197
01	F 0379	Fluids for use with abrasives (Auxiliary—)	F 0317	010004
09	F 0380	Fluorescent screens	E 0129	090208
01	F 0381	Fluorine	F 0320	010302
01	F 0382	Fluorspar compounds	F 0321	010303
11	F 0383	Flushing apparatus	C 0562	110272
11	F 0384	Flushing tanks	R 0251	110075
15	F 0385	Flutes	F 0324	150036
15	F 0386	Flutes (Bamboo—)	F 0325	150082
01	F 0387	Fluxes (Brazing—)	F 0333	010583
01	F 0388	Fluxes (Soldering—)	F 0334	010584
21	F 0389	Fly catchers [traps or whisks]	C 0558	210069
05	F 0390	Fly catching adhesives	G 0234	050217
05	F 0391	Fly catching paper	A 0821	050035
05	F 0392	Fly destroying preparations	T 0569	050218
05	F 0393	Fly glue	G 0234	050217
21	F 0394	Fly swatters	C 0558	210069
16	F 0395	Flyers	F 0326	160360
28	F 0396	Flying discs [toys]	D 0243	280158
07	F 0397	Fly-wheels (Machine—)	V 0310	070337
17	F 0398	Foam supports for flower arrangements [semi-finished products]	P 0522	170112
31	F 0399	Fodder	F 0399	310060
07	F 0400	Fodder presses	P 0954	070195
20	F 0401	Fodder racks	R 0092	200117
13	F 0402	Fog signals, explosive	S 0316	130064
09	F 0403	Fog signals, non-explosive	S 0317	090524
06	F 0404	Foil (Aluminium—)	A 0394	060270
02	F 0405	Foil (Metal—) for painters, decorators, printers and artists	M 0307	020092
17	F 0406	Foil of regenerated cellulose, other than for packing	C 0380	170053
02	F 0407	Foil (Silver—) [leaf]	A 0694	020013
17	F 0408	Foils of metal for insulating	F 0133	170059
06	F 0409	Foils of metal for wrapping and packaging	F 0134	060416
16	F 0410	Folders for papers	C 0700	160085
16	F 0411	Folders [stationery]	P 0642	160224

Cl.	SERIAL No. (E)	INDICATION OF GOODS	SERIAL No. (F)	BASIC No.
19	F 0412	Folding doors, not of metal	B 0259	190022
30	F 0413	Fondants [confectionery]	F 0332	300067
09	F 0414	Food analysis apparatus	A 0338	090029
02	F 0415	Food colorants	C 1055	020005
21	F 0416	Food cooling devices, containing heat exchange fluids, for household purposes	R 0175	210293
02	F 0417	Food dyes	C 1055	020005
05	F 0418	Food for babies	A 0344	050298
31	F 0419	Food (Pet—)	N 0107	310138
07	F 0420	Food preparation machines, electromechanical	A 0337	070423
07	F 0421	Food processors, electric	R 0353	070475
30	F 0422	Foods (Farinaceous—)	M 0334	300064
29	F 0423	Foods prepared from fish	M 0335	290125
31	F 0424	Foodstuffs (Animal—)	A 0343	310007
01	F 0425	Foodstuffs (Chemical substances for preserving—)	C 1185	010044
20	F 0426	Foodstuffs (Decorations of plastic for—)	D 0037	200003
30	F 0427	Foodstuffs (Essences for—), except etheric essences and essential oils	E 0452	300048
05	F 0428	Foot perspiration (Remedies for—)	P 0440	050247
03	F 0429	Foot perspiration (Soap for—)	P 0441	030143
06	F 0430	Foot scrapers	D 0045	060113
25	F 0431	Football boots	C 0637	250075
25	F 0432	Football boots (Studs for—)	C 1506	250134
25	F 0433	Football shoes	C 0637	250075
28	F 0434	Football (Tables for indoor—)	T 0043	280070
11	F 0435	Footmuffs, electrically heated	C 0477	110088
25	F 0436	Footmuffs, not electrically heated	C 0478	250133
20	F 0437	Footstools	T 0052	200235
11	F 0438	Footwarmers, electric or non-electric	C 0615	110087
25	F 0439	Footwear *	C 0626	250003
10	F 0440	Footwear (Arch supports for—)	R 0281	100040
21	F 0441	Footwear (Brushes for—)	C 0630	210071
01	F 0442	Footwear (Cement for—)	M 0206	010170
24	F 0443	Footwear (Fabric for—)	T 0308	240021
25	F 0444	Footwear (Fittings of metal for—)	F 0091	250048
25	F 0445	Footwear (Heelpieces for—)	T 0072	250116
25	F 0446	Footwear (Non-slipping devices for—)	A 0580	250001
10	F 0447	Footwear (Orthopaedic [orthopedic]—)	C 0653	100051
25	F 0448	Footwear (Tips for—)	B 0771	250016
25	F 0449	Footwear uppers	E 0266	250061
25	F 0450	Footwear (Welts for—)	T 0502	250118
31	F 0451	Forage	F 0399	310060
11	F 0452	Forage drying apparatus	F 0394	110141
10	F 0453	Forceps	F 0353	100090
01	F 0454	Forestry (Chemicals for—), except fungicides, herbicides, insecticides and parasiticides	S 0618	010505
07	F 0455	Forge bellows	S 0442	070351
11	F 0456	Forges, portable	F 0360	110149

Cl.	SERIAL No. (E)	INDICATION OF GOODS	SERIAL No. (F)	BASIC No.
12	F 0457	Fork lift trucks	C 0540	120001
08	F 0458	Forks	F 0382	080220
01	F 0459	Formic acid	F 0364	010310
01	F 0460	Formic aldehyde for chemical purposes	F 0365	010311
05	F 0461	Formic aldehyde for pharmaceutical purposes	F 0366	050335
16	F 0462	Forms, printed	F 0367	160158
20	F 0463	Foundations for beehives	R 0109	200004
08	F 0464	Foundry ladles [hand tools]	F 0345	080176
07	F 0465	Foundry machines	F 0337	070196
01	F 0466	Foundry molding [moulding] preparations	F 0340	010307
19	F 0467	Foundry molds [moulds], not of metal	M 0533	190091
06	F 0468	Foundry molds [moulds] of metal	M 0532	060384
01	F 0469	Foundry sand	S 0004	010467
16	F 0470	Fountain pens	S 0553	160225
11	F 0471	Fountains	F 0343	110126
11	F 0472	Fountains (Ornamental—)	J 0030	110175
20	F 0473	Frames (Embroidery—)	M 0328	200032
12	F 0474	Frames for bicycles, cycles	C 0061	120221
08	F 0475	Frames for handsaws	C 0570	080054
09	F 0476	Frames for photographic transparencies	C 0069	090099
18	F 0477	Frames for umbrellas or parasols	C 0255	180018
18	F 0478	Frames (Handbag—)	C 0256	180065
25	F 0479	Frames (Hat—) [skeletons]	C 0254	250028
06	F 0480	Frames of metal for building	C 0575	060074
20	F 0481	Frames (Picture—)	C 0067	200225
19	F 0482	Framework, not of metal, for building	C 0546	190050
06	F 0483	Framework of metal for building	C 0545	060328
11	F 0484	Framework of metal for ovens	A 0717	110025
01	F 0485	Francium	F 0420	010314
09	F 0486	Franking (Apparatus to check—)	A 0157	090149
16	F 0487	Franking machines for office use	A 0158	160009
12	F 0488	Freewheels for land vehicles	R 0388	120148
07	F 0489	Freewheels other than for land vehicles	R 0387	070279
11	F 0490	Freezers	C 1175	110106
16	F 0491	French curves	P 0542	160107
09	F 0492	Frequency meters	F 0432	090268
11	F 0493	Friction lighters for igniting gas	B 0825	110018
24	F 0494	Frieze [cloth]	F 0441	240052
07	F 0495	Friezing machines	R 0096	070325
26	F 0496	Frills for clothing	R 0448	260086
26	F 0497	Frills [lacework]	J 0001	260066
26	F 0498	Fringes	F 0421	260060
05	F 0499	Frostbite salve for pharmaceutical purposes	A 0591	050023
29	F 0500	Frosted fruits	C 1172	290035
01	F 0501	Frosting chemicals (Glass—)	M 0216	010386
30	F 0502	Frosting [icing] (Cake—)	G 0201	300203
29	F 0503	Frozen fruits	C 1176	290025
30	F 0504	Frozen yoghurt [confectionery ices]	Y 0003	300181
30	F 0505	Frozen yogurt [confectionery ices]	Y 0003	300181
33	F 0506	Fruit (Alcoholic beverages containing—)	B 0568	330031
26	F 0507	Fruit (Artificial—)	F 0452	260061
29	F 0508	Fruit chips	T 0460	290131
21	F 0509	Fruit cups	C 1395	210089
33	F 0510	Fruit extracts, alcoholic	E 0569	330002
32	F 0511	Fruit extracts (Non-alcoholic—)	E 0570	320001
31	F 0512	Fruit, fresh	F 0464	310062
01	F 0513	Fruit (Hormones for hastening the ripening of—)	H 0092	010346
29	F 0514	Fruit jellies	F 0465	290044
30	F 0515	Fruit jellies [confectionery]	P 0207	300176
32	F 0516	Fruit juice beverages (Non-alcoholic—)	F 0454	320006
32	F 0517	Fruit juices	J 0068	320010
32	F 0518	Fruit nectars, non-alcoholic	N 0040	320044
29	F 0519	Fruit peel	E 0119	290115
08	F 0520	Fruit pickers [hand tools]	C 1589	080079
29	F 0521	Fruit, preserved	F 0455	290017
29	F 0522	Fruit preserved in alcohol	F 0456	290133
07	F 0523	Fruit presses, electric, for household purposes	P 0949	070460
21	F 0524	Fruit presses, non-electric, for household purposes	P 0950	210138
29	F 0525	Fruit pulp	P 1035	290045
31	F 0526	Fruit residue [marc]	M 0141	310086
11	F 0527	Fruit roasters	F 0472	110159
29	F 0528	Fruit salads	S 0060	290104
29	F 0529	Fruit, stewed	F 0459	290043
29	F 0530	Fruit-based snack food	E 0284	290160
29	F 0531	Fruits (Crystallized—)	C 1172	290035
29	F 0532	Fruits (Frosted—)	C 1172	290035
29	F 0533	Fruits, tinned [canned (Am.)]	C 1195	290146
21	F 0534	Frying pans	P 0694	210136
04	F 0535	Fuel	C 1072	040025
07	F 0536	Fuel conversion apparatus for internal combustion engines	C 1230	070463
07	F 0537	Fuel dispensing pumps for service stations	D 0255	070542
11	F 0538	Fuel economisers *	E 0114	110102
07	F 0539	Fuel economisers for motors and engines	E 0113	070400
01	F 0540	Fuel for atomic piles	C 1077	010087
04	F 0541	Fuel gas	G 0115	040049
04	F 0542	Fuel mixtures (Vaporized—)	C 0249	040020
04	F 0543	Fuel oil	H 0145	040084
07	F 0544	Fuel pumps (Self-regulating—)	P 0773	070543
04	F 0545	Fuel with an alcoholic base	A 0294	040004
01	F 0546	Fuel-saving preparations	C 1078	010257
01	F 0547	Fuller's earth for use in textile industry	T 0211	010525
08	F 0548	Fullers [hand tools]	C 0564	080051
01	F 0549	Fulling preparations	F 0381	010313
01	F 0550	Fulling preparations for use in textile industry	F 0378	010312
08	F 0551	Fulling tools [hand tools]	F 0380	080052

Cl.	SERIAL No. (E)	INDICATION OF GOODS	SERIAL No. (F)	BASIC No.
05	F 0552	Fumigating pastilles	C 0968	050085
05	F 0553	Fumigating sticks	C 0968	050085
10	F 0554	Fumigation apparatus for medical purposes	F 0487	100182
11	F 0555	Fumigation apparatus, not for medical purposes	F 0488	110278
05	F 0556	Fumigation preparations for medical purposes	F 0489	050337
03	F 0557	Fumigation preparations [perfumes]	F 0490	030106
20	F 0558	Funerary urns	U 0016	200267
05	F 0559	Fungicides	F 0341	050151
01	F 0560	Fungicides (Chemical additives to—)	F 0342	010309
12	F 0561	Funiculars	F 0501	120189
21	F 0562	Funnels	E 0354	210121
12	F 0563	Funnels for locomotives	C 0673	120229
12	F 0564	Funnels for ships	C 0674	120073
18	F 0565	Fur	F 0402	180067
25	F 0566	Fur stoles	E 0514	250074
03	F 0567	Furbishing preparations	A 0803	030044
11	F 0568	Furnace ash boxes	C 0388	110154
06	F 0569	Furnace fire screens	E 0127	060117
06	F 0570	Furnace fireguards	G 0066	060390
11	F 0571	Furnace grates	G 0350	110152
19	F 0572	Furnaces (Cement for—)	C 0858	190092
11	F 0573	Furnaces (Coolers for—)	B 0010	110032
11	F 0574	Furnaces (Cooling vats for—)	B 0010	110032
09	F 0575	Furnaces for laboratory use	F 0409	090568
11	F 0576	Furnaces (Loading apparatus for—)	C 0524	110074
11	F 0577	Furnaces, other than for laboratory use	F 0404	110150
11	F 0578	Furnaces (Shaped fittings for—)	G 0089	110151
20	F 0579	Furniture	M 0336	200041
20	F 0580	Furniture casters, not of metal	R 0410	200149
06	F 0581	Furniture casters of metal	R 0409	060187
18	F 0582	Furniture coverings of leather	R 0293	180116
24	F 0583	Furniture coverings of plastic	R 0294	240075
24	F 0584	Furniture coverings of textile	R 0295	240117
21	F 0585	Furniture dusters	E 0463	210125
09	F 0586	Furniture especially made for laboratories	M 0429	090315
10	F 0587	Furniture especially made for medical purposes	M 0428	100119
20	F 0588	Furniture fittings, not of metal	G 0083	200113
06	F 0589	Furniture (Fittings of metal for—)	G 0082	060380
18	F 0590	Furniture (Leather trimmings for—)	G 0073	180041
24	F 0591	Furniture (Loose covers for—)	H 0109	240059
20	F 0592	Furniture of metal	M 0345	200132
20	F 0593	Furniture (Office—)	M 0337	200037
20	F 0594	Furniture partitions of wood	M 0346	200148
20	F 0595	Furniture (Partitions of wood for—)	M 0346	200148
20	F 0596	Furniture (School—)	M 0427	200094
20	F 0597	Furniture shelves	R 0105	200172
19	F 0598	Furrings of wood	B 0040	190015
25	F 0599	Furs [clothing]	F 0403	250049
18	F 0600	Fur-skins	F 0402	180067
09	F 0601	Fuse wire	A 0356	090505
21	F 0602	Fused silica [semi-worked product], other than for building	S 0323	210308
09	F 0603	Fuses	F 0510	090269
13	F 0604	Fuses for explosives	E 0518	130060
13	F 0605	Fuses for explosives, for use in mines	M 0245	130044
24	F 0606	Fustian	B 0226	240054

Cl.	SERIAL No. (E)	INDICATION OF GOODS	SERIAL No. (F)	BASIC No.
25	G 0001	Gabardines [clothing]	G 0001	250077
01	G 0002	Gadolinium	G 0007	010318
25	G 0003	Gaiter straps	S 0472	250083
25	G 0004	Gaiters	G 0367	250062
09	G 0005	Galena crystals [detectors]	G 0018	090271
06	G 0006	Galena [ore]	G 0017	060145
01	G 0007	Gallate (Basic—) of bismuth	G 0022	010126
16	G 0008	Galley racks [printing]	G 0016	160162
05	G 0009	Gallic acid for pharmaceutical purposes	G 0024	050338
01	G 0010	Gallic acid for the manufacture of ink	G 0025	010320
01	G 0011	Gallium	G 0026	010321
01	G 0012	Gallnuts	N 0096	010319
01	G 0013	Gallotannic acid	G 0027	010323
25	G 0014	Galoshes	G 0028	250080
09	G 0015	Galvanic batteries	P 0480	090272
10	G 0016	Galvanic belts for medical purposes	B 0157	100023
09	G 0017	Galvanic cells	E 0208	090218
10	G 0018	Galvanic therapeutic appliances	T 0243	100091
01	G 0019	Galvanizing baths	B 0079	010098
07	G 0020	Galvanizing machines	G 0036	070536
01	G 0021	Galvanizing preparations	G 0037	010324
09	G 0022	Galvanometers	G 0038	090092
01	G 0023	Gambier	G 0042	010325
05	G 0024	Gamboge for medical purposes	G 0275	050341
02	G 0025	Gamboge for painting	G 0276	020076
18	G 0026	Game bags [hunting accessories]	G 0187	180019
28	G 0027	Game calls (Hunting—)	A 0624	280180
29	G 0028	Game, not live	C 0557	290050
28	G 0029	Games *	J 0035	280079
28	G 0030	Games (Apparatus for—)	J 0036	280128
28	G 0031	Games (Balls for—)	B 0113	280011
28	G 0032	Games (Bats for—)	R 0075	280081
28	G 0033	Games (Counters [discs] for—)	J 0028	280040
28	G 0034	Games (Marbles for—)	B 0430	280023
28	G 0035	Gaming machines for gambling	M 0014	280202
16	G 0036	Garbage bags of paper or of plastics	S 0026	160292
21	G 0037	Garbage cans	P 0905	210194
07	G 0038	Garbage disposals	B 0877	070414
31	G 0039	Garden herbs, fresh	H 0066	310070
30	G 0040	Garden herbs, preserved [seasonings]	H 0065	300201
08	G 0041	Garden tools, hand-operated	J 0014	080145
21	G 0042	Gardening gloves	G 0050	210321
26	G 0043	Garlands (Artificial—)	G 0378	260065
29	G 0044	Garlic (Preserved—)	A 0218	290173
21	G 0045	Garlic presses [kitchen utensils]	P 0948	210332
18	G 0046	Garment bags for travel	S 0052	180111
20	G 0047	Garment covers [storage]	H 0119	200252
09	G 0048	Garments for protection against fire	V 0209	090413
25	G 0049	Garters	J 0017	250038
11	G 0050	Gas apparatus (Regulating and safety accessories for—)	G 0107	110259
11	G 0051	Gas boilers	G 0114	110162
11	G 0052	Gas burners	B 0296	110161
11	G 0053	Gas burners (Brackets for—)	A 0625	110251
11	G 0054	Gas condensers, other than parts of machines	C 1135	110294
34	G 0055	Gas containers for cigar lighters	R 0250	340008
04	G 0056	Gas for lighting	G 0117	040040
11	G 0057	Gas lamps	L 0091	110163
11	G 0058	Gas lighters	A 0371	110019
04	G 0059	Gas oil	G 0091	040048
11	G 0060	Gas pipes (Regulating and safety accessories for—)	C 1146	110240
04	G 0061	Gas (Producer—)	G 0122	040103
01	G 0062	Gas propellents for aerosols	G 0124	010026
01	G 0063	Gas purifying preparations	G 0123	010275
11	G 0064	Gas scrubbers [parts of gas installations]	L 0168	110160
11	G 0065	Gas scrubbing apparatus	G 0111	110138
04	G 0066	Gas (Solidified—) [fuel]	G 0128	040088
09	G 0067	Gas testing instruments	G 0110	090278
13	G 0068	Gas weapons (Tear—)	A 0737	130008
07	G 0069	Gases (Blowing machines for the compression, exhaustion and transport of—)	S 0439	070199
05	G 0070	Gases for medical purposes	G 0106	050314
01	G 0071	Gases (Protective—) for welding	G 0125	010326
01	G 0072	Gases (Solidified—) for industrial purposes	G 0127	010328
07	G 0073	Gasifiers	G 0134	070432
17	G 0074	Gaskets	J 0046	170043
22	G 0075	Gaskets (Fibrous—) for ships	G 0063	220036
04	G 0076	Gasoline	G 0140	040051
01	G 0077	Gasoline (Detergent additives to—)	A 0099	010021
09	G 0078	Gasoline gauges	N 0078	090243
09	G 0079	Gasometers [measuring instruments]	G 0141	090279
07	G 0080	Gas-operated blow torches	C 0453	070522
10	G 0081	Gastroscopes	G 0092	100093
06	G 0082	Gate stops of metal	A 0757	060036
19	G 0083	Gates, not of metal	P 0796	190153
06	G 0084	Gates of metal	P 0795	060218
09	G 0085	Gauges	J 0020	090242
03	G 0086	Gaultheria oil	H 0133	030108
28	G 0087	Gauntlets (Fencing—)	G 0056	280132
24	G 0088	Gauze [cloth]	G 0133	240056
05	G 0089	Gauze for dressings	G 0132	050155
12	G 0090	Gear boxes for land vehicles	B 0617	120217
07	G 0091	Gear boxes other than for land vehicles	B 0616	070409
12	G 0092	Gearing for land vehicles	E 0329	120103
12	G 0093	Gears for cycles	C 1689	120085
07	G 0094	Gears for weaving looms	H 0032	070212
07	G 0095	Gears, other than for land vehicles	E 0328	070443
29	G 0096	Gelatine*	G 0146	290003
01	G 0097	Gelatine for industrial purposes	G 0147	010330
05	G 0098	Gelatine for medical purposes	G 0148	050157

Cl.	SERIAL No. (E)	INDICATION OF GOODS	SERIAL No. (F)	BASIC No.
01	G 0099	Gelatine for photographic purposes	G 0149	010329
03	G 0100	Gels (Dental bleaching—)	G 0159	030210
01	G 0101	Gels (Electrophoresis—), other than for medical or veterinary purposes	G 0158	010650
11	G 0102	Generators (Acetylene—)	G 0161	110004
07	G 0103	Generators (Current—)	C 1408	070124
07	G 0104	Generators of electricity	G 0163	070171
01	G 0105	Genes of seeds for agricultural production	G 0164	010656
05	G 0106	Gentian for pharmaceutical purposes	G 0170	050158
16	G 0107	Geographical maps	C 0294	160164
19	G 0108	Geotextiles	G 0173	190236
03	G 0109	Geraniol	G 0174	030110
31	G 0110	Germ (Seed—) for botanical purposes	G 0178	310065
06	G 0111	German silver	M 0032	060031
06	G 0112	Germanium	G 0177	060147
11	G 0113	Germicidal burners	B 0885	110061
11	G 0114	Germicidal lamps for purifying air	L 0105	110166
05	G 0115	Germicides	G 0182	050159
01	G 0116	Getters [chemically active substances]	G 0186	010332
29	G 0117	Gherkins	C 1300	290028
02	G 0118	Gildings	D 0281	020063
08	G 0119	Gimlets [hand tools]	V 0332	080124
33	G 0120	Gin	G 0166	330014
32	G 0121	Ginger ale	G 0194	320003
32	G 0122	Ginger beer	G 0194	320003
29	G 0123	Ginger jam	G 0196	290051
30	G 0124	Ginger [spice]	G 0195	300073
30	G 0125	Gingerbread	P 0022	300055
19	G 0126	Girders, not of metal	P 0938	190083
06	G 0127	Girders of metal	P 0937	060224
25	G 0128	Girdles	G 0015	250079
19	G 0129	Glass (Alabaster—)	V 0135	190002
21	G 0130	Glass bowls	B 0728	210044
19	G 0131	Glass (Building—)	V 0140	190063
21	G 0132	Glass bulbs [receptacles]	A 0482	210009
21	G 0133	Glass caps	B 0677	210042
03	G 0134	Glass cloth	T 0328	030161
24	G 0135	Glass cloths [towels]	E 0465	240048
09	G 0136	Glass covered with an electrical conductor	V 0161	090224
22	G 0137	Glass fibers [fibres] for textile use	F 0155	220093
21	G 0138	Glass flasks [containers]	B 0120	210022
21	G 0139	Glass for vehicle windows [semi-finished product]	V 0157	210231
19	G 0140	Glass granules for road marking	G 0324	190121
21	G 0141	Glass incorporating fine electrical conductors	V 0138	210229
21	G 0142	Glass jars [carboys]	B 0510	210033
01	G 0143	Glass (Opacifiers for—)	V 0160	010263
21	G 0144	Glass (Opal—)	V 0177	210166
03	G 0145	Glass paper	P 0094	030140

Cl.	SERIAL No. (E)	INDICATION OF GOODS	SERIAL No. (F)	BASIC No.
01	G 0146	Glass (Preparations for preventing the tarnishing of—)	V 0159	010522
21	G 0147	Glass [receptacles]	V 0178	210085
20	G 0148	Glass (Silvered—) [mirrors]	V 0136	200013
21	G 0149	Glass stoppers	B 0677	210042
21	G 0150	Glass, unworked or semi-worked, except building glass	V 0139	210149
21	G 0151	Glass vials [receptacles]	A 0482	210009
01	G 0152	Glass (Water—) [soluble glass]	V 0162	010544
17	G 0153	Glass wool for insulation	L 0031	170063
21	G 0154	Glass wool other than for insulation	L 0030	210152
07	G 0155	Glass working machines	V 0152	070382
01	G 0156	Glass-frosting chemicals	M 0216	010386
01	G 0157	Glass-staining chemicals	V 0158	010521
09	G 0158	Glassware (Graduated—)	V 0165	090285
21	G 0159	Glassware (Painted—)	V 0155	210230
03	G 0160	Glaze (Laundry—)	G 0200	030029
02	G 0161	Glazes [paints, lacquers]	G 0224	020075
08	G 0162	Glaziers' diamonds [parts of hand tools]	D 0192	080089
07	G 0163	Glaziers' diamonds [parts of machines]	D 0191	070494
01	G 0164	Glaziers' putty	M 0199	010651
09	G 0165	Glazing apparatus for photographic prints	E 0407	090283
08	G 0166	Glazing irons	F 0102	080118
01	G 0167	Glazings (Ceramic—)	G 0225	010160
09	G 0168	Global Positioning System [GPS] apparatus	G 0292	090701
16	G 0169	Globes (Terrestrial—)	G 0232	160165
21	G 0170	Glove stretchers	O 0158	210141
28	G 0171	Gloves (Baseball—)	G 0047	280141
28	G 0172	Gloves (Boxing—)	G 0048	280032
25	G 0173	Gloves [clothing]	G 0057	250067
28	G 0174	Gloves (Fencing—)	G 0056	280132
09	G 0175	Gloves for divers	G 0052	090275
28	G 0176	Gloves for games	G 0046	280072
21	G 0177	Gloves for household purposes	G 0051	210290
10	G 0178	Gloves for massage	G 0061	100092
10	G 0179	Gloves for medical purposes	G 0045	100043
09	G 0180	Gloves for protection against accidents	G 0060	090274
09	G 0181	Gloves for protection against X-rays for industrial purposes	G 0053	090276
21	G 0182	Gloves (Gardening—)	G 0050	210321
28	G 0183	Gloves (Golf—)	G 0049	280153
17	G 0184	Gloves (Insulating—)	G 0058	170049
21	G 0185	Gloves (Polishing—)	G 0044	210294
07	G 0186	Glow plugs for Diesel engines	B 0706	070061
06	G 0187	Glucinium [beryllium]	B 0325	060043
05	G 0188	Glucose dietary supplements	G 0239	050430
30	G 0189	Glucose for culinary purposes	G 0236	300077
01	G 0190	Glucose for industrial purposes	G 0237	010614
05	G 0191	Glucose for medical purposes	G 0238	050340
01	G 0192	Glucose for the food industry	G 0240	010662
01	G 0193	Glucosides	G 0241	010335
05	G 0194	Glue (Fly—)	G 0234	050217
01	G 0195	Glue for industrial purposes	C 1035	010600

Cl.	SERIAL No. (E)	INDICATION OF GOODS	SERIAL No. (F)	BASIC No.
16	G 0196	Glue for stationery or household purposes	C 1034	160290
07	G 0197	Glue guns, electric	P 0533	070476
11	G 0198	Glue-heating appliances	C 1025	110100
21	G 0199	Glue-pots	C 1027	210084
30	G 0200	Gluten additives for culinary purposes	G 0243	300216
01	G 0201	Gluten for industrial purposes	G 0242	010671
01	G 0202	Gluten for the food industry	G 0246	010670
16	G 0203	Gluten [glue] for stationery or household purposes	G 0245	160264
01	G 0204	Gluten [glue], other than for stationery or household purposes	G 0244	010615
30	G 0205	Gluten prepared as foodstuff	G 0247	300078
01	G 0206	Glutinous tree-banding preparations	A 0649	010079
01	G 0207	Glutinous tree-grafting preparations	A 0649	010079
01	G 0208	Glycerides	G 0248	010336
01	G 0209	Glycerine for industrial purposes	G 0249	010252
05	G 0210	Glycerine for medical purposes	G 0250	050331
05	G 0211	Glycerophosphates	G 0251	050160
01	G 0212	Glycol	G 0252	010337
01	G 0213	Glycol ether	G 0253	010283
21	G 0214	Goblets	G 0254	210232
08	G 0215	Goffering irons	F 0101	080117
09	G 0216	Goggles for sports	L 0389	090654
18	G 0217	Gold beaters' skin	B 0273	180008
05	G 0218	Gold (Dental amalgams of —)	O 0082	050230
26	G 0219	Gold embroidery	O 0083	260094
01	G 0220	Gold salts	S 0209	010409
06	G 0221	Gold solder	S 0432	060417
14	G 0222	Gold thread [jewellery, jewelry (Am.)]	O 0086	140064
14	G 0223	Gold, unwrought or beaten	O 0084	140063
30	G 0224	Golden syrup	S 0337	300096
28	G 0225	Golf bags, with or without wheels	S 0050	280061
12	G 0226	Golf carts	C 0549	120068
28	G 0227	Golf clubs	C 1577	280034
28	G 0228	Golf gloves	G 0049	280153
25	G 0229	Goloshes	G 0028	250080
15	G 0230	Gongs	G 0280	150037
08	G 0231	Gouges [hand tools]	G 0287	080129
05	G 0232	Goulard water	E 0007	050054
21	G 0233	Gourds (Bottle —)	B 0399	210144
25	G 0234	Gowns (Dressing —)	P 0269	250033
09	G 0235	Gradient indicators	I 0068	090299
01	G 0236	Grafting mastic for trees	M 0197	010341
08	G 0237	Grafting tools [hand tools]	G 0342	080134
01	G 0238	Grafting wax for trees	C 0879	010198
07	G 0239	Grain (Blowing machines or fans for the compression, sucking and carrying of —)	S 0440	070203
07	G 0240	Grain husking machines	D 0039	070089
07	G 0241	Grain separators	E 0175	070169
16	G 0242	Graining combs	P 0265	160122
31	G 0243	Grains [cereals]	G 0299	310066
31	G 0244	Grains for animal consumption	G 0296	310067
31	G 0245	Grains [seeds]	G 0298	310068
19	G 0246	Granite	G 0323	190098
19	G 0247	Granules for marking out roads (Glass —)	G 0324	190121
32	G 0248	Grape must, unfermented	R 0059	320026
31	G 0249	Grapes, fresh	R 0060	310115
16	G 0250	Graphic prints	D 0144	160121
16	G 0251	Graphic representations	R 0239	160168
16	G 0252	Graphic reproductions	R 0246	160167
01	G 0253	Graphite for industrial purposes	G 0326	010305
04	G 0254	Graphite (Lubricating —)	G 0327	040052
07	G 0255	Grapnels (Automatic —) for marine purposes	G 0328	070073
22	G 0256	Grass (Esparto —)	S 0483	220070
22	G 0257	Grasses for upholstering	H 0067	220044
21	G 0258	Graters [household utensils]	R 0072	210197
11	G 0259	Grates (Furnace —)	G 0350	110152
07	G 0260	Grating machines for vegetables	R 0070	070455
06	G 0261	Gratings of metal	G 0351	060152
19	G 0262	Grave or tomb enclosures, not of metal	E 0282	190081
19	G 0263	Gravel	G 0335	190099
19	G 0264	Gravestone slabs, not of metal	P 0608	190088
06	G 0265	Gravestone slabs of metal	F 0493	060385
19	G 0266	Gravestones	P 0466	190144
06	G 0267	Gravestones of metal	F 0493	060385
30	G 0268	Gravies (Meat —)	J 0070	300193
08	G 0269	Graving tools [hand tools]	B 0908	080043
07	G 0270	Grease boxes [parts of machines]	B 0614	070204
04	G 0271	Grease for arms [weapons]	A 0739	040011
04	G 0272	Grease for belts	C 1431	040033
04	G 0273	Grease for boots	G 0317	040026
04	G 0274	Grease for leather	G 0318	040034
04	G 0275	Grease for shoes	G 0317	040026
04	G 0276	Grease (Illuminating —)	G 0319	040039
06	G 0277	Grease nipples	R 0005	060151
07	G 0278	Grease rings [parts of machines]	B 0030	070031
01	G 0279	Grease-removing preparations for use in manufacturing processes	D 0054	010231
02	G 0280	Greases (Anti-rust —)	G 0315	020079
03	G 0281	Greases for cosmetic purposes	G 0310	030111
05	G 0282	Greases for medical purposes	G 0311	050163
05	G 0283	Greases for veterinary purposes	G 0312	050164
01	G 0284	Greases (Preparations for the separation of —)	G 0321	010604
19	G 0285	Greenhouse frames, not of metal	C 0572	190210
06	G 0286	Greenhouse frames of metal	C 0571	060316
06	G 0287	Greenhouses of metal, transportable	S 0250	060236
19	G 0288	Greenhouses, transportable, not of metal	S 0251	190167
16	G 0289	Greeting cards	S 0446	160250
11	G 0290	Griddles [cooking appliances]	G 0354	110172

Cl.	SERIAL No. (E)	INDICATION OF GOODS	SERIAL No. (F)	BASIC No.
21	G 0291	Griddles [cooking utensils]	G 0356	210145
21	G 0292	Gridiron supports	G 0355	210146
09	G 0293	Grids for batteries	G 0353	090287
21	G 0294	Grill supports	G 0355	210146
06	G 0295	Grilles of metal	G 0351	060152
11	G 0296	Grills [cooking appliances]	G 0354	110172
21	G 0297	Grills [cooking utensils]	G 0356	210145
07	G 0298	Grinders/crushers, electric, for household purposes	B 0879	070256
07	G 0299	Grinding machines	B 0878	070263
03	G 0300	Grinding preparations	A 0217	030003
08	G 0301	Grinding wheels (Emery—)	E 0258	080226
08	G 0302	Grindstones [hand tools]	M 0356	080201
07	G 0303	Grindstones [parts of machines]	M 0357	070389
30	G 0304	Groats for human food	G 0362	300080
31	G 0305	Groats for poultry	G 0361	310069
19	G 0306	Grog [fired refractory material]	C 0471	190048
19	G 0307	Grout	M 0481	190053
01	G 0308	Growth regulating preparations (Plant—)	R 0200	010634
30	G 0309	Gruel, with a milk base, for food	B 0713	300021
05	G 0310	Guaiacol for pharmaceutical purposes	G 0009	050153
01	G 0311	Guano	G 0366	010342
06	G 0312	Guard rails of metal	C 1221	060095
20	G 0313	Guards (Fire—)	E 0126	200046
07	G 0314	Guards [parts of machines]	C 0208	070075
07	G 0315	Guides for machines	G 0369	070209
10	G 0316	Guidewires (Medical—)	F 0224	100213
15	G 0317	Guitars	G 0379	150039
01	G 0318	Gum arabic for industrial purposes	A 0640	010078
05	G 0319	Gum for medical purposes	G 0271	050161
17	G 0320	Gum, raw or partly processed	G 0265	170017
02	G 0321	Gum resins	G 0278	020078
01	G 0322	Gum solvents	D 0044	010234
01	G 0323	Gum (Tragacanth—) for use in manufactures	A 0122	010024
02	G 0324	Gum-lac	G 0277	020077
16	G 0325	Gummed cloth for stationery purposes	T 0334	160312
24	G 0326	Gummed cloth, other than for stationery	T 0333	240057
16	G 0327	Gummed tape [stationery]	B 0158	160036
16	G 0328	Gums [adhesives] for stationery or household purposes	G 0273	160311
01	G 0329	Gums [adhesives], other than for stationery or household purposes	G 0272	010616
13	G 0330	Gun barrels	C 0184	130021
13	G 0331	Gun carriages [artillery]	A 0163	130002
13	G 0332	Gun cases	E 0530	130033
13	G 0333	Gun cotton	C 1354	130030
20	G 0334	Gun racks	R 0093	200118
13	G 0335	Gunpowder	C 0181	130050
13	G 0336	Guns (Artillery—) [cannons]	P 0431	130014
07	G 0337	Guns (Glue—), electric	P 0533	070476
13	G 0338	Guns (Hammers for—)	C 0749	130028
08	G 0339	Guns [hand tools]	P 0539	080174
08	G 0340	Guns, hand-operated, for the extrusion of mastics	P 0535	080232
28	G 0341	Guns (Harpoon—) [sports articles]	F 0519	280071
13	G 0342	Guns (Harpoon—) [weapons]	F 0518	130069
13	G 0343	Guns (Noise-suppressors for—)	A 0741	130070
28	G 0344	Guns (Paintball—) [sports apparatus]	P 0534	280170
13	G 0345	Guns (Sighting mirrors for—)	M 0409	130038
07	G 0346	Guns (Spray—) for paint	P 0541	070298
07	G 0347	Guns [tools using explosives]	P 0540	070477
13	G 0348	Guns [weapons]	F 0512	130036
13	G 0349	Gunstocks	F 0528	130037
01	G 0350	Gurjun [gurjon, gurjan] (Balm of—) for making varnish	B 0275	010343
05	G 0351	Gurjun [gurjon, gurjan] balsam for medical purposes	B 0274	050342
28	G 0352	Gut for fishing	R 0013	280107
18	G 0353	Gut for making sausages	B 0778	180009
28	G 0354	Gut for rackets	B 0775	280033
17	G 0355	Guttapercha	G 0384	170050
19	G 0356	Gutter pipes, not of metal	T 0590	190075
06	G 0357	Gutter pipes of metal	D 0117	060356
06	G 0358	Gutters of metal	C 0702	060332
19	G 0359	Gutters (Roof—), not of metal	C 0703	190044
19	G 0360	Gutters (Street—), not of metal	C 0168	190245
27	G 0361	Gymnasium mats	T 0115	270004
27	G 0362	Gymnastic mats	T 0115	270004
25	G 0363	Gymnastic shoes	G 0388	250085
28	G 0364	Gymnastics (Appliances for—)	G 0387	280129
19	G 0365	Gypsum	G 0390	190102

Cl.	SERIAL No. (E)	INDICATION OF GOODS	SERIAL No. (F)	BASIC No.
26	H 0001	Haberdashery *, except thread	M 0283	260070
08	H 0002	Hackles [hand tools]	S 0234	080187
05	H 0003	Haematogen	H 0059	050168
05	H 0004	Haemoglobin	H 0060	050169
05	H 0005	Haemorrhoid preparations	A 0595	050025
05	H 0006	Haemostatic pencils	C 1519	050104
06	H 0007	Hafnium [celtium]	C 0382	060067
08	H 0008	Hainault scythes	S 0086	080183
26	H 0009	Hair bands	B 0143	260013
08	H 0010	Hair clippers for animals [hand instruments]	P 0704	080222
08	H 0011	Hair clippers for personal use, electric and non-electric	T 0389	080219
07	H 0012	Hair clipping machines for animals	T 0390	070431
03	H 0013	Hair colorants	C 0736	030040
26	H 0014	Hair coloring caps	B 0644	260115
26	H 0015	Hair colouring caps	B 0644	260115
26	H 0016	Hair curlers, other than hand implements	B 0412	260127
08	H 0017	Hair curling (Hand implements for—)	F 0443	080126
26	H 0018	Hair curling papers	P 0133	260121
26	H 0019	Hair curling pins	C 0728	260039
07	H 0020	Hair cutting machines for animals	T 0390	070431
11	H 0021	Hair driers [dryers]	S 0159	110095
03	H 0022	Hair dyes	C 0736	030040
26	H 0023	Hair extensions	E 0563	260125
26	H 0024	Hair (False—)	C 0732	260043
21	H 0025	Hair for brushes	P 0706	210055
26	H 0026	Hair grips [slides]	P 0501	260015
05	H 0027	Hair growth preparations (Medicinal—)	C 0733	050394
03	H 0028	Hair lotions	L 0371	030034
26	H 0029	Hair nets	F 0202	260042
26	H 0030	Hair ornaments	C 0721	260038
26	H 0031	Hair pins	C 0727	260041
26	H 0032	Hair (Plaited—)	T 0506	260044
10	H 0033	Hair prostheses	P 1018	100192
03	H 0034	Hair spray	L 0141	030201
26	H 0035	Hair (Tresses of—)	T 0506	260044
03	H 0036	Hair waving preparations	C 0734	030041
24	H 0037	Haircloth [sackcloth]	H 0017	240058
20	H 0038	Hairdressers' chairs	C 1011	200241
08	H 0039	Hair-removing tweezers	P 0504	080102
25	H 0040	Half-boots	B 0665	250015
18	H 0041	Halters	L 0238	180059
30	H 0042	Halvah	H 0021	300191
29	H 0043	Ham	J 0011	290063
30	H 0044	Ham glaze	G 0199	300210
13	H 0045	Hammers for guns and rifles	C 0749	130028
08	H 0046	Hammers [hand tools]	M 0173	080156
07	H 0047	Hammers [parts of machines]	M 0174	070247
07	H 0048	Hammers (Pneumatic—)	M 0175	070249
22	H 0049	Hammocks	H 0022	220043
20	H 0050	Hampers [baskets]	M 0118	200143
12	H 0051	Hand cars	D 0303	120106
08	H 0052	Hand drills [hand tools]	B 0235	080028
11	H 0053	Hand drying apparatus for washrooms	S 0161	110223
13	H 0054	Hand grenades	G 0344	130078
16	H 0055	Hand labelling appliances	E 0503	160176
08	H 0056	Hand pumps*	G 0279	080245
08	H 0057	Hand tools, hand-operated	O 0144	080072
18	H 0058	Handbag frames	C 0256	180065
18	H 0059	Handbags	S 0025	180077
15	H 0060	Handbells [musical instruments]	C 0956	150086
16	H 0061	Handbooks [manuals]	M 0125	160180
06	H 0062	Handcuffs	M 0271	060181
20	H 0063	Hand-held mirrors [toilet mirrors]	M 0416	200274
07	H 0064	Hand-held tools, other than hand-operated	O 0154	070284
16	H 0065	Handkerchiefs of paper	M 0516	160198
24	H 0066	Handkerchiefs of textile	M 0515	240078
12	H 0067	Handle bars for bicycles, cycles	G 0371	120080
20	H 0068	Handles (Door—), not of metal	P 0702	200273
06	H 0069	Handles (Ferrules of metal for—)	M 0084	060172
20	H 0070	Handles, not of metal (Knife—)	M 0079	200075
18	H 0071	Handles (Suitcase—)	P 0703	180086
20	H 0072	Handles (Tool—) not of metal	M 0083	200142
18	H 0073	Handles (Walking stick—)	P 0699	180060
07	H 0074	Handling apparatus for loading and unloading	M 0126	070245
12	H 0075	Handling carts	C 0537	120065
07	H 0076	Handling machines, automatic [manipulators]	M 0111	070421
20	H 0077	Handling pallets, not of metal	P 0035	200146
06	H 0078	Handling pallets of metal	P 0034	060175
16	H 0079	Hand-rests for painters	A 0629	160019
14	H 0080	Hands (Clock—) [clock and watch making]	A 0204	140002
09	H 0081	Hands free kits for phones	N 0037	090688
16	H 0082	Handwriting specimens for copying	E 0155	160303
28	H 0083	Hang gliders	A 0219	280127
20	H 0084	Hangers (Coat—)	C 0868	200059
07	H 0085	Hangers [parts of machines]	C 0443	070092
27	H 0086	Hangings (Wall—), not of textile	T 0125	270013
01	H 0087	Hardening preparations (Metal—)	M 0318	010249
01	H 0088	Hardening substances (Limestone—)	F 0315	010301
06	H 0089	Hardware * of metal, small	Q 0019	060227
15	H 0090	Harmonicas	H 0028	150014
15	H 0091	Harmoniums	H 0029	150040
28	H 0092	Harness (Climbers'—)	B 0272	280142
18	H 0093	Harness fittings	G 0079	180120
18	H 0094	Harness for animals	H 0031	180055
28	H 0095	Harness for sailboards	H 0036	280167
22	H 0096	Harness, not of metal, for handling loads	B 0807	220081
06	H 0097	Harness of metal for handling loads	B 0806	060026
12	H 0098	Harness (Security—) for vehicle seats	H 0034	120244
18	H 0099	Harness straps	C 1423	180033

Cl.	SERIAL No. (E)	INDICATION OF GOODS	SERIAL No. (F)	BASIC No.
18	H 0100	Harness traces	C 1423	180033
15	H 0101	Harp strings	H 0038	150042
28	H 0102	Harpoon guns [sports articles]	F 0519	280071
13	H 0103	Harpoon guns [weapons]	F 0518	130069
08	H 0104	Harpoons	H 0039	080140
08	H 0105	Harpoons for fishing	P 0252	080170
15	H 0106	Harps	H 0037	150041
07	H 0107	Harrows	H 0072	070213
07	H 0108	Harvesting machines	F 0024	070051
16	H 0109	Hat boxes of cardboard	C 0308	160076
18	H 0110	Hat boxes of leather	B 0594	180023
25	H 0111	Hat frames [skeletons]	C 0254	250028
24	H 0112	Hat linings, of textile, in the piece	C 1010	240019
26	H 0113	Hat ornaments, not of precious metal	O 0124	260016
14	H 0114	Hat ornaments of precious metal	O 0123	140117
20	H 0115	Hat stands	P 0803	200053
08	H 0116	Hatchets	H 0010	080137
25	H 0117	Hats	C 0492	250046
25	H 0118	Hats (Paper —) [clothing]	C 0499	250162
15	H 0119	Hats with bells [musical instruments]	C 0496	150019
07	H 0120	Haulage apparatus [mining]	E 0566	070185
07	H 0121	Hauling machines (Net —) [fishing]	T 0511	070478
18	H 0122	Haversacks	H 0050	180100
31	H 0123	Hay	F 0330	310058
31	H 0124	Hazelnuts	N 0089	310087
09	H 0125	Head cleaning tapes [recording]	B 0154	090535
05	H 0126	Headache (Articles for —)	A 0598	050027
05	H 0127	Headache pencils	C 1514	050101
25	H 0128	Headbands [clothing]	B 0142	250142
25	H 0129	Headgear for wear	C 1012	250047
12	H 0130	Headlight wipers	E 0460	120262
11	H 0131	Headlights for automobiles	A 0854	110031
09	H 0132	Headphones	C 0324	090671
12	H 0133	Head-rests for vehicle seats	A 0631	120015
20	H 0134	Head-rests [furniture]	A 0630	200052
18	H 0135	Head-stalls	L 0238	180059
10	H 0136	Hearing aids for the deaf	A 0082	100005
10	H 0137	Hearing protectors	O 0140	100124
10	H 0138	Heart pacemakers	S 0540	100203
11	H 0139	Hearths	F 0414	110153
11	H 0140	Heat accumulators	A 0032	110002
26	H 0141	Heat adhesive patches for repairing textile articles	P 0428	260081
17	H 0142	Heat (Compositions to prevent the radiation of —)	C 0449	170024
11	H 0143	Heat exchangers, not parts of machines	E 0079	110129
07	H 0144	Heat exchangers [parts of machines]	E 0080	070450
17	H 0145	Heat (Non-conducting materials for retaining —)	C 0137	170016
11	H 0146	Heat pumps	P 0769	110268
11	H 0147	Heat regenerators	R 0158	110069
09	H 0148	Heat regulating apparatus	C 0448	090116

Cl.	SERIAL No. (E)	INDICATION OF GOODS	SERIAL No. (F)	BASIC No.
11	H 0149	Heaters, electric, for feeding bottles	C 0610	110257
11	H 0150	Heaters for baths	C 0609	110038
21	H 0151	Heaters for feeding bottles, non-electric	C 0611	210239
11	H 0152	Heaters for heating irons	C 0613	110086
11	H 0153	Heaters for vehicles	C 0605	110081
11	H 0154	Heaters (Immersion —)	T 0250	110090
11	H 0155	Heating apparatus	C 0136	110067
11	H 0156	Heating apparatus, electric	C 0598	110082
11	H 0157	Heating apparatus for defrosting windows of vehicles	V 0071	110250
11	H 0158	Heating apparatus for solid, liquid or gaseous fuels	C 0597	110080
11	H 0159	Heating boilers	C 0582	110077
10	H 0160	Heating cushions [pads], electric, for medical purposes	C 1447	100050
11	H 0161	Heating cushions [pads], electric, not for medical purposes	C 1448	110296
11	H 0162	Heating elements	C 1309	110085
11	H 0163	Heating filaments, electric	F 0181	110293
11	H 0164	Heating installations	C 0608	110073
11	H 0165	Heating installations (Hot water —)	C 0595	110076
11	H 0166	Heating installations [water]	C 0595	110076
11	H 0167	Heating plates	P 0600	110201
21	H 0168	Heat-insulated containers	R 0141	210062
01	H 0169	Heavy water	E 0035	010253
16	H 0170	Hectographs	H 0052	160171
07	H 0171	Heel-making machines	T 0071	070361
25	H 0172	Heelpieces for footwear	T 0072	250116
25	H 0173	Heelpieces for stockings	T 0073	250008
25	H 0174	Heels	T 0074	250131
09	H 0175	Heliographic apparatus	H 0055	090290
03	H 0176	Heliotropine	H 0056	030113
01	H 0177	Helium	H 0057	010344
09	H 0178	Helmets (Protective —)	C 0325	090112
09	H 0179	Helmets (Protective —) for sports	C 0326	090656
09	H 0180	Helmets (Riding —)	B 0632	090690
10	H 0181	Hematimeters	H 0058	100095
05	H 0182	Hematogen	H 0059	050168
09	H 0183	Hemline markers	A 0758	090313
07	H 0184	Hemming machines	O 0141	070283
05	H 0185	Hemoglobin	H 0060	050169
05	H 0186	Hemorrhoid preparations	A 0595	050025
05	H 0187	Hemostatic pencils	C 1519	050104
22	H 0188	Hemp	C 0488	220013
22	H 0189	Hemp bands	S 0077	220015
24	H 0190	Hemp cloth	C 0491	240018
24	H 0191	Hemp fabric	C 0490	240017
23	H 0192	Hemp thread and yarn	C 0489	230005
26	H 0193	Hems (False —)	F 0034	260056
05	H 0194	Herbal teas for medicinal purposes	T 0288	050240
05	H 0195	Herbicides	H 0069	050204
34	H 0196	Herbs for smoking *	H 0062	340028
31	H 0197	Herbs, fresh (Garden —)	H 0066	310070

Cl.	SERIAL No. (E)	INDICATION OF GOODS	SERIAL No. (F)	BASIC No.
05	H 0198	Herbs (Medicinal –)	H 0064	050170
05	H 0199	Herbs (Smoking –) for medical purposes	H 0063	050336
10	H 0200	Hernia bandages	B 0802	100039
29	H 0201	Herrings	H 0027	290055
20	H 0202	High chairs for babies	C 0440	200257
07	H 0203	High pressure washers	N 0047	070495
09	H 0204	High tension batteries	B 0261	090044
09	H 0205	High-frequency apparatus	F 0431	090267
30	H 0206	High-protein cereal bars	B 0203	300214
20	H 0207	Hinges, not of metal	C 0544	200056
06	H 0208	Hinges of metal	C 0543	060327
19	H 0209	Hips for roofing	C 0744	190009
16	H 0210	Histological sections for teaching purposes	C 1397	160106
28	H 0211	Hockey sticks	C 1579	280048
08	H 0212	Hoes [hand tools]	S 0089	080185
07	H 0213	Hoists	M 0459	070095
16	H 0214	Holders for checkbooks [cheque books]	P 0804	160333
09	H 0215	Holders for electric coils	B 0504	090514
21	H 0216	Holders for flowers and plants [flower arranging]	P 0594	210132
16	H 0217	Holders for stamps [seals]	T 0271	160258
16	H 0218	Holders (Passport –)	P 0180	160340
21	H 0219	Holders (Toilet paper –)	P 0830	210335
07	H 0220	Holding devices for machine tools	P 0826	070286
08	H 0221	Holing axes	B 0326	080030
08	H 0222	Hollowing bits [parts of hand tools]	E 0547	080108
01	H 0223	Holmium	H 0076	010345
09	H 0224	Holograms	H 0077	090291
30	H 0225	Hominy	B 0714	300197
30	H 0226	Hominy grits	S 0229	300198
30	H 0227	Honey	M 0376	300098
32	H 0228	Honey-based beverages (Non-alcoholic –)	B 0589	320049
20	H 0229	Honeycombs	R 0106	200150
25	H 0230	Hoods [clothing]	C 0222	250027
11	H 0231	Hoods (Extractor –) for kitchens	H 0094	110314
12	H 0232	Hoods for baby carriages	V 0301	120165
12	H 0233	Hoods for vehicle engines	C 0207	120054
12	H 0234	Hoods for vehicles	C 0206	120055
07	H 0235	Hoods [parts of machines]	C 0208	070075
26	H 0236	Hook and pile fastening tapes	B 0151	260116
12	H 0237	Hooks (Boat –)	C 1568	120036
20	H 0238	Hooks (Curtain –)	C 1572	200176
26	H 0239	Hooks (Embroidering crochet –)	C 1566	260051
28	H 0240	Hooks (Fish –)	H 0023	280076
26	H 0241	Hooks for corsets	C 1328	260098
06	H 0242	Hooks for slate [metal hardware]	A 0684	060351
26	H 0243	Hooks [haberdashery]	C 1573	260052
06	H 0244	Hooks [metal hardware]	C 1575	060105
20	H 0245	Hooks, not of metal, for clothes rails	C 1571	200080
06	H 0246	Hooks of metal for clothes rails	C 1570	060352
26	H 0247	Hooks (Rug –)	C 1567	260122
26	H 0248	Hooks (Shoe –)	C 1574	260033
08	H 0249	Hoop cutters [hand tools]	H 0015	080139
06	H 0250	Hoop iron	F 0125	060131
06	H 0251	Hoop steel	F 0124	060003
20	H 0252	Hoops, not of metal (Barrel –)	C 0404	200211
20	H 0253	Hoops, not of metal (Cask –)	C 0404	200211
06	H 0254	Hoops of metal (Barrel –)	C 0403	060288
20	H 0255	Hooves (Animal –)	S 0008	200179
05	H 0256	Hooves (Cement for animal –)	C 0859	050083
31	H 0257	Hop cones	C 1166	310038
07	H 0258	Hoppers [mechanical discharging]	T 0497	070145
06	H 0259	Hoppers of metal, non-mechanical	T 0496	060418
31	H 0260	Hops	H 0097	310073
32	H 0261	Hops (Extracts of –) for making beer	H 0099	320021
05	H 0262	Hops (Extracts of –) for pharmaceutical purposes	H 0098	050343
01	H 0263	Hormones for hastening the ripening of fruit	H 0092	010346
05	H 0264	Hormones for medical purposes	H 0091	050171
20	H 0265	Horn, unworked or semi-worked	C 1286	200074
20	H 0266	Horns (Animal –)	C 1290	200035
21	H 0267	Horns (Drinking –)	C 1287	210086
09	H 0268	Horns for loudspeakers	P 0232	090575
12	H 0269	Horns for vehicles	A 0869	120212
15	H 0270	Horns [musical instruments]	C 1322	150030
13	H 0271	Horns (Powder –)	C 1289	130029
18	H 0272	Horse blankets	C 1477	180026
21	H 0273	Horse brushes	C 0715	210073
18	H 0274	Horse collars	C 0716	180025
22	H 0275	Horsehair	C 1560	220027
15	H 0276	Horsehair for bows for musical instruments	C 1561	150007
28	H 0277	Horseshoe games	F 0099	280159
06	H 0278	Horseshoe nails	F 0098	060077
18	H 0279	Horseshoes	F 0097	180121
19	H 0280	Horticultural frames, not of metal	C 0572	190210
01	H 0281	Horticulture chemicals, except fungicides, herbicides, insecticides and parasiticides	H 0093	010347
12	H 0282	Hose carts	C 0539	120066
09	H 0283	Hose (Fire –)	T 0585	090708
17	H 0284	Hose (Watering –)	T 0586	170006
17	H 0285	Hoses of textile material	T 0596	170025
20	H 0286	Hoses (Reels, not of metal, non-mechanical, for flexible –)	D 0179	200103
20	H 0287	Hoses (Winding spools, not of metal, non-mechanical, for flexible –)	E 0343	200104
25	H 0288	Hosiery	B 0640	250013
22	H 0289	Hosiery (Bags for washing –)	S 0034	220106
07	H 0290	Hosiery looms	B 0641	070057
20	H 0291	Hospital beds	L 0344	200138
11	H 0292	Hot air apparatus	A 0228	110016

Cl.	SERIAL No. (E)	INDICATION OF GOODS	SERIAL No. (F)	BASIC No.
11	H 0293	Hot air bath fittings	B 0077	110017
11	H 0294	Hot air ovens	A 0147	110008
10	H 0295	Hot air therapeutic apparatus	A 0230	100011
10	H 0296	Hot air vibrators for medical purposes	V 0229	100012
11	H 0297	Hot plates	P 0597	110170
21	H 0298	Hot pots, not electrically heated	C 0988	210322
11	H 0299	Hot water bottles	B 0720	110302
09	H 0300	Hourglasses	S 0006	090683
11	H 0301	House numbers (Luminous —)	N 0109	110196
20	H 0302	House numbers, not of metal, non-luminous	N 0111	200155
06	H 0303	House numbers of metal, non-luminous	N 0110	060196
16	H 0304	House painters' rollers	R 0398	160215
24	H 0305	Household linen	L 0289	240071
20	H 0306	Household pets (Nesting boxes for —)	N 0068	200008
07	H 0307	Housings [parts of machines]	C 0088	070040
12	H 0308	Hub caps	E 0330	120124
12	H 0309	Hubs for vehicle wheels	M 0562	120060
12	H 0310	Hulls (Ships' —)	C 1240	120035
26	H 0311	Human hair	C 0722	260126
11	H 0312	Humidifiers for central heating radiators	H 0178	110084
16	H 0313	Humidity control sheets of paper or plastic for foodstuff packaging	F 0136	160356
34	H 0314	Humidors	B 0596	340038
29	H 0315	Hummus [chickpea paste]	H 0105	290158
01	H 0316	Humus	T 0215	010355
01	H 0317	Humus top dressing	H 0182	010641
13	H 0318	Hunting firearms	A 0728	130026
28	H 0319	Hunting game calls	A 0624	280180
08	H 0320	Hunting knives	C 0556	080053
15	H 0321	Huqin [Chinese violins]	H 0183	150081
30	H 0322	Husked barley	O 0116	300100
30	H 0323	Husked oats	A 0883	300143
07	H 0324	Husking machines (Corn and grain —)	D 0039	070089
19	H 0325	Huts	B 0180	190019
11	H 0326	Hydrants	B 0673	110049
05	H 0327	Hydrastine	H 0184	050174
05	H 0328	Hydrastinine	H 0185	050175
05	H 0329	Hydrated chloral for pharmaceutical purposes	C 0784	050079
01	H 0330	Hydrates	H 0186	010356
01	H 0331	Hydraulic circuits (Fluids for —)	L 0315	010197
12	H 0332	Hydraulic circuits for vehicles	C 0873	120079
01	H 0333	Hydraulic circuits (Liquids for —)	L 0315	010197
07	H 0334	Hydraulic door openers and closers [parts of machines]	P 0840	070515
07	H 0335	Hydraulic engines and motors	H 0190	070461
07	H 0336	Hydraulic turbines	H 0191	070215
01	H 0337	Hydrazine	H 0193	010358
01	H 0338	Hydrochlorates	C 0788	010184
01	H 0339	Hydrochloric acid	C 0789	010185
01	H 0340	Hydrofluoric acid	F 0323	010304
01	H 0341	Hydrogen	H 0195	010359

Cl.	SERIAL No. (E)	INDICATION OF GOODS	SERIAL No. (F)	BASIC No.
01	H 0342	Hydrogen peroxide	E 0036	010414
03	H 0343	Hydrogen peroxide for cosmetic purposes	P 0340	030112
05	H 0344	Hydrogen peroxide for medical purposes	P 0341	050345
11	H 0345	Hydromassage bath apparatus	H 0199	110334
33	H 0346	Hydromel [mead]	H 0200	330016
09	H 0347	Hydrometers	H 0201	090011
12	H 0348	Hydroplanes	H 0198	120135
10	H 0349	Hydrostatic beds for medical purposes	L 0347	100096
20	H 0350	Hydrostatic beds, not for medical purposes	L 0348	200230
05	H 0351	Hygienic bandages	B 0160	050047
10	H 0352	Hygienic basins	B 0230	100025
16	H 0353	Hygienic paper	P 0098	160094
09	H 0354	Hygrometers	H 0211	090292
03	H 0355	Hypochloride (Potassium —)	E 0019	030089
01	H 0356	Hypochlorite of soda	H 0212	010360
10	H 0357	Hypodermic syringes	H 0213	100097
10	H 0358	Hypogastric belts	H 0214	100002
01	H 0359	Hyposulphites	H 0216	010361

Cl.	SERIAL No. (E)	INDICATION OF GOODS	SERIAL No. (F)	BASIC No.
10	I 0001	Ice bags for medical purposes	S 0024	100094
11	I 0002	Ice boxes	G 0221	110168
21	I 0003	Ice buckets	G 0210	210196
11	I 0004	Ice chests	G 0221	110168
30	I 0005	Ice cream	C 1539	300046
30	I 0006	Ice cream (Binding agents for—)	L 0230	300074
21	I 0007	Ice cube molds [moulds]	M 0525	210099
01	I 0008	Ice (Dry—) [carbon dioxide]	G 0211	010333
30	I 0009	Ice for refreshment	G 0202	300076
11	I 0010	Ice machines and apparatus	G 0203	110167
06	I 0011	Ice moulds of metal	M 0524	060150
06	I 0012	Ice nails [climbing irons]	C 1505	060149
30	I 0013	Ice, natural or artificial	G 0204	300075
21	I 0014	Ice pails	G 0210	210196
08	I 0015	Ice picks	P 0514	080128
28	I 0016	Ice skates	P 0214	280099
30	I 0017	Iced tea	T 0235	300186
30	I 0018	Ices (Binding agents for edible—)	L 0230	300074
30	I 0019	Ices (Edible—)	G 0214	300136
30	I 0020	Ices (Powder for edible—)	G 0216	300137
09	I 0021	Identification bracelets (Encoded—), magnetic	B 0785	090692
20	I 0022	Identification bracelets, not of metal, for hospitals	B 0784	200221
06	I 0023	Identification bracelets of metal, for hospitals	B 0783	060051
09	I 0024	Identification sheaths for electric wires	G 0013	090294
09	I 0025	Identification threads for electric wires	F 0229	090293
09	I 0026	Identity cards, magnetic	C 0296	090529
20	I 0027	Identity plates, not of metal	P 0603	200154
06	I 0028	Identity plates of metal	P 0602	060399
09	I 0029	Igniting apparatus, electric, for igniting at a distance	A 0358	090030
07	I 0030	Igniting devices for internal combustion engines	A 0365	070016
07	I 0031	Igniting magnetos	M 0029	070244
09	I 0032	Ignition (Electric apparatus for remote—)	A 0358	090030
04	I 0033	Illuminating grease	G 0319	040039
04	I 0034	Illuminating wax	C 0890	040029
18	I 0035	Imitation leather	C 1603	180042
11	I 0036	Immersion heaters	T 0250	110090
05	I 0037	Implants (Surgical—) [living tissues]	I 0022	050397
01	I 0038	Impregnating chemicals (Leather-—)	C 1609	010224
01	I 0039	Impregnating chemicals (Textile-—)	T 0228	010363
16	I 0040	Imprinters (Credit card—), non-electric	P 0953	160345
11	I 0041	Incandescent burners	B 0294	110043
03	I 0042	Incense	E 0288	030095
05	I 0043	Incense (Insect repellent—)	E 0290	050386
11	I 0044	Incinerators	I 0057	110173
12	I 0045	Inclined ways for boats	P 0586	120039
09	I 0046	Inclinometers	I 0068	090299
10	I 0047	Incontinence sheets	D 0309	100014
05	I 0048	Incontinents (Napkins for—)	C 1358	050351
05	I 0049	Incontinents (Pants, absorbent, for—)	C 1648	050372
10	I 0050	Incubators for babies	C 1487	100177
09	I 0051	Incubators for bacteria culture	C 1488	090556
07	I 0052	Incubators for eggs	I 0064	070442
10	I 0053	Incubators for medical purposes	C 1486	100067
20	I 0054	Index cabinets [furniture]	F 0171	200043
16	I 0055	Index cards [stationery]	F 0167	160072
16	I 0056	Indexes	R 0234	160154
16	I 0057	Indian inks	C 0772	160089
09	I 0058	Indicators (Quantity—)	I 0071	090301
09	I 0059	Indicators (Speed—)	I 0074	090303
09	I 0060	Indicators (Water level—)	I 0067	090204
02	I 0061	Indigo [colorant]	I 0076	020086
06	I 0062	Indium	I 0077	060154
21	I 0063	Indoor aquaria	A 0635	210336
28	I 0064	Indoor football (Tables for—)	T 0043	280070
21	I 0065	Indoor terrariums [plant cultivation]	T 0205	210305
21	I 0066	Indoor terrariums [vivariums]	T 0206	210338
20	I 0067	Indoor window blinds [shades] [furniture]	S 0545	200272
09	I 0068	Inductors [electricity]	I 0078	090304
01	I 0069	Industrial chemicals	C 0770	010176
04	I 0070	Industrial grease	G 0316	040035
04	I 0071	Industrial oil	H 0155	040087
04	I 0072	Industrial wax	C 0896	040030
20	I 0073	Infant playpens (Mats for—)	T 0121	200275
20	I 0074	Infant walkers	T 0535	200258
18	I 0075	Infants (Slings for carrying—)	E 0086	180122
20	I 0076	Inflatable publicity objects	O 0003	200259
05	I 0077	Infusions (Medicinal—)	I 0084	050148
30	I 0078	Infusions, not medicinal	I 0085	300009
06	I 0079	Ingots of common metal	L 0303	060164
14	I 0080	Ingots of precious metals	L 0304	140003
10	I 0081	Inhalers	I 0086	100099
07	I 0082	Injectors for engines	I 0088	070077
10	I 0083	Injectors for medical purposes	I 0087	100100
16	I 0084	Ink *	E 0298	160142
02	I 0085	Ink for leather	E 0302	020033
02	I 0086	Ink for skin-dressing	E 0301	020069
02	I 0087	Ink (Printing—)	E 0300	020066
16	I 0088	Ink sticks	E 0295	160334
16	I 0089	Ink stones [ink reservoirs]	E 0296	160335
02	I 0090	Ink [toner] for photocopiers	E 0304	020121
07	I 0091	Inking apparatus for printing machines	E 0305	070175
16	I 0092	Inking pads	T 0092	160054
16	I 0093	Inking ribbons	R 0436	160143
16	I 0094	Inking ribbons for computer printers	R 0438	160326
16	I 0095	Inking sheets for document reproducing machines	T 0331	160241
16	I 0096	Inking sheets for duplicators	T 0332	160199
02	I 0097	Inks (Marking—) for animals	E 0303	020067
16	I 0098	Inkstands	E 0151	160301

Cl.	SERIAL No. (E)	INDICATION OF GOODS	SERIAL No. (F)	BASIC No.
16	I 0099	Inkwells	E 0309	160144
28	I 0100	In-line roller skates	P 0216	280182
25	I 0101	Inner soles	S 0221	250041
12	I 0102	Inner tubes (Adhesive rubber patches for repairing —)	C 0461	120194
12	I 0103	Inner tubes for bicycles, cycles	B 0381	120214
12	I 0104	Inner tubes for pneumatic tires [tyres]	C 0460	120007
01	I 0105	Inner tubes of tires [tyres] (Compositions for repairing —)	C 0458	010032
12	I 0106	Inner tubes (Repair outfits for —)	T 0546	120008
05	I 0107	Insect repellent incense	E 0290	050386
05	I 0108	Insect repellents	I 0098	050178
19	I 0109	Insect screens not of metal	M 0553	190239
06	I 0110	Insect screens of metal	M 0552	060428
21	I 0111	Insect traps	P 0445	210150
08	I 0112	Insecticide atomizers [hand tools]	P 1041	080144
08	I 0113	Insecticide sprayers [hand tools]	P 1041	080144
08	I 0114	Insecticide vaporizers [hand tools]	P 1041	080144
05	I 0115	Insecticides	I 0093	050055
01	I 0116	Insecticides (Chemical additives to —)	I 0094	010308
21	I 0117	Insects (Electric devices for attracting and killing —)	A 0820	210345
05	I 0118	Insemination (Semen for artificial —)	S 0491	050177
10	I 0119	Instrument cases for use by surgeons and doctors	C 0783	100055
15	I 0120	Instruments (Musical —)	I 0106	150025
10	I 0121	Insufflators	I 0110	100103
17	I 0122	Insulating buildings against moisture (Substances for —)	H 0179	170058
17	I 0123	Insulating fabrics	T 0306	170056
17	I 0124	Insulating felt	F 0140	170045
21	I 0125	Insulating flasks	B 0752	210046
19	I 0126	Insulating glass [building]	V 0149	190180
17	I 0127	Insulating gloves	G 0058	170049
17	I 0128	Insulating materials	I 0138	170023
17	I 0129	Insulating oils	H 0156	170052
17	I 0130	Insulating paints	P 0291	170060
17	I 0131	Insulating paper	P 0101	170055
17	I 0132	Insulating plaster	E 0311	170110
17	I 0133	Insulating refractory materials	M 0222	170116
17	I 0134	Insulating tape and band	B 0161	170107
17	I 0135	Insulating varnish	V 0132	170057
17	I 0136	Insulation (Metal foil for —)	F 0133	170059
17	I 0137	Insulators	I 0145	170099
17	I 0138	Insulators for electric mains	C 1155	170098
09	I 0139	Integrated circuit cards [smart cards]	C 0288	090640
09	I 0140	Integrated circuits	C 0875	090538
15	I 0141	Intensity regulators for mechanical pianos	R 0197	150045
09	I 0142	Intercommunication apparatus	I 0111	090308
09	I 0143	Interfaces for computers	I 0112	090603
20	I 0144	Interior textile window blinds	S 0541	200282
01	I 0145	Internal combustion engines (Anti-knock substances for —)	A 0582	010071
10	I 0146	Invalids' hoists	D 0229	100204
09	I 0147	Inverters [electricity]	I 0115	090310
09	I 0148	Invoicing machines	F 0002	090252
01	I 0149	Iodic acid	I 0121	010367
05	I 0150	Iodides for pharmaceutical purposes	I 0124	050347
01	I 0151	Iodine for chemical purposes	I 0116	010365
01	I 0152	Iodine for industrial purposes	I 0123	010368
05	I 0153	Iodine for pharmaceutical purposes	I 0117	050346
01	I 0154	Iodised albumen	A 0273	010034
01	I 0155	Iodised salts	I 0118	010366
05	I 0156	Iodoform	I 0122	050181
01	I 0157	Ion exchangers [chemical preparations]	E 0078	010255
11	I 0158	Ionization apparatus for the treatment of air or water	A 0251	110174
09	I 0159	Ionization apparatus not for the treatment of air or water	I 0125	090311
03	I 0160	Ionone [perfumery]	I 0127	030121
14	I 0161	Iridium	I 0129	140045
05	I 0162	Irish moss for medical purposes	M 0544	050182
06	I 0163	Iron bands (Stretchers for —) [tension links]	F 0060	060284
06	I 0164	Iron (Chrome —)	F 0084	060080
06	I 0165	Iron (Molybdenum —)	F 0086	060136
06	I 0166	Iron ores	F 0057	060134
01	I 0167	Iron salts	F 0059	010290
06	I 0168	Iron (Silicon —)	F 0087	060137
06	I 0169	Iron slabs	B 0790	060052
06	I 0170	Iron strip	F 0125	060131
06	I 0171	Iron, unwrought or semi-wrought	F 0054	060115
06	I 0172	Iron wire	F 0056	060132
21	I 0173	Ironing board covers, shaped	H 0116	210093
21	I 0174	Ironing boards	P 0569	210179
07	I 0175	Ironing machines	R 0232	070328
06	I 0176	Ironmongery *	Q 0019	060227
06	I 0177	Irons (Beak-—) [bick-irons]	B 0411	060045
08	I 0178	Irons (Flat —)	R 0229	080224
08	I 0179	Irons [non-electric hand tools]	F 0114	080116
06	I 0180	Ironwork for doors	F 0093	060347
06	I 0181	Ironwork for windows	F 0092	060106
29	I 0182	Isinglass for food	I 0001	290062
16	I 0183	Isinglass for stationery or household purposes	I 0003	160313
01	I 0184	Isinglass other than for stationery, household or alimentary purposes	I 0002	010618
21	I 0185	Isothermic bags	S 0045	210323
32	I 0186	Isotonic beverages	B 0582	320045
01	I 0187	Isotopes for industrial purposes	I 0147	010369
05	I 0188	Isotopes for medical purposes	I 0148	050349
14	I 0189	Ivory [jewellery, jewelry (Am.)]	I 0151	140046
20	I 0190	Ivory, unworked or semi-worked	I 0150	200131

Cl.	SERIAL No. (E)	INDICATION OF GOODS	SERIAL No. (F)	BASIC No.
25	J 0001	Jackets [clothing]	V 0185	250121
16	J 0002	Jackets for papers	C 0700	160085
17	J 0003	Jackets (Pipe—), not of metal	M 0091	170067
25	J 0004	Jackets (Stuff—) [clothing]	V 0035	250120
21	J 0005	Jacks (Boot—)	T 0278	210041
08	J 0006	Jacks (Lifting—), hand-operated	C 1557	080024
07	J 0007	Jacks [machines]	V 0125	070135
16	J 0008	Jacquard looms (Perforated cards for—)	C 0310	160077
05	J 0009	Jalap	J 0005	050183
19	J 0010	Jalousies, not of metal	J 0008	190103
06	J 0011	Jalousies of metal	J 0007	060156
29	J 0012	Jams	C 1174	290024
02	J 0013	Japan (Black—)	A 0790	020017
17	J 0014	Jar lids (Bands of rubber for unscrewing—)	B 0511	170012
09	J 0015	Jars (Accumulator—)	B 0007	090008
21	J 0016	Jars (Glass—) [carboys]	B 0510	210033
03	J 0017	Jasmine oil	J 0018	030115
03	J 0018	Javelle water	E 0019	030089
10	J 0019	Jaws (Artificial—)	M 0017	100111
29	J 0020	Jellies for food	G 0156	290048
30	J 0021	Jellies (Fruit—) [confectionery]	P 0207	300176
03	J 0022	Jelly (Petroleum—) for cosmetic purposes	G 0150	030109
05	J 0023	Jelly (Petroleum—) for medical purposes	G 0152	050339
24	J 0024	Jersey [fabric]	J 0023	240062
25	J 0025	Jerseys [clothing]	J 0024	250089
12	J 0026	Jet engines for land vehicles	R 0128	120145
07	J 0027	Jet engines other than for land vehicles	R 0127	070272
14	J 0028	Jet (Ornaments of—)	O 0125	140047
14	J 0029	Jet, unwrought or semi-wrought	J 0003	140048
06	J 0030	Jets of metal	A 0260	060021
03	J 0031	Jewellers' rouge	R 0392	030011
14	J 0032	Jewellery	B 0413	140050
14	J 0033	Jewellery cases [caskets]	C 1001	140166
14	J 0034	Jewellery of yellow amber	A 0420	140004
14	J 0035	Jewellery (Paste—)	S 0549	140097
14	J 0036	Jewelry	B 0413	140050
14	J 0037	Jewelry cases [caskets]	C 1001	140166
14	J 0038	Jewelry of yellow amber	A 0420	140004
14	J 0039	Jewelry (Paste—) [costume jewelry]	S 0549	140097
15	J 0040	Jews' harps [musical instruments]	G 0374	150038
09	J 0041	Jigs [measuring instruments]	G 0005	090105
28	J 0042	Jigsaw puzzles	P 1058	280168
08	J 0043	Jig-saws	C 0487	080048
17	J 0044	Joint packings	J 0046	170043
17	J 0045	Joints (Fillers for expansion—)	J 0047	170041
07	J 0046	Joints [parts of engines]	J 0049	070118
07	J 0047	Joints (Universal—) [Cardan joints]	J 0048	070479
19	J 0048	Joists, not of metal	P 0936	190157
06	J 0049	Joists of metal	P 0935	060225
28	J 0050	Jokes (Practical—) [novelties]	F 0008	280062
03	J 0051	Joss sticks	B 0257	030213
07	J 0052	Journal boxes [parts of machines]	T 0421	070289
12	J 0053	Journals (Axle—)	F 0506	120120
07	J 0054	Journals [parts of machines]	T 0419	070366
21	J 0055	Jugs	C 1583	210271
32	J 0056	Juice (Fruit—)	J 0068	320010
29	J 0057	Juices (Vegetable—) for cooking	J 0072	290067
05	J 0058	Jujube, medicated	P 0197	050184
09	J 0059	Juke boxes for computers	C 0483	090604
09	J 0060	Juke boxes, musical	A 0841	090062
25	J 0061	Jumper dresses	R 0346	250169
25	J 0062	Jumpers [pullovers]	P 1034	250107
09	J 0063	Junction boxes [electricity]	B 0615	090145
09	J 0064	Junction sleeves for electric cables	M 0088	090626
17	J 0065	Junctions, not of metal, for pipes	R 0008	170073
06	J 0066	Junctions of metal for pipes	R 0007	060229
31	J 0067	Juniper berries	G 0165	310064
22	J 0068	Jute	J 0074	220046
24	J 0069	Jute fabric	J 0076	240063
23	J 0070	Jute thread and yarn	J 0075	230011

Cl.	SERIAL No. (E)	INDICATION OF GOODS	SERIAL No. (F)	BASIC No.
01	K 0001	Kainite	K 0001	010140
28	K 0002	Kaleidoscopes	K 0002	280190
01	K 0003	Kaolin	K 0003	010370
22	K 0004	Kapok	C 0205	220047
29	K 0005	Kefir [milk beverage]	K 0006	290070
20	K 0006	Kennels for household pets	N 0063	200009
29	K 0007	Kephir [milk beverage]	K 0006	290070
04	K 0008	Kerosene	K 0007	040059
30	K 0009	Ketchup [sauce]	K 0008	300082
01	K 0010	Ketones	C 0424	010164
15	K 0011	Kettledrum frames	T 0262	150020
15	K 0012	Kettledrums	T 0263	150069
11	K 0013	Kettles, electric	B 0715	110303
21	K 0014	Kettles, non-electric	B 0716	210246
20	K 0015	Key cards (Plastic —), not encoded	C 0298	200260
18	K 0016	Key cases	E 0529	180113
14	K 0017	Key rings [trinkets or fobs]	P 0807	140162
20	K 0018	Keyboards for hanging keys	T 0020	200197
15	K 0019	Keyboards for musical instruments	C 0930	150024
06	K 0020	Keys	C 0933	060083
15	K 0021	Keys for musical instruments	T 0412	150077
06	K 0022	Keys (Rings of common metal for —)	A 0559	060221
12	K 0023	Kick sledges	T 0448	120253
07	K 0024	Kick starters for motorcycles	D 0065	070516
18	K 0025	Kid	C 0743	180027
01	K 0026	Kieselgur	K 0009	010371
11	K 0027	Kiln furniture [supports]	S 0594	110279
11	K 0028	Kilns	C 1623	110048
09	K 0029	Kilometer recorders for vehicles	E 0338	090232
33	K 0030	Kirsch	K 0010	330017
21	K 0031	Kitchen containers	C 1627	210272
07	K 0032	Kitchen machines, electric *	C 1625	070445
21	K 0033	Kitchen mixers, non-electric	B 0880	210158
11	K 0034	Kitchen ranges [ovens]	P 0881	110204
21	K 0035	Kitchen utensils	U 0019	210273
28	K 0036	Kite reels	T 0432	280037
28	K 0037	Kites	C 0418	280036
03	K 0038	Kits (Cosmetic —)	N 0033	030064
09	K 0039	Kits (Hands free —) for phones	N 0037	090688
07	K 0040	Kneading machines	P 0362	070295
10	K 0041	Knee bandages, orthopedic	G 0167	100193
28	K 0042	Knee guards [sports articles]	P 1011	280144
18	K 0043	Knee-pads for horses	G 0168	180053
09	K 0044	Knee-pads for workers	G 0169	090605
05	K 0045	Knickers (Menstruation —)	C 1647	050200
05	K 0046	Knickers (Sanitary —)	C 1647	050200
20	K 0047	Knife handles, not of metal	M 0079	200075
06	K 0048	Knife handles of metal	M 0078	060342
21	K 0049	Knife rests for the table	P 0808	210090
08	K 0050	Knife steels	F 0511	080037
24	K 0051	Knitted fabric	T 0519	240092
07	K 0052	Knitting machines	T 0517	070374
26	K 0053	Knitting needles	A 0192	260009
25	K 0054	Knitwear [clothing]	T 0520	250071
08	K 0055	Knives *	C 1453	080205
10	K 0056	Knives (Corn —)	C 1386	100062
07	K 0057	Knives, electric	C 1455	070131
07	K 0058	Knives for mowing machines	F 0025	070188
10	K 0059	Knives for surgical purposes	C 1454	100029
16	K 0060	Knives (Paper —) [office requisites]	C 1391	160291
07	K 0061	Knives [parts of machines]	C 1458	070080
20	K 0062	Knobs, not of metal	B 0768	200277
06	K 0063	Knobs of metal	B 0767	060301
06	K 0064	Knockers (Door —)	M 0171	060180
08	K 0065	Knuckle dusters	C 1407	080015
31	K 0066	Kola nuts	N 0095	310074
29	K 0067	Koumiss [kumiss] [milk beverage]	K 0012	290071
01	K 0068	Krypton	K 0013	010372
29	K 0069	Kumys [kumyss] [milk beverage]	K 0012	290071
32	K 0070	Kvass [non-alcoholic beverage]	K 0014	320048

Cl.	SERIAL No. (E)	INDICATION OF GOODS	SERIAL No. (F)	BASIC No.
07	L 0001	Labellers [machines]	E 0504	070182
16	L 0002	Labels, not of textile	E 0507	160308
24	L 0003	Labels of cloth	E 0506	240102
09	L 0004	Laboratories (Clothing especially made for—)	V 0212	090691
11	L 0005	Laboratory burners	B 0884	110058
09	L 0006	Laboratory centrifuges	C 0392	090698
11	L 0007	Laboratory lamps	L 0097	110176
09	L 0008	Laboratory trays	P 0629	090177
25	L 0009	Lace boots	B 0841	250019
26	L 0010	Lace for edgings	B 0649	260019
07	L 0011	Lace making machines	D 0086	070151
26	L 0012	Lace trimmings	P 0179	260068
18	L 0013	Laces (Leather—)	C 1279	180031
26	L 0014	Laces (Shoe—)	L 0008	260034
26	L 0015	Laces (Woollen—)	L 0026	260067
05	L 0016	Lacquer (Dental—)	L 0138	050112
03	L 0017	Lacquer-removing preparations	L 0143	030085
02	L 0018	Lacquers	L 0137	020115
02	L 0019	Lacquers (Thinners for—)	D 0218	020054
05	L 0020	Lacteal flour for babies	F 0020	050145
01	L 0021	Lactic acid	L 0015	010373
09	L 0022	Lactodensimeters	L 0018	090316
09	L 0023	Lactometers	L 0019	090317
01	L 0024	Lactose for industrial purposes	L 0020	010673
05	L 0025	Lactose for pharmaceutical purposes	S 0566	050192
01	L 0026	Lactose for the food industry	L 0023	010672
01	L 0027	Lactose [raw material]	L 0022	010674
22	L 0028	Ladder tapes for venetian blinds	R 0431	220045
06	L 0029	Ladders of metal	E 0091	060361
20	L 0030	Ladders of wood or plastics	E 0090	200092
22	L 0031	Ladders (Rope—)	E 0088	220023
12	L 0032	Ladle carriages	C 0536	120067
12	L 0033	Ladle cars	C 0536	120067
08	L 0034	Ladles for wine	L 0374	080260
08	L 0035	Ladles [hand tools]	C 1593	080081
16	L 0036	Laminators (Document—) for office use	D 0271	160346
01	L 0037	Lamp black for industrial purposes	N 0086	010316
02	L 0038	Lamp black [pigment]	N 0087	020073
11	L 0039	Lamp casings	M 0089	110042
11	L 0040	Lamp chimneys	T 0562	110092
11	L 0041	Lamp glasses	V 0172	110091
11	L 0042	Lamp globes	G 0231	110169
11	L 0043	Lamp mantles	M 0089	110042
11	L 0044	Lamp reflectors	R 0164	110183
11	L 0045	Lamp shades	A 0001	110237
04	L 0046	Lamp wicks	L 0108	040061
21	L 0047	Lamp-glass brushes	V 0173	210052
11	L 0048	Lamps	L 0100	110040
11	L 0049	Lamps (Burners for—)	B 0298	110044
09	L 0050	Lamps (Darkroom—) [photography]	L 0111	090318
11	L 0051	Lamps (Electric—)	L 0102	110024
11	L 0052	Lamps for directional signals of automobiles	A 0845	110255
10	L 0053	Lamps for medical purposes	L 0094	100108
11	L 0054	Lamps (Globes for—)	G 0231	110169
11	L 0055	Lampshade holders	A 0002	110238
10	L 0056	Lancets	L 0125	100077
28	L 0057	Landing nets for anglers	E 0410	280060
04	L 0058	Lanolin	S 0576	040074
11	L 0059	Lanterns for lighting	L 0132	110041
09	L 0060	Lanterns (Magic—)	L 0133	090321
09	L 0061	Lanterns (Optical—)	L 0109	090319
01	L 0062	Lanthanum	L 0136	010375
09	L 0063	Laptop computers	O 0096	090707
29	L 0064	Lard for food	S 0057	290103
05	L 0065	Larvae exterminating preparations	L 0145	050193
10	L 0066	Lasers for medical purposes	L 0146	100106
09	L 0067	Lasers, not for medical purposes	L 0147	090323
26	L 0068	Lasts (Darning—)	B 0724	260020
07	L 0069	Lasts for shoes [parts of machines]	F 0363	070352
08	L 0070	Lasts [shoemakers' hand tools]	F 0362	080056
06	L 0071	Latch bars of metal	C 0937	060022
20	L 0072	Latches, not of metal	L 0366	200140
06	L 0073	Latches of metal	L 0365	060167
17	L 0074	Latex [rubber]	L 0148	170064
07	L 0075	Lathes [machine tools]	T 0439	070098
19	L 0076	Laths, not of metal	L 0150	190109
06	L 0077	Laths of metal	L 0149	060160
19	L 0078	Latticework, not of metal	T 0494	190177
06	L 0079	Latticework of metal	T 0493	060256
12	L 0080	Launches	C 0451	120064
03	L 0081	Laundry bleach	B 0483	030028
03	L 0082	Laundry blueing	C 1056	030059
11	L 0083	Laundry dryers, electric	S 0163	110316
03	L 0084	Laundry glaze	G 0200	030029
03	L 0085	Laundry preparations	L 0205	030124
11	L 0086	Laundry room boilers	C 0581	110063
03	L 0087	Laundry soaking preparations	L 0296	030098
03	L 0088	Laundry starch	A 0445	030010
03	L 0089	Laundry wax	C 0889	030051
11	L 0090	Lava rocks for use in barbecue grills	P 0462	110326
03	L 0091	Lavender oil	L 0162	030116
03	L 0092	Lavender water	E 0020	030090
29	L 0093	Laver (Toasted—)	V 0033	290159
08	L 0094	Lawn clippers [hand instruments]	T 0385	080127
07	L 0095	Lawnmowers [machines]	T 0386	070201
05	L 0096	Laxatives	L 0169	050156
25	L 0097	Layettes [clothing]	L 0170	250092
21	L 0098	Lazy susans	C 0281	210324
01	L 0099	Lead acetate	P 0643	010440
01	L 0100	Lead arsenate	A 0767	010083
02	L 0101	Lead (Orange—)	L 0329	020089
01	L 0102	Lead oxide	O 0167	010441
02	L 0103	Lead (Red—)	M 0403	020095
06	L 0104	Lead seals	P 0650	060146
13	L 0105	Lead shot for hunting	G 0345	130041

Cl.	SERIAL No. (E)	INDICATION OF GOODS	SERIAL No. (F)	BASIC No.
06	L 0106	Lead, unwrought or semi-wrought	P 0645	060214
05	L 0107	Lead water	E 0007	050054
02	L 0108	Lead (White —)	C 0422	020038
18	L 0109	Leads (Leather —)	L 0040	180005
17	L 0110	Leaks (Chemical compositions for repairing —)	F 0474	170042
18	L 0111	Leashes (Leather —)	L 0040	180005
09	L 0112	Leather (Appliances for measuring the thickness of —)	C 1620	090171
03	L 0113	Leather bleaching preparations	C 1611	030025
25	L 0114	Leather (Clothing of —)	V 0196	250151
25	L 0115	Leather (Clothing of imitations of —)	V 0197	250150
03	L 0116	Leather (Creams for —)	C 1541	030074
01	L 0117	Leather (Currying preparations for —)	C 1317	010215
01	L 0118	Leather glues	C 1598	010222
04	L 0119	Leather (Grease for —)	G 0318	040034
18	L 0120	Leather (Imitation —)	C 1603	180042
02	L 0121	Leather (Ink for —)	E 0302	020033
18	L 0122	Leather leads	L 0040	180005
18	L 0123	Leather leashes	L 0040	180005
01	L 0124	Leather (Mastic for —)	M 0208	010192
02	L 0125	Leather (Mordants for —)	C 1607	020057
07	L 0126	Leather paring machines	D 0276	070157
21	L 0127	Leather (Polishing —)	C 1595	210100
04	L 0128	Leather (Preservatives for —) [oils and greases]	C 1613	040086
03	L 0129	Leather preservatives [polishes]	C 1612	030061
18	L 0130	Leather shoulder belts	B 0176	180096
02	L 0131	Leather (Stains for —)	C 1607	020057
18	L 0132	Leather straps	L 0129	180036
08	L 0133	Leather strops	C 1617	080006
18	L 0134	Leather thongs	L 0129	180036
18	L 0135	Leather thread	C 1601	180040
18	L 0136	Leather twist	C 1601	180040
18	L 0137	Leather, unworked or semi-worked	C 1596	180039
18	L 0138	Leatherboard	C 0306	180022
01	L 0139	Leather-dressing chemicals	C 1622	010223
01	L 0140	Leather-impregnating chemicals	C 1609	010224
01	L 0141	Leather-renovating chemicals	C 1610	010175
18	L 0142	Leathers (Stirrup —)	E 0524	180046
01	L 0143	Leather-waterproofing chemicals	C 1608	010364
07	L 0144	Leather-working machines	C 1605	070136
30	L 0145	Leaven	L 0218	300086
03	L 0146	Leaves of plants (Preparations to make shiny the —)	P 0591	030212
05	L 0147	Lecithin dietary supplements	L 0175	050431
29	L 0148	Lecithin for culinary purposes	L 0172	290177
01	L 0149	Lecithin for industrial purposes	L 0173	010664
05	L 0150	Lecithin for medical purposes	L 0174	050313
01	L 0151	Lecithin for the food industry	L 0177	010663
01	L 0152	Lecithin [raw material]	L 0176	010588
20	L 0153	Lecterns	L 0400	200141
16	L 0154	Ledgers [books]	R 0180	160153
05	L 0155	Leeches for medical purposes	S 0083	050266
31	L 0156	Leeks, fresh	P 0719	310108
25	L 0157	Leg warmers	J 0010	250088
25	L 0158	Leggings [leg warmers]	J 0010	250088
25	L 0159	Leggings [trousers]	L 0184	250168
03	L 0160	Lemon (Essential oils of —)	C 0913	030056
32	L 0161	Lemonades	L 0267	320020
31	L 0162	Lemons, fresh	C 0912	310032
19	L 0163	Lengthening pieces, not of metal, for chimneys	C 0682	190217
09	L 0164	Lens hoods	B 0646	090088
09	L 0165	Lenses for astrophotography	A 0806	090059
10	L 0166	Lenses [intraocular prostheses] for surgical implantation	L 0200	100194
09	L 0167	Lenses (Optical —)	L 0198	090324
01	L 0168	Lenses (Preparations for preventing the tarnishing of —)	L 0199	010377
31	L 0169	Lentils, fresh	L 0197	310076
29	L 0170	Lentils, preserved	L 0196	290077
20	L 0171	Letter boxes, not of metal or masonry	B 0610	200244
19	L 0172	Letter boxes of masonry	B 0608	190228
06	L 0173	Letter boxes of metal	B 0609	060120
09	L 0174	Letter scales	P 0350	090325
16	L 0175	Letter trays	C 1250	160101
06	L 0176	Letters and numerals of common metal, except type	L 0211	060419
26	L 0177	Letters for marking linen	L 0214	260069
16	L 0178	Letters [type]	C 0224	160097
31	L 0179	Lettuce, fresh	L 0067	310075
11	L 0180	Level controlling valves in tanks	S 0459	110194
09	L 0181	Levelling instruments	N 0080	090363
09	L 0182	Levelling staffs [surveying instruments]	J 0006	090281
09	L 0183	Levels [instruments for determining the horizontal]	N 0079	090362
08	L 0184	Levers	L 0220	080153
22	L 0185	Liber	L 0236	220054
20	L 0186	Library shelves	B 0366	200024
09	L 0187	Life belts	C 0355	090547
09	L 0188	Life buoys	B 0698	090517
09	L 0189	Life jackets	G 0192	090546
09	L 0190	Life nets	F 0198	090260
09	L 0191	Life saving apparatus and equipment	S 0167	090295
09	L 0192	Life-saving rafts	R 0017	090073
07	L 0193	Lift belts	C 1429	070127
07	L 0194	Lift operating apparatus	A 0786	070540
07	L 0195	Lifting apparatus	L 0217	070237
12	L 0196	Lifting cars [lift cars]	C 0540	120001
08	L 0197	Lifting jacks, hand-operated	C 1557	080024
07	L 0198	Lifts, other than ski-lifts	A 0785	070023
12	L 0199	Lifts (Ski —)	R 0217	120170
12	L 0200	Lifts (Tailboard —) [parts of land vehicles]	H 0051	120243
11	L 0201	Light bulbs	A 0479	110021
11	L 0202	Light bulbs, electric	A 0481	110022
11	L 0203	Light bulbs for directional signals for vehicles	A 0480	110071

Cl.	SERIAL No. (E)	INDICATION OF GOODS	SERIAL No. (F)	BASIC No.
09	L 0204	Light conducting filaments [optical fibers [fibres]]	F 0163	090571
11	L 0205	Light diffusers	D 0213	110118
09	L 0206	Light dimmers [regulators], electric	V 0036	090606
09	L 0207	Light (Traffic-—) apparatus [signalling devices]	F 0143	090687
09	L 0208	Light-emitting diodes [LED]	D 0220	090704
11	L 0209	Light-emitting diodes [LED] lighting apparatus	D 0221	110333
09	L 0210	Light-emitting electronic pointers	P 0716	090679
11	L 0211	Lighters *	A 0376	110020
34	L 0212	Lighters for smokers	B 0824	340007
11	L 0213	Lighters (Gas—)	A 0371	110019
11	L 0214	Lighting apparatus and installations	E 0099	110130
11	L 0215	Lighting apparatus for vehicles	E 0098	110229
09	L 0216	Lighting ballasts	B 0112	090672
09	L 0217	Lighting (Batteries for—)	B 0260	090031
04	L 0218	Lighting fuel	E 0106	040041
04	L 0219	Lighting (Gas for—)	G 0117	040040
11	L 0220	Lighting installations for air vehicles	A 0130	110007
04	L 0221	Lighting (Paper spills for—)	A 0359	040005
19	L 0222	Lighting slabs	P 0229	190115
04	L 0223	Lighting (Wood spills for—)	C 1238	040006
09	L 0224	Lightning arresters	P 0143	090381
09	L 0225	Lightning conductors [rods]	P 0143	090381
11	L 0226	Lights (Diving—)	P 0982	110322
11	L 0227	Lights, electric, for Christmas trees	L 0104	110195
11	L 0228	Lights for automobiles	A 0852	110256
11	L 0229	Lights for vehicles	F 0144	110027
04	L 0230	Lignite	L 0259	040062
04	L 0231	Ligroin	L 0260	040045
10	L 0232	Limbs (Artificial—)	P 1017	100117
19	L 0233	Lime	C 0660	190052
01	L 0234	Lime acetate	C 0661	010171
01	L 0235	Lime carbonate	C 0663	010172
01	L 0236	Lime chloride	C 0664	010173
31	L 0237	Lime for animal forage	C 0666	310028
01	L 0238	Lime (Nitrogenous—) [manure]	C 1678	010141
05	L 0239	Lime (Preparations of—) for pharmaceutical purposes	C 0667	050074
02	L 0240	Lime wash	L 0052	020042
19	L 0241	Limestone	C 0115	190043
01	L 0242	Limestone hardening substances	F 0315	010301
09	L 0243	Limiters [electricity]	L 0266	090165
06	L 0244	Limonite	L 0269	060163
24	L 0245	Linen (Bed—)	L 0288	240068
25	L 0246	Linen (Body—) [garments]	L 0300	250026
24	L 0247	Linen cloth	L 0283	240067
24	L 0248	Linen (Diapered—)	L 0297	240069
24	L 0249	Linen (Household—)	L 0289	240071
26	L 0250	Linen (Letters for marking—)	L 0214	260069
26	L 0251	Linen (Numerals for marking—)	C 0758	260045
22	L 0252	Linen (Raw—) [flax]	L 0272	220056
03	L 0253	Linen (Sachets for perfuming—)	L 0299	030150
23	L 0254	Linen thread and yarn	L 0278	230013
28	L 0255	Lines for fishing	L 0256	280084
24	L 0256	Lingerie fabric	L 0302	240038
05	L 0257	Liniments	L 0305	050196
24	L 0258	Lining fabric for shoes	C 0644	240020
17	L 0259	Lining materials (Brake—), partly processed	F 0426	170048
12	L 0260	Linings (Brake—) for vehicles	G 0078	120215
17	L 0261	Linings (Clutch—)	G 0086	170039
24	L 0262	Linings (Hat—), of textile, in the piece	C 1010	240019
19	L 0263	Linings, not of metal, for building	R 0291	190150
06	L 0264	Linings of metal [building]	R 0290	060211
25	L 0265	Linings (Ready-made—) [parts of clothing]	D 0286	250068
24	L 0266	Linings [textile]	D 0287	240039
06	L 0267	Linkages of metal (Cable—), non-electric	R 0009	060059
14	L 0268	Links (Cuff—)	B 0765	140122
27	L 0269	Linoleum	T 0322	270014
05	L 0270	Linseed dietary supplements	L 0273	050421
31	L 0271	Linseed for animal consumption	L 0280	310150
30	L 0272	Linseed for human consumption	L 0281	300212
05	L 0273	Linseed for pharmaceutical purposes	G 0293	050162
31	L 0274	Linseed meal for animal consumption	L 0277	310151
05	L 0275	Linseed meal for pharmaceutical purposes	F 0010	050190
05	L 0276	Linseed oil dietary supplements	L 0274	050422
29	L 0277	Linseed oil for culinary purposes	L 0282	290175
05	L 0278	Lint for medical purposes	C 0547	050073
19	L 0279	Lintels, not of metal	L 0308	190114
06	L 0280	Lintels of metal	L 0307	060165
22	L 0281	Linters	L 0309	220101
03	L 0282	Lip glosses	B 0816	030221
03	L 0283	Lipsticks	R 0391	030018
21	L 0284	Liqueur sets	L 0313	210155
33	L 0285	Liqueurs	L 0310	330015
02	L 0286	Liqueurs (Colorants for—)	L 0311	020088
32	L 0287	Liqueurs (Preparations for making—)	L 0312	320024
20	L 0288	Liquid fuel (Containers, not of metal, for—)	R 0151	200065
17	L 0289	Liquid rubber	C 0197	170113
03	L 0290	Liquids for floors (Non-slipping—)	L 0314	030208
01	L 0291	Liquids for removing sulphates from accumulators	A 0038	010500
01	L 0292	Liquids for removing sulphates from batteries	A 0038	010500
01	L 0293	Liquifying chemicals (Starch-—) [ungluing agents]	A 0444	010056
30	L 0294	Liquorice [confectionery]	R 0188	300118
05	L 0295	Liquorice for pharmaceutical purposes	R 0187	050185

Cl.	SERIAL No. (E)	INDICATION OF GOODS	SERIAL No. (F)	BASIC No.
02	L 0296	Litharge	L 0329	020089
01	L 0297	Lithia [lithium oxide]	L 0330	010378
32	L 0298	Lithia water	E 0056	320014
01	L 0299	Lithium	L 0332	010379
16	L 0300	Lithographic stones	P 0467	160188
16	L 0301	Lithographic works of art	A 0776	160029
16	L 0302	Lithographs	L 0334	160187
01	L 0303	Litmus paper	P 0093	010419
21	L 0304	Litter boxes [trays] for pets	B 0008	210306
31	L 0305	Litter peat	T 0418	310081
31	L 0306	Litter (Products for animal—)	L 0338	310080
31	L 0307	Live animals	A 0545	310006
29	L 0308	Liver	F 0327	290124
29	L 0309	Liver pâté	P 0206	290088
25	L 0310	Liveries	L 0352	250093
31	L 0311	Livestock fattening preparations	E 0327	310052
08	L 0312	Livestock marking tools	B 0330	080031
06	L 0313	Load handling (Braces of metal for—)	B 0806	060026
06	L 0314	Load handling (Harness of metal for—)	B 0806	060026
06	L 0315	Load handling (Straps of metal for—)	S 0080	060305
11	L 0316	Loading apparatus for furnaces	C 0524	110074
20	L 0317	Loading gauge rods, not of metal, for railway waggons [wagons]	G 0004	200055
06	L 0318	Loading gauge rods, of metal, for railway waggons	G 0003	060326
06	L 0319	Loading gauge rods, of metal, for railway wagons	G 0003	060326
20	L 0320	Loading pallets, not of metal	P 0039	200054
06	L 0321	Loading pallets, of metal	P 0038	060325
07	L 0322	Loading ramps	P 0787	070096
22	L 0323	Loads (Belts, not of metal, for handling—)	S 0081	220082
22	L 0324	Loads (Slings, not of metal, for handling—)	E 0218	220083
06	L 0325	Loads (Slings of metal for handling—)	E 0217	060306
22	L 0326	Loads (Straps, not of metal, for handling—)	S 0081	220082
01	L 0327	Loam	T 0214	010527
31	L 0328	Lobsters, live	H 0081	310135
29	L 0329	Lobsters, not live	H 0080	290057
31	L 0330	Lobsters (Spiny—), live	L 0127	310140
29	L 0331	Lobsters (Spiny—), not live	L 0126	290075
20	L 0332	Lockers	T 0285	200192
09	L 0333	Locks, electric	S 0252	090443
20	L 0334	Locks, not of metal, for vehicles	S 0256	200181
06	L 0335	Locks of metal for bags	F 0079	060379
06	L 0336	Locks of metal for vehicles	S 0254	060237
06	L 0337	Locks of metal, other than electric	S 0253	060144
20	L 0338	Locks, other than electric, not of metal	S 0255	200240
12	L 0339	Locomotives	L 0360	120138
31	L 0340	Locust beans	C 0271	310022
09	L 0341	Logs [measuring instruments]	L 0358	090326
07	L 0342	Loom shafts	L 0074	070224

Cl.	SERIAL No. (E)	INDICATION OF GOODS	SERIAL No. (F)	BASIC No.
07	L 0343	Looms	M 0331	070259
16	L 0344	Loose-leaf binders	B 0368	160035
12	L 0345	Lorries	C 0147	120022
09	L 0346	Loss indicators (Electric—)	I 0069	090213
03	L 0347	Lotions for cosmetic purposes	L 0367	030122
05	L 0348	Lotions for pharmaceutical purposes	L 0368	050191
05	L 0349	Lotions for veterinary purposes	L 0369	050220
03	L 0350	Lotions (Tissues impregnated with cosmetic—)	S 0271	030197
05	L 0351	Lotions (Tissues impregnated with pharmaceutical—)	S 0272	050374
09	L 0352	Loudspeakers	H 0044	090190
10	L 0353	Love dolls [sex dolls]	P 0924	100219
29	L 0354	Low-fat potato chips	C 0774	290176
30	L 0355	Lozenges [confectionery]	P 0186	300107
05	L 0356	Lozenges for pharmaceutical purposes	P 0185	050214
04	L 0357	Lubricants	L 0379	040063
04	L 0358	Lubricating graphite	G 0327	040052
04	L 0359	Lubricating grease	G 0303	040060
04	L 0360	Lubricating oil	H 0149	040042
07	L 0361	Lubricating pumps	P 0776	070205
07	L 0362	Lubricators [parts of machines]	G 0322	070085
12	L 0363	Luggage carriers for vehicles	P 0799	120029
12	L 0364	Luggage nets for vehicles	F 0200	120123
12	L 0365	Luggage trucks	D 0182	120050
19	L 0366	Lumber	B 0530	190027
11	L 0367	Luminous house numbers	N 0109	110196
16	L 0368	Luminous paper	P 0102	160190
19	L 0369	Luminous paving	P 0229	190115
11	L 0370	Luminous tubes for lighting	T 0565	110189
21	L 0371	Lunch boxes	B 0593	210325
05	L 0372	Lupulin for pharmaceutical purposes	L 0396	050197
28	L 0373	Lures for hunting or fishing	L 0216	280082
28	L 0374	Lures (Scent—) for hunting or fishing	L 0215	280194
17	L 0375	Lute	L 0398	170066
01	L 0376	Lutetium [cassiopium]	C 0338	010153
15	L 0377	Lyres	L 0401	150046

Cl.	SERIAL No. (E)	INDICATION OF GOODS	SERIAL No. (F)	BASIC No.
19	M 0001	Macadam	M 0001	190116
30	M 0002	Macaroni	M 0002	300090
30	M 0003	Macaroons [pastry]	M 0003	300089
08	M 0004	Machetes	M 0005	080154
06	M 0005	Machine belt fasteners of metal	A 0176	060012
06	M 0006	Machine belts (Reinforcing materials of metal for —)	A 0722	060277
07	M 0007	Machine fly-wheels	V 0310	070337
13	M 0008	Machine guns	M 0419	130046
07	M 0009	Machine tools	M 0016	070243
07	M 0010	Machine wheels	R 0382	070336
07	M 0011	Machine wheelwork	R 0378	070335
07	M 0012	Machines for the textile industry	I 0082	070496
07	M 0013	Machining (Apparatus for —)	D 0311	070159
20	M 0014	Magazine racks	P 0829	200135
16	M 0015	Magazines [periodicals]	R 0302	160243
09	M 0016	Magic lanterns	L 0133	090321
19	M 0017	Magnesia cement	M 0023	190118
05	M 0018	Magnesia for pharmaceutical purposes	M 0021	050127
01	M 0019	Magnesite	M 0024	010382
06	M 0020	Magnesium	M 0025	060169
01	M 0021	Magnesium carbonate	M 0022	010147
01	M 0022	Magnesium chloride	M 0026	010383
11	M 0023	Magnesium filaments for lighting	F 0225	110190
09	M 0024	Magnetic data media	S 0592	090607
09	M 0025	Magnetic encoders	E 0292	090608
01	M 0026	Magnetic fluid for industrial purposes	F 0316	010642
09	M 0027	Magnetic tape units for computers	U 0006	090609
09	M 0028	Magnetic tapes	B 0171	090078
09	M 0029	Magnetic wires	F 0238	090256
09	M 0030	Magnets	A 0220	090023
09	M 0031	Magnets (Decorative —)	A 0222	090660
09	M 0032	Magnifying glasses [optics]	L 0377	090328
28	M 0033	Mah-jong	M 0031	280160
22	M 0034	Mail bags	S 0048	220104
31	M 0035	Maize	M 0038	310082
31	M 0036	Maize cake for cattle	M 0048	310083
30	M 0037	Maize flakes	F 0307	300043
30	M 0038	Maize flour	M 0040	300059
30	M 0039	Maize meal	M 0040	300059
30	M 0040	Maize, milled	M 0045	300091
29	M 0041	Maize oil	M 0044	290058
30	M 0042	Maize, roasted	M 0042	300092
21	M 0043	Majolica	M 0055	210157
03	M 0044	Make-up	F 0009	030102
24	M 0045	Make-up (Napkins for removing —) [cloth]	S 0259	240101
03	M 0046	Make-up powder	P 0911	030147
03	M 0047	Make-up preparations	M 0137	030033
21	M 0048	Make-up removing appliances	D 0061	210344
03	M 0049	Make-up removing preparations	D 0062	030078
08	M 0050	Mallets [hand instruments]	B 0264	080155
01	M 0051	Malt albumen	A 0272	010035
32	M 0052	Malt beer	M 0063	320004
30	M 0053	Malt biscuits	M 0064	300017
02	M 0054	Malt caramel [food colorant]	M 0065	020035
02	M 0055	Malt colorants	M 0071	020048
30	M 0056	Malt extract for food	E 0571	300164
31	M 0057	Malt for brewing and distilling	M 0068	310084
30	M 0058	Malt for human consumption	M 0069	300165
05	M 0059	Malt for pharmaceutical purposes	M 0061	050203
11	M 0060	Malt roasters	M 0070	110191
32	M 0061	Malt wort	M 0067	320025
05	M 0062	Malted milk beverages for medical purposes	L 0056	050188
30	M 0063	Maltose	M 0073	300094
15	M 0064	Mandolins	M 0095	150049
01	M 0065	Manganate	M 0099	010384
06	M 0066	Manganese	M 0100	060174
01	M 0067	Manganese dioxide	B 0444	010124
21	M 0068	Mangers for animals	M 0103	210074
07	M 0069	Mangles	C 0113	070292
01	M 0070	Mangrove bark for industrial purposes	M 0106	010385
05	M 0071	Mangrove bark for pharmaceutical purposes	M 0107	050199
19	M 0072	Manhole covers, not of metal	C 1471	190070
06	M 0073	Manhole covers of metal	C 1470	060349
08	M 0074	Manicure sets	T 0543	080231
08	M 0075	Manicure sets, electric	N 0034	080243
07	M 0076	Manifold (Exhaust —) for engines	M 0109	070497
06	M 0077	Manifolds of metal for pipelines	M 0110	060420
16	M 0078	Manifolds [stationery]	M 0108	160192
25	M 0079	Maniples	M 0112	250098
20	M 0080	Mannequins	M 0115	200064
09	M 0081	Mannequins (Resuscitation —) [teaching apparatus]	M 0117	090680
09	M 0082	Manometers	M 0119	090336
25	M 0083	Mantillas	M 0122	250152
19	M 0084	Mantlepieces	M 0121	190049
16	M 0085	Manuals [handbooks]	M 0125	160180
01	M 0086	Manure for agriculture	E 0326	010271
16	M 0087	Maps (Geographical —)	C 0294	160164
24	M 0088	Marabouts [cloth]	M 0138	240073
19	M 0089	Marble	M 0139	190120
28	M 0090	Marbles for games	B 0430	280023
31	M 0091	Marc	M 0141	310086
29	M 0092	Margarine	M 0147	290078
30	M 0093	Marinades	M 0149	300207
09	M 0094	Marine compasses	C 1098	090133
09	M 0095	Marine depth finders	S 0397	090668
28	M 0096	Marionettes	M 0150	280087
28	M 0097	Markers (Billiard —)	B 0424	280021
09	M 0098	Marking buoys	B 0697	090583
16	M 0099	Marking chalk	C 1497	160193
09	M 0100	Marking gauges [joinery]	T 0550	090490
02	M 0101	Marking ink for animals	E 0303	020067
26	M 0102	Marking linen (Numerals or letters for —)	M 0161	260032
16	M 0103	Marking pens [stationery]	M 0165	160359
19	M 0104	Marl (Calcareous —)	M 0156	190211
08	M 0105	Marline spikes	E 0397	080103

Cl.	SERIAL No. (E)	INDICATION OF GOODS	SERIAL No. (F)	BASIC No.
29	M 0106	Marmalade	M 0151	290079
29	M 0107	Marrow (Animal —) for food	M 0440	290081
31	M 0108	Marrows	C 1412	310043
30	M 0109	Marzipan	M 0194	300039
03	M 0110	Mascara	M 0179	030202
31	M 0111	Mash for fattening livestock	P 0199	310102
03	M 0112	Masks (Beauty —)	M 0181	030020
09	M 0113	Masks (Divers' —)	M 0183	090597
28	M 0114	Masks (Fencing —)	M 0186	280131
10	M 0115	Masks for use by medical personnel	M 0190	100205
09	M 0116	Masks (Protective —)*	M 0184	090338
25	M 0117	Masks (Sleep —)	M 0187	250163
28	M 0118	Masks (Theatrical —)	M 0185	280089
28	M 0119	Masks (Toy —)	M 0182	280090
04	M 0120	Masonry (Oil for the preservation of —)	H 0157	040055
01	M 0121	Masonry preservatives, except paints and oils	M 0020	010380
08	M 0122	Masons' hammers	M 0196	080158
25	M 0123	Masquerade costumes	C 1339	250153
10	M 0124	Massage apparatus	M 0191	100113
03	M 0125	Massage gels other than for medical purposes	G 0157	030220
10	M 0126	Massage (Gloves for —)	G 0061	100092
20	M 0127	Massage tables	T 0037	200229
14	M 0128	Master clocks	C 1226	140043
01	M 0129	Mastic for leather	M 0208	010192
01	M 0130	Mastic for tires [tyres]	M 0209	010193
01	M 0131	Mastic (Grafting —) for trees	M 0197	010341
02	M 0132	Mastic [natural resin]	M 0202	020091
05	M 0133	Mastics (Dental —)	M 0203	050113
08	M 0134	Mastics (Guns, hand-operated, for the extrusion of —)	P 0535	080232
12	M 0135	Masts for boats	M 0236	120259
28	M 0136	Masts for sailboards	M 0237	280169
09	M 0137	Masts for wireless aerials	P 1060	090471
06	M 0138	Masts of metal	M 0234	060023
19	M 0139	Masts [poles], not of metal	M 0235	190124
34	M 0140	Match boxes	A 0373	340035
34	M 0141	Match holders	P 0798	340031
34	M 0142	Matches	A 0372	340001
09	M 0143	Material testing instruments and machines	E 0440	090240
24	M 0144	Material (Textile —)	T 0224	240012
06	M 0145	Materials of metal for funicular railway permanent ways	F 0502	060330
10	M 0146	Maternity belts	G 0358	100046
09	M 0147	Mathematical instruments	M 0223	090339
07	M 0148	Matrices (Boxes for —) [printing]	C 0336	070081
07	M 0149	Matrices for use in printing	M 0232	070436
27	M 0150	Mats *	N 0015	270006
16	M 0151	Mats for beer glasses	D 0149	160037
20	M 0152	Mats for infant playpens	T 0121	200275
27	M 0153	Mats of woven rope for ski slopes	N 0017	270017
24	M 0154	Mats (Place —), not of paper	S 0282	240113
20	M 0155	Mats, removable, for sinks	R 0289	200099
08	M 0156	Mattocks	H 0123	080142
24	M 0157	Mattress covers	E 0359	240030
20	M 0158	Mattress (Straw —)	P 0002	200159
20	M 0159	Mattresses *	M 0210	200079
10	M 0160	Mattresses (Childbirth —)	M 0214	100004
20	M 0161	Mattresses (Spring —)	S 0386	200185
30	M 0162	Mayonnaise	M 0239	300172
04	M 0163	Mazut	M 0240	040064
33	M 0164	Mead [hydromel]	H 0200	330016
30	M 0165	Meal *	F 0017	300057
31	M 0166	Meal for animals	F 0021	310088
05	M 0167	Meal for pharmaceutical purposes	F 0019	050144
09	M 0168	Measures	M 0297	090201
09	M 0169	Measuring apparatus	M 0298	090202
09	M 0170	Measuring devices, electric	M 0291	090214
09	M 0171	Measuring glassware	V 0165	090285
09	M 0172	Measuring instruments	M 0296	090347
09	M 0173	Measuring spoons	C 1592	090641
29	M 0174	Meat	V 0217	290046
01	M 0175	Meat (Chemical preparations for smoking —)	V 0228	010317
20	M 0176	Meat chests, not of metal	G 0068	200122
08	M 0177	Meat choppers [hand tools]	H 0012	080236
07	M 0178	Meat choppers [machines]	H 0011	070211
29	M 0179	Meat extracts	V 0220	290068
30	M 0180	Meat gravies	J 0070	300193
29	M 0181	Meat jellies	V 0221	290049
07	M 0182	Meat mincers [machines]	H 0011	070211
30	M 0183	Meat pies	V 0225	300133
29	M 0184	Meat, preserved	V 0218	290137
06	M 0185	Meat safes of metal	G 0067	060392
30	M 0186	Meat tenderizers, for household purposes	V 0226	300135
01	M 0187	Meat tenderizers for industrial purposes	V 0227	010545
29	M 0188	Meat, tinned [canned (Am.)]	C 1198	290147
29	M 0189	Meats (Salted —)	S 0064	290098
09	M 0190	Mechanical signs	E 0352	090234
07	M 0191	Mechanized livestock feeders	A 0339	070517
14	M 0192	Medallions [jewellery, jewelry (Am.)]	M 0249	140051
14	M 0193	Medals	M 0248	140052
05	M 0194	Media for bacteriological cultures	B 0718	050036
10	M 0195	Medical apparatus and instruments	M 0257	100114
10	M 0196	Medical guidewires	F 0224	100213
03	M 0197	Medicated soap	S 0120	030130
05	M 0198	Medicinal alcohol	A 0304	050008
05	M 0199	Medicinal drinks	P 0895	050332
05	M 0200	Medicinal hair growth preparations	C 0733	050394
05	M 0201	Medicinal herbs	H 0064	050170
05	M 0202	Medicinal infusions	I 0084	050148
05	M 0203	Medicinal oils	H 0142	050167
05	M 0204	Medicinal roots	R 0012	050260
05	M 0205	Medicinal tea	T 0236	050149
20	M 0206	Medicine cabinets	A 0744	200015
05	M 0207	Medicine cases, portable, filled	D 0315	050126

Cl.	SERIAL No. (E)	INDICATION OF GOODS	SERIAL No. (F)	BASIC No.
10	M 0208	Medicine (Spoons for administering —)	C 1594	100069
05	M 0209	Medicines for dental purposes	M 0252	050327
05	M 0210	Medicines for human purposes	M 0255	050328
05	M 0211	Medicines for veterinary purposes	M 0253	050329
05	M 0212	Mediums (Bacteriological culture —)	B 0718	050036
20	M 0213	Meerschaum	E 0159	200098
09	M 0214	Megaphones	M 0259	090341
05	M 0215	Melissa water for pharmaceutical purposes	E 0021	050128
19	M 0216	Memorial plaques, not of metal	P 0599	190089
06	M 0217	Memorial plaques, of metal	P 0598	060389
06	M 0218	Memorial plates of metal	P 0598	060389
28	M 0219	Men's athletic supporters [sports articles]	S 0353	280196
31	M 0220	Menagerie animals	A 0523	310005
05	M 0221	Menstruation bandages	B 0167	050233
05	M 0222	Menstruation knickers	C 1647	050200
05	M 0223	Menstruation tampons	T 0093	050232
05	M 0224	Menthol	M 0278	050210
21	M 0225	Menu card holders	P 0801	210064
05	M 0226	Mercurial ointments	M 0288	050211
01	M 0227	Mercuric oxide	O 0166	010389
01	M 0228	Mercury	M 0284	010387
09	M 0229	Mercury levels	M 0285	090344
01	M 0230	Mercury salts	M 0287	010388
21	M 0231	Mess-tins	G 0043	210140
09	M 0232	Metal alloys (Wires of —) [fuse wire]	A 0356	090505
01	M 0233	Metal annealing preparations	M 0321	010393
08	M 0234	Metal band stretchers [hand tools]	T 0184	080160
09	M 0235	Metal detectors for industrial or military purposes	D 0166	090178
07	M 0236	Metal drawing machines	E 0508	070183
01	M 0237	Metal earths	M 0323	010392
02	M 0238	Metal foil for painters, decorators, printers and artists	M 0307	020092
01	M 0239	Metal hardening preparations	M 0318	010249
01	M 0240	Metal tempering preparations	M 0321	010393
01	M 0241	Metalloids	M 0299	010390
01	M 0242	Metals (Alkaline —)	M 0301	010560
01	M 0243	Metals (Alkaline-earth —)	M 0300	010039
06	M 0244	Metals in powder form *	M 0308	060434
02	M 0245	Metals in powder form for painters, decorators, printers and artists	M 0309	020090
07	M 0246	Metalworking machines	M 0310	070258
09	M 0247	Meteorological balloons	B 0121	090075
09	M 0248	Meteorological instruments	M 0325	090348
09	M 0249	Meters	C 1124	090138
01	M 0250	Methane	M 0326	010394
01	M 0251	Methyl benzene	B 0312	010577
01	M 0252	Methyl benzol	B 0317	010576
01	M 0253	Methyl ether	M 0327	010284
04	M 0254	Methylated spirit	A 0290	040002
09	M 0255	Metronomes	M 0333	090139
17	M 0256	Mica, raw or partly processed	M 0359	170070
26	M 0257	Mica spangles	M 0360	260071
05	M 0258	Mice (Preparations for destroying —)	S 0468	050120
10	M 0259	Microdermabrasion apparatus	M 0361	100220
09	M 0260	Micrometer gauges	M 0362	090379
09	M 0261	Micrometer screws for optical instruments	V 0257	090350
09	M 0262	Micrometers	M 0362	090379
05	M 0263	Microorganisms (Cultures of —) for medical and veterinary use	C 1655	050213
01	M 0264	Microorganisms (Cultures of —) other than for medical and veterinary use	C 1656	010596
05	M 0265	Microorganisms (Nutritive substances for —)	M 0370	050212
05	M 0266	Microorganisms (Preparations of —) for medical and veterinary use	C 1655	050213
01	M 0267	Microorganisms (Preparations of —) other than for medical and veterinary use	C 1656	010596
09	M 0268	Microphones	M 0371	090351
09	M 0269	Microprocessors	M 0372	090610
09	M 0270	Microscope slides (Containers for —)	C 1007	090128
09	M 0271	Microscopes	M 0373	090193
09	M 0272	Microtomes	M 0375	090352
16	M 0273	Microwave cooking (Bags for —)	S 0020	160323
11	M 0274	Microwave ovens [cooking apparatus]	C 1631	110317
11	M 0275	Microwave ovens for industrial purposes	F 0405	110328
09	M 0276	Milage recorders for vehicles	E 0338	090232
01	M 0277	Mildew (Chemical preparations to prevent —)	M 0380	010395
05	M 0278	Mildew (Chemical preparations to treat —)	M 0381	050202
12	M 0279	Military vehicles for transport	V 0085	120144
29	M 0280	Milk	L 0041	290039
29	M 0281	Milk (Albumin —)	L 0042	290174
29	M 0282	Milk beverages, milk predominating	B 0583	290072
03	M 0283	Milk (Cleansing —) for toilet purposes	L 0066	030123
11	M 0284	Milk cooling installations	L 0055	110177
01	M 0285	Milk ferments for chemical purposes	L 0016	010374
05	M 0286	Milk ferments for pharmaceutical purposes	L 0017	050187
32	M 0287	Milk of almonds [beverage]	L 0050	320032
05	M 0288	Milk of almonds for pharmaceutical purposes	L 0049	050300
32	M 0289	Milk (Peanut —) [non-alcoholic beverage]	L 0051	320046
29	M 0290	Milk products	L 0064	290074
29	M 0291	Milk shakes	M 0383	290164
05	M 0292	Milk sugar for pharmaceutical purposes	S 0566	050192
05	M 0293	Milking grease	G 0307	050165
07	M 0294	Milking machines	T 0453	070367

Cl.	SERIAL No. (E)	INDICATION OF GOODS	SERIAL No. (F)	BASIC No.
07	M 0295	Milking machines (Teat cups [suction cups] for —)	V 0123	070368
17	M 0296	Millboards (Asbestos —)	C 0309	170087
08	M 0297	Milling cutters [hand tools]	F 0418	080085
07	M 0298	Milling machines	F 0419	070090
21	M 0299	Mills for domestic purposes, hand-operated	M 0537	210162
07	M 0300	Mills for household purposes, other than hand-operated	M 0538	070277
07	M 0301	Mills [machines]	M 0539	070042
07	M 0302	Millstones	M 0358	070262
16	M 0303	Mimeograph apparatus and machines	P 0752	160230
08	M 0304	Mincing knives [hand tools]	H 0012	080236
07	M 0305	Mine borers	T 0132	070264
12	M 0306	Mine cart wheels	B 0307	120043
01	M 0307	Mineral acids	M 0393	010396
05	M 0308	Mineral food supplements	S 0590	050382
04	M 0309	Mineral fuel	M 0394	040032
32	M 0310	Mineral water [beverages]	E 0059	320015
07	M 0311	Mineral water making machines	E 0058	070164
32	M 0312	Mineral water (Preparations for making —)	E 0060	320016
05	M 0313	Mineral water salts	S 0208	050130
05	M 0314	Mineral waters for medical purposes	E 0057	050129
17	M 0315	Mineral wool [insulator]	L 0037	170062
11	M 0316	Miners' lamps	M 0402	110192
13	M 0317	Mines [explosives]	M 0397	130045
07	M 0318	Mineworking machines	M 0398	070342
02	M 0319	Minium	M 0403	020095
03	M 0320	Mint essence [essential oil]	M 0275	030128
30	M 0321	Mint for confectionery	M 0276	300097
03	M 0322	Mint for perfumery	M 0277	030129
05	M 0323	Mint for pharmaceutical purposes	M 0272	050201
20	M 0324	Mirror tiles	M 0413	200261
10	M 0325	Mirrors for dentists	M 0415	100078
09	M 0326	Mirrors for inspecting work	M 0410	090307
10	M 0327	Mirrors for surgeons	M 0414	100118
20	M 0328	Mirrors (Hand-held —) [toilet mirrors]	M 0416	200274
20	M 0329	Mirrors [looking glasses]	G 0219	200193
09	M 0330	Mirrors [optics]	M 0412	090354
12	M 0331	Mirrors (Rearview —)	R 0284	120173
13	M 0332	Mirrors (Sighting —) for guns and rifles	M 0409	130038
13	M 0333	Missiles (Ballistic —)	E 0323	130015
25	M 0334	Miters [hats]	M 0422	250100
08	M 0335	Mitre [Miter (Am.)] boxes [hand tools]	B 0603	080253
25	M 0336	Mitres [hats]	M 0422	250100
25	M 0337	Mittens	M 0417	250099
24	M 0338	Mitts (Washing —)	G 0055	240055
11	M 0339	Mixer taps for water pipes	R 0351	110239
07	M 0340	Mixers [machines]	M 0423	070267
21	M 0341	Mixers, manual [cocktail shakers]	M 0261	210082
07	M 0342	Mixing machines	M 0056	070026
21	M 0343	Mixing machines, non-electric, for household purposes	B 0880	210158
21	M 0344	Mixing spoons [kitchen utensils]	C 1591	210326
20	M 0345	Mobiles [decoration]	M 0426	200151
28	M 0346	Mobiles [toys]	M 0425	280145
28	M 0347	Model vehicles (Scale —)	M 0435	280091
16	M 0348	Modelling clay	A 0711	160026
16	M 0349	Modelling clays (Molds for —) [artists' materials]	M 0531	160352
16	M 0350	Modelling clays (Moulds for —) [artists' materials]	M 0531	160352
16	M 0351	Modelling materials	M 0430	160196
16	M 0352	Modelling paste	P 0189	160197
16	M 0353	Modelling wax, not for dental purposes	C 0895	160091
16	M 0354	Models (Architects' —)	M 0136	160021
09	M 0355	Modems	M 0437	090611
01	M 0356	Moderating materials for nuclear reactors	M 0439	010179
16	M 0357	Moisteners for gummed surfaces [office requisites]	H 0177	160173
16	M 0358	Moisteners [office requisites]	M 0522	160049
04	M 0359	Moistening oil	H 0150	040056
01	M 0360	Moistening [wetting] preparations for use in bleaching	M 0519	010127
01	M 0361	Moistening [wetting] preparations for use in dyeing	M 0521	010398
01	M 0362	Moistening [wetting] preparations for use in the textile industry	M 0520	010530
17	M 0363	Moisture (Substances for insulating buildings against —)	H 0179	170058
30	M 0364	Molasses for food	M 0262	300095
19	M 0365	Moldable wood	B 0554	190127
08	M 0366	Molding irons	F 0104	080120
07	M 0367	Molding machines	M 0541	070278
01	M 0368	Molding preparations (Foundry —)	F 0340	010307
05	M 0369	Molding wax for dentists	C 0894	050084
20	M 0370	Moldings for picture frames	M 0543	200190
19	M 0371	Moldings, not of metal, for building	M 0542	190128
19	M 0372	Moldings, not of metal, for cornices	C 1298	190065
06	M 0373	Moldings of metal for cornices	C 1297	060344
01	M 0374	Mold-release preparations	D 0069	010237
17	M 0375	Molds (Ebonite —)	M 0527	170100
16	M 0376	Molds for modelling clays [artists' materials]	M 0531	160352
21	M 0377	Molds (Ice cube —)	M 0525	210099
21	M 0378	Molds [kitchen utensils]	M 0534	210079
07	M 0379	Molds [parts of machines]	M 0530	070276
24	M 0380	Moleskin [fabric]	M 0447	240077
05	M 0381	Moleskin for medical purposes	M 0445	050392
18	M 0382	Moleskin [imitation of leather]	M 0446	180063
06	M 0383	Molybdenum	M 0451	060189
25	M 0384	Money belts [clothing]	C 0363	250160
16	M 0385	Money clips	P 0500	160353

Cl.	SERIAL No. (E)	INDICATION OF GOODS	SERIAL No. (F)	BASIC No.
09	M 0386	Money counting and sorting machines	A 0697	090053
08	M 0387	Money scoops	R 0063	080162
09	M 0388	Monitoring apparatus, electric	S 0610	090151
09	M 0389	Monitors [computer hardware]	M 0452	090612
09	M 0390	Monitors [computer programs]	M 0453	090613
26	M 0391	Monogram tabs for marking linen	M 0161	260032
19	M 0392	Monuments, not of metal	M 0472	190117
06	M 0393	Monuments of metal	M 0471	060190
19	M 0394	Mooring boats (Floating docks, not of metal, for—)	Q 0002	190188
06	M 0395	Mooring boats (Floating docks of metal, for—)	Q 0001	060272
19	M 0396	Mooring bollards, not of metal	P 0474	190187
06	M 0397	Mooring bollards of metal	P 0473	060271
20	M 0398	Mooring buoys, not of metal	B 0696	200251
06	M 0399	Mooring buoys of metal	B 0695	060412
21	M 0400	Mop wringers	E 0458	210339
12	M 0401	Mopeds	V 0112	120196
21	M 0402	Mops	B 0092	210135
02	M 0403	Mordants *	M 0474	020002
02	M 0404	Mordants for leather	C 1607	020057
01	M 0405	Mordants for metals	M 0475	010633
19	M 0406	Mortar for building	M 0481	190053
20	M 0407	Mortar (Troughs, not of metal, for mixing—)	A 0826	200206
06	M 0408	Mortar (Troughs of metal for mixing—)	A 0825	060279
13	M 0409	Mortars [firearms]	M 0482	130047
08	M 0410	Mortars for pounding	M 0483	080163
08	M 0411	Mortise axes	B 0326	080030
08	M 0412	Mortise chisels	B 0301	080029
07	M 0413	Mortising machines	M 0477	070071
19	M 0414	Mosaics for building	M 0486	190126
21	M 0415	Mosaics of glass, not for building	M 0485	210161
24	M 0416	Mosquito nets	M 0551	240079
05	M 0417	Moss (Irish—) for medical purposes	M 0544	050182
20	M 0418	Mother-of-pearl, unworked or semi-worked	N 0001	200153
05	M 0419	Mothproofing paper	P 0082	050286
05	M 0420	Mothproofing preparations	A 0599	050028
12	M 0421	Motor buses	A 0831	120018
12	M 0422	Motor cars	V 0298	120199
12	M 0423	Motor coaches	A 0833	120019
09	M 0424	Motor fire engines	A 0859	090297
04	M 0425	Motor fuel	C 0245	040081
04	M 0426	Motor fuel (Additives, non-chemical, to—)	A 0100	040085
01	M 0427	Motor fuel (Chemical additives to—)	A 0097	010020
12	M 0428	Motor homes	A 0832	120249
04	M 0429	Motor oil	H 0167	040104
12	M 0430	Motorcycles	M 0505	120147
07	M 0431	Motorcycles (Kick starters for—)	D 0065	070516
25	M 0432	Motorists' clothing	A 0857	250002
07	M 0433	Motorized cultivators	M 0502	070513
13	M 0434	Motorized weapons	A 0734	130007

Cl.	SERIAL No. (E)	INDICATION OF GOODS	SERIAL No. (F)	BASIC No.
12	M 0435	Motors, electric, for land vehicles	E 0193	120109
07	M 0436	Motors, electric, other than for land vehicles	E 0192	070452
07	M 0437	Motors for boats	B 0243	070402
12	M 0438	Motors for cycles	C 1696	120090
12	M 0439	Motors for land vehicles	M 0497	120130
07	M 0440	Motors, other than for land vehicles	M 0489	070433
19	M 0441	Mouldable wood	B 0554	190127
08	M 0442	Moulding irons	F 0104	080120
07	M 0443	Moulding machines	M 0541	070278
01	M 0444	Moulding preparations (Foundry—)	F 0340	010307
05	M 0445	Moulding wax for dentists	C 0894	050084
20	M 0446	Mouldings for picture frames	M 0543	200190
19	M 0447	Mouldings, not of metal, for building	M 0542	190128
19	M 0448	Mouldings, not of metal, for cornices	C 1298	190065
06	M 0449	Mouldings of metal for cornices	C 1297	060344
01	M 0450	Mould-release preparations	D 0069	010237
17	M 0451	Moulds (Ebonite—)	M 0527	170100
16	M 0452	Moulds for modelling clays [artists' materials]	M 0531	160352
21	M 0453	Moulds (Ice cube—)	M 0525	210099
21	M 0454	Moulds [kitchen utensils]	M 0534	210079
07	M 0455	Moulds [parts of machines]	M 0530	070276
18	M 0456	Mountaineering sticks	A 0382	180001
16	M 0457	Mounting photographs (Apparatus for—)	C 1018	160219
09	M 0458	Mouse [data processing equipment]	S 0467	090614
09	M 0459	Mouse pads	T 0116	090662
21	M 0460	Mouse traps	S 0466	210216
30	M 0461	Mousses (Chocolate—)	M 0545	300204
30	M 0462	Mousses (Dessert—) [confectionery]	M 0548	300205
29	M 0463	Mousses (Fish—)	M 0547	290167
29	M 0464	Mousses (Vegetable—)	M 0546	290169
03	M 0465	Moustache wax	C 0880	030052
26	M 0466	Moustaches (False—)	M 0550	260072
03	M 0467	Mouth washes, not for medical purposes	B 0671	030031
34	M 0468	Mouthpieces for cigarette holders	B 0773	340023
15	M 0469	Mouthpieces for musical instruments	E 0244	150034
05	M 0470	Mouthwashes for medical purposes	S 0370	050383
14	M 0471	Movements for clocks and watches	M 0561	140060
07	M 0472	Moving pavements [sidewalks]	T 0122	070518
07	M 0473	Moving staircases [escalators]	E 0426	070178
07	M 0474	Mowing and reaping machines	F 0024	070051
07	M 0475	Mowing machines (Knives for—)	F 0025	070188
07	M 0476	Mud catchers and collectors [machines]	C 1028	070059
05	M 0477	Mud for baths	B 0075	050059

Cl.	SERIAL No. (E)	INDICATION OF GOODS	SERIAL No. (F)	BASIC No.
05	M 0478	Mud (Medicinal —)	B 0701	050058
12	M 0479	Mudguards	G 0064	120049
01	M 0480	Muds (Drilling —)	B 0702	010136
30	M 0481	Muesli	M 0564	300177
07	M 0482	Mufflers for motors and engines	S 0321	070519
25	M 0483	Muffs [clothing]	M 0093	250097
17	M 0484	Muffs (Pipe —), not of metal	M 0091	170067
21	M 0485	Mugs	G 0254	210232
31	M 0486	Mulch (Straw —)	P 0016	310046
31	M 0487	Mushroom spawn for propagation	B 0464	310025
31	M 0488	Mushrooms, fresh	C 0475	310024
29	M 0489	Mushrooms, preserved	C 0474	290120
18	M 0490	Music cases	P 0825	180013
15	M 0491	Music rolls [piano]	B 0165	150078
15	M 0492	Music stands	P 1045	150080
15	M 0493	Music synthesizers	S 0619	150087
09	M 0494	Musical automata (Coin-operated —) [juke boxes]	A 0841	090062
15	M 0495	Musical boxes	B 0602	150052
16	M 0496	Musical greeting cards	C 0293	160336
15	M 0497	Musical instruments	I 0106	150025
03	M 0498	Musk [perfumery]	M 0571	030132
31	M 0499	Mussels, live	M 0529	310136
29	M 0500	Mussels, not live	M 0449	290083
32	M 0501	Must	M 0559	320019
03	M 0502	Mustache wax	C 0880	030052
30	M 0503	Mustard	M 0554	300101
05	M 0504	Mustard for pharmaceutical purposes	M 0555	050219
30	M 0505	Mustard meal	M 0556	300060
05	M 0506	Mustard oil for medical purposes	M 0557	050172
05	M 0507	Mustard plasters	S 0334	050271
05	M 0508	Mustard poultices	S 0334	050271
01	M 0509	Must-fining preparations	C 1017	010200
15	M 0510	Mutes for musical instruments	S 0465	150065
18	M 0511	Muzzles	M 0573	180028
05	M 0512	Myrobalan bark for pharmaceutical purposes	M 0596	050221

Cl.	SERIAL No. (E)	INDICATION OF GOODS	SERIAL No. (F)	BASIC No.
03	N 0001	Nail art stickers	A 0837	030224
21	N 0002	Nail brushes	O 0061	210050
08	N 0003	Nail buffers, electric or non-electric	P 0747	080214
03	N 0004	Nail care preparations	O 0067	030137
08	N 0005	Nail clippers, electric or non-electric	C 1390	080221
08	N 0006	Nail drawers [hand tools]	P 0443	080034
08	N 0007	Nail extractors	A 0753	080023
08	N 0008	Nail files	O 0064	080168
08	N 0009	Nail files, electric	L 0264	080213
08	N 0010	Nail nippers	P 0507	080074
03	N 0011	Nail polish	L 0142	030032
08	N 0012	Nail punches	C 0560	080050
03	N 0013	Nail varnish	L 0142	030032
06	N 0014	Nails	C 0965	060085
03	N 0015	Nails (False —)	O 0066	030136
20	N 0016	Nameplates, not of metal	P 0603	200154
04	N 0017	Naphtha	N 0006	040066
01	N 0018	Naphthalene	N 0005	010399
21	N 0019	Napkin holders	P 0858	210210
21	N 0020	Napkin rings	R 0362	210200
05	N 0021	Napkin-pants (Babies' —)	C 1360	050413
05	N 0022	Napkins (Babies' —) [diapers]	C 1359	050412
05	N 0023	Napkins for incontinents	C 1358	050351
24	N 0024	Napkins, of cloth, for removing make-up	S 0259	240101
16	N 0025	Napkins of paper for removing make-up	S 0260	160294
16	N 0026	Napkins of paper (Table —)	S 0263	160295
24	N 0027	Napkins of textile (Table —)	S 0262	240076
05	N 0028	Narcotics	N 0009	050223
09	N 0029	Nautical apparatus and instruments	N 0018	090356
09	N 0030	Naval signalling apparatus	N 0020	090357
09	N 0031	Navigation apparatus for vehicles [on-board computers]	V 0051	090659
09	N 0032	Navigational instruments	N 0027	090358
14	N 0033	Necklaces [jewellery, jewelry (Am.)]	C 1039	140031
25	N 0034	Neckties	C 1508	250060
32	N 0035	Nectars (Fruit —), non-alcoholic	N 0040	320044
26	N 0036	Needle cases	A 0209	260091
26	N 0037	Needle cushions	P 0306	260078
08	N 0038	Needle files	A 0205	080005
26	N 0039	Needles *	A 0188	260002
26	N 0040	Needles (Binding —)	A 0190	260006
10	N 0041	Needles for medical purposes	A 0193	100008
09	N 0042	Needles for record players	S 0087	090462
26	N 0043	Needles for wool combing machines	A 0207	260005
26	N 0044	Needles (Shoemakers' —)	A 0199	260003
08	N 0045	Needle-threaders	E 0321	080004
01	N 0046	Neodymium	N 0042	010400
01	N 0047	Neon	N 0043	010401
09	N 0048	Neon signs	T 0564	090330
01	N 0049	Neptunium	N 0044	010402
05	N 0050	Nervines	N 0045	050152
21	N 0051	Nest eggs, artificial	N 0064	210164
20	N 0052	Nesting boxes	N 0065	200109
20	N 0053	Nesting boxes for household pets	N 0068	200008
18	N 0054	Net bags for shopping	F 0192	180114
24	N 0055	Net curtains	V 0277	240093
07	N 0056	Net hauling machines [fishing]	T 0511	070478
22	N 0057	Nets *	F 0190	220094
28	N 0058	Nets (Butterfly —)	F 0191	280165
09	N 0059	Nets for protection against accidents	F 0197	090259
28	N 0060	Nets for sports	F 0193	280064
26	N 0061	Nets (Hair —)	F 0202	260042
28	N 0062	Nets (Landing —) for anglers	E 0410	280060
24	N 0063	Nets (Mosquito —)	M 0551	240079
09	N 0064	Nets (Safety —)	F 0198	090260
22	N 0065	Nets (Twine for —)	F 0223	220039
31	N 0066	Nettles	O 0128	310096
22	N 0067	Network	L 0011	220049
03	N 0068	Neutralizers for permanent waving	N 0062	030133
01	N 0069	Neutralizers (Toxic gas —)	N 0061	010403
16	N 0070	Newsletters	C 0876	160337
20	N 0071	Newspaper display stands	J 0060	200134
16	N 0072	Newspapers	J 0058	160032
16	N 0073	Nibs	P 0664	160131
16	N 0074	Nibs of gold	P 0665	160134
06	N 0075	Nickel	N 0066	060193
06	N 0076	Nickel-silver	A 0350	060016
04	N 0077	Nightlights [candles]	V 0111	040076
28	N 0078	Ninepins	Q 0018	280106
06	N 0079	Niobium	N 0071	060194
08	N 0080	Nippers	P 0512	080207
06	N 0081	Nipples (Grease —)	R 0005	060151
13	N 0082	Nitrate of ammonia explosives	N 0072	130005
01	N 0083	Nitrate of uranium	U 0009	010405
01	N 0084	Nitrate paper	P 0106	010416
01	N 0085	Nitrates	N 0073	010572
01	N 0086	Nitric acid	A 0889	010095
01	N 0087	Nitric monoxide	P 1024	010093
01	N 0088	Nitrite (Bismuth —) for chemical purposes	B 0453	010494
13	N 0089	Nitrocellulose (Acetyl —)	A 0058	130001
01	N 0090	Nitrogen	A 0886	010092
01	N 0091	Nitrogenous fertilisers	A 0888	010094
01	N 0092	Nitrogenous lime [manure]	C 1678	010141
01	N 0093	Nitrous oxide	P 1024	010093
13	N 0094	Noise-suppressors for guns	A 0741	130070
32	N 0095	Non-alcoholic beverages	B 0588	320031
32	N 0096	Non-alcoholic fruit extracts	E 0570	320001
32	N 0097	Non-alcoholic fruit juice beverages	F 0454	320006
32	N 0098	Non-alcoholic honey-based beverages	B 0589	320049
17	N 0099	Non-conducting materials for retaining heat	C 0137	170016
12	N 0100	Non-skid devices for vehicle tires [tyres]	A 0579	120013
27	N 0101	Non-slip mats	T 0110	270012

Cl.	SERIAL No. (E)	INDICATION OF GOODS	SERIAL No. (F)	BASIC No.
25	N 0102	Non-slipping devices for footwear	A 0580	250001
03	N 0103	Non-slipping liquids for floors	L 0314	030208
04	N 0104	Non-slipping preparations for belts	A 0581	040009
03	N 0105	Non-slipping wax for floors	C 0884	030207
24	N 0106	Non-woven textile fabrics	N 0101	240098
21	N 0107	Noodle machines, hand-operated	N 0105	210327
30	N 0108	Noodle-based prepared meals	N 0106	300202
30	N 0109	Noodles	N 0104	300103
18	N 0110	Nose bags [feed bags]	M 0575	180050
09	N 0111	Nose clips for divers and swimmers	P 0510	090655
07	N 0112	Notchers [machine tools]	G 0364	070208
16	N 0113	Note books	C 0269	160068
09	N 0114	Notebook computers	O 0092	090642
09	N 0115	Notice boards (Electronic —)	T 0023	090643
28	N 0116	Novelties for parties, dances [party favors, favours]	C 1342	280045
05	N 0117	Noxious animals (Preparations for destroying —)	P 0353	050021
05	N 0118	Noxious plants (Preparations for destroying —)	H 0069	050204
11	N 0119	Nozzles (Anti-splash tap —)	B 0832	110055
09	N 0120	Nozzles (Fire hose —)	L 0122	090296
21	N 0121	Nozzles for sprinkler hose	L 0123	210012
21	N 0122	Nozzles for watering cans	P 0758	210183
06	N 0123	Nozzles of metal	T 0612	060014
11	N 0124	Nuclear fuel and nuclear moderating material (Installations for processing —)	M 0438	110193
11	N 0125	Nuclear reactors	R 0122	110253
01	N 0126	Nuclear reactors (Moderating materials for —)	M 0439	010179
16	N 0127	Numbering apparatus	N 0113	160203
08	N 0128	Numbering punches	P 0506	080167
20	N 0129	Numberplates, not of metal	P 0605	200130
06	N 0130	Numberplates, of metal	P 0604	060400
26	N 0131	Numbers (Competitors' —)	D 0284	260112
16	N 0132	Numbers [type]	C 0756	160088
26	N 0133	Numerals for marking linen	C 0758	260045
06	N 0134	Numerals (Letters and —) of common metal, except type	L 0211	060419
10	N 0135	Nursing appliances	A 0349	100016
08	N 0136	Nutcrackers	C 0328	080215
30	N 0137	Nutmegs	N 0099	300102
05	N 0138	Nutritional supplements	C 1103	050384
05	N 0139	Nutritive substances for microorganisms	M 0370	050212
31	N 0140	Nuts [fruits]	N 0090	310004
01	N 0141	Nuts (Gall —)	N 0096	010319
20	N 0142	Nuts, not of metal	E 0157	200097
06	N 0143	Nuts of metal	E 0156	060364
29	N 0144	Nuts, prepared	N 0100	290085
07	N 0145	Nut-tapping machines	T 0128	070167

Cl.	SERIAL No. (E)	INDICATION OF GOODS	SERIAL No. (F)	BASIC No.

Cl.	SERIAL No. (E)	INDICATION OF GOODS	SERIAL No. (F)	BASIC No.
12	O 0001	Oars	R 0064	120041
30	O 0002	Oat flakes	F 0304	300145
30	O 0003	Oat-based food	A 0879	300144
30	O 0004	Oatmeal	A 0882	300146
31	O 0005	Oats	A 0878	310012
30	O 0006	Oats (Crushed —)	A 0880	300142
30	O 0007	Oats (Husked —)	A 0883	300143
09	O 0008	Objectives [lenses] [optics]	O 0001	090160
16	O 0009	Obliterating stamps	C 1110	160098
15	O 0010	Oboes	H 0043	150043
09	O 0011	Observation instruments	O 0004	090366
10	O 0012	Obstetric apparatus	O 0005	100120
15	O 0013	Ocarinas	O 0008	150056
09	O 0014	Octants	O 0009	090367
01	O 0015	Oenological bactericides [chemical preparations used in wine making]	B 0012	010096
20	O 0016	Office furniture	M 0337	200037
16	O 0017	Office perforators	P 0330	160093
16	O 0018	Office requisites, except furniture	B 0902	160159
09	O 0019	Ohmmeters	O 0029	090368
11	O 0020	Oil burners	H 0128	110199
31	O 0021	Oil cake	T 0440	310026
01	O 0022	Oil cement [putty]	M 0198	010655
05	O 0023	Oil (Cod liver —)	H 0132	050150
21	O 0024	Oil cruets	H 0170	210292
01	O 0025	Oil dispersants	H 0144	010352
04	O 0026	Oil for the preservation of leather	H 0160	040090
04	O 0027	Oil for the preservation of masonry	H 0157	040055
11	O 0028	Oil lamps	L 0092	110179
03	O 0029	Oil of turpentine for degreasing	E 0446	030158
05	O 0030	Oil of turpentine for pharmaceutical purposes	E 0445	050283
07	O 0031	Oil refining machines	R 0047	070498
01	O 0032	Oil (Synthetic materials for absorbing —)	A 0015	010620
01	O 0033	Oil-bleaching chemicals	H 0168	010353
24	O 0034	Oilcloth for use as tablecloths	T 0330	240025
04	O 0035	Oil-gas	G 0118	040050
01	O 0036	Oil-purifying chemicals	P 1057	010354
02	O 0037	Oils (Anti-rust —)	H 0147	020083
01	O 0038	Oils (Chemical additives for —)	A 0098	010654
03	O 0039	Oils for cleaning purposes	H 0151	030117
03	O 0040	Oils for cosmetic purposes	H 0141	030114
01	O 0041	Oils for currying leather	H 0164	010601
04	O 0042	Oils for paints	H 0162	040102
03	O 0043	Oils for perfumes and scents	H 0161	030118
01	O 0044	Oils for preparing leather in the course of manufacture	H 0166	010349
04	O 0045	Oils for releasing form work [building]	H 0148	040036
01	O 0046	Oils for tanning leather	H 0163	010350
01	O 0047	Oils for the preservation of food	H 0158	010348
02	O 0048	Oils for the preservation of wood	H 0159	020082
03	O 0049	Oils for toilet purposes	H 0152	030120

Cl.	SERIAL No. (E)	INDICATION OF GOODS	SERIAL No. (F)	BASIC No.
17	O 0050	Oils (Insulating —)	H 0156	170052
05	O 0051	Oils (Medicinal —)	H 0142	050167
11	O 0052	Oil-scrubbing apparatus	H 0127	110277
01	O 0053	Oil-separating chemicals	H 0169	010233
06	O 0054	Oilwells (Casings of metal for —)	C 0991	060337
05	O 0055	Ointments for pharmaceutical purposes	O 0070	050225
01	O 0056	Oleic acid	O 0044	010407
04	O 0057	Oleine	O 0043	040068
16	O 0058	Oleographs	O 0045	160204
29	O 0059	Olive oil for food	O 0048	290091
31	O 0060	Olives, fresh	O 0050	310093
29	O 0061	Olives, preserved	O 0049	290090
01	O 0062	Olivine [chemical preparations]	O 0053	010408
19	O 0063	Olivine for building	O 0052	190132
14	O 0064	Olivine [gems]	O 0051	140062
12	O 0065	Omnibuses	O 0056	120152
31	O 0066	Onions, fresh vegetables	O 0033	310092
29	O 0067	Onions, preserved	O 0032	290089
01	O 0068	Opacifiers for enamel or glass	O 0071	010264
21	O 0069	Opal glass	V 0177	210166
21	O 0070	Opaline glass	O 0073	210167
07	O 0071	Openers (Can —), electric	O 0155	070287
07	O 0072	Openers (Tin —), electric	O 0155	070287
10	O 0073	Operating tables	T 0040	100150
10	O 0074	Ophthalmometers	O 0075	100122
05	O 0075	Opiates	O 0077	050226
05	O 0076	Opium	O 0078	050227
05	O 0077	Opodeldoc	O 0079	050228
05	O 0078	Opotherapy preparations	O 0080	050229
10	O 0079	Opthalmoscopes	O 0076	100123
09	O 0080	Optical apparatus and instruments	O 0081	090370
09	O 0081	Optical character readers	L 0183	090615
09	O 0082	Optical condensers	C 1132	090592
09	O 0083	Optical data media	S 0593	090616
09	O 0084	Optical discs	D 0238	090617
09	O 0085	Optical fibers [fibres] [light conducting filaments]	F 0163	090571
09	O 0086	Optical glass	V 0153	090371
09	O 0087	Optical goods	L 0385	090335
09	O 0088	Optical lamps	L 0109	090319
09	O 0089	Optical lanterns	L 0109	090319
09	O 0090	Optical lenses	L 0198	090324
02	O 0091	Orange lead	L 0329	020089
31	O 0092	Oranges	O 0089	310094
07	O 0093	Ore treating machines	M 0384	070265
06	O 0094	Ores of metal	M 0385	060183
01	O 0095	Organic-bleaching chemicals	B 0479	010129
05	O 0096	Organotherapy preparations	O 0080	050229
15	O 0097	Organs	O 0118	150057
32	O 0098	Orgeat	O 0117	320027
11	O 0099	Ornamental fountains	J 0030	110175
26	O 0100	Ornamental novelty badges [buttons]	B 0020	260113
14	O 0101	Ornamental pins	E 0395	140069

Cl.	SERIAL No. (E)	INDICATION OF GOODS	SERIAL No. (F)	BASIC No.
28	O 0102	Ornaments for Christmas trees, except illumination articles and confectionery	D 0038	280119
26	O 0103	Ornaments (Hair—)	C 0721	260038
26	O 0104	Ornaments (Hat—), not of precious metal	O 0124	260016
14	O 0105	Ornaments (Hat—) of precious metal	O 0123	140117
14	O 0106	Ornaments [jewellery, jewelry (Am.)]	P 0174	140068
14	O 0107	Ornaments of jet	O 0125	140047
26	O 0108	Ornaments (Shoe—), not of precious metal	P 0176	260035
14	O 0109	Ornaments (Shoe—) of precious metal	P 0175	140119
26	O 0110	Orsedew [trimmings for clothing]	C 0949	260075
10	O 0111	Orthodontic appliances	O 0126	100214
10	O 0112	Orthopaedic articles	O 0127	100038
10	O 0113	Orthopaedic belts	C 0362	100047
10	O 0114	Orthopaedic footwear [shoes]	C 0653	100051
10	O 0115	Orthopaedic soles	S 0222	100171
10	O 0116	Orthopedic articles	O 0127	100038
10	O 0117	Orthopedic belts	C 0362	100047
10	O 0118	Orthopedic footwear [shoes]	C 0653	100051
10	O 0119	Orthopedic soles	S 0222	100171
09	O 0120	Oscillographs	O 0133	090374
14	O 0121	Osmium	O 0135	140066
26	O 0122	Ostrich feathers [clothing accessories]	A 0861	260011
06	O 0123	Outdoor blinds of metal	S 0542	060158
25	O 0124	Outerclothing	D 0156	250066
11	O 0125	Oven fittings made of fireclay	C 0472	110070
09	O 0126	Ovens for laboratory use	F 0409	090568
11	O 0127	Ovens (Microwave—) for industrial purposes	F 0405	110328
11	O 0128	Ovens, other than for laboratory use	F 0404	110150
11	O 0129	Ovens (Shaped fittings for—)	G 0089	110151
25	O 0130	Overalls	B 0498	250010
25	O 0131	Overcoats	P 0150	250115
01	O 0132	Oxalates	O 0160	010411
01	O 0133	Oxalic acid	O 0161	010412
11	O 0134	Oxhydrogen burners	O 0162	110197
02	O 0135	Oxide (Zinc—) [pigment]	G 0357	020081
01	O 0136	Oxygen	O 0168	010413
05	O 0137	Oxygen baths	B 0083	050043
05	O 0138	Oxygen for medical purposes	O 0169	050399
09	O 0139	Oxygen transvasing apparatus	O 0170	090377
08	O 0140	Oyster openers	O 0159	080143
20	O 0141	Oyster shells	E 0074	200090
31	O 0142	Oysters, live	H 0176	310137
29	O 0143	Oysters, not live	H 0174	290061
04	O 0144	Ozocerite [ozokerite]	O 0173	040069
09	O 0145	Ozonisers [ozonators]	O 0174	090378

Cl.	SERIAL No. (E)	INDICATION OF GOODS	SERIAL No. (F)	BASIC No.
28	P 0001	Pachinkos	J 0040	280199
10	P 0002	Pacifiers for babies	S 0560	100145
06	P 0003	Packaging containers of metal	R 0143	060231
20	P 0004	Packaging containers of plastic	R 0142	200100
07	P 0005	Packaging machines	E 0230	070499
16	P 0006	Packaging material made of starches	E 0227	160338
17	P 0007	Packing (Asbestos —)	T 0505	170081
22	P 0008	Packing [cushioning, stuffing] materials, not of rubber or plastics	E 0235	220031
17	P 0009	Packing [cushioning, stuffing] materials of rubber or plastics	E 0234	170101
07	P 0010	Packing machines	E 0265	070294
22	P 0011	Packing, of straw, for bottles	E 0239	220080
16	P 0012	Packing paper	E 0231	160130
22	P 0013	Packing rope	E 0226	220091
22	P 0014	Packing string	E 0229	220032
06	P 0015	Packings (Tin-plate —)	E 0238	060119
22	P 0016	Padding materials, not of rubber or plastics	R 0211	220030
17	P 0017	Padding materials of rubber or plastics	R 0210	170014
28	P 0018	Paddings (Protective —) [parts of sports suits]	R 0213	280147
12	P 0019	Paddles for canoes	P 0001	120153
06	P 0020	Padlocks	C 0054	060062
10	P 0021	Pads (Abdominal —)	P 0308	100098
05	P 0022	Pads (Breast-nursing —)	C 1438	050378
05	P 0023	Pads (Bunion —)	C 1441	050391
11	P 0024	Pads [cushions] (Heating —), electric, not for medical purposes	C 1448	110296
21	P 0025	Pads for cleaning	T 0085	210168
18	P 0026	Pads for horse saddles	D 0152	180117
10	P 0027	Pads (Heating —), electric, for medical purposes	C 1447	100050
09	P 0028	Pads (Mouse —)	T 0116	090662
10	P 0029	Pads [pouches] for preventing pressure sores on patient bodies	C 1440	100195
16	P 0030	Pads [stationery]	B 0497	160042
16	P 0031	Pads (Writing —)	S 0471	160255
21	P 0032	Pails	S 0154	210023
06	P 0033	Paint (Booths of metal for spraying —)	C 0007	060310
16	P 0034	Paint boxes [articles for use in school]	P 0276	160217
02	P 0035	Paint patches (Repositionable —)	P 0187	020125
07	P 0036	Paint (Spray guns for —)	P 0541	070298
19	P 0037	Paint spraying booths, not of metal	C 0008	190205
06	P 0038	Paint spraying booths, of metal	C 0007	060310
03	P 0039	Paint stripping preparations	P 0284	030179
16	P 0040	Paint trays	B 0005	160358
28	P 0041	Paintball guns [sports apparatus]	P 0534	280170
28	P 0042	Paintballs [ammunition for paintball guns] [sports apparatus]	M 0566	280171
16	P 0043	Paintbrushes	P 0492	160273
16	P 0044	Painters' brushes	P 0271	160050
16	P 0045	Painters' easels	C 0712	160087
07	P 0046	Painting machines	P 0280	070297
16	P 0047	Paintings [pictures], framed or unframed	T 0029	160030
02	P 0048	Paints *	P 0286	020001
02	P 0049	Paints (Anti-fouling —)	P 0287	020122
02	P 0050	Paints (Bactericidal —)	P 0288	020019
02	P 0051	Paints (Ceramic —)	C 0395	020037
01	P 0052	Paints (Chemical preparations for the manufacture of —)	C 1374	010575
02	P 0053	Paints (Enamel —)	E 0222	020065
02	P 0054	Paints (Fireproof —)	P 0290	020085
17	P 0055	Paints (Insulating —)	P 0291	170060
04	P 0056	Paints (Oils for —)	H 0162	040102
02	P 0057	Paints (Thickeners for —)	E 0379	020055
02	P 0058	Paints (Thinners for —)	D 0219	020053
25	P 0059	Pajamas (Am.)	P 1059	250108
08	P 0060	Palette knives	A 0417	080013
16	P 0061	Palettes for painters	P 0040	160207
19	P 0062	Palings, not of metal	P 0046	190134
06	P 0063	Palings of metal	P 0045	060198
19	P 0064	Palisading, not of metal	P 0046	190134
01	P 0065	Palladious chlorides	P 0048	010415
14	P 0066	Palladium	P 0047	140067
20	P 0067	Pallets, not of metal (Loading —)	P 0039	200054
20	P 0068	Pallets, not of metal (Transport —)	P 0037	200145
06	P 0069	Pallets of metal (Handling —)	P 0034	060175
06	P 0070	Pallets of metal (Loading —)	P 0038	060325
06	P 0071	Pallets of metal (Transport —)	P 0036	060176
29	P 0072	Palm kernel oil for food	N 0098	290059
29	P 0073	Palm oil for food	P 0049	290084
31	P 0074	Palm trees	P 0053	310101
31	P 0075	Palms [leaves of the palm tree]	P 0051	310100
16	P 0076	Pamphlets	B 0839	160046
30	P 0077	Pancakes	C 1548	300047
19	P 0078	Panels (Building —) not of metal	P 0066	190223
06	P 0079	Panels of metal (Building —)	P 0065	060381
12	P 0080	Panniers adapted for cycles	C 0999	120254
21	P 0081	Pans (Frying —)	P 0694	210136
05	P 0082	Panties (Sanitary —)	C 1647	050200
19	P 0083	Pantiles	T 0572	190151
16	P 0084	Pantographs [drawing instruments]	P 0071	160208
25	P 0085	Pants	C 0124	250023
05	P 0086	Pants, absorbent, for incontinents	C 1648	050372
05	P 0087	Pants (Sanitary —)	C 1647	050200
05	P 0088	Panty liners [sanitary]	P 1012	050315
16	P 0089	Paper *	P 0075	160006
17	P 0090	Paper (Asbestos —)	P 0124	170071
20	P 0091	Paper blinds	S 0547	200281
16	P 0092	Paper bows	N 0081	160351

Cl.	SERIAL No. (E)	INDICATION OF GOODS	SERIAL No. (F)	BASIC No.
19	P 0093	Paper (Building—)	P 0092	190062
16	P 0094	Paper clasps	C 1569	160116
25	P 0095	Paper clothing	V 0198	250122
16	P 0096	Paper (Electro-cardiograph—)	P 0112	160140
07	P 0097	Paper feeders [printing]	M 0148	070246
02	P 0098	Paper for dyeing Easter eggs	P 0116	020096
17	P 0099	Paper for electrical capacitors	P 0111	170029
05	P 0100	Paper for mustard plasters	P 0079	050237
05	P 0101	Paper for mustard poultices	P 0079	050237
16	P 0102	Paper for recording machines	P 0110	160067
25	P 0103	Paper hats [clothing]	C 0499	250162
17	P 0104	Paper (Insulating—)	P 0101	170055
16	P 0105	Paper knives [cutters] [office requisites]	C 1391	160291
07	P 0106	Paper machines	P 0104	070293
05	P 0107	Paper (Mothproof—)	P 0082	050286
28	P 0108	Paper party hats	C 0498	280204
21	P 0109	Paper plates	P 0640	210173
01	P 0110	Paper pulp	P 0190	010156
16	P 0111	Paper ribbons	R 0433	160244
16	P 0112	Paper sheets [stationery]	F 0135	160074
16	P 0113	Paper shredders for office use	D 0025	160287
04	P 0114	Paper spills for lighting	A 0359	040005
16	P 0115	Paper tapes and cards for the recordal of computer programmes	P 0978	160231
22	P 0116	Paper (Twine made of—)	P 0097	220038
16	P 0117	Paper (Waxed—)	P 0107	160339
19	P 0118	Paperboard for building	C 0304	190045
16	P 0119	Paper-clips	P 0498	160202
01	P 0120	Paperhanging (Adhesives for—)	C 1036	010203
07	P 0121	Papermaking machines	P 0105	070291
01	P 0122	Papers (Diazo—)	P 0095	010245
26	P 0123	Papers (Hair curling—)	P 0133	260121
16	P 0124	Paperweights	P 0951	160183
16	P 0125	Papier mâché	P 0103	160191
12	P 0126	Parachutes	P 0134	120113
04	P 0127	Paraffin	P 0135	040070
28	P 0128	Paragliders	P 0137	280146
05	P 0129	Parasiticides	P 0141	050238
18	P 0130	Parasols	P 0142	180066
16	P 0131	Parchment paper	P 0122	160210
08	P 0132	Paring irons [hand tools]	B 0763	080039
08	P 0133	Paring knives	T 0462	080133
07	P 0134	Paring machines	M 0477	070071
25	P 0135	Parkas	P 0165	250143
19	P 0136	Parking bicycles (Installations, not of metal, for—)	B 0391	190199
09	P 0137	Parking meters	P 0147	090383
28	P 0138	Parlor games	S 0357	280078
28	P 0139	Parlour games	S 0357	280078
19	P 0140	Parquet floor boards	L 0076	190106
03	P 0141	Parquet floor wax	C 0881	030053
19	P 0142	Parquet flooring	P 0170	190112
07	P 0143	Parquet wax-polishers, electric	C 0899	070500
09	P 0144	Particle accelerators	A 0017	090002
19	P 0145	Partitions, not of metal	C 0961	190060
06	P 0146	Partitions of metal	C 0960	060336
26	P 0147	Passementerie	P 0179	260068
16	P 0148	Passport holders	P 0180	160340
30	P 0149	Pasta	P 0204	300003
30	P 0150	Paste (Almond—)	P 0191	300004
30	P 0151	Paste (Cake—)	P 0198	300072
14	P 0152	Paste jewellery [costume jewelry (Am.)]	S 0549	140097
02	P 0153	Paste (Silver—)	A 0701	020014
30	P 0154	Paste (Soya bean—) [condiment]	P 0196	300194
16	P 0155	Pastels [crayons]	P 0183	160211
30	P 0156	Pastes (Farinaceous food—)	P 0204	300003
03	P 0157	Pastes for razor strops	P 0211	030073
16	P 0158	Pastes for stationery or household purposes	C 1034	160290
29	P 0159	Pastes (Liver—)	P 0206	290088
11	P 0160	Pasteurisers	P 0184	110178
30	P 0161	Pasties	P 0210	300134
30	P 0162	Pastilles [confectionery]	P 0186	300107
32	P 0163	Pastilles for effervescing beverages	P 0188	320033
05	P 0164	Pastilles for pharmaceutical purposes	P 0185	050214
05	P 0165	Pastilles (Fumigating—)	C 0968	050085
30	P 0166	Pastries	P 0219	300108
30	P 0167	Pastry	P 0198	300072
21	P 0168	Pastry cutters	C 1392	210328
12	P 0169	Patches (Adhesive rubber—) for repairing inner tubes	C 0461	120194
26	P 0170	Patches (Heat adhesive—) for decoration of textile articles [haberdashery]	P 0429	260111
26	P 0171	Patches (Heat adhesive—) for repairing textile articles	P 0428	260081
29	P 0172	Pâté (Liver—)	P 0206	290088
30	P 0173	Pâté [pastries]	P 0210	300134
16	P 0174	Patterns for dressmaking	P 0224	160212
16	P 0175	Patterns for making clothes	V 0207	160213
19	P 0176	Paving blocks, not of metal	P 0231	190200
06	P 0177	Paving blocks of metal	P 0230	060294
19	P 0178	Paving (Luminous—)	P 0229	190115
19	P 0179	Paving slabs, not of metal	D 0003	190219
25	P 0180	Peaks (Cap—)	V 0267	250030
29	P 0181	Peanut butter	B 0355	290007
31	P 0182	Peanut cake for animals	A 0647	310128
30	P 0183	Peanut confectionery	A 0643	300139
31	P 0184	Peanut meal for animals	A 0644	310127
32	P 0185	Peanut milk [non-alcoholic beverage]	L 0051	320046
31	P 0186	Peanuts, fresh	A 0645	310126
29	P 0187	Peanuts, processed	A 0646	290118
05	P 0188	Pearl powder for medical purposes	P 0909	050410
14	P 0189	Pearls [jewellery, jewelry (Am.)]	P 0336	140070
14	P 0190	Pearls made of ambroid [pressed amber]	A 0423	140005
31	P 0191	Peas, fresh	P 0722	310109
29	P 0192	Peas, preserved	P 0721	290096
04	P 0193	Peat (Blocks of—) [fuel]	B 0829	040017
04	P 0194	Peat briquettes [fuel]	B 0829	040017
01	P 0195	Peat [fertiliser]	T 0416	010539

Cl.	SERIAL No. (E)	INDICATION OF GOODS	SERIAL No. (F)	BASIC No.
04	P 0196	Peat [fuel]	T 0415	040024
31	P 0197	Peat (Litter—)	T 0418	310081
01	P 0198	Peat pots for horticulture	P 0903	010445
29	P 0199	Pectin for culinary purposes	P 0256	290093
01	P 0200	Pectin for industrial purposes	P 0257	010666
05	P 0201	Pectin for pharmaceutical purposes	P 0258	050231
01	P 0202	Pectin for the food industry	P 0260	010665
01	P 0203	Pectin [photography]	P 0259	010420
07	P 0204	Pedal drives for sewing machines	C 1087	070111
12	P 0205	Pedals for cycles	P 0261	120092
15	P 0206	Pedals for musical instruments	P 0262	150060
20	P 0207	Pedestals (Flower-pot—)	P 0433	200116
08	P 0208	Pedicure sets	T 0544	080106
09	P 0209	Pedometers	P 0693	090137
29	P 0210	Peel (Fruit—)	E 0119	290115
07	P 0211	Peeling machines	E 0398	070454
09	P 0212	Peepholes [magnifying lenses] for doors	J 0061	090312
15	P 0213	Pegs for musical instruments	C 0741	150021
20	P 0214	Pegs, not of metal (Tent—)	P 0525	200168
06	P 0215	Pegs of metal	C 0739	060078
20	P 0216	Pegs [pins], not of metal	C 0740	200217
25	P 0217	Pelerines	P 0293	250102
25	P 0218	Pelisses	P 0294	250103
18	P 0219	Pelts	P 0244	180002
16	P 0220	Pen cases	P 0671	160133
16	P 0221	Pen clips	A 0177	160011
16	P 0222	Pen wipers	E 0464	160148
16	P 0223	Pencil holders	P 0810	160113
16	P 0224	Pencil lead holders	P 0822	160114
16	P 0225	Pencil leads	M 0396	160105
16	P 0226	Pencil sharpeners, electric or non-electric	T 0062	160293
16	P 0227	Pencil sharpening machines, electric or non-electric	C 1520	160017
16	P 0228	Pencils	C 1512	160031
03	P 0229	Pencils (Cosmetic—)	C 1513	030069
03	P 0230	Pencils (Eyebrow—)	S 0464	030154
14	P 0231	Pendulums [clock and watch making]	B 0099	140013
16	P 0232	Penholders	P 0828	160299
08	P 0233	Penknives	C 0167	080046
09	P 0234	Pens (Electronic—) [visual display units]	C 1518	090598
16	P 0235	Pens [office requisites]	P 0667	160242
19	P 0236	Penstock pipes, not of metal	C 1158	190232
06	P 0237	Penstock pipes of metal	C 1157	060421
30	P 0238	Pepper	P 0730	300113
21	P 0239	Pepper mills, hand-operated	P 0731	210184
07	P 0240	Pepper mills other than hand-operated	P 0732	070307
21	P 0241	Pepper pots	P 0733	210185
33	P 0242	Peppermint liqueurs	A 0295	330001
30	P 0243	Peppermint sweets	M 0274	300019
31	P 0244	Peppers [plants]	P 0488	310106
30	P 0245	Peppers [seasonings]	P 0487	300111
05	P 0246	Pepsins for pharmaceutical purposes	P 0316	050242
05	P 0247	Peptones for pharmaceutical purposes	P 0317	050180
12	P 0248	Perambulator covers (Fitted—)	B 0003	120164
01	P 0249	Perborate of soda	P 0318	010421
01	P 0250	Percarbonates	P 0319	010422
19	P 0251	Perches	P 0326	190140
01	P 0252	Perchlorates	P 0325	010423
11	P 0253	Percolators (Coffee—), electric	P 0328	110261
21	P 0254	Percolators (Coffee—), non-electric	P 0329	210257
13	P 0255	Percussion caps other than toys	A 0466	130066
28	P 0256	Percussion caps [toys]	A 0467	280118
16	P 0257	Perforated cards for Jacquard looms	C 0310	160077
15	P 0258	Perforated music rolls	B 0166	150079
08	P 0259	Perforating tools [hand tools]	P 0331	080062
21	P 0260	Perfume burners	B 0882	210056
21	P 0261	Perfume sprayers	V 0029	210228
21	P 0262	Perfume vaporizers	V 0029	210228
04	P 0263	Perfumed candles	B 0708	040105
03	P 0264	Perfumery	P 0160	030141
03	P 0265	Perfumes	P 0161	030135
16	P 0266	Periodicals	P 0332	160033
09	P 0267	Peripheral devices (Computer—)	P 0333	090590
09	P 0268	Periscopes	P 0334	090337
03	P 0269	Permanent waving (Neutralizers for—)	N 0062	030133
33	P 0270	Perry	P 0718	330021
05	P 0271	Personal sexual lubricants	L 0380	050408
09	P 0272	Personal stereos	B 0089	090663
01	P 0273	Persulphates	P 0343	010424
01	P 0274	Persulphuric acid	P 0344	010425
10	P 0275	Pessaries	P 0352	100010
05	P 0276	Pesticides	P 0353	050021
08	P 0277	Pestles for pounding	P 0484	080172
30	P 0278	Pesto [sauce]	P 0354	300209
20	P 0279	Pet cushions	C 1452	200271
31	P 0280	Pet food	N 0107	310138
30	P 0281	Petit-beurre biscuits	P 0361	300109
30	P 0282	Petits fours [cakes]	P 0359	300068
04	P 0283	Petrol	E 0449	040043
11	P 0284	Petrol burners	B 0295	110248
09	P 0285	Petrol gauges	N 0078	090243
01	P 0286	Petroleum dispersants	P 0363	010351
04	P 0287	Petroleum ether	E 0496	040044
03	P 0288	Petroleum jelly for cosmetic purposes	G 0150	030109
04	P 0289	Petroleum jelly for industrial purposes	G 0151	040047
05	P 0290	Petroleum jelly for medical purposes	G 0152	050339
04	P 0291	Petroleum, raw or refined	P 0365	040071
31	P 0292	Pets (Aromatic sand for—) [litter]	S 0003	310147
21	P 0293	Pets (Cages for household—)	C 0090	210302
18	P 0294	Pets (Clothing for—)	H 0006	180054

Cl.	SERIAL No. (E)	INDICATION OF GOODS	SERIAL No. (F)	BASIC No.
21	P 0295	Pets (Litter boxes [trays] for—)	B 0008	210306
31	P 0296	Pets (Sanded paper for—) [litter]	P 0118	310146
03	P 0297	Pets (Shampoos for—)	S 0287	030196
25	P 0298	Petticoats	J 0067	250144
05	P 0299	Pharmaceutical preparations	P 0371	050069
05	P 0300	Pharmaceutical preparations for treating dandruff	P 0304	050241
01	P 0301	Phenol for industrial purposes	P 0376	010426
05	P 0302	Phenol for pharmaceutical purposes	P 0377	050236
10	P 0303	Phials (Drop counting—), for medical purposes	F 0282	100089
09	P 0304	Phonograph records	D 0231	090016
01	P 0305	Phonograph records (Compositions for the manufacture of—)	C 1108	010603
01	P 0306	Phonograph records (Renovating preparations for—)	D 0234	010246
01	P 0307	Phosphates [fertilisers]	P 0380	010427
05	P 0308	Phosphates for pharmaceutical purposes	P 0379	050245
01	P 0309	Phosphatides	P 0381	010429
01	P 0310	Phosphoric acid	P 0383	010433
01	P 0311	Phosphorus	P 0382	010430
09	P 0312	Photocopiers [photographic, electrostatic, thermic]	P 0389	090154
02	P 0313	Photocopiers (Toner cartridges, filled, for printers and—)	E 0297	020123
16	P 0314	Photo-engravings	P 0410	160221
16	P 0315	Photograph stands	P 0396	160220
01	P 0316	Photographic developers	R 0286	010435
01	P 0317	Photographic emulsions	E 0279	010267
01	P 0318	Photographic paper	P 0113	010322
09	P 0319	Photographic prints (Drying apparatus for—)	E 0408	090282
09	P 0320	Photographic prints (Glazing apparatus for—)	E 0407	090283
01	P 0321	Photographic sensitizers	S 0230	010436
09	P 0322	Photographic transparencies (Centering apparatus for—)	D 0197	090183
09	P 0323	Photographic transparencies (Frames for—)	C 0069	090099
16	P 0324	Photographs (Apparatus for mounting—)	C 1018	160219
16	P 0325	Photographs [printed]	P 0395	160147
01	P 0326	Photography (Chemical preparations for use in—)	P 0392	010211
01	P 0327	Photography (Reducing agents for use in—)	A 0148	010027
09	P 0328	Photometers	P 0411	090393
01	P 0329	Photometric paper	P 0109	010417
01	P 0330	Photosensitive plates	P 0612	010213
09	P 0331	Phototelegraphy apparatus	P 0414	090394
09	P 0332	Photovoltaic cells	C 0368	090531
05	P 0333	Phylloxera (Chemical preparations for treating—)	P 0415	050246
10	P 0334	Physical exercise apparatus, for medical purposes	E 0551	100176
28	P 0335	Physical exercises (Machines for—)	E 0324	280043
09	P 0336	Physics (Apparatus and instruments for—)	P 0417	090395
10	P 0337	Physiotherapy apparatus	P 0416	100196
15	P 0338	Piano keyboards	P 0419	150061
15	P 0339	Piano keys	P 0422	150063
15	P 0340	Piano strings	P 0420	150062
15	P 0341	Pianos	P 0418	150008
29	P 0342	Piccalilli	P 0423	290094
08	P 0343	Pickaxes	P 0513	080044
08	P 0344	Pickhammers	B 0669	080036
29	P 0345	Pickles	P 0424	290095
10	P 0346	Picks (Ear—)	C 1668	100071
15	P 0347	Picks for stringed instruments	M 0251	150048
08	P 0348	Picks [hand tools]	P 0427	080171
21	P 0349	Picnic baskets (Fitted—), including dishes	N 0039	210170
26	P 0350	Picot [lace]	P 0425	260080
01	P 0351	Picric acid	P 0426	010437
20	P 0352	Picture frame brackets	L 0325	200226
20	P 0353	Picture frames	C 0067	200225
20	P 0354	Picture frames (Moldings [mouldings] for—)	M 0543	200190
16	P 0355	Pictures	I 0014	160014
21	P 0356	Pie servers	P 0295	210177
08	P 0357	Piercing apparatus (Ear—)	P 0320	080241
30	P 0358	Pies	T 0441	300104
30	P 0359	Pies (Meat—)	V 0225	300133
21	P 0360	Pig bristles	P 0789	210188
21	P 0361	Piggy banks	T 0284	210224
02	P 0362	Pigments	P 0476	020059
01	P 0363	Pigments (Chemical preparations for the manufacture of—)	C 1374	010575
19	P 0364	Pigsties	P 0792	190084
19	P 0365	Pilings, not of metal	P 0056	190136
06	P 0366	Pilings of metal	P 0055	060188
06	P 0367	Pillars of metal for buildings	C 1049	060090
24	P 0368	Pillow shams	H 0113	240112
24	P 0369	Pillowcases	T 0060	240080
20	P 0370	Pillows	O 0100	200157
10	P 0371	Pillows (Soporific—) for insomnia	O 0103	100101
26	P 0372	Pin cushions	P 0307	260055
08	P 0373	Pin punches	R 0238	080180
25	P 0374	Pinafore dresses	R 0346	250169
28	P 0375	Piñatas	P 0490	280183
09	P 0376	Pince-nez	P 0493	090397
09	P 0377	Pince-nez cases	E 0535	090248
09	P 0378	Pince-nez chains	C 0438	090115
09	P 0379	Pince-nez cords	C 1276	090156
09	P 0380	Pince-nez mountings	M 0470	090364
08	P 0381	Pincers	P 0512	080207
10	P 0382	Pincers (Castrating—)	T 0182	100049
31	P 0383	Pine cones	P 0759	310105
06	P 0384	Pins (Cotter—) of metal	C 0929	060082
10	P 0385	Pins for artificial teeth	P 0548	100074
06	P 0386	Pins [hardware]	F 0168	060141

Cl.	SERIAL No. (E)	INDICATION OF GOODS	SERIAL No. (F)	BASIC No.
14	P 0387	Pins [jewellery, jewelry (Am.)]	E 0393	140150
21	P 0388	Pins of metal (Cooking—)	B 0837	210049
14	P 0389	Pins (Ornamental—)	E 0395	140069
26	P 0390	Pins, other than jewellery [jewelry (Am.)]	E 0392	260100
20	P 0391	Pins [pegs], not of metal	C 0740	200217
14	P 0392	Pins (Tie—)	E 0394	140151
15	P 0393	Pipa [Chinese guitars]	P 0515	150083
34	P 0394	Pipe cleaners for tobacco pipes	C 1669	340026
17	P 0395	Pipe gaskets	C 1159	170030
17	P 0396	Pipe jackets, not of metal	M 0091	170067
11	P 0397	Pipe line cocks [spigots]	R 0348	110068
17	P 0398	Pipe muffs, not of metal	M 0091	170067
06	P 0399	Pipe muffs of metal	M 0090	060173
20	P 0400	Pipe or cable clips of plastics	P 0225	200016
34	P 0401	Pipe racks for tobacco pipes	R 0094	340030
06	P 0402	Pipelines (Manifolds of metal for—)	M 0110	060420
06	P 0403	Pipes (Clips of metal for—)	C 1040	060312
19	P 0404	Pipes (Drain—) not of metal	T 0594	190220
19	P 0405	Pipes (Gutter—) not of metal	T 0590	190075
17	P 0406	Pipes (Joint packings for—)	C 1159	170030
17	P 0407	Pipes (Junctions for—), not of metal	R 0008	170073
06	P 0408	Pipes of metal	T 0608	060127
06	P 0409	Pipes of metal, for central heating installations	C 1161	060076
11	P 0410	Pipes [parts of sanitary installations]	C 1164	110103
19	P 0411	Pipes (Penstock—), not of metal	C 1158	190232
06	P 0412	Pipes (Penstock—) of metal	C 1157	060421
17	P 0413	Pipes (Reinforcing materials, not of metal for—)	A 0724	170089
06	P 0414	Pipes (Reinforcing materials of metal for—)	A 0721	060275
19	P 0415	Pipes (Rigid—), not of metal [building]	T 0611	190178
34	P 0416	Pipes (Tobacco—)	P 0517	340009
19	P 0417	Pipes (Water--) not of metal	C 1152	190076
09	P 0418	Pipettes	P 0520	090398
21	P 0419	Pipettes [wine-tasters]	T 0142	210178
06	P 0420	Pipework of metal	T 0584	060258
33	P 0421	Piquette	P 0526	330020
13	P 0422	Pistols [arms]	P 0537	130049
28	P 0423	Pistols (Caps for—) [toys]	A 0468	280003
28	P 0424	Pistols (Toy—)	P 0538	280058
07	P 0425	Piston segments	S 0177	070032
07	P 0426	Pistons for cylinders	C 1713	070197
07	P 0427	Pistons for engines	M 0496	070274
07	P 0428	Pistons [parts of machines or engines]	P 0545	070302
19	P 0429	Pitch	P 0734	190037
28	P 0430	Pitch mark repair tools [golf accessories]	O 0148	280179
21	P 0431	Pitchers	C 1583	210271
06	P 0432	Pitons of metal [mountaineering equipment]	P 0547	060430
08	P 0433	Pizza cutters, non-electric	C 1393	080249
30	P 0434	Pizzas	P 0549	300112
16	P 0435	Placards of paper or cardboard	E 0150	160305
20	P 0436	Placards of wood or plastics	E 0149	200096
24	P 0437	Place mats, not of paper	S 0282	240113
16	P 0438	Place mats of paper	S 0281	160296
26	P 0439	Plaited hair	T 0506	260044
20	P 0440	Plaited straw, except matting	P 0011	200160
20	P 0441	Plaits (Straw—)	T 0507	200161
08	P 0442	Plane irons	F 0113	080177
09	P 0443	Plane tables [surveying instruments]	P 0582	090399
08	P 0444	Planes	R 0002	080071
09	P 0445	Planimeters	P 0584	090400
07	P 0446	Planing machines	R 0001	070321
19	P 0447	Planks [wood for building]	P 0575	190149
16	P 0448	Plans	P 0585	160223
01	P 0449	Plant growth regulating preparations	R 0200	010634
08	P 0450	Plant parasite killing apparatus	P 0140	080088
31	P 0451	Plant seeds	G 0298	310068
31	P 0452	Plants	P 0588	310071
31	P 0453	Plants, dried, for decoration	P 0593	310107
05	P 0454	Plants (Preparations for destroying noxious—)	H 0069	050204
03	P 0455	Plants (Preparations to make shiny the leaves of—)	P 0591	030212
05	P 0456	Plasma (Blood—)	P 0618	050248
19	P 0457	Plaster *	P 0636	190054
10	P 0458	Plaster bandages for orthopaedic purposes [casts (Am.)]	B 0136	100206
17	P 0459	Plaster (Insulating—)	E 0311	170110
05	P 0460	Plasters for medical purposes	E 0268	050097
05	P 0461	Plasters (Mustard—)	S 0334	050271
16	P 0462	Plastic cling film, extensible, for palletization	P 0300	160325
22	P 0463	Plastic fibers [fibres] for textile use	F 0160	220092
17	P 0464	Plastic fibers [fibres], not for textile use	F 0161	170102
16	P 0465	Plastic film for wrapping	P 0302	160218
17	P 0466	Plastic film other than for wrapping	P 0301	170072
24	P 0467	Plastic material [substitute for fabrics]	M 0228	240081
17	P 0468	Plastic sheeting for agricultural purposes	F 0132	170111
17	P 0469	Plastic substances, semi-processed	M 0226	170097
01	P 0470	Plasticizers	P 0619	010143
01	P 0471	Plastics (Dispersions of—)	D 0226	010605
16	P 0472	Plastics for modelling	M 0227	160195
01	P 0473	Plastics, unprocessed	M 0224	010438
01	P 0474	Plastisols	P 0625	010439
21	P 0475	Plate glass [raw material]	G 0218	210143
19	P 0476	Plate glass [windows], for building	G 0220	190095
20	P 0477	Plate racks	V 0005	200198
11	P 0478	Plate warmers	C 0616	110089
09	P 0479	Plates (Carriers for dark—) [photography]	I 0113	090309

Cl.	SERIAL No. (E)	INDICATION OF GOODS	SERIAL No. (F)	BASIC No.
16	P 0480	Plates for addressing machines (Address —)	P 0596	160268
09	P 0481	Plates for batteries	A 0039	090012
01	P 0482	Plates for offset printing (Sensitized —)	P 0613	010406
11	P 0483	Plates (Hot —)	P 0597	110170
20	P 0484	Plates, not of metal (Registration —)	P 0605	200130
21	P 0485	Plates (Paper —)	P 0640	210173
01	P 0486	Plates (Photosensitive —)	P 0612	010213
07	P 0487	Plates (Printing —)	P 0580	070217
06	P 0488	Plates (Registration —) of metal	P 0604	060400
01	P 0489	Plates (Sensitized photographic —)	P 0611	010269
21	P 0490	Plates to prevent milk boiling over	L 0059	210107
13	P 0491	Platforms (Firing —)	T 0509	130057
19	P 0492	Platforms, prefabricated, not of metal	Q 0004	190158
06	P 0493	Platforms, prefabricated, of metal	Q 0003	060226
14	P 0494	Platinum [metal]	P 0635	140075
28	P 0495	Play balloons	B 0117	280012
09	P 0496	Players (DVD —)	L 0181	090685
28	P 0497	Playing balls	B 0727	280030
28	P 0498	Playing cards	C 0287	280191
20	P 0499	Playpens for babies	P 0148	200022
20	P 0500	Playpens (Mats for infant —)	T 0121	200275
15	P 0501	Plectrums	M 0251	150048
08	P 0502	Pliers	P 0499	080206
09	P 0503	Plotters	T 0045	090596
07	P 0504	Ploughs	C 0550	070028
07	P 0505	Ploughshares	S 0359	070100
13	P 0506	Plugs (Detonating —)	B 0678	130018
20	P 0507	Plugs [dowels], not of metal	T 0089	200232
10	P 0508	Plugs (Ear —) [ear protection devices]	O 0107	100224
20	P 0509	Plugs, not of metal	B 0639	200213
06	P 0510	Plugs of metal	B 0638	060296
06	P 0511	Plugs of metal (Wall —)	T 0088	060087
09	P 0512	Plugs, sockets and other contacts [electric connections]	P 0974	090166
09	P 0513	Plumb bobs	P 0649	090257
09	P 0514	Plumb lines	F 0217	090258
07	P 0515	Plunger pistons	A 0470	070395
21	P 0516	Plungers for clearing blocked drains	D 0013	210329
28	P 0517	Plush toys	P 0310	280161
01	P 0518	Plutonium	P 0672	010442
19	P 0519	Plywood	C 1220	190028
07	P 0520	Pneumatic door openers and closers [parts of machines]	P 0842	070520
07	P 0521	Pneumatic hammers	M 0175	070249
12	P 0522	Pneumatic tires [tyres]	P 0684	120157
07	P 0523	Pneumatic transporters	P 0680	070304
07	P 0524	Pneumatic tube conveyors	T 0481	070370
09	P 0525	Pocket calculators	C 0121	090644
11	P 0526	Pocket searchlights	L 0098	110051
25	P 0527	Pocket squares	P 0689	250161
11	P 0528	Pocket torches, electric	L 0098	110051
18	P 0529	Pocket wallets	P 0814	180069
11	P 0530	Pocket warmers	C 0618	110280
25	P 0531	Pockets for clothing	P 0686	250106
16	P 0532	Pointers (Chart —), non-electronic	B 0046	160350
09	P 0533	Pointers (Light-emitting electronic —)	P 0716	090679
06	P 0534	Points (Railway —)	C 0482	060013
05	P 0535	Poisons	P 0723	050249
09	P 0536	Polarimeters	P 0736	090404
28	P 0537	Poles for pole vaulting	P 0324	280210
20	P 0538	Poles, not of metal	P 0323	200242
19	P 0539	Poles, not of metal, for electric power lines	P 0888	190079
06	P 0540	Poles of metal	P 0322	060024
06	P 0541	Poles of metal, for electric lines	P 0887	060365
08	P 0542	Police batons	M 0230	080130
03	P 0543	Polish for furniture and flooring	E 0287	030047
01	P 0544	Polish removing substances	D 0104	010238
03	P 0545	Polishes (Denture —)	P 1022	030198
21	P 0546	Polishing apparatus and machines, for household purposes, non-electric	P 0737	210186
03	P 0547	Polishing creams	C 1537	030070
21	P 0548	Polishing gloves	G 0044	210294
08	P 0549	Polishing irons [glazing tools]	F 0102	080118
21	P 0550	Polishing leather	C 1595	210100
07	P 0551	Polishing (Machines and apparatus for —) [electric]	P 0740	070308
21	P 0552	Polishing materials for making shiny, except preparations, paper and stone	P 0744	210187
03	P 0553	Polishing paper	P 0078	030139
03	P 0554	Polishing preparations	P 0743	030045
03	P 0555	Polishing rouge	R 0392	030011
03	P 0556	Polishing stones	P 0448	030144
03	P 0557	Polishing wax	C 0883	030054
05	P 0558	Pollen dietary supplements	P 0748	050428
29	P 0559	Pollen prepared as foodstuff	P 0750	290134
31	P 0560	Pollen [raw material]	P 0749	310057
01	P 0561	Polonium	P 0751	010443
11	P 0562	Polymerisation installations	P 0753	110203
03	P 0563	Pomades for cosmetic purposes	P 0754	030146
05	P 0564	Pomades for medical purposes	P 0755	050207
25	P 0565	Ponchos	P 0784	250165
12	P 0566	Pontoons	P 0786	120159
06	P 0567	Pools (Swimming —) [metal structures]	P 0528	060290
28	P 0568	Pools (Swimming —) [play articles]	P 0527	280095
19	P 0569	Pools (Swimming —) [structures, not of metal]	P 0529	190196
30	P 0570	Popcorn	M 0043	300044
05	P 0571	Porcelain for dental prostheses	P 0790	050115
21	P 0572	Porcelain ware	P 0791	210189
19	P 0573	Porches, not of metal, for building	M 0166	190123
06	P 0574	Porches of metal [building]	M 0169	060179
29	P 0575	Pork	V 0219	290142

Cl.	SERIAL No. (E)	INDICATION OF GOODS	SERIAL No. (F)	BASIC No.
19	P 0576	Porphyry [stone]	P 0793	190244
28	P 0577	Portable games with liquid crystal displays	J 0044	280215
09	P 0578	Portable media players	B 0090	090702
09	P 0579	portable telephones	T 0164	090661
12	P 0580	Portholes	H 0124	120133
16	P 0581	Portraits	P 0865	160228
16	P 0582	Postage meters for office use	A 0158	160009
16	P 0583	Postage stamps	T 0272	160260
16	P 0584	Postcards	P 0867	160174
16	P 0585	Posters	A 0152	160007
19	P 0586	Posts, not of metal	P 0890	190206
19	P 0587	Posts, not of metal, for electric power lines	P 0888	190079
06	P 0588	Posts of metal	P 0889	060205
06	P 0589	Posts of metal for electric lines	P 0887	060365
06	P 0590	Pot hooks of metal	C 1525	060103
21	P 0591	Pot lids	C 1469	210092
01	P 0592	Potash	P 0883	010446
01	P 0593	Potash water	E 0063	010448
01	P 0594	Potassium	P 0885	010447
01	P 0595	Potassium dioxalate	B 0443	010123
05	P 0596	Potassium salts for medical purposes	P 0886	050251
29	P 0597	Potato chips	P 0756	290019
29	P 0598	Potato crisps	P 0756	290019
29	P 0599	Potato flakes	F 0308	290154
30	P 0600	Potato flour for food	P 0761	300114
01	P 0601	Potato flour for industrial purposes	P 0762	010444
29	P 0602	Potato fritters	B 0302	290148
31	P 0603	Potatoes, fresh	P 0760	310110
03	P 0604	Potpourris [fragrances]	P 0904	030203
21	P 0605	Pots	P 0896	210153
21	P 0606	Pots (Flower —)	P 0897	210133
01	P 0607	Pots (Peat —) for horticulture	P 0903	010445
19	P 0608	Potters' clay	A 0712	190011
07	P 0609	Potters' wheels	T 0437	070420
21	P 0610	Pottery	P 0893	210193
01	P 0611	Potting soil	T 0215	010355
18	P 0612	Pouch baby carriers	S 0046	180123
13	P 0613	Pouches (Cartridge —)	C 0317	130025
11	P 0614	Pouches (Disposable sterilization —)	P 0687	110324
18	P 0615	Pouches, of leather, for packaging	S 0040	180079
34	P 0616	Pouches (Tobacco —)	B 0461	340004
05	P 0617	Poultices	C 0342	050070
05	P 0618	Poultices (Mustard —)	S 0334	050271
31	P 0619	Poultry, live	V 0306	310123
29	P 0620	Poultry, not live	V 0309	290114
21	P 0621	Poultry rings	A 0562	210011
02	P 0622	Powder (Aluminium —) for painters, artists and decorators	P 0908	020008
02	P 0623	Powder (Bronze —) [paint]	B 0856	020032
30	P 0624	Powder (Cake —)	P 0910	300071
21	P 0625	Powder compacts	P 0914	210195
06	P 0626	Powder form (Metals in —) *	M 0308	060434
02	P 0627	Powder form (Metals in —) for painters, decorators, printers and artists	M 0309	020090
13	P 0628	Powder horns	C 1289	130029
03	P 0629	Powder (Make-up —)	P 0911	030147
05	P 0630	Powder of cantharides	C 0188	050065
21	P 0631	Powder puffs	H 0106	210148
29	P 0632	Powdered eggs	O 0025	290087
21	P 0633	Powdered glass for decoration	V 0142	210114
13	P 0634	Powders (Explosive —)	P 0913	130051
32	P 0635	Powders for effervescing beverages	B 0581	320034
30	P 0636	Powders for ice cream	G 0216	300137
02	P 0637	Powders (Silvering —)	A 0705	020016
07	P 0638	Power hammers	M 0176	070248
01	P 0639	Power steering fluid	F 0318	010643
12	P 0640	Power tailgates (Am.) [parts of land vehicles]	H 0051	120243
28	P 0641	Practical jokes [novelties]	F 0008	280062
30	P 0642	Pralines	P 0940	300116
12	P 0643	Prams [baby carriages]	V 0299	120163
01	P 0644	Praseodymium	P 0941	010449
29	P 0645	Prawns, not live	B 0733	290135
01	P 0646	Precious metals (Salts of —) for industrial purposes	S 0206	010391
14	P 0647	Precious metals, unwrought or semi-wrought	M 0313	140055
14	P 0648	Precious stones	P 0469	140074
09	P 0649	Precision balances	T 0491	090489
09	P 0650	Precision measuring apparatus	M 0294	090346
19	P 0651	Prefabricated houses [kits]	M 0054	190243
05	P 0652	Pregnancy (Chemical preparations for the diagnosis of —)	G 0359	050166
33	P 0653	Pre-mixed alcoholic beverages, other than beer-based	B 0569	330035
04	P 0654	Preservation of masonry (Oil for the —)	H 0157	040055
01	P 0655	Preservatives (Brickwork —), except paints and oils	B 0821	010381
01	P 0656	Preservatives (Cement —), except paints and oils	C 0861	010196
01	P 0657	Preservatives (Concrete —), except paints and oils	B 0347	010117
01	P 0658	Preservatives (Flower —)	F 0301	010209
04	P 0659	Preservatives for leather [oils and greases]	C 1613	040086
03	P 0660	Preservatives for leather [polishes]	C 1612	030061
01	P 0661	Preservatives for pharmaceutical preparations	C 1188	010210
01	P 0662	Preservatives for tiles, except paints and oils	T 0573	010540
01	P 0663	Preservatives (Masonry —), except paints and oils	M 0020	010380
02	P 0664	Preservatives (Wood —)	B 0553	020049
06	P 0665	Preserve tins	B 0599	060093
06	P 0666	Preserving boxes of metal	B 0599	060093
01	P 0667	Preserving foodstuffs (Chemical substances for —)	C 1185	010044

Cl.	SERIAL No. (E)	INDICATION OF GOODS	SERIAL No. (F)	BASIC No.
30	P 0668	Preserving foodstuffs (Salt for—)	S 0189	300014
01	P 0669	Preserving (Salt for—), other than for foodstuffs	S 0188	010003
21	P 0670	Presses (Garlic—) [kitchen utensils]	P 0948	210332
07	P 0671	Presses [machines for industrial purposes]	P 0957	070316
07	P 0672	Presses (Smoothing—)	L 0319	070240
21	P 0673	Presses (Trouser—)	P 0958	210171
07	P 0674	Presses (Wine—)	P 0968	070102
11	P 0675	Pressure cookers [autoclaves], electric	M 0153	110254
21	P 0676	Pressure cookers [autoclaves], non-electric	A 0839	210236
11	P 0677	Pressure cooking saucepans, electric	C 0331	110029
09	P 0678	Pressure gauges	M 0119	090336
09	P 0679	Pressure in vehicle tires [tyres] (Automatic indicators of low—)	A 0864	090069
09	P 0680	Pressure indicator plugs for valves	B 0681	090090
09	P 0681	Pressure indicators	E 0337	090410
09	P 0682	Pressure measuring apparatus	P 0964	090409
07	P 0683	Pressure reducers [parts of machines]	D 0167	070154
07	P 0684	Pressure regulators [parts of machines]	R 0190	070317
07	P 0685	Pressure valves [parts of machines]	P 0966	070318
11	P 0686	Pressure water tanks	R 0252	110127
02	P 0687	Primers	A 0628	020108
08	P 0688	Priming irons [hand tools]	T 0461	080196
13	P 0689	Primings [fuses]	A 0465	130061
09	P 0690	Printed circuit boards	C 0290	090699
09	P 0691	Printed circuits	C 0874	090125
16	P 0692	Printed matter	I 0043	160175
16	P 0693	Printed publications	P 1029	160179
16	P 0694	Printed timetables	H 0083	160172
02	P 0695	Printers and photocopiers (Toner cartridges, filled, for—)	E 0297	020123
16	P 0696	Printers' blankets, not of textile	B 0471	160177
24	P 0697	Printers' blankets of textile	B 0470	240106
09	P 0698	Printers for use with computers	I 0028	090618
02	P 0699	Printers' pastes [ink]	P 0208	020043
16	P 0700	Printers' reglets	R 0186	160235
16	P 0701	Printing blocks	C 0942	160040
02	P 0702	Printing compositions [ink]	P 0208	020043
07	P 0703	Printing cylinders	C 1711	070140
02	P 0704	Printing ink	E 0300	020066
07	P 0705	Printing machines	I 0032	070218
07	P 0706	Printing machines for use on sheet metal	T 0367	070216
07	P 0707	Printing plates	P 0580	070217
01	P 0708	Printing plates (Sensitized—) for offset	P 0613	010406
07	P 0709	Printing presses	P 0955	070219
07	P 0710	Printing rollers for machines	R 0400	070220
16	P 0711	Printing sets, portable [office requisites]	I 0046	160178

Cl.	SERIAL No. (E)	INDICATION OF GOODS	SERIAL No. (F)	BASIC No.
16	P 0712	Printing type	I 0035	160065
16	P 0713	Prints [engravings]	P 0578	160015
09	P 0714	Prisms [optics]	P 0975	090365
26	P 0715	Prize ribbons	R 0444	260117
10	P 0716	Probes for medical purposes	S 0393	100085
09	P 0717	Probes for scientific purposes	S 0394	090436
11	P 0718	Processing installations for fuel and nuclear moderating material	M 0438	110193
09	P 0719	Processors [central processing units]	P 0977	090619
04	P 0720	Producer gas	G 0122	040103
09	P 0721	Programs (Computer—) [downloadable software]	P 0980	090658
09	P 0722	Programs (Computer game—)	L 0362	090670
09	P 0723	Programs (Computer operating—) recorded	P 0981	090589
13	P 0724	Projectiles [weapons]	P 0983	130052
09	P 0725	Projection apparatus	P 0984	090411
09	P 0726	Projection screens	E 0128	090209
11	P 0727	Projector lamps	L 0110	110132
01	P 0728	Promethium	P 0987	010450
30	P 0729	Propolis*	P 0988	300166
05	P 0730	Propolis dietary supplements	P 0990	050427
05	P 0731	Propolis for pharmaceutical purposes	P 0989	050426
19	P 0732	Props, not of metal	E 0488	190086
06	P 0733	Props of metal	E 0487	060372
12	P 0734	Propulsion mechanisms for land vehicles	P 0993	120143
07	P 0735	Propulsion mechanisms other than for land vehicles	P 0992	070252
16	P 0736	Prospectuses	P 0994	160232
10	P 0737	Prostheses (Hair—)	P 1018	100192
10	P 0738	Prostheses (Intraocular—) [lenses] for surgical implantation	L 0200	100194
01	P 0739	Protactinium	P 0995	010451
10	P 0740	Protection devices against X-rays, for medical purposes	R 0118	100137
09	P 0741	Protection devices against X-rays, not for medical purposes	R 0119	090422
09	P 0742	Protection devices for personal use against accidents	P 1005	090004
01	P 0743	Protective gases for welding	G 0125	010326
09	P 0744	Protective helmets	C 0325	090112
09	P 0745	Protective helmets for sports	C 0326	090656
09	P 0746	Protective masks *	M 0184	090338
28	P 0747	Protective paddings [parts of sports suits]	R 0213	280147
02	P 0748	Protective preparations for metals	P 0999	020094
09	P 0749	Protective suits for aviators	C 1067	090070
09	P 0750	Protectors (Voltage surge—)	R 0189	090676
05	P 0751	Protein dietary supplements	P 1014	050435
29	P 0752	Protein milk	L 0042	290174
01	P 0753	Protein [raw material]	P 1016	010452
05	P 0754	Protein supplements for animals	P 1015	050436

Cl.	SERIAL No. (E)	INDICATION OF GOODS	SERIAL No. (F)	BASIC No.
09	P 0755	Protractors [measuring instruments]	R 0074	090419
08	P 0756	Pruning knives	S 0241	080146
08	P 0757	Pruning scissors	S 0156	080097
08	P 0758	Pruning shears	E 0094	080098
01	P 0759	Prussiates	C 1680	010228
09	P 0760	Publications (Electronic —), downloadable	P 1028	090657
16	P 0761	Publications (Printed —)	P 1029	160179
29	P 0762	Pudding (Black —) [blood sausage]	B 0690	290013
30	P 0763	Puddings	P 0906	300115
07	P 0764	Puddling machines	P 1032	070319
07	P 0765	Pulleys *	P 0031	070099
07	P 0766	Pulleys (Adhesive bands for —)	B 0126	070314
06	P 0767	Pulleys of metal, other than for machines	P 0919	060207
20	P 0768	Pulleys of plastics for blinds	P 0918	200262
07	P 0769	Pulleys [parts of machines]	P 0920	070117
25	P 0770	Pullovers	P 1034	250107
29	P 0771	Pulp (Fruit —)	P 1035	290045
01	P 0772	Pulp (Paper —)	P 0190	010156
01	P 0773	Pulp (Wood —)	P 0192	010132
10	P 0774	Pulse meters	S 0494	100222
07	P 0775	Pulverisers [machines]	P 1039	070214
07	P 0776	Pulverisers (Sewage —)	P 1040	070162
03	P 0777	Pumice stone	P 0451	030145
07	P 0778	Pump diaphragms	M 0265	070257
12	P 0779	Pumps (Air —) [vehicle accessories]	P 0765	120009
12	P 0780	Pumps for bicycles, cycles	B 0394	120093
07	P 0781	Pumps for heating installations	P 0780	070311
10	P 0782	Pumps for medical purposes	P 0771	100086
08	P 0783	Pumps (Hand —)*	G 0279	080245
07	P 0784	Pumps [machines]	P 0777	070309
07	P 0785	Pumps [parts of machines, engines or motors]	P 0779	070179
07	P 0786	Pumps (Vacuum —) [machines]	P 0772	070312
08	P 0787	Punch pliers [hand tools]	E 0271	080228
08	P 0788	Punch rings [knuckle dusters]	C 1407	080015
09	P 0789	Punched card machines for offices	B 0903	090097
07	P 0790	Punches for punching machines	P 0709	070305
08	P 0791	Punches [hand tools]	P 0710	080229
16	P 0792	Punches [office requisites]	E 0270	160141
28	P 0793	Punching bags	P 1043	280184
07	P 0794	Punching machines	P 0707	070306
28	P 0795	Puppets	M 0150	280087
05	P 0796	Purgatives	P 1048	050143
11	P 0797	Purification installations for sewage	P 1056	110135
01	P 0798	Purification of gas (Preparations for the —)	G 0123	010275
01	P 0799	Purification preparations	C 0925	010254
01	P 0800	Purifying chemicals (Oil- —)	P 1057	010354
01	P 0801	Purifying chemicals (Water- —)	P 1055	010608
18	P 0802	Purses	B 0738	180010
09	P 0803	Push buttons for bells	B 0766	090093
12	P 0804	Pushchair covers	B 0003	120164
12	P 0805	Pushchair hoods	V 0301	120165
12	P 0806	Pushchairs	V 0299	120163
01	P 0807	Putty (Glaziers' —)	M 0199	010651
25	P 0808	Pyjamas	P 1059	250108
05	P 0809	Pyrethrum powder	P 1061	050252
01	P 0810	Pyrogallic acid	P 1062	010453
01	P 0811	Pyroligneous acid [wood vinegar]	V 0244	010133
09	P 0812	Pyrometers	P 1064	090415
06	P 0813	Pyrophoric metals	M 0322	060185
13	P 0814	Pyrophoric substances	P 1065	130053
13	P 0815	Pyrotechnic products	P 1067	130054
13	P 0816	Pyroxylin	C 1354	130030

Cl.	SERIAL No. (E)	INDICATION OF GOODS	SERIAL No. (F)	BASIC No.
09	Q 0001	Quantity indicators	I 0071	090301
19	Q 0002	Quartz	Q 0005	190073
10	Q 0003	Quartz lamps for medical purposes	Q 0006	100130
05	Q 0004	Quassia for medical purposes	Q 0007	050254
01	Q 0005	Quebracho for industrial purposes	Q 0009	010454
05	Q 0006	Quebracho for medical purposes	Q 0010	050253
30	Q 0007	Quiches	Q 0015	300192
03	Q 0008	Quillaia bark for washing	E 0115	030093
24	Q 0009	Quilts	C 1490	240029
05	Q 0010	Quinine for medical purposes	Q 0020	050256
05	Q 0011	Quinquina for medical purposes	Q 0022	050255
28	Q 0012	Quoits	P 0033	280097

Cl.	SERIAL No. (E)	INDICATION OF GOODS	SERIAL No. (F)	BASIC No.

Cl.	SERIAL No. (E)	INDICATION OF GOODS	SERIAL No. (F)	BASIC No.
08	R 0001	Rabbeting planes	G 0372	080135
07	R 0002	Rack and pinion jacks	C 1524	070132
07	R 0003	Racket stringing machines	R 0079	070511
28	R 0004	Rackets	R 0075	280081
28	R 0005	Rackets (Guts for—)	B 0775	280033
28	R 0006	Rackets (Strings for—)	C 1264	280042
20	R 0007	Racks [furniture]	E 0477	200108
09	R 0008	Racks (Photographic—)	E 0173	090212
09	R 0009	Radar apparatus	R 0016	090416
17	R 0010	Radiation of heat (Compositions to prevent the—)	C 0449	170024
11	R 0011	Radiator caps	B 0676	110050
01	R 0012	Radiator flushing chemicals	R 0024	010648
07	R 0013	Radiators [cooling] for motors and engines	R 0021	070464
11	R 0014	Radiators, electric	R 0023	110137
11	R 0015	Radiators [heating]	R 0019	110198
09	R 0016	Radio pagers	T 0153	090673
01	R 0017	Radioactive elements for scientific purposes	R 0028	010456
05	R 0018	Radioactive substances for medical purposes	R 0029	050258
28	R 0019	Radio-controlled toy vehicles	V 0103	280185
16	R 0020	Radiograms (Paper for—)	P 0115	160233
09	R 0021	Radiological apparatus for industrial purposes	R 0036	090418
10	R 0022	Radiological apparatus for medical purposes	R 0037	100133
05	R 0023	Radiological contrast substances for medical purposes	C 1218	050096
09	R 0024	Radiology screens for industrial purposes	E 0132	090526
10	R 0025	Radiology screens for medical purposes	E 0133	100083
09	R 0026	Radios	R 0025	090270
09	R 0027	Radios (Vehicle—)	R 0026	090417
09	R 0028	Radiotelegraphy sets	P 0870	090408
09	R 0029	Radiotelephony sets	P 0871	090407
10	R 0030	Radiotherapy apparatus	R 0043	100134
05	R 0031	Radium for medical purposes	R 0044	050259
01	R 0032	Radium for scientific purposes	R 0045	010458
10	R 0033	Radium tubes for medical purposes	A 0483	100017
01	R 0034	Radon	R 0046	010457
22	R 0035	Raffia	R 0073	220067
21	R 0036	Rags for cleaning	T 0404	210077
07	R 0037	Rail-laying machines	R 0057	070322
07	R 0038	Railroad constructing machines	V 0292	070383
19	R 0039	Railroad ties, not of metal	T 0489	190176
06	R 0040	Railroad ties of metal	T 0488	060245
21	R 0041	Rails and rings for towels	B 0206	210334
20	R 0042	Rails (Curtain—)	R 0058	200171
06	R 0043	Rails of metal	R 0053	060129
12	R 0044	Railway cars (Bogies for—)	B 0515	120047
12	R 0045	Railway couplings	A 0815	120002
06	R 0046	Railway material of metal	V 0293	060089
06	R 0047	Railway points	C 0482	060013
19	R 0048	Railway sleepers, not of metal	T 0489	190176
06	R 0049	Railway sleepers of metal	T 0488	060245
06	R 0050	Railway switches	C 0482	060013
17	R 0051	Railway tracks (Insulators for—)	V 0291	170084
09	R 0052	Railway traffic safety appliances	T 0447	090254
20	R 0053	Railway waggons [wagons] (Loading gauge rods, not of metal, for—)	G 0004	200055
12	R 0054	Railway wheel tires [tyres] (Flanges of—)	B 0691	120033
29	R 0055	Raisins	R 0061	290027
07	R 0056	Rakes for raking machines	R 0088	070323
08	R 0057	Rakes [hand tools]	R 0089	080109
08	R 0058	Rakes (Sand trap—)	R 0087	080254
07	R 0059	Raking machines	R 0090	070324
24	R 0060	Ramie fabric	R 0066	240083
22	R 0061	Ramie fibre	R 0065	220066
08	R 0062	Rammers (Earth—) [hand tools]	D 0007	080083
08	R 0063	Rammers [hand tools]	P 0484	080172
07	R 0064	Rammers [machines]	B 0878	070263
08	R 0065	Rams [hand tools]	B 0304	080211
07	R 0066	Rams [machines]	B 0303	070404
09	R 0067	Range finders	T 0161	090195
31	R 0068	Rape cake for cattle	C 1063	310036
29	R 0069	Rape oil for food	C 1062	290022
04	R 0070	Rape oil for industrial purposes	N 0022	040065
01	R 0071	Rare earth metals (Salts from—)	S 0205	010162
01	R 0072	Rare earths	T 0216	010526
08	R 0073	Rasps [hand tools]	R 0071	080178
05	R 0074	Rat poison	M 0478	050216
21	R 0075	Rat traps	R 0095	210198
08	R 0076	Ratchets [hand tools]	C 0950	080065
20	R 0077	Rattan	R 0375	200133
28	R 0078	Rattles [playthings]	H 0074	280077
30	R 0079	Ravioli	R 0100	300117
31	R 0080	Raw barks	E 0117	310139
22	R 0081	Raw cotton	C 1345	220025
22	R 0082	Raw fibrous textile	T 0225	220010
22	R 0083	Raw linen [flax]	L 0272	220056
22	R 0084	Raw or treated wool	L 0024	220050
22	R 0085	Raw silk	S 0363	220008
24	R 0086	Rayon fabric	R 0103	240084
23	R 0087	Rayon thread and yarn	R 0102	230014
08	R 0088	Razor blades	L 0077	080148
08	R 0089	Razor cases	E 0536	080107
08	R 0090	Razor strops	C 1618	080082
03	R 0091	Razor strops (Pastes for—)	P 0211	030073
08	R 0092	Razors, electric or non-electric	R 0084	080179
11	R 0093	Reactors (Nuclear—)	R 0122	110253
09	R 0094	Readers (Bar code—)	L 0179	090581
09	R 0095	Readers [data processing equipment]	L 0182	090620
09	R 0096	Readers (Optical character—)	L 0183	090615
25	R 0097	Ready-made clothing	C 1168	250057
25	R 0098	Ready-made linings [parts of clothing]	D 0286	250068
01	R 0099	Reagent paper	P 0117	010259

Cl.	SERIAL No. (E)	INDICATION OF GOODS	SERIAL No. (F)	BASIC No.
05	R 0100	Reagents (Chemical —) for medical or veterinary purposes	R 0125	050364
01	R 0101	Reagents (Chemical —) other than for medical or veterinary purposes	R 0126	010178
08	R 0102	Reamer sockets	M 0087	080011
08	R 0103	Reamers	A 0311	080010
07	R 0104	Reapers	M 0442	070268
07	R 0105	Reapers and binders	M 0444	070269
07	R 0106	Reapers and threshers	M 0443	070270
12	R 0107	Rearview mirrors	R 0284	120173
09	R 0108	Receivers (Audio-- and video--)	R 0131	090289
09	R 0109	Receivers (Telephone —)	E 0121	090207
10	R 0110	Receptacles for applying medicines	R 0152	100115
01	R 0111	Recharging accumulators (Acidulated water for —)	E 0002	010251
09	R 0112	Record player needles (Apparatus for changing —)	A 0201	090503
09	R 0113	Record players	T 0424	090192
09	R 0114	Recording distance (Apparatus for —)	E 0332	090194
01	R 0115	Records (Renovating preparations for phonograph —)	D 0234	010246
02	R 0116	Red lead	M 0403	020095
09	R 0117	Reducers [electricity]	R 0161	090168
07	R 0118	Reducers (Pressure —) [parts of machines]	D 0167	070154
01	R 0119	Reducing agents for use in photography	A 0148	010027
05	R 0120	Reducing sexual activity (Preparations for —)	R 0162	050411
12	R 0121	Reduction gears for land vehicles	D 0071	120235
07	R 0122	Reduction gears other than for land vehicles	D 0070	070447
27	R 0123	Reed mats	R 0370	270009
15	R 0124	Reeds	A 0492	150003
19	R 0125	Reeds, for building	R 0371	190163
20	R 0126	Reeds [plaiting materials]	R 0369	200178
07	R 0127	Reeling apparatus, mechanical	D 0176	070155
28	R 0128	Reels for fishing	M 0536	280092
07	R 0129	Reels for weaving looms	B 0502	070054
07	R 0130	Reels, mechanical, for flexible hoses	E 0341	070376
20	R 0131	Reels, not of metal, non-mechanical, for flexible hoses	D 0179	200103
06	R 0132	Reels of metal, non-mechanical, for flexible hoses	D 0178	060357
20	R 0133	Reels of wood for yarn, silk, cord	B 0505	200025
07	R 0134	Reels [parts of machines]	B 0507	070408
11	R 0135	Refining towers for distillation	T 0438	110208
09	R 0136	Reflecting discs for wear, for the prevention of traffic accidents	D 0241	090003
11	R 0137	Reflectors (Lamp —)	R 0164	110183
11	R 0138	Reflectors (Vehicle —)	R 0165	110212
09	R 0139	Refractometers	R 0170	090250
09	R 0140	Refractors	R 0169	090424
19	R 0141	Refractory construction materials, not of metal	M 0220	190242
06	R 0142	Refractory construction materials of metal	M 0219	060435
17	R 0143	Refractory materials (Insulating —)	M 0222	170116
01	R 0144	Refrigerants	F 0437	010459
12	R 0145	Refrigerated vehicles	V 0077	120128
11	R 0146	Refrigerating apparatus and machines	F 0434	110155
11	R 0147	Refrigerating appliances and installations	R 0174	110213
21	R 0148	Refrigerating bottles	B 0759	210047
11	R 0149	Refrigerating cabinets	A 0746	110026
11	R 0150	Refrigerating chambers	C 0465	110156
11	R 0151	Refrigerating containers	R 0147	110157
11	R 0152	Refrigerating display cabinets [display cases]	V 0286	110330
01	R 0153	Refrigerating preparations	F 0437	010459
11	R 0154	Refrigerators	R 0173	110274
21	R 0155	Refuse bins	P 0905	210194
11	R 0156	Regenerators (Heat —)	R 0158	110069
09	R 0157	Registers (Cash —)	C 0102	090525
20	R 0158	Registration plates, not of metal	P 0605	200130
06	R 0159	Registration plates, of metal	P 0604	060400
11	R 0160	Regulating accessories for water or gas apparatus and pipes	R 0181	110216
11	R 0161	Regulating and safety accessories for gas apparatus	G 0107	110259
11	R 0162	Regulating and safety accessories for gas pipes	C 1146	110240
11	R 0163	Regulating and safety accessories for water apparatus	E 0001	110241
09	R 0164	Regulating apparatus, electric	C 1222	090150
09	R 0165	Regulators [dimmers] (Light —), electric	V 0036	090606
07	R 0166	Regulators [parts of machines]	R 0198	070254
28	R 0167	Rehabilitation apparatus (Body —)	C 1660	280044
10	R 0168	Rehabilitation apparatus (Body —) for medical purposes	R 0163	100221
11	R 0169	Reheaters (Air —)	R 0137	110012
19	R 0170	Reinforcing materials, not of metal, for building	A 0725	190191
17	R 0171	Reinforcing materials, not of metal, for pipes	A 0724	170089
06	R 0172	Reinforcing materials of metal for building	A 0723	060276
06	R 0173	Reinforcing materials, of metal, for concrete	A 0720	060033
06	R 0174	Reinforcing materials of metal for machine belts	A 0722	060277
06	R 0175	Reinforcing materials of metal for pipes	A 0721	060275
18	R 0176	Reins	R 0222	180072
26	R 0177	Reins for guiding children	B 0814	260025

Cl.	SERIAL No. (E)	INDICATION OF GOODS	SERIAL No. (F)	BASIC No.
09	R 0178	Relays, electric	R 0201	090222
09	R 0179	Releases (Shutter —) [photography]	D 0027	090174
30	R 0180	Relish [condiment]	R 0202	300167
05	R 0181	Remedies for foot perspiration	P 0440	050247
05	R 0182	Remedies for perspiration	T 0478	050285
09	R 0183	Remote control apparatus	T 0160	090470
09	R 0184	Remote control of industrial operations (Electric installations for the —)	C 1079	090130
09	R 0185	Remote control of railway points (Electro-dynamic apparatus for the —)	A 0198	090022
09	R 0186	Remote control of signals (Electro-dynamic apparatus for the —)	S 0313	090447
12	R 0187	Remote control vehicles, other than toys	V 0102	120257
03	R 0188	Removers (Floor wax —) [scouring preparations]	D 0018	030206
01	R 0189	Removing polish (Substances for —)	D 0104	010238
29	R 0190	Rennet	P 0970	290042
01	R 0191	Renovating chemicals (Leather- —)	C 1610	010175
01	R 0192	Renovating preparations for phonograph records	D 0234	010246
12	R 0193	Repair outfits for inner tubes	T 0546	120008
01	R 0194	Repairing tires [tyres] (Compositions for —)	P 0676	010465
05	R 0195	Repellents for dogs	R 0248	050076
05	R 0196	Repellents (Insect —)	I 0098	050178
16	R 0197	Reproductions (Graphic —)	R 0246	160167
20	R 0198	Reservoirs, not of metal nor of masonry	R 0255	200174
31	R 0199	Residue in a still after distillation	V 0247	310122
01	R 0200	Resins (Acrylic —), unprocessed	A 0090	010461
17	R 0201	Resins (Artificial —) [semi-finished products]	R 0268	170075
01	R 0202	Resins (Artificial —), unprocessed	R 0263	010462
01	R 0203	Resins (Epoxy —), unprocessed	E 0406	010274
02	R 0204	Resins (Gum —)	G 0278	020078
02	R 0205	Resins (Natural —), raw	R 0266	020061
17	R 0206	Resins (Synthetic —) [semi-finished products]	R 0268	170075
01	R 0207	Resins (Synthetic —), unprocessed	R 0267	010455
09	R 0208	Resistances, electric	R 0269	090427
10	R 0209	Respirators for artificial respiration	R 0270	100138
09	R 0210	Respirators for filtering air	R 0271	090430
09	R 0211	Respirators, other than for artificial respiration	M 0188	090113
09	R 0212	Respiratory masks, other than for artificial respiration	M 0188	090113
09	R 0213	Restraints (Safety —), other than for vehicle seats and sports equipment	H 0033	090621
10	R 0214	Resuscitation apparatus	R 0130	100135
09	R 0215	Resuscitation mannequins [teaching apparatus]	M 0117	090680
09	R 0216	Retorts	C 1303	090157
09	R 0217	Retorts' stands	D 0150	090158
12	R 0218	Reversing alarms for vehicles	A 0867	120026
09	R 0219	Revolution counters	C 1123	090485
13	R 0220	Revolvers	R 0301	130055
01	R 0221	Rhenium	R 0304	010463
09	R 0222	Rheostats	R 0305	090432
14	R 0223	Rhodium	R 0306	140083
31	R 0224	Rhubarb	R 0307	310116
05	R 0225	Rhubarb roots for pharmaceutical purposes	R 0308	050261
30	R 0226	Ribbon vermicelli	N 0104	300103
26	R 0227	Ribbons (Elastic —)	R 0435	260095
26	R 0228	Ribbons [haberdashery]	R 0442	260076
16	R 0229	Ribbons (Paper —)	R 0433	160244
26	R 0230	Ribbons (Prize —)	R 0444	260117
18	R 0231	Ribs (Umbrella or parasol —)	B 0106	180007
30	R 0232	Rice	R 0338	300119
33	R 0233	Rice alcohol	A 0296	330032
30	R 0234	Rice cakes	C 0108	300178
31	R 0235	Rice meal for forage	F 0015	310053
31	R 0236	Rice, unprocessed	R 0342	310144
30	R 0237	Rice-based snack food	E 0285	300196
09	R 0238	Riding helmets	B 0632	090690
18	R 0239	Riding saddles	S 0199	180081
13	R 0240	Rifle barrels	C 0184	130021
13	R 0241	Rifle cases	E 0530	130033
13	R 0242	Rifles	C 0223	130022
13	R 0243	Rifles (Hammers for —)	C 0749	130028
13	R 0244	Rifles (Sighting mirrors for —)	M 0409	130038
13	R 0245	Rifles (Trigger guards for —)	S 0470	130040
26	R 0246	Rimming (Cords for —), for clothing	C 1274	260096
12	R 0247	Rims for vehicle wheels	J 0012	120174
12	R 0248	Rims for wheels of bicycles, cycles	B 0392	120088
28	R 0249	Ring games	A 0557	280005
05	R 0250	Rings (Anti-rheumatism —)	A 0551	050016
07	R 0251	Rings (Ball —) for bearings	B 0027	070339
20	R 0252	Rings (Curtain —)	A 0554	200011
21	R 0253	Rings for birds	B 0035	210018
07	R 0254	Rings (Grease —) [parts of machines]	B 0030	070031
14	R 0255	Rings [jewellery, jewelry (Am.)]	B 0028	140107
06	R 0256	Rings of common metal for keys	A 0559	060221
06	R 0257	Rings of metal *	A 0558	060038
17	R 0258	Rings of rubber	A 0555	170004
07	R 0259	Rings (Piston —)	S 0177	070032
21	R 0260	Rings (Rails and —) for towels	B 0206	210334
17	R 0261	Rings (Stuffing —)	B 0032	170009
10	R 0262	Rings (Teething —)	A 0560	100018
17	R 0263	Rings (Water-tight —)	B 0032	170009
07	R 0264	Rinsing machines	R 0330	070063
08	R 0265	Riveters [hand tools]	R 0334	080182
08	R 0266	Riveting hammers [hand tools]	B 0761	080038
07	R 0267	Riveting machines	R 0333	070332

Cl.	SERIAL No. (E)	INDICATION OF GOODS	SERIAL No. (F)	BASIC No.
20	R 0268	Rivets, not of metal	R 0336	200216
06	R 0269	Rivets of metal	R 0335	060217
19	R 0270	Road coating materials	R 0288	190161
07	R 0271	Road making machines	R 0420	070340
19	R 0272	Road marking sheets and strips of synthetic material	M 0157	190122
19	R 0273	Road repair (Binding material for—)	L 0233	190110
07	R 0274	Road rollers	R 0397	070014
09	R 0275	Road signs, luminous or mechanical	B 0655	090516
07	R 0276	Road sweeping machines [self-propelled]	B 0103	070034
19	R 0277	Roads (Materials for making and coating—)	C 0619	190051
11	R 0278	Roasters	T 0408	110230
11	R 0279	Roasters (Coffee—)	B 0886	110062
11	R 0280	Roasting apparatus	G 0354	110172
11	R 0281	Roasting jacks	T 0423	110056
11	R 0282	Roasting spits	B 0836	110057
25	R 0283	Robes (Bath—)	B 0066	250127
07	R 0284	Robots [machines]	R 0354	070422
19	R 0285	Rock crystal	Q 0005	190073
01	R 0286	Rock salt	S 0187	010331
13	R 0287	Rocket launchers	L 0121	130043
19	R 0288	Rocket launching platforms, not of metal	R 0068	190108
06	R 0289	Rocket launching platforms of metal	R 0067	060159
13	R 0290	Rockets [projectiles]	F 0507	130068
13	R 0291	Rockets (Signal—)	F 0505	130035
28	R 0292	Rocking horses	C 0714	280014
07	R 0293	Rods (Connecting—) for machines, motors and engines	B 0400	070048
20	R 0294	Rods (Curtain—)	T 0524	200175
28	R 0295	Rods for fishing	C 0172	280035
09	R 0296	Rods for water diviners	B 0038	090072
06	R 0297	Rods of metal for brazing and welding	B 0043	060303
20	R 0298	Rods (Picture—) [frames]	L 0325	200226
20	R 0299	Rods (Stair—)	T 0525	200105
09	R 0300	Rods [surveying instruments]	J 0006	090281
07	R 0301	Roller bearings	R 0405	070338
06	R 0302	Roller blinds of steel	A 0076	060009
07	R 0303	Roller bridges	P 0788	070313
28	R 0304	Roller skates	P 0215	280098
20	R 0305	Rollers (Curtain—)	G 0021	200121
28	R 0306	Rollers for stationary exercise bicycles	R 0401	280059
16	R 0307	Rollers for typewriters	C 1709	160118
16	R 0308	Rollers (House painters'—)	R 0398	160215
07	R 0309	Rollers (Printing—) for machines	R 0400	070220
07	R 0310	Rolling mill cylinders	L 0086	070141
07	R 0311	Rolling mills	L 0085	070228
21	R 0312	Rolling pins, domestic	R 0396	210175
12	R 0313	Rolling stock for funicular railways	F 0503	120071
12	R 0314	Rolling stock for railways	C 0694	120072

Cl.	SERIAL No. (E)	INDICATION OF GOODS	SERIAL No. (F)	BASIC No.
30	R 0315	Rolls (Bread—)	P 0360	300110
15	R 0316	Rolls (Perforated music—)	B 0166	150079
19	R 0317	Roof coverings, not of metal	C 1481	190071
06	R 0318	Roof coverings of metal	C 1480	060350
19	R 0319	Roof flashing, not of metal	T 0362	190066
06	R 0320	Roof flashing of metal	T 0361	060098
19	R 0321	Roofing (Hips for—)	C 0744	190009
19	R 0322	Roofing, not of metal	T 0365	190173
19	R 0323	Roofing, not of metal, incorporating solar cells	T 0366	190240
06	R 0324	Roofing of metal	T 0364	060252
19	R 0325	Roofing shingles	B 0192	190021
19	R 0326	Roofing slates	A 0686	190007
28	R 0327	Rooms (Dolls'—)	C 0464	280104
31	R 0328	Roots for food	R 0011	310114
05	R 0329	Roots (Medicinal—)	R 0012	050260
22	R 0330	Rope ladders	E 0088	220023
06	R 0331	Rope thimbles of metal	C 1337	060058
22	R 0332	Ropes *	C 1261	220021
22	R 0333	Ropes (Car towing—)	V 0065	220103
22	R 0334	Ropes, not of metal	C 1257	220020
06	R 0335	Ropes of metal	C 1256	060341
16	R 0336	Rosaries	C 0503	160083
31	R 0337	Rose bushes	R 0373	310117
03	R 0338	Rose oil	R 0368	030119
21	R 0339	Roses for watering cans	P 0758	210183
26	R 0340	Rosettes [haberdashery]	R 0372	260085
28	R 0341	Rosin used by athletes	R 0262	280186
07	R 0342	Rotary printing presses	R 0374	070334
07	R 0343	Rotary steam presses, portable, for fabrics	C 0112	070480
11	R 0344	Rotisseries	R 0377	110220
03	R 0345	Rouge (Jewellers'—)	R 0392	030011
31	R 0346	Rough cork	L 0241	310078
28	R 0347	Roulette wheels	P 0634	280181
12	R 0348	Rowlocks	T 0370	120182
30	R 0349	Royal jelly*	G 0153	300168
05	R 0350	Royal jelly dietary supplements	G 0155	050425
05	R 0351	Royal jelly for pharmaceutical purposes	G 0154	050316
16	R 0352	Rubber erasers	G 0268	160139
05	R 0353	Rubber for dental purposes	C 0190	050066
17	R 0354	Rubber (Liquid—)	C 0197	170113
17	R 0355	Rubber material for recapping tires [tyres]	R 0133	170109
01	R 0356	Rubber preservatives	C 0198	010145
17	R 0357	Rubber, raw or semi-worked	G 0265	170017
17	R 0358	Rubber sleeves for protecting parts of machines	M 0092	170068
17	R 0359	Rubber solutions	D 0246	170114
17	R 0360	Rubber stoppers	B 0679	170018
17	R 0361	Rubber (Synthetic—)	C 0200	170020
23	R 0362	Rubber thread for textile use	F 0220	230018
19	R 0363	Rubble	M 0441	190237
01	R 0364	Rubidium	R 0445	010466
18	R 0365	Rucksacks	S 0023	180058
12	R 0366	Rudders	G 0291	120070
26	R 0367	Rug hooks	C 1567	260122
27	R 0368	Rugs*	T 0109	270011

Cl.	SERIAL No. (E)	INDICATION OF GOODS	SERIAL No. (F)	BASIC No.
24	R 0369	Rugs (Travelling —) [lap robes]	C 1482	240034
16	R 0370	Rulers (Drawing —)	R 0183	160234
09	R 0371	Rulers [measuring instruments]	R 0184	090284
16	R 0372	Rulers (Square —)	C 0278	160069
09	R 0373	Rules [measuring instruments]	M 0332	090349
33	R 0374	Rum	R 0309	330033
06	R 0375	Runners of metal for sliding doors	G 0020	060348
24	R 0376	Runners (Table —)	C 0697	240022
12	R 0377	Running boards (Vehicle —)	M 0142	120141
01	R 0378	Runs in stockings (Substances for preventing —)	D 0060	010105
30	R 0379	Rusks	B 0446	300015
03	R 0380	Rust removing preparations	D 0113	030170
14	R 0381	Ruthenium	R 0451	140085
31	R 0382	Rye	S 0179	310118

Cl.	SERIAL No. (E)	INDICATION OF GOODS	SERIAL No. (F)	BASIC No.
08	S 0001	Sabres	S 0012	080209
01	S 0002	Saccharin	S 0015	010114
09	S 0003	Saccharometers	S 0014	090435
03	S 0004	Sachets for perfuming linen	L 0299	030150
12	S 0005	Sack-barrows	D 0182	120050
22	S 0006	Sacks [bags] of textile, for packaging	S 0041	220069
18	S 0007	Saddle cloths for horses	H 0111	180097
12	S 0008	Saddle covers for bicycles or motorcycles	H 0110	120232
18	S 0009	Saddle trees	A 0678	180004
26	S 0010	Saddlers' needles	A 0200	260008
18	S 0011	Saddlery	S 0193	180082
12	S 0012	Saddles for bicycles, cycles or motorcycles	S 0198	120175
18	S 0013	Saddles (Pads for horse—)	D 0152	180117
06	S 0014	Safes [strong boxes]	C 1000	060034
11	S 0015	Safety accessories for water or gas apparatus and pipes	S 0601	110217
12	S 0016	Safety belts for vehicle seats	C 0356	120059
06	S 0017	Safety cashboxes	C 0335	060066
06	S 0018	Safety chains of metal	C 0432	060071
17	S 0019	Safety curtains (Asbestos—)	R 0319	170003
19	S 0020	Safety glass	V 0137	190192
11	S 0021	Safety lamps	L 0099	110182
09	S 0022	Safety nets	F 0198	090260
09	S 0023	Safety restraints, other than for vehicle seats and sports equipment	H 0033	090621
12	S 0024	Safety seats for children, for vehicles	S 0296	120112
09	S 0025	Safety tarpaulins	B 0002	090261
02	S 0026	Saffron [colorant]	S 0054	020099
30	S 0027	Saffron [seasoning]	S 0053	300120
03	S 0028	Safrol	S 0055	030151
30	S 0029	Sago	S 0056	300121
28	S 0030	Sailboards	P 0572	280126
28	S 0031	Sailboards (Harness for—)	H 0036	280167
28	S 0032	Sailboards (Masts for—)	M 0237	280169
22	S 0033	Sails	V 0294	220059
22	S 0034	Sails for ski sailing	V 0295	220105
33	S 0035	Sake	S 0058	330022
01	S 0036	Sal ammoniac	A 0454	010057
01	S 0037	Sal ammoniac spirits	E 0439	010058
21	S 0038	Salad bowls	S 0063	210203
30	S 0039	Salad (Dressings for—)	S 0099	300188
29	S 0040	Salads (Fruit—)	S 0060	290104
29	S 0041	Salads (Vegetable—)	S 0061	290102
01	S 0042	Salicylic acid	S 0065	010468
09	S 0043	Salinometers	P 0351	090389
29	S 0044	Salmon	S 0107	290107
01	S 0045	Salpetre	S 0067	010469
21	S 0046	Salt cellars	S 0066	210204
30	S 0047	Salt (Cooking—)	S 0184	300049
31	S 0048	Salt for cattle	S 0190	310014
30	S 0049	Salt for preserving foodstuffs	S 0189	300014
01	S 0050	Salt for preserving, other than for foodstuffs	S 0188	010003
01	S 0051	Salt, raw	S 0183	010476
21	S 0052	Salt shakers	S 0066	210204
29	S 0053	Salted fish	P 0727	290149
29	S 0054	Salted meats	S 0064	290098
01	S 0055	Saltpeter	S 0067	010469
01	S 0056	Salts [chemical preparations]	S 0217	010475
01	S 0057	Salts [fertilisers]	S 0210	010478
01	S 0058	Salts for coloring [colouring] metal	S 0213	010207
01	S 0059	Salts for galvanic cells	S 0214	010261
01	S 0060	Salts for industrial purposes	S 0201	010397
05	S 0061	Salts for medical purposes	S 0202	050137
05	S 0062	Salts for mineral water baths	B 0082	050042
01	S 0063	Salts from rare earth metals	S 0205	010162
05	S 0064	Salts (Mineral water—)	S 0208	050130
01	S 0065	Salts of alkaline metals	A 0285	010561
01	S 0066	Salts of precious metals for industrial purposes	S 0206	010391
01	S 0067	Samarium	S 0070	010470
19	S 0068	Sand, except foundry sand	S 0001	190166
01	S 0069	Sand (Foundry—)	S 0004	010467
19	S 0070	Sand (Silver—)	S 0002	190010
08	S 0071	Sand trap rakes	R 0087	080254
25	S 0072	Sandals	S 0071	250111
02	S 0073	Sandarac	S 0072	020100
03	S 0074	Sandcloth	T 0321	030160
31	S 0075	Sanded paper for pets [litter]	P 0118	310146
03	S 0076	Sandpaper	P 0094	030140
19	S 0077	Sandstone for building	G 0346	190100
19	S 0078	Sandstone tubes	G 0347	190101
30	S 0079	Sandwiches	S 0073	300106
11	S 0080	Sanitary apparatus and installations	S 0085	110221
24	S 0081	Sanitary flannel	F 0284	240051
05	S 0082	Sanitary knickers	C 1647	050200
05	S 0083	Sanitary napkins	S 0270	050234
05	S 0084	Sanitary pads	B 0167	050233
05	S 0085	Sanitary panties	C 1647	050200
05	S 0086	Sanitary tampons	T 0093	050232
05	S 0087	Sanitary towels	S 0270	050234
29	S 0088	Sardines	S 0090	290106
25	S 0089	Saris	S 0091	250154
25	S 0090	Sarongs	S 0092	250166
05	S 0091	Sarsaparilla for medical purposes	S 0068	050264
32	S 0092	Sarsaparilla [non-alcoholic beverage]	S 0069	320041
22	S 0093	Sash cords	C 1275	220088
06	S 0094	Sash fasteners of metal for windows	A 0756	060035
06	S 0095	Sash pulleys	G 0019	060075
25	S 0096	Sashes for wear	E 0084	250070
18	S 0097	Satchels (School—)	S 0266	180020
09	S 0098	Satellite navigational apparatus	N 0025	090674
09	S 0099	Satellites for scientific purposes	S 0094	090437
07	S 0100	Satinizing machines	S 0095	070345
01	S 0101	Sauce for preparing tobacco	S 0097	010471
30	S 0102	Sauce (Tomato—)	S 0098	300171
21	S 0103	Saucepan scourers of metal	R 0159	210066
21	S 0104	Saucepans (Earthenware—)	P 0696	210181

Cl.	SERIAL No. (E)	INDICATION OF GOODS	SERIAL No. (F)	BASIC No.
11	S 0105	Saucepans (Pressure cooking —), electric	C 0331	110029
21	S 0106	Saucers	S 0408	210212
16	S 0107	Saucers (Watercolor [watercolour] —) for artists	G 0257	160166
30	S 0108	Sauces [condiments]	S 0100	300122
29	S 0109	Sauerkraut	C 0798	290020
11	S 0110	Sauna bath installations	S 0108	110297
30	S 0111	Sausage binding materials	L 0235	300088
07	S 0112	Sausage machines	S 0104	070346
29	S 0113	Sausages	S 0101	290097
18	S 0114	Sausages (Gut for making —)	B 0778	180009
29	S 0115	Sausages in batter	S 0105	290153
07	S 0116	Saw benches [parts of machines]	C 0713	070035
08	S 0117	Saw blades [parts of hand tools]	L 0079	080151
07	S 0118	Saw blades [parts of machines]	L 0078	070226
08	S 0119	Saw holders	P 0857	080186
20	S 0120	Saw horses	C 0710	200263
22	S 0121	Sawdust	S 0146	220006
10	S 0122	Saws for surgical purposes	S 0141	100140
08	S 0123	Saws [hand tools]	S 0145	080055
07	S 0124	Saws [machines]	S 0144	070341
15	S 0125	Saxophones	S 0122	150089
08	S 0126	Scabbards (Sword —)	F 0401	080125
19	S 0127	Scaffolding, not of metal	E 0076	190078
06	S 0128	Scaffolding of metal	E 0075	060360
07	S 0129	Scale collectors (Machine boiler —)	C 1029	070110
28	S 0130	Scale model kits [toys]	M 0436	280198
28	S 0131	Scale model vehicles	M 0435	280091
03	S 0132	Scale removing preparations for household purposes	D 0160	030081
01	S 0133	Scale removing preparations, other than for household purposes	D 0161	010635
09	S 0134	Scales	B 0098	090074
09	S 0135	Scales (Lever —) [steelyards]	R 0358	090433
08	S 0136	Scaling knives	E 0073	080095
10	S 0137	Scalpels	S 0123	100030
01	S 0138	Scandium	S 0124	010473
09	S 0139	Scanners [data processing equipment]	E 0554	090622
19	S 0140	Scantlings [carpentry]	V 0323	190185
05	S 0141	Scapulars for surgical purposes	S 0127	050267
25	S 0142	Scarfs	F 0379	250069
25	S 0143	Scarves	F 0379	250069
28	S 0144	Scent lures for hunting or fishing	L 0215	280194
03	S 0145	Scented water	E 0048	030091
03	S 0146	Scented wood	B 0547	030030
22	S 0147	Schappe [raw silk waste]	S 0132	220016
19	S 0148	Schists	S 0133	190059
18	S 0149	School bags	S 0266	180020
20	S 0150	School furniture	M 0427	200094
18	S 0151	School satchels	S 0266	180020
16	S 0152	School supplies [stationery]	F 0393	160248
08	S 0153	Scissors *	C 0906	080040
07	S 0154	Scissors, electric	C 0908	070106
10	S 0155	Scissors for surgery	C 0909	100058
21	S 0156	Scoops [tableware]	P 0296	210102
28	S 0157	Scooters [toys]	T 0536	280115
12	S 0158	Scooters [vehicles]	T 0537	120258
21	S 0159	Scouring pads	T 0085	210168
03	S 0160	Scouring solutions	D 0017	030076
16	S 0161	Scrapbooks	A 0277	160013
16	S 0162	Scrapers [erasers] for offices	G 0331	160169
28	S 0163	Scrapers for skis	R 0015	280108
08	S 0164	Scrapers [hand tools]	G 0332	080235
10	S 0165	Scrapers (Tongue —)	C 1667	100070
08	S 0166	Scraping tools [hand tools]	R 0014	080237
28	S 0167	Scratch cards for playing lottery games	T 0259	280207
20	S 0168	Scratching posts for cats	A 0650	200264
28	S 0169	Screens (Camouflage —) [sports articles]	E 0125	280195
09	S 0170	Screens for firemen (Asbestos —)	P 0144	090689
09	S 0171	Screens for photoengraving	T 0457	090286
06	S 0172	Screens (Furnace —)	E 0127	060117
20	S 0173	Screens [furniture]	P 0145	200165
19	S 0174	Screens (Insect —) not of metal	M 0553	190239
06	S 0175	Screens of metal (Insect —)	M 0552	060428
09	S 0176	Screens [photography]	E 0130	090211
06	S 0177	Screw rings	T 0281	060143
08	S 0178	Screw stocks [hand tools]	F 0203	080066
08	S 0179	Screw taps (Extension pieces for braces for —)	A 0357	080012
08	S 0180	Screwdrivers	T 0433	080195
12	S 0181	Screw-propellers	P 0991	120166
12	S 0182	Screw-propellers for boats	B 0245	120040
20	S 0183	Screws, not of metal	V 0258	200215
06	S 0184	Screws of metal	V 0256	060118
12	S 0185	Screws [propellers] for ships	H 0054	120151
09	S 0186	Screw-tapping gauges	T 0127	090466
08	S 0187	Screw-thread cutters [hand tools]	F 0203	080066
11	S 0188	Scrubbers [parts of gas installations]	L 0168	110160
21	S 0189	Scrubbing brushes	F 0451	210137
12	S 0190	Sculls	G 0258	120131
20	S 0191	Scythe handles, not of metal	M 0081	200111
06	S 0192	Scythe handles of metal	M 0080	060378
08	S 0193	Scythe rings	F 0031	080114
08	S 0194	Scythe stones	P 0457	080115
08	S 0195	Scythes	F 0030	080113
30	S 0196	Sea water for cooking	E 0025	300169
01	S 0197	Sea water for industrial purposes	E 0022	010636
05	S 0198	Sea water for medicinal bathing	E 0024	050044
22	S 0199	Sea wrack	A 0322	220074
31	S 0200	Sea-cucumbers, live	H 0079	310145
29	S 0201	Sea-cucumbers, not live	H 0078	290150
28	S 0202	Seal skins [coverings for skis]	P 0246	280100
17	S 0203	Sealant compounds for joints	M 0207	170069
20	S 0204	Sealing caps, not of metal	C 0213	200214
06	S 0205	Sealing caps of metal	C 0212	060297

Cl.	SERIAL No. (E)	INDICATION OF GOODS	SERIAL No. (F)	BASIC No.
06	S 0206	Sealing caps of metal for bottles	C 0214	060299
16	S 0207	Sealing compounds for stationery purposes	C 0043	160057
07	S 0208	Sealing joints [parts of engines]	J 0049	070118
07	S 0209	Sealing machines for industrial purposes	S 0130	070347
16	S 0210	Sealing machines for offices	C 0042	160056
07	S 0211	Sealing plastics (Electrical apparatus for —) [packaging]	S 0422	070541
16	S 0212	Sealing stamps	T 0267	160053
16	S 0213	Sealing wafers	P 0028	160206
16	S 0214	Sealing wax	C 0877	160055
17	S 0215	Seals	J 0046	170043
06	S 0216	Seals (Lead —)	P 0650	060146
16	S 0217	Seals [stamps]	S 0128	160149
12	S 0218	Seaplanes	H 0192	120134
11	S 0219	Searchlights	T 0403	110202
30	S 0220	Seasonings	A 0798	300012
12	S 0221	Seat covers for vehicles	H 0118	120132
20	S 0222	Seats	C 0444	200050
20	S 0223	Seats of metal	S 0302	200182
12	S 0224	Seats (Safety —) for children, for vehicles	S 0296	120112
11	S 0225	Seats (Toilet —)	S 0297	110236
12	S 0226	Seats (Vehicle —)	S 0298	120177
22	S 0227	Seaweed for stuffing	A 0322	220074
01	S 0228	Seaweeds [fertilizers]	A 0324	010043
01	S 0229	Sebacic acid	S 0155	010474
08	S 0230	Secateurs	S 0156	080097
20	S 0231	Sections of wood for beehives	C 0066	200040
12	S 0232	Security harness for vehicle seats	H 0034	120244
05	S 0233	Sedatives	C 0134	050268
05	S 0234	Sediment (Medicinal —) [mud]	B 0701	050058
01	S 0235	Seed preserving substances	S 0225	010480
31	S 0236	Seedlings	P 0595	310072
31	S 0237	Seeds (Plant —)	G 0298	310068
29	S 0238	Seeds (Processed —)	G 0297	290171
29	S 0239	Seeds (Processed sunflower —)	G 0295	290166
12	S 0240	Segments (Brake —) for vehicles	S 0176	120236
01	S 0241	Selenium	S 0191	010479
16	S 0242	Self-adhesive tapes for stationery or household purposes	A 0829	160274
17	S 0243	Self-adhesive tapes, other than stationery and not for medical or household purposes	A 0828	170092
07	S 0244	Self-oiling bearings	A 0840	070027
07	S 0245	Self-regulating fuel pumps	P 0773	070543
01	S 0246	Self-toning paper [photography]	P 0083	010090
32	S 0247	Seltzer water	E 0026	320017
05	S 0248	Semen for artificial insemination	S 0491	050177
09	S 0249	Semi-conductors	S 0226	090539
14	S 0250	Semi-precious stones	P 0465	140073
30	S 0251	Semolina	S 0228	300124
01	S 0252	Sensitized cloth for photography	T 0327	010212
01	S 0253	Sensitized films, unexposed	F 0213	010581
01	S 0254	Sensitized paper	P 0119	010418
01	S 0255	Sensitized photographic plates	P 0611	010269
01	S 0256	Sensitized plates for offset printing	P 0613	010406
01	S 0257	Sensitizers (Photographic —)	S 0230	010436
01	S 0258	Separating and unsticking [ungluing] preparations	D 0031	010232
07	S 0259	Separators	S 0233	070142
07	S 0260	Separators (Steam/oil —)	D 0121	070152
05	S 0261	Serotherapeutic medicines	S 0238	050270
05	S 0262	Serums	S 0257	050209
21	S 0263	Services [dishes]	S 0258	210207
24	S 0264	Serviettes of textile	S 0262	240076
31	S 0265	Sesame	S 0279	310120
29	S 0266	Sesame oil	S 0280	290060
20	S 0267	Settees	C 0161	200184
07	S 0268	Sewage pulverizers	P 1040	070162
11	S 0269	Sewage (Purification installations for —)	P 1056	110135
26	S 0270	Sewing boxes	B 0600	260049
07	S 0271	Sewing machines	C 1367	070440
26	S 0272	Sewing needles	A 0189	260004
26	S 0273	Sewing thimbles	D 0114	260050
23	S 0274	Sewing thread and yarn	C 1366	230009
09	S 0275	Sextants	S 0285	090444
20	S 0276	Shades (Indoor window —) [furniture]	S 0545	200272
07	S 0277	Shaft couplings [machines]	A 0652	070001
07	S 0278	Shafts (Bearings for transmission —)	P 0044	070290
07	S 0279	Shafts (Loom —)	L 0074	070224
21	S 0280	Shakers	M 0261	210082
03	S 0281	Shampoos	S 0286	030134
03	S 0282	Shampoos for pets	S 0287	030196
24	S 0283	Shams (Pillow —)	H 0113	240112
07	S 0284	Shares (Plough —)	S 0359	070100
08	S 0285	Sharpening instruments	A 0210	080092
07	S 0286	Sharpening machines	A 0160	070387
03	S 0287	Sharpening preparations	A 0217	030003
08	S 0288	Sharpening steels	F 0511	080037
08	S 0289	Sharpening stones	P 0454	080003
08	S 0290	Sharpening wheels [hand tools]	M 0356	080201
07	S 0291	Sharpening wheels [parts of machines]	M 0357	070389
21	S 0292	Shaving brush stands	P 0800	210241
21	S 0293	Shaving brushes	B 0462	210240
08	S 0294	Shaving cases	N 0035	080166
03	S 0295	Shaving preparations	R 0081	030148
03	S 0296	Shaving soap	B 0185	030017
03	S 0297	Shaving stones [astringents]	P 0455	030005
22	S 0298	Shavings (Wood —)	C 1236	220004
25	S 0299	Shawls	C 0446	250032
06	S 0300	Sheaf binders of metal	G 0175	060396
07	S 0301	Sheaf-binding machines	L 0250	070052
22	S 0302	Sheaf-binding yarns	G 0176	220042
08	S 0303	Shear blades	L 0072	080061
08	S 0304	Shearers [hand instruments]	T 0387	080223
07	S 0305	Shearing machines for animals	T 0390	070431

Cl.	SERIAL No. (E)	INDICATION OF GOODS	SERIAL No. (F)	BASIC No.
08	S 0306	Shears	C 0903	080060
07	S 0307	Shears, electric	C 0904	070105
09	S 0308	Sheaths for electric cables	G 0014	090098
15	S 0309	Sheet music (Turning apparatus for—)	M 0577	150053
19	S 0310	Sheet piles, not of metal	P 0056	190136
06	S 0311	Sheet piles of metal	P 0055	060188
06	S 0312	Sheets and plates of metal	T 0368	060376
17	S 0313	Sheets (Asbestos—)	D 0308	170035
10	S 0314	Sheets (Incontinence—)	D 0309	100014
16	S 0315	Sheets of reclaimed cellulose for wrapping	C 0381	160288
17	S 0316	Sheets of reclaimed cellulose, other than for packing	C 0380	170053
24	S 0317	Sheets [textile]	D 0306	240040
31	S 0318	Shell (Cocoanut—)	C 1242	310033
02	S 0319	Shellac	G 0277	020077
31	S 0320	Shellfish, live	C 1246	310041
29	S 0321	Shellfish, not live	C 1245	290082
20	S 0322	Shells	C 1247	200233
13	S 0323	Shells [projectiles]	O 0007	130048
20	S 0324	Shelves for filing-cabinets [furniture]	C 0928	200062
20	S 0325	Shelves for storage	T 0047	200191
20	S 0326	Shelves for typewriters	T 0048	200095
15	S 0327	Sheng [Chinese musical wind instruments]	S 0290	150084
32	S 0328	Sherbets [beverages]	S 0406	320029
30	S 0329	Sherbets [ices]	S 0407	300125
25	S 0330	Shields (Dress—)	D 0154	250017
16	S 0331	Shields (Erasing—)	G 0002	160138
16	S 0332	Shields [paper seals]	E 0161	160137
06	S 0333	Shims	C 0111	060063
28	S 0334	Shin guards [sports articles]	P 1013	280046
03	S 0335	Shining preparations [polish]	B 0818	030048
03	S 0336	Shiny (Preparations to make the leaves of plants—)	P 0591	030212
12	S 0337	Ships	N 0028	120150
12	S 0338	Ships' hulls	C 1240	120035
12	S 0339	Ships' steering gears	B 0239	120037
12	S 0340	Ships (Timbers [frames] for—)	C 1402	120082
25	S 0341	Shirt fronts	P 0626	250043
25	S 0342	Shirt yokes	E 0267	250072
25	S 0343	Shirts	C 0698	250042
07	S 0344	Shock absorber plungers [parts of machines]	A 0470	070395
12	S 0345	Shock absorbers for automobiles	A 0844	120210
12	S 0346	Shock absorbers (Suspension—) for vehicles	A 0469	120010
17	S 0347	Shock absorbing buffers of rubber	T 0087	170021
12	S 0348	Shock absorbing springs for vehicles	R 0276	120011
21	S 0349	Shoe brushes	C 0630	210071
26	S 0350	Shoe buckles	B 0686	260088
03	S 0351	Shoe cream	C 1540	030039
02	S 0352	Shoe dyes	C 0658	020041
26	S 0353	Shoe eyelets	O 0013	260036
26	S 0354	Shoe fasteners	A 0178	260001

Cl.	SERIAL No. (E)	INDICATION OF GOODS	SERIAL No. (F)	BASIC No.
26	S 0355	Shoe hooks	C 1574	260033
21	S 0356	Shoe horns	C 0620	210213
26	S 0357	Shoe laces	L 0008	260034
07	S 0358	Shoe lasts [parts of machines]	F 0363	070352
26	S 0359	Shoe ornaments, not of precious metal	P 0176	260035
14	S 0360	Shoe ornaments of precious metal	P 0175	140119
03	S 0361	Shoe polish	C 1540	030039
07	S 0362	Shoe polishers, electric	C 0901	070501
21	S 0363	Shoe trees [stretchers]	C 0646	210120
03	S 0364	Shoe wax	C 0870	030046
26	S 0365	Shoemakers' needles	A 0199	260003
03	S 0366	Shoemakers' wax	C 0887	030049
25	S 0367	Shoes *	S 0447	250130
12	S 0368	Shoes (Brake—) for vehicles	S 0011	120216
09	S 0369	Shoes for protection against accidents, irradiation and fire	C 0640	090645
04	S 0370	Shoes (Grease for—)	G 0317	040026
10	S 0371	Shoes (Orthopaedic [orthopedic]—)	C 0653	100051
18	S 0372	Shopping bags	S 0027	180071
12	S 0373	Shopping trolleys [carts (Am.)]	C 0535	120255
22	S 0374	Shorn wool	T 0402	220073
25	S 0375	Short-sleeve shirts	C 0701	250044
13	S 0376	Shot for hunting (Lead—)	G 0345	130041
18	S 0377	Shoulder belts [straps] of leather	B 0176	180096
26	S 0378	Shoulder pads for clothing	E 0381	260118
20	S 0379	Shoulder poles [yokes]	P 0030	200265
13	S 0380	Shoulder straps for weapons	B 0177	130063
25	S 0381	Shoulder wraps	C 1059	250020
08	S 0382	Shovels [hand tools]	P 0298	080110
07	S 0383	Shovels, mechanical	P 0297	070070
20	S 0384	Showcases [furniture]	V 0287	200200
25	S 0385	Shower caps	B 0645	250158
11	S 0386	Shower cubicles [enclosures (Am.)]	C 0005	110298
24	S 0387	Shower curtains of textile or plastic	R 0317	240119
11	S 0388	Showers	D 0290	110121
07	S 0389	Shredders [machines] for industrial use	D 0026	070419
29	S 0390	Shrimps, not live	C 1551	290138
24	S 0391	Shrouds	L 0285	240041
31	S 0392	Shrubs	A 0667	310011
09	S 0393	Shutter releases [photography]	D 0027	090174
19	S 0394	Shuttering, not of metal, for concrete	C 0993	190198
06	S 0395	Shuttering of metal for concrete	C 0992	060292
19	S 0396	Shutters, not of metal	V 0319	190133
06	S 0397	Shutters of metal	V 0318	060197
09	S 0398	Shutters [photography]	O 0006	090181
28	S 0399	Shuttlecocks	V 0313	280116
26	S 0400	Shuttles for making fishing nets	N 0024	260058
07	S 0401	Shuttles [parts of machines]	N 0023	070280
05	S 0402	Siccatives [drying agents] for medical purposes	S 0291	050373
02	S 0403	Siccatives [drying agents] for paints	S 0292	020068

Cl.	SERIAL No. (E)	INDICATION OF GOODS	SERIAL No. (F)	BASIC No.
08	S 0404	Sickles	F 0026	080189
13	S 0405	Side arms [firearms]	A 0736	130077
08	S 0406	Side arms, other than firearms	A 0735	080022
12	S 0407	Side cars	S 0293	120176
20	S 0408	Sideboards	B 0894	200034
07	S 0409	Sidewalks [moving pavements]	T 0122	070518
02	S 0410	Sienna earth	T 0212	020029
21	S 0411	Sieves [household utensils]	T 0082	210097
07	S 0412	Sieves [machines or parts of machines]	T 0081	070187
07	S 0413	Sifters	C 1555	070134
21	S 0414	Sifters [household utensils]	C 1554	210061
07	S 0415	Sifting installations	C 1553	070133
07	S 0416	Sifting machines	E 0398	070454
13	S 0417	Sighting mirrors for guns and rifles	M 0409	130038
09	S 0418	Sighting telescopes for firearms	L 0390	090509
13	S 0419	Sights, other than telescopic sights, for firearms	V 0263	130058
13	S 0420	Sights, other than telescopic sights, for guns [artillery]	C 0185	130065
09	S 0421	Signal bells	C 0954	090127
09	S 0422	Signal lanterns	L 0131	090322
13	S 0423	Signal rockets	F 0505	130035
09	S 0424	Signalling buoys	B 0699	090518
09	S 0425	Signalling panels, luminous or mechanical	P 0062	090380
19	S 0426	Signalling panels, non-luminous and non-mechanical, not of metal	P 0064	190137
06	S 0427	Signalling panels, non-luminous and non-mechanical, of metal	P 0063	060200
09	S 0428	Signalling whistles	S 0304	090445
12	S 0429	Signals (Direction—) for vehicles	I 0066	120228
09	S 0430	Signals, luminous or mechanical	S 0309	090434
09	S 0431	Signals (Transmitters of electronic—)	E 0261	090227
06	S 0432	Signboards of metal	E 0348	060370
16	S 0433	Signboards of paper or cardboard	E 0349	160327
21	S 0434	Signboards of porcelain or glass	E 0350	210279
20	S 0435	Signboards of wood or plastics	E 0347	200253
09	S 0436	Signs, luminous	E 0351	090329
19	S 0437	Signs, non-luminous and non-mechanical, not of metal, for roads	B 0657	190164
06	S 0438	Signs, non-luminous and non-mechanical, of metal	S 0310	060235
06	S 0439	Signs, non-luminous and non-mechanical, of metal, for roads	B 0656	060228
19	S 0440	Signs, not of metal (Non-luminous and non-mechanical—)	S 0311	190165
07	S 0441	Silencers for motors and engines	S 0321	070519
21	S 0442	Silica (Fused—) [semi-worked product], other than for building	S 0323	210308
19	S 0443	Silica [quartz]	S 0324	190168
01	S 0444	Silicates	S 0322	010481
01	S 0445	Silicon	S 0327	010483
03	S 0446	Silicon carbide [abrasive]	S 0328	030036
06	S 0447	Silicon iron	F 0087	060137
01	S 0448	Silicones	S 0329	010484
24	S 0449	Silk [cloth]	S 0367	240088
24	S 0450	Silk fabrics for printing patterns	P 0222	240060
22	S 0451	Silk flock	F 0292	220040
22	S 0452	Silk (Raw—)	S 0363	220008
23	S 0453	Silk thread and yarn	S 0365	230007
22	S 0454	Silk waste	S 0132	220016
29	S 0455	Silkworm chrysalis, for human consumption	C 0818	290151
31	S 0456	Silkworm eggs	O 0023	310090
31	S 0457	Silkworms	V 0181	310119
19	S 0458	Sills, not of metal	S 0284	190162
06	S 0459	Sills of metal	S 0283	060233
19	S 0460	Silos, not of metal	S 0331	190169
06	S 0461	Silos of metal	S 0330	060239
26	S 0462	Silver embroidery	A 0690	260093
02	S 0463	Silver emulsions [pigments]	E 0278	020015
02	S 0464	Silver foil [leaf]	A 0694	020013
01	S 0465	Silver nitrate	A 0698	010569
16	S 0466	Silver paper	P 0090	160025
02	S 0467	Silver paste	A 0701	020014
08	S 0468	Silver plate [knives, forks and spoons]	A 0706	080203
06	S 0469	Silver plated tin alloy	A 0703	060032
01	S 0470	Silver salt solutions for silvering	S 0204	010081
19	S 0471	Silver sand	S 0002	190010
06	S 0472	Silver solder	S 0431	060030
14	S 0473	Silver thread	A 0696	140009
14	S 0474	Silver, unwrought or beaten	A 0691	140163
20	S 0475	Silvered glass [mirrors]	V 0136	200013
02	S 0476	Silvering powders	A 0705	020016
09	S 0477	Simulators for the steering and control of vehicles	S 0333	090448
25	S 0478	Singlets	M 0034	250094
11	S 0479	Sinks	E 0548	110299
20	S 0480	Sinks (Removable mats or covers for—)	R 0289	200099
01	S 0481	Sintering (Ceramic compositions for—) [granules and powders]	C 1107	010646
21	S 0482	Siphons for carbonated water	S 0335	210118
09	S 0483	Sirens	S 0336	090449
22	S 0484	Sisal	S 0340	220077
11	S 0485	Sitz-baths (Bath tubs for—)	B 0056	110035
01	S 0486	Size for finishing and priming	C 1032	010202
07	S 0487	Sizing machines	A 0259	070013
01	S 0488	Sizing preparations	E 0293	010270
28	S 0489	Skateboards	P 0571	280148
28	S 0490	Skates (Ice—)	P 0214	280099
28	S 0491	Skates (In-line roller—)	P 0216	280182
28	S 0492	Skates (Roller—)	P 0215	280098

Cl.	SERIAL No. (E)	INDICATION OF GOODS	SERIAL No. (F)	BASIC No.
18	S 0493	Skates (Straps for—)	C 1426	180035
28	S 0494	Skating boots with skates attached	B 0666	280028
19	S 0495	Skating rinks [structures, not of metal]	P 0213	190139
06	S 0496	Skating rinks [structures of metal]	P 0212	060203
28	S 0497	Ski bindings	F 0278	280066
25	S 0498	Ski boots	C 0641	250145
12	S 0499	Ski carriers for cars	P 0861	120161
25	S 0500	Ski gloves	G 0054	250167
12	S 0501	Ski lifts	R 0217	120170
27	S 0502	Ski slopes (Mats of woven rope for—)	N 0017	270017
21	S 0503	Skin (Abrasive sponges for scrubbing the—)	E 0399	210331
03	S 0504	Skin care (Cosmetic preparations for—)	P 0238	030142
05	S 0505	Skin care (Pharmaceutical preparations for—)	P 0239	050239
18	S 0506	Skin (Goldbeaters'—)	B 0273	180008
03	S 0507	Skin whitening creams	P 0235	030023
02	S 0508	Skin-dressing (Ink for—)	E 0301	020069
08	S 0509	Skinning animals (Instruments and tools for—)	D 0106	080019
08	S 0510	Skinning butcher's animals (Apparatus and instruments for—)	D 0105	080018
18	S 0511	Skins (Animal—)	P 0244	180002
09	S 0512	Skins (Apparatus for measuring the thickness of—)	P 0241	090386
18	S 0513	Skins (Cattle—)	B 0672	180088
01	S 0514	Skins (Currying preparations for—)	P 0248	010216
01	S 0515	Skins (Dressing, except oils, for—)	C 1173	010208
15	S 0516	Skins for drums	P 0247	150059
21	S 0517	Skins of chamois for cleaning	P 0245	210263
18	S 0518	Skins of chamois, other than for cleaning purposes	P 0242	180094
26	S 0519	Skirt flounces	V 0311	260084
25	S 0520	Skirts	J 0065	250090
28	S 0521	Skis	S 0344	280110
28	S 0522	Skis and surfboards (Bags especially designed for—)	H 0121	280166
28	S 0523	Skis (Edges of—)	A 0687	280009
28	S 0524	Skis (Sole coverings for—)	R 0298	280109
28	S 0525	Skis (Wax for—)	F 0022	280063
28	S 0526	Skittles	Q 0017	280022
28	S 0527	Skittles [games]	Q 0018	280106
25	S 0528	Skorts	J 0066	250164
25	S 0529	Skull caps	C 0139	250024
19	S 0530	Slabs (Cement—)	C 0856	190057
19	S 0531	Slabs (Lighting—)	P 0229	190115
19	S 0532	Slabs, not of metal	D 0003	190219
19	S 0533	Slag [building material]	S 0152	190104
01	S 0534	Slag [fertilisers]	S 0151	010428
19	S 0535	Slag stone	P 0463	190143
17	S 0536	Slag wool [insulator]	L 0028	170061
19	S 0537	Slate	A 0680	190006
17	S 0538	Slate asbestos	A 0682	170005
16	S 0539	Slate pencils	C 1517	160024
19	S 0540	Slate powder	A 0683	190008
20	S 0541	Slatted indoor blinds	S 0544	200136
08	S 0542	Slaughtering butchers' animals (Apparatus and instruments for—)	A 0003	080001
08	S 0543	Sledgehammers	M 0195	080157
25	S 0544	Sleep masks	M 0187	250163
19	S 0545	Sleepers, not of metal (Railway—)	T 0489	190176
06	S 0546	Sleepers of metal (Railway—)	T 0488	060245
20	S 0547	Sleeping bags for camping	S 0032	200234
24	S 0548	Sleeping bags [sheeting]	S 0031	240100
12	S 0549	Sleeping berths for vehicles	C 1362	120081
12	S 0550	Sleeping cars	W 0008	120136
09	S 0551	Sleeves (Junction—) for electric cables	M 0088	090626
06	S 0552	Sleeves [metal hardware]	M 0094	060092
17	S 0553	Sleeves of rubber for protecting parts of machines	M 0092	170068
28	S 0554	Sleighs [sports articles]	T 0449	280113
12	S 0555	Sleighs [vehicles]	T 0450	120186
08	S 0556	Slicers (Cheese—), non-electric	T 0463	080248
08	S 0557	Slicers (Egg—), non-electric	T 0464	080251
09	S 0558	Slide calipers	P 0434	090104
26	S 0559	Slide fasteners [zippers]	F 0071	260053
26	S 0560	Slide locks for bags	S 0043	260087
09	S 0561	Slide projectors	D 0198	090186
07	S 0562	Slide rests [parts of machines]	S 0591	070365
07	S 0563	Sliders for knitting machines	C 0542	070097
09	S 0564	Slide-rules	R 0182	090102
07	S 0565	Slides for knitting machines	C 0542	070097
26	S 0566	Slides [hair grips]	P 0501	260015
09	S 0567	Slides [photography]	D 0196	090185
28	S 0568	Slides [playthings]	T 0315	280149
05	S 0569	Slimming pills	A 0402	050416
03	S 0570	Slimming purposes (Cosmetic preparations for—)	C 1334	030177
05	S 0571	Slimming purposes (Medical preparations for—)	A 0450	050317
18	S 0572	Sling bags for carrying infants	S 0022	180044
28	S 0573	Sling shots [sports articles]	L 0120	280188
18	S 0574	Slings for carrying infants	E 0086	180122
22	S 0575	Slings, not of metal, for handling loads	E 0218	220083
06	S 0576	Slings of metal for handling loads	E 0217	060306
10	S 0577	Slings [supporting bandages]	E 0085	100217
25	S 0578	Slippers	P 0072	250101
25	S 0579	Slips [undergarments]	C 1066	250146
09	S 0580	Slope indicators	I 0068	090299
28	S 0581	Slot machines [gaming machines]	M 0009	280203
05	S 0582	Slug exterminating preparations	L 0261	050195
09	S 0583	Smart cards [integrated circuit cards]	C 0288	090640
05	S 0584	Smelling salts	S 0203	050224
25	S 0585	Smocks	B 0498	250010

Cl.	SERIAL No. (E)	INDICATION OF GOODS	SERIAL No. (F)	BASIC No.
21	S 0586	Smoke absorbers for household purposes	F 0492	210139
09	S 0587	Smoke detectors	D 0164	090623
34	S 0588	Smokers (Lighters for —)	B 0824	340007
05	S 0589	Smoking herbs for medical purposes	H 0063	050336
01	S 0590	Smoking meat (Chemical preparations for —)	V 0228	010317
32	S 0591	Smoothies	B 0575	320050
03	S 0592	Smoothing preparations [starching]	L 0318	030127
07	S 0593	Smoothing presses	L 0319	070240
03	S 0594	Smoothing stones	P 0447	030002
30	S 0595	Snack food (Cereal-based —)	E 0283	300195
29	S 0596	Snack food (Fruit-based —)	E 0284	290160
30	S 0597	Snack food (Rice-based —)	E 0285	300196
29	S 0598	Snail eggs for consumption	O 0024	290139
26	S 0599	Snap fasteners	B 0770	260022
22	S 0600	Snares [nets]	L 0010	220048
28	S 0601	Snow for Christmas trees (Artificial —)	N 0041	280096
28	S 0602	Snow globes	B 0723	280175
07	S 0603	Snow ploughs	C 0559	070502
28	S 0604	Snowboards	S 0356	280197
12	S 0605	Snowmobiles	A 0858	120256
28	S 0606	Snowshoes	R 0076	280187
34	S 0607	Snuff	P 0973	340033
34	S 0608	Snuff boxes	T 0009	340034
03	S 0609	Soaking laundry (Preparations for —)	L 0296	030098
03	S 0610	Soap	S 0115	030012
03	S 0611	Soap (Antiperspirant —)	S 0116	030163
21	S 0612	Soap boxes	B 0606	210037
28	S 0613	Soap bubbles [toys]	B 0900	280162
03	S 0614	Soap (Cakes of —)	S 0114	030152
03	S 0615	Soap (Deodorant —)	S 0119	030149
03	S 0616	Soap (Disinfectant —)	S 0118	030080
21	S 0617	Soap dispensers	D 0260	210117
03	S 0618	Soap for brightening textile	S 0117	030013
03	S 0619	Soap for foot perspiration	P 0441	030143
21	S 0620	Soap holders	P 0856	210191
01	S 0621	Soap [metallic] for industrial purposes	S 0121	010472
25	S 0622	Sock suspenders	F 0279	250037
11	S 0623	Sockets for electric lights	D 0293	110122
09	S 0624	Sockets, plugs and other contacts [electric connections]	P 0974	090166
25	S 0625	Socks	C 0621	250036
09	S 0626	Socks, electrically heated	C 0622	090121
31	S 0627	Sod	G 0143	310063
01	S 0628	Soda ash	S 0415	010100
03	S 0629	Soda (Bleaching —)	S 0417	030027
01	S 0630	Soda (Calcined —)	S 0413	010488
03	S 0631	Soda lye	S 0416	030153
32	S 0632	Soda water	S 0360	320028
01	S 0633	Sodium	S 0361	010485
01	S 0634	Sodium salts [chemical preparations]	S 0419	010491
05	S 0635	Sodium salts for medical purposes	S 0418	050274
20	S 0636	Sofas	S 0362	200183
03	S 0637	Softeners (Fabric —) for laundry use	A 0801	030193
11	S 0638	Softening apparatus (Water —)	A 0120	110243
01	S 0639	Softening preparations (Water —)	A 0118	010023
09	S 0640	Software (Computer —), recorded	L 0363	090591
01	S 0641	Soil conditioning preparations	A 0426	010053
05	S 0642	Soil-sterilising preparations	S 0383	050272
09	S 0643	Solar batteries	P 0481	090557
11	S 0644	Solar furnaces	F 0412	110270
11	S 0645	Solar thermal collectors [heating]	C 0219	110269
06	S 0646	Solder (Gold —)	S 0432	060417
06	S 0647	Solder (Silver —)	S 0431	060030
09	S 0648	Solderers' helmets	S 0430	090114
07	S 0649	Soldering apparatus, electric	S 0421	070528
07	S 0650	Soldering apparatus, gas-operated	S 0420	070503
07	S 0651	Soldering blow pipes, gas-operated	C 0454	070504
01	S 0652	Soldering chemicals	S 0412	010487
01	S 0653	Soldering fluxes	F 0334	010584
07	S 0654	Soldering irons, electric	F 0109	070529
07	S 0655	Soldering irons, gas-operated	F 0108	070505
07	S 0656	Soldering lamps	L 0093	070532
17	S 0657	Soldering threads of plastic	S 0426	170047
06	S 0658	Soldering wire of metal	S 0427	060242
18	S 0659	Soldiers' equipment (Straps for —)	B 0897	180012
28	S 0660	Sole coverings for skis	R 0298	280109
09	S 0661	Solenoid valves [electromagnetic switches]	V 0014	090675
17	S 0662	Soles (Asbestos —)	S 0220	170027
25	S 0663	Soles for footwear	S 0219	250129
10	S 0664	Soles (Orthopaedic [orthopedic] —)	S 0222	100171
01	S 0665	Solidified gases for industrial purposes	G 0127	010328
04	S 0666	Solidified gases [fuel]	G 0128	040088
05	S 0667	Solutions for contact lenses	V 0171	050094
05	S 0668	Solvents for removing adhesive plasters	S 0385	050134
01	S 0669	Solvents for varnishes	D 0247	010606
09	S 0670	Sonars	S 0390	090179
16	S 0671	Song books	C 0484	160082
02	S 0672	Soot [colorant]	S 0574	020101
01	S 0673	Soot for industrial or agricultural purposes	S 0573	010499
10	S 0674	Soporific pillows for insomnia	O 0103	100101
05	S 0675	Soporifics	S 0387	050273
32	S 0676	Sorbets [beverages]	S 0406	320029
30	S 0677	Sorbets [ices]	S 0407	300125
10	S 0678	Sores (Pads [pouches] for preventing pressure —) on patient bodies	C 1440	100195
01	S 0679	Sorrel salt	S 0185	010410

Cl.	SERIAL No. (E)	INDICATION OF GOODS	SERIAL No. (F)	BASIC No.
07	S 0680	Sorting machines for industry	T 0523	070143
09	S 0681	Sound alarms	A 0863	090014
09	S 0682	Sound locating instruments	S 0404	090455
09	S 0683	Sound recording apparatus	E 0334	090451
09	S 0684	Sound recording carriers	E 0335	090111
09	S 0685	Sound recording discs	D 0231	090016
09	S 0686	Sound recording strips	F 0210	090231
09	S 0687	Sound reproduction apparatus	R 0245	090452
09	S 0688	Sound transmitting apparatus	S 0388	090450
09	S 0689	Sounding apparatus and machines	S 0391	090453
09	S 0690	Sounding leads	P 0651	090454
09	S 0691	Sounding lines	L 0252	090327
17	S 0692	Soundproofing materials	I 0103	170008
21	S 0693	Soup bowls	S 0460	210214
29	S 0694	Soup (Preparations for making —)	P 0880	290099
29	S 0695	Soup preparations (Vegetable —)	J 0063	290066
29	S 0696	Soups	P 0882	290026
07	S 0697	Sowers [machines]	S 0227	070348
04	S 0698	Soya bean oil preparations for non-stick treatment of cooking utensils	S 0378	040058
30	S 0699	Soya bean paste [condiment]	P 0196	300194
29	S 0700	Soya beans, preserved, for food	G 0294	290052
30	S 0701	Soya flour	S 0374	300062
29	S 0702	Soya milk [milk substitute]	L 0054	290163
30	S 0703	Soya sauce	S 0096	300179
11	S 0704	Spa baths [vessels]	B 0073	110291
12	S 0705	Space vehicles	V 0101	120117
08	S 0706	Spades [hand tools]	B 0291	080111
30	S 0707	Spaghetti	S 0480	300126
26	S 0708	Spangles for clothing	P 0015	260077
08	S 0709	Spanners [hand tools]	C 0934	080064
12	S 0710	Spare tire covers	H 0117	120264
12	S 0711	Spare tyre covers	H 0117	120264
12	S 0712	Spare wheel covers	H 0117	120264
09	S 0713	Spark-guards	P 0155	090245
07	S 0714	Sparking plugs for internal combustion engines	B 0705	070394
12	S 0715	Spars for ships	E 0435	120118
25	S 0716	Spats	G 0367	250062
08	S 0717	Spatulas [hand tools]	S 0487	080014
21	S 0718	Spatulas [kitchen utensils]	S 0488	210330
31	S 0719	Spawn (Fish —)	O 0022	310089
09	S 0720	Speaking tubes	P 0863	090017
09	S 0721	Spectacle cases	E 0528	090567
09	S 0722	Spectacle frames	M 0468	090359
09	S 0723	Spectacle glasses	V 0174	090334
09	S 0724	Spectacles [optics]	L 0394	090331
09	S 0725	Spectrograph apparatus	S 0489	090457
09	S 0726	Spectroscopes	S 0490	090426
09	S 0727	Speed checking apparatus for vehicles	C 1227	090152
07	S 0728	Speed governors for machines, engines and motors	R 0192	070275
09	S 0729	Speed indicators	I 0074	090303
09	S 0730	Speed measuring apparatus [photography]	V 0270	090345
09	S 0731	Speed regulators for record players	R 0193	090486
09	S 0732	Spherometers	S 0492	090458
10	S 0733	Sphygmomanometers	S 0495	100129
10	S 0734	Sphygmotensiometers	S 0495	100129
21	S 0735	Spice sets	E 0386	210122
30	S 0736	Spices	E 0385	300054
12	S 0737	Spikes for tires [tyres]	C 0969	120155
07	S 0738	Spin driers [not heated]	E 0457	070084
31	S 0739	Spinach, fresh	E 0391	310149
01	S 0740	Spinel [chemical preparations]	S 0497	010496
14	S 0741	Spinel [precious stones]	S 0496	140095
07	S 0742	Spinning frames	F 0184	070260
07	S 0743	Spinning machines	F 0182	070190
28	S 0744	Spinning tops [toys]	T 0414	280112
07	S 0745	Spinning wheels	R 0390	070191
31	S 0746	Spiny lobsters, live	L 0127	310140
29	S 0747	Spiny lobsters, not live	L 0126	290075
09	S 0748	Spirit levels	B 0899	090096
33	S 0749	Spirits [beverages]	S 0498	330018
01	S 0750	Spirits of salt	E 0439	010058
01	S 0751	Spirits of vinegar [dilute acetic acid]	E 0436	010277
10	S 0752	Spirometers [medical apparatus]	S 0499	100197
10	S 0753	Spittoons for medical purposes	C 1493	100034
34	S 0754	Spittoons for tobacco users	C 1494	340037
10	S 0755	Splints, surgical	E 0108	100021
12	S 0756	Spoilers for vehicles	S 0500	120261
12	S 0757	Spoke clips for wheels	T 0186	120169
12	S 0758	Spokes for bicycles, cycles	B 0395	120094
12	S 0759	Spokes (Vehicle wheel —)	R 0107	120168
21	S 0760	Sponge holders	P 0813	210124
21	S 0761	Sponges for household purposes	E 0401	210280
10	S 0762	Sponges (Surgical —)	E 0400	100053
05	S 0763	Sponges (Vulnerary —)	E 0404	050136
16	S 0764	Spools for inking ribbons	B 0508	160043
09	S 0765	Spools [photography]	E 0344	090233
08	S 0766	Spoons *	C 1590	080080
21	S 0767	Spoons (Basting —), for kitchen use	L 0375	210156
10	S 0768	Spoons for administering medicine	C 1594	100069
13	S 0769	Sporting firearms	A 0728	130026
18	S 0770	Sports (Bags for —)*	S 0036	180118
25	S 0771	Sports (Boots for —) *	C 0642	250141
12	S 0772	Sports cars	S 0506	120178
09	S 0773	Sports (Goggles for —)	L 0389	090654
25	S 0774	Sports jerseys	M 0034	250094
09	S 0775	Sports (Protective helmets for —)	C 0326	090656
25	S 0776	Sports shoes *	S 0505	250132
21	S 0777	Spouts	B 0300	210027
07	S 0778	Spray guns for paint	P 0541	070298
10	S 0779	Sprayers for medical purposes	V 0030	100109

Cl.	SERIAL No. (E)	INDICATION OF GOODS	SERIAL No. (F)	BASIC No.
08	S 0780	Sprayers (Insecticide—) [hand tools]	P 1041	080144
07	S 0781	Spraying machines	P 1039	070214
03	S 0782	Sprays (Breath freshening—)	A 0142	030204
13	S 0783	Sprays for personal defence purposes	S 0508	130073
13	S 0784	Sprays for personal defense purposes	S 0508	130073
28	S 0785	Spring boards [sports articles]	T 0499	280150
06	S 0786	Spring locks	H 0122	060153
20	S 0787	Spring mattresses	S 0386	200185
30	S 0788	Spring rolls	R 0399	300183
18	S 0789	Springs (Casings, of leather, for plate—)	G 0012	180052
06	S 0790	Springs [metal hardware]	R 0282	060206
07	S 0791	Springs [parts of machines]	R 0280	070330
12	S 0792	Springs (Shock absorbing—) for vehicles	R 0276	120011
14	S 0793	Springs (Watch—)	R 0277	140058
09	S 0794	Sprinkler systems for fire protection	G 0189	090646
21	S 0795	Sprinklers	A 0763	210015
21	S 0796	Sprinklers for watering flowers and plants	S 0236	210206
21	S 0797	Sprinkling devices	A 0760	210013
12	S 0798	Sprinkling trucks	A 0764	120016
23	S 0799	Spun cotton	C 1349	230008
23	S 0800	Spun silk	S 0364	230016
14	S 0801	Spun silver [silver wire]	A 0695	140008
23	S 0802	Spun thread and yarn	F 0186	230010
23	S 0803	Spun wool	L 0034	230012
06	S 0804	Spurs	E 0383	060122
16	S 0805	Square rulers	C 0278	160069
16	S 0806	Squares (Drawing—)	E 0414	160297
08	S 0807	Squares [hand tools]	E 0416	080017
31	S 0808	Squashes	C 1412	310043
19	S 0809	Stables	E 0473	190085
11	S 0810	Stacks (Flare—) for use in oil refineries	T 0597	110059
20	S 0811	Stag antlers	R 0069	200049
09	S 0812	Stage lighting regulators	R 0196	090682
03	S 0813	Stain removers	D 0159	030068
19	S 0814	Stained-glass windows	V 0278	190182
01	S 0815	Staining-chemicals (Enamel and glass-—)	T 0202	010520
01	S 0816	Stain-preventing chemicals for use on fabrics	T 0053	010286
02	S 0817	Stains for leather	C 1607	020057
02	S 0818	Stains (Wood—)	B 0557	020028
20	S 0819	Stair rods	T 0525	200105
06	S 0820	Stair treads [steps] of metal	M 0145	060355
07	S 0821	Staircases (Moving—) [escalators]	E 0426	070178
19	S 0822	Staircases, not of metal	E 0425	190222
06	S 0823	Staircases of metal	E 0424	060124
20	S 0824	Stairs (Mobile boarding—), not of metal, for passengers	E 0093	200093
19	S 0825	Stair-treads [steps], not of metal	D 0058	190074
20	S 0826	Stakes for plants or trees	E 0077	200091
07	S 0827	Stalk separators [machines]	E 0174	070168
31	S 0828	Stall food for animals	P 0939	310112
16	S 0829	Stamp pads	S 0129	160247
16	S 0830	Stamp stands	T 0265	160261
07	S 0831	Stamping machines	T 0264	070180
09	S 0832	Stamping mail (Apparatus to check—)	A 0157	090149
08	S 0833	Stamping-out tools [hand tools]	E 0485	080084
16	S 0834	Stamps (Address—)	C 0941	160004
08	S 0835	Stamps [hand tools]	E 0485	080084
16	S 0836	Stamps [seals]	T 0269	160052
16	S 0837	Stamps [seals] (Cases for—)	C 1003	160259
11	S 0838	Standard lamps	L 0087	110263
20	S 0839	Stands (Costume—)	B 0914	200038
21	S 0840	Stands (Flat-iron—)	F 0107	210112
12	S 0841	Stands for bicycles, cycles [parts of bicycles, cycles]	B 0379	120046
20	S 0842	Stands for calculating machines	B 0250	200212
07	S 0843	Stands for machines	B 0251	070041
15	S 0844	Stands for musical instruments	S 0358	150088
16	S 0845	Stands for pens and pencils	S 0595	160281
09	S 0846	Stands for photographic apparatus	P 0438	090391
21	S 0847	Stands for shaving brushes	P 0800	210241
15	S 0848	Stands (Music—)	P 1045	150080
06	S 0849	Stands of metal (Cask—)	C 0485	060391
16	S 0850	Staples for offices	A 0175	160010
16	S 0851	Stapling presses [office requisites]	B 0838	160012
30	S 0852	Star aniseed	A 0546	300007
05	S 0853	Starch for dietetic or pharmaceutical purposes	A 0442	050013
30	S 0854	Starch for food	A 0441	300065
01	S 0855	Starch for industrial purposes	A 0443	010055
03	S 0856	Starch for laundry purposes	A 0445	030010
03	S 0857	Starch glaze for laundry purposes	A 0440	030009
16	S 0858	Starch paste [adhesive] for stationery or household purposes	A 0447	160271
01	S 0859	Starch paste [adhesive], other than for stationery or household purposes	A 0446	010566
01	S 0860	Starch size [chemical preparations]	A 0627	010077
16	S 0861	Starches (Packaging material made of—)	E 0227	160338
01	S 0862	Starch-liquifying chemicals [ungluing agents]	A 0444	010056
09	S 0863	Starter cables for motors	C 0019	090647
07	S 0864	Starters for motors and engines	D 0066	070150
28	S 0865	Starting blocks for sports	B 0496	280174
28	S 0866	Stationary exercise bicycles	B 0385	280017
16	S 0867	Stationery	P 0073	160209
16	S 0868	Stationery (Cabinets for—) [office requisites]	C 1006	160289
07	S 0869	Stators [parts of machines]	S 0512	070354
06	S 0870	Statues of common metal	S 0514	060244
21	S 0871	Statues of porcelain, earthenware, ceramic or glass	S 0517	210217

Cl.	SERIAL No. (E)	INDICATION OF GOODS	SERIAL No. (F)	BASIC No.
14	S 0872	Statues of precious metal	S 0515	140096
19	S 0873	Statues of stone, concrete or marble	S 0516	190170
20	S 0874	Statues of wood, wax, plaster or plastic	S 0513	200187
06	S 0875	Statuettes of common metal	F 0173	060382
21	S 0876	Statuettes of porcelain, ceramic, earthenware or glass	F 0177	210285
14	S 0877	Statuettes of precious metal	F 0174	140146
19	S 0878	Statuettes of stone, concrete or marble	F 0176	190224
20	S 0879	Statuettes of wood, wax, plaster or plastic	F 0172	200239
19	S 0880	Stave wood	M 0289	190125
20	S 0881	Staves of wood	D 0294	200087
11	S 0882	Steam accumulators	A 0033	110242
11	S 0883	Steam boilers, other than parts of machines	G 0162	110165
07	S 0884	Steam engine boilers	C 0586	070429
07	S 0885	Steam engines	M 0010	070242
11	S 0886	Steam facial apparatus [saunas]	V 0031	110300
11	S 0887	Steam generating installations	V 0027	110232
07	S 0888	Steam presses (Rotary—), portable, for fabrics	C 0112	070480
07	S 0889	Steam traps	P 1049	070320
11	S 0890	Steamers (Fabric—)	D 0049	110331
07	S 0891	Steam/oil separators	D 0121	070152
07	S 0892	Steamrollers	R 0397	070014
01	S 0893	Stearic acid	S 0525	010497
04	S 0894	Stearine	S 0524	040073
16	S 0895	Steatite [tailor's chalk]	S 0526	160251
06	S 0896	Steel alloys	A 0064	060002
06	S 0897	Steel buildings	A 0068	060266
01	S 0898	Steel (Finishing preparations for use in the manufacture of—)	A 0075	010017
16	S 0899	Steel letters	A 0072	160001
06	S 0900	Steel masts	A 0073	060006
16	S 0901	Steel pens	A 0074	160002
06	S 0902	Steel pipes	A 0079	060011
06	S 0903	Steel sheets	A 0077	060010
06	S 0904	Steel strip	F 0124	060003
06	S 0905	Steel tubes	A 0079	060011
06	S 0906	Steel, unwrought or semi-wrought	A 0067	060001
06	S 0907	Steel wire	A 0070	060004
21	S 0908	Steel wool for cleaning	P 0004	210005
07	S 0909	Steelworks (Converters for—)	C 1229	070003
09	S 0910	Steelyards [lever scales]	R 0358	090433
09	S 0911	Steering apparatus, automatic, for vehicles	P 0485	090396
12	S 0912	Steering gears for ships	B 0239	120037
12	S 0913	Steering wheels (Covers for vehicle—)	H 0120	120260
12	S 0914	Steering wheels for vehicles	V 0314	120230
05	S 0915	Stem cells for medical purposes	C 0369	050403
05	S 0916	Stem cells for veterinary purposes	C 0370	050404
01	S 0917	Stem cells other than for medical or veterinary purposes	C 0371	010657
16	S 0918	Stencil cases	E 0533	160214
16	S 0919	Stencil plates	P 0692	160226
16	S 0920	Stencils	S 0529	160227
16	S 0921	Stencils [stationery]	G 0006	160161
10	S 0922	Stents	S 0530	100223
20	S 0923	Steps [ladders], not of metal	M 0144	200147
06	S 0924	Steps [ladders] of metal	M 0143	060177
09	S 0925	Step-up transformers	S 0611	090706
09	S 0926	Stereos (Personal—)	B 0089	090663
09	S 0927	Stereoscopes	S 0531	090460
09	S 0928	Stereoscopic apparatus	S 0532	090461
07	S 0929	Stereotype machines	S 0533	070355
10	S 0930	Sterile sheets, surgical	C 0476	100172
05	S 0931	Sterilising preparations	S 0537	050275
05	S 0932	Sterilising (Soil--) preparations	S 0383	050272
11	S 0933	Sterilizers	S 0535	110226
12	S 0934	Stern oars	G 0258	120131
05	S 0935	Steroids	S 0538	050395
10	S 0936	Stethoscopes	S 0539	100144
21	S 0937	Stew-pans	C 0330	210065
30	S 0938	Stick liquorice [confectionery]	B 0256	300147
05	S 0939	Stick liquorice for pharmaceutical purposes	B 0255	050303
16	S 0940	Stickers [stationery]	A 0836	160328
05	S 0941	Sticking plasters	S 0481	050019
15	S 0942	Sticks (Drum—)	B 0039	150010
15	S 0943	Sticks for bows for musical instruments	B 0036	150006
05	S 0944	Sticks (Fumigating—)	C 0968	050085
18	S 0945	Sticks (Mountaineering—)	A 0382	180001
05	S 0946	Sticks (Sulphur—) [disinfectants]	M 0247	050205
30	S 0947	Stiffening whipped cream (Preparations for—)	C 1534	300045
11	S 0948	Stills *	A 0264	110246
09	S 0949	Stills for laboratory experiments	A 0265	090504
18	S 0950	Stirrup leathers	E 0524	180046
18	S 0951	Stirrups	E 0521	180119
18	S 0952	Stirrups (Parts of rubber for—)	E 0522	180045
07	S 0953	Stitching machines	C 1436	070128
25	S 0954	Stocking suspenders	J 0016	250039
25	S 0955	Stockings	B 0216	250006
10	S 0956	Stockings (Elastic—) [surgery]	B 0217	100165
10	S 0957	Stockings for varices	B 0218	100166
25	S 0958	Stockings (Heel pieces for—)	T 0073	250008
01	S 0959	Stockings (Substances for preventing runs in—)	D 0060	010105
25	S 0960	Stockings (Sweat-absorbent—)	B 0220	250007
13	S 0961	Stocks (Gun—)	F 0528	130037
25	S 0962	Stoles (Fur—)	E 0514	250074
19	S 0963	Stone	P 0446	190094
08	S 0964	Stone hammers	C 0329	080047
07	S 0965	Stone working machines	P 0450	070301
19	S 0966	Stonemasonry (Works of—)	P 0468	190146
19	S 0967	Stones (Binding agents for making—)	L 0232	190040
16	S 0968	Stones (Lithographic—)	P 0467	160188

Cl.	SERIAL No. (E)	INDICATION OF GOODS	SERIAL No. (F)	BASIC No.
08	S 0969	Stones (Sharpening—)	P 0454	080003
20	S 0970	Stools	T 0052	200235
06	S 0971	Stop collars of metal *	A 0558	060038
20	S 0972	Stoppers for bottles, not of glass, metal or rubber	F 0075	200220
21	S 0973	Stoppers (Glass—)	B 0677	210042
20	S 0974	Stoppers, not of metal	C 0213	200214
17	S 0975	Stoppers (Rubber—)	B 0679	170018
06	S 0976	Stops of metal	B 0917	060238
17	S 0977	Stops of rubber	B 0916	170093
14	S 0978	Stopwatches	C 0815	140164
11	S 0979	Stoves	C 0617	110140
11	S 0980	Stoves [heating apparatus]	P 0695	110143
21	S 0981	Strainers	P 0182	210174
21	S 0982	Strainers for household purposes	F 0268	210088
10	S 0983	Strait jackets	C 0150	100041
06	S 0984	Strap-hinges of metal	P 0315	060039
18	S 0985	Straps for skates	C 1426	180035
18	S 0986	Straps for soldiers' equipment	B 0897	180012
14	S 0987	Straps for wristwatches	B 0782	140017
25	S 0988	Straps (Gaiter—)	S 0472	250083
18	S 0989	Straps (Harness—)	C 1423	180033
18	S 0990	Straps (Leather—)	L 0129	180036
18	S 0991	Straps (Leather shoulder—)	B 0176	180096
22	S 0992	Straps, not of metal, for handling loads	S 0081	220082
18	S 0993	Straps of leather [saddlery]	C 1430	180034
06	S 0994	Straps of metal for handling loads	S 0080	060305
07	S 0995	Straw [chaff] cutters	H 0008	070210
20	S 0996	Straw edgings	R 0432	200162
22	S 0997	Straw for stuffing upholstery	P 0008	220062
31	S 0998	Straw [forage]	P 0005	310099
31	S 0999	Straw litter	P 0010	310098
20	S 1000	Straw mattresses	P 0002	200159
31	S 1001	Straw mulch	P 0016	310046
20	S 1002	Straw plaits	T 0507	200161
22	S 1003	Straw wrappers for bottles	E 0239	220080
21	S 1004	Straws for drinking	P 0013	210342
11	S 1005	Street lamps	L 0087	110263
31	S 1006	Strengthening animal forage	F 0369	310059
10	S 1007	Stretchers (Ambulance—)	B 0791	100037
21	S 1008	Stretchers for clothing	T 0187	210221
06	S 1009	Stretchers for metal bands [tension links]	B 0163	060383
08	S 1010	Stretchers for wire and metal bands [hand tools]	T 0184	080160
21	S 1011	Stretchers (Glove—)	O 0158	210141
06	S 1012	Stretchers of metal (Belt—)	T 0183	060101
10	S 1013	Stretchers, wheeled	B 0792	100036
22	S 1014	String	F 0165	220035
15	S 1015	Stringed musical instruments	C 1268	150029
19	S 1016	Stringers [parts of staircases], not of metal	L 0271	190113
06	S 1017	Stringers [parts of staircases] of metal	L 0270	060162
15	S 1018	Strings for musical instruments	C 1266	150028
28	S 1019	Strings for rackets	C 1264	280042
06	S 1020	Strip (Iron—)	F 0125	060131
06	S 1021	Strip (Steel—)	F 0124	060003
03	S 1022	Strips (Breath freshening—)	B 0145	030216
22	S 1023	Strips for tying-up vines	B 0144	220003
09	S 1024	Strips (Sound recording—)	F 0210	090231
12	S 1025	Stroller covers [pushchairs]	B 0003	120164
12	S 1026	Strollers	V 0299	120163
01	S 1027	Strontium	S 0550	010498
08	S 1028	Stropping instruments	A 0156	080091
07	S 1029	Stropping machines	L 0081	070225
11	S 1030	Structural plates for ovens	A 0717	110025
05	S 1031	Strychnine	S 0551	050276
25	S 1032	Studs for football boots	C 1506	250134
12	S 1033	Studs for tires [tyres]	C 0969	120155
25	S 1034	Stuff jackets [clothing]	V 0035	250120
20	S 1035	Stuffed animals	A 0531	200006
28	S 1036	Stuffed toys	J 0057	280208
07	S 1037	Stuffing boxes [parts of machines]	B 0601	070198
22	S 1038	Stuffing, not of rubber or plastic	R 0211	220030
17	S 1039	Stuffing of rubber or plastic	R 0210	170014
08	S 1040	Stunning apparatus (Cattle—)	B 0333	080032
09	S 1041	Styli for record players	S 0087	090462
05	S 1042	Styptic preparations	S 0556	050277
01	S 1043	Substrates for soil-free growing [agriculture]	S 0558	010589
07	S 1044	Suction cups for milking machines	V 0123	070368
07	S 1045	Suction machines for industrial purposes	A 0797	070282
29	S 1046	Suet for food	S 0575	290108
30	S 1047	Sugar *	S 0561	300069
21	S 1048	Sugar bowls	S 0571	210218
30	S 1049	Sugar confectionery	C 1170	300042
05	S 1050	Sugar for medical purposes	S 0562	050278
07	S 1051	Sugar making machines	S 0570	070356
08	S 1052	Sugar tongs	P 0508	080173
31	S 1053	Sugarcane	C 0173	310021
18	S 1054	Suitcase handles	P 0703	180086
18	S 1055	Suitcases	M 0058	180115
25	S 1056	Suits	C 1338	250056
25	S 1057	Suits (Bathing—)	B 0065	250126
01	S 1058	Sulphates	S 0578	010555
01	S 1059	Sulphides	S 0582	010486
09	S 1060	Sulphitometers	S 0580	090463
05	S 1061	Sulphonamides [medicines]	S 0577	050279
01	S 1062	Sulphonic acids	S 0581	010501
01	S 1063	Sulphur	S 0443	010493
05	S 1064	Sulphur sticks [disinfectants]	M 0247	050205
01	S 1065	Sulphuric acid	S 0584	010503
01	S 1066	Sulphuric ether	S 0585	010285
01	S 1067	Sulphurous acid	S 0583	010502
01	S 1068	Sumac for use in tanning	S 0586	010504
02	S 1069	Sumac for varnishes	S 0587	020102
25	S 1070	Sun visors	V 0267	250030
12	S 1071	Sun-blinds adapted for automobiles	S 0548	120245
05	S 1072	Sunburn ointments	A 0615	050301

Cl.	SERIAL No. (E)	INDICATION OF GOODS	SERIAL No. (F)	BASIC No.
05	S 1073	Sunburn preparations for pharmaceutical purposes	S 0381	050100
14	S 1074	Sundials	C 0057	140022
29	S 1075	Sunflower oil for food	T 0429	290111
04	S 1076	Sunflower oil for industrial purposes	T 0430	040075
09	S 1077	Sunglasses	L 0388	090648
03	S 1078	Sunscreen preparations	E 0134	030225
03	S 1079	Sun-tanning preparations [cosmetics]	B 0853	030171
15	S 1080	Suona [Chinese trumpets]	S 0588	150085
07	S 1081	Superchargers	S 0599	070358
07	S 1082	Superheaters	S 0598	070357
01	S 1083	Superphosphates [fertilisers]	S 0589	010431
28	S 1084	Supporters (Men's athletic—) [sports articles]	S 0353	280196
10	S 1085	Supportive bandages	B 0135	100020
26	S 1086	Supports (Collar—)	B 0045	260046
10	S 1087	Supports for flat feet	P 0439	100146
05	S 1088	Suppositories	S 0597	050280
28	S 1089	Surf boards	P 0579	280102
28	S 1090	Surf skis	K 0005	280125
01	S 1091	Surface-active chemical agents	T 0190	010518
19	S 1092	Surfacings, not of metal, for building	R 0291	190150
28	S 1093	Surfboard leashes	S 0082	280172
28	S 1094	Surfboards (Bags especially designed for skis and—)	H 0121	280166
10	S 1095	Surgical apparatus and instruments	C 0779	100054
01	S 1096	Surgical bandages (Adhesive preparations for—)	A 0106	010022
05	S 1097	Surgical cloth [tissues]	T 0299	050078
10	S 1098	Surgical drapes	D 0307	100207
05	S 1099	Surgical dressings	E 0511	050140
10	S 1100	Surgical implants [artificial materials]	I 0021	100208
05	S 1101	Surgical implants [living tissues]	I 0022	050397
05	S 1102	Surgical tissues	T 0299	050078
09	S 1103	Surveying apparatus and instruments	G 0171	090280
09	S 1104	Surveying chains	C 0427	090056
09	S 1105	Surveying instruments	A 0751	090055
09	S 1106	Surveyors' levels	L 0393	090333
30	S 1107	Sushi	S 0612	300170
25	S 1108	Suspenders	B 0804	250018
26	S 1109	Suspenders (Fastenings for—)	B 0805	260026
12	S 1110	Suspension shock absorbers for vehicles	A 0469	120010
12	S 1111	Suspension springs (Vehicle—)	R 0278	120171
10	S 1112	Suspensory bandages	S 0615	100148
10	S 1113	Suture materials	S 0617	100149
10	S 1114	Suture needles	S 0616	100009
03	S 1115	Swabs [toiletries]	B 0252	030019
07	S 1116	Swaging machines	E 0247	070173
25	S 1117	Sweat-absorbent underclothing [underwear]	S 0475	250054
25	S 1118	Sweaters	C 0479	250034
04	S 1119	Sweeping (Dust binding compositions for—)	B 0102	040012
07	S 1120	Sweeping machines (Road—) [self-propelled]	B 0103	070034
01	S 1121	Sweeteners (Artificial—) [chemical preparations]	E 0165	010607
30	S 1122	Sweeteners (Natural—)	E 0166	300053
30	S 1123	Sweetmeats [candy]	B 0635	300020
30	S 1124	Sweets (Peppermint—)	M 0274	300019
28	S 1125	Swimming belts	C 0354	280212
28	S 1126	Swimming jackets	G 0191	280213
28	S 1127	Swimming kick boards	P 0576	280205
11	S 1128	Swimming pool chlorinating apparatus	C 0786	110318
06	S 1129	Swimming pools [metal structures]	P 0528	060290
28	S 1130	Swimming pools [play articles]	P 0527	280095
19	S 1131	Swimming pools [structures, not of metal]	P 0529	190196
28	S 1132	Swimming webs [flippers]	P 0052	280093
25	S 1133	Swimsuits	B 0065	250126
28	S 1134	Swings	B 0100	280010
09	S 1135	Switchboards	T 0025	090146
09	S 1136	Switchboxes [electricity]	B 0598	090131
09	S 1137	Switches, electric	I 0114	090164
06	S 1138	Switches (Railway—)	C 0482	060013
08	S 1139	Sword scabbards	F 0401	080125
08	S 1140	Swords	E 0382	080208
15	S 1141	Synthesizers (Music—)	S 0619	150087
17	S 1142	Synthetic resins [semi-finished products]	R 0268	170075
01	S 1143	Synthetic resins, unprocessed	R 0267	010455
17	S 1144	Synthetic rubber	C 0200	170020
10	S 1145	Syringes for injections	B 0512	100080
10	S 1146	Syringes for medical purposes	S 0235	100164
08	S 1147	Syringes for spraying insecticides	S 0237	080202
21	S 1148	Syringes for watering flowers and plants	S 0236	210206
32	S 1149	Syrups for beverages	S 0339	320011
32	S 1150	Syrups for lemonade	L 0268	320023
05	S 1151	Syrups for pharmaceutical purposes	S 0338	050067

Cl.	SERIAL No. (E)	INDICATION OF GOODS	SERIAL No. (F)	BASIC No.
30	T 0001	Tabbouleh	T 0051	300190
08	T 0002	Table cutlery [knives, forks and spoons]	C 1473	080059
08	T 0003	Table forks	F 0383	080070
24	T 0004	Table linen, not of paper	L 0291	240070
16	T 0005	Table linen of paper	L 0290	160186
16	T 0006	Table napkins of paper	S 0263	160295
24	T 0007	Table napkins of textile	S 0262	240076
21	T 0008	Table plates	A 0799	210235
21	T 0009	Table plates (Disposable —)	A 0800	210333
24	T 0010	Table runners	C 0697	240022
28	T 0011	Table tennis (Tables for —)	T 0044	280111
20	T 0012	Table tops	P 0630	200169
32	T 0013	Table waters	E 0049	320018
24	T 0014	Tablecloths, not of paper	N 0008	240033
16	T 0015	Tablecloths of paper	N 0007	160200
24	T 0016	Tablemats, not of paper	R 0364	240097
16	T 0017	Tablemats of paper	R 0363	160254
20	T 0018	Tables *	T 0030	200070
16	T 0019	Tables (Arithmetical —)	T 0033	160027
16	T 0020	Tables (Calculating —)	T 0033	160027
28	T 0021	Tables for indoor football	T 0043	280070
07	T 0022	Tables for machines	T 0036	070359
28	T 0023	Tables for table tennis	T 0044	280111
20	T 0024	Tables of metal	T 0041	200188
10	T 0025	Tables (Operating —)	T 0040	100150
08	T 0026	Tableware [knives, forks and spoons]	C 1473	080059
21	T 0027	Tableware, other than knives, forks and spoons	V 0006	210227
26	T 0028	Tabs (Monogram —) for marking linen	M 0161	260032
09	T 0029	Tachometers	T 0054	090465
28	T 0030	Tackle (Fishing —)	P 0250	280083
06	T 0031	Tacks [nails]	P 0715	060086
30	T 0032	Tacos	T 0056	300184
24	T 0033	Taffeta [cloth]	T 0058	240091
05	T 0034	Taffeta plasters (Gummed —)	S 0481	050019
16	T 0035	Tags for index cards	C 0348	160081
29	T 0036	Tahini [sesame seed paste]	T 0059	290157
12	T 0037	Tailboard lifts [parts of land vehicles]	H 0051	120243
12	T 0038	Tailgates (Am.) (Elevating -, Power —) [parts of land vehicles]	H 0051	120243
16	T 0039	Tailors' chalk	C 1504	160111
20	T 0040	Tailors' dummies	M 0115	200064
03	T 0041	Tailors' wax	C 0891	030055
01	T 0042	Talc [magnesium silicate]	T 0069	010506
03	T 0043	Talcum powder, for toilet use	T 0068	030155
04	T 0044	Tallow	D 0056	040037
15	T 0045	Tambourines	T 0075	150067
07	T 0046	Tambours for embroidery machines	T 0080	070067
01	T 0047	Tan	T 0097	010507
21	T 0048	Tankards	H 0025	210291
21	T 0049	Tanks [indoor aquaria]	A 0635	210336
20	T 0050	Tanks, not of metal nor of masonry	R 0255	200174
19	T 0051	Tanks of masonry	R 0253	190160
06	T 0052	Tanks of metal	R 0254	060232
13	T 0053	Tanks [weapons]	C 0553	130071
01	T 0054	Tannic acid	T 0103	010511
01	T 0055	Tannin	T 0102	010508
11	T 0056	Tanning apparatus [sun beds]	B 0857	110271
05	T 0057	Tanning pills	A 0830	050417
01	T 0058	Tanning substances	T 0099	010509
06	T 0059	Tantalum [metal]	T 0104	060246
01	T 0060	Tan-wood	B 0518	010130
08	T 0061	Tap wrenches	T 0422	080063
17	T 0062	Tape (Insulating —)	B 0161	170107
09	T 0063	Tape recorders	E 0336	090077
09	T 0064	Tape units (Magnetic —) for computers	U 0006	090609
04	T 0065	Tapers	B 0707	040015
05	T 0066	Tapes (Adhesive —), for medical purposes	B 0149	050294
17	T 0067	Tapes (Adhesive —), other than stationery and not for medical or household purposes	B 0148	170085
09	T 0068	Tapes (Demagnetizing apparatus for magnetic —)	D 0059	090076
26	T 0069	Tapes for curtain headings	R 0439	260120
27	T 0070	Tapestry [wall hangings], not of textile	T 0125	270013
24	T 0071	Tapestry [wall hangings], of textile	T 0196	240103
30	T 0072	Tapioca	T 0106	300127
30	T 0073	Tapioca flour for food	T 0107	300128
01	T 0074	Tapioca flour for industrial purposes	T 0108	010512
11	T 0075	Taps [cocks, spigots] [faucets (Am.)] for pipes	R 0348	110068
11	T 0076	Taps [faucets] *	R 0347	110218
20	T 0077	Taps for casks, not of metal	R 0350	200042
06	T 0078	Taps for casks, of metal	R 0349	060402
08	T 0079	Taps [hand tools]	T 0130	080193
07	T 0080	Taps [parts of machines, engines or motors]	R 0352	070333
19	T 0081	Tar	G 0282	190171
21	T 0082	Tar-brushes, long handled	G 0377	210147
28	T 0083	Targets	C 0820	280038
28	T 0084	Targets (Electronic —)	C 0821	280193
22	T 0085	Tarpaulins	B 0001	220002
22	T 0086	Tarred brattice cloth	C 0959	220001
02	T 0087	Tarred felt (Coatings for —) [paints]	C 0301	020036
19	T 0088	Tarred strips, for building	B 0159	190018
07	T 0089	Tarring machines	G 0286	070202
21	T 0090	Tart scoops	P 0295	210177
05	T 0091	Tartar for pharmaceutical purposes	T 0137	050281
01	T 0092	Tartar other than for pharmaceutical purposes	T 0138	010514
01	T 0093	Tartaric acid	T 0139	010515
30	T 0094	Tarts	T 0134	300129
26	T 0095	Tassels [haberdashery]	H 0107	260063
08	T 0096	Tattooing (Apparatus for —)	T 0143	080256
09	T 0097	Taximeters	T 0144	090300

Cl.	SERIAL No. (E)	INDICATION OF GOODS	SERIAL No. (F)	BASIC No.
30	T 0098	Tea*	T 0230	300037
21	T 0099	Tea balls	B 0725	210248
21	T 0100	Tea caddies	B 0607	210038
20	T 0101	Tea carts	D 0138	200082
21	T 0102	Tea cosies	C 1341	210343
30	T 0103	Tea (Iced —)	T 0235	300186
21	T 0104	Tea infusers	B 0725	210248
21	T 0105	Tea services [tableware]	T 0238	210209
21	T 0106	Tea strainers	P 0181	210288
20	T 0107	Tea trolleys	D 0138	200082
30	T 0108	Tea-based beverages	B 0565	300187
09	T 0109	Teaching apparatus	E 0345	090440
16	T 0110	Teaching materials [except apparatus]	I 0105	160071
21	T 0111	Teapots	T 0240	210222
13	T 0112	Tear-gas weapons	A 0737	130008
07	T 0113	Teat cups for milking machines	V 0123	070368
10	T 0114	Teats	S 0560	100145
10	T 0115	Teats (Feeding bottle —)	T 0220	100170
01	T 0116	Technetium	T 0145	010516
25	T 0117	Teddies [undergarments]	B 0514	250147
07	T 0118	Tedding machines	F 0005	070186
28	T 0119	Teddy bears	O 0143	280151
25	T 0120	Tee-shirts	T 0146	250155
10	T 0121	Teeth (Artificial —)	D 0093	100052
05	T 0122	Teeth filling material	D 0097	050110
09	T 0123	Teeth protectors	P 1010	090414
05	T 0124	Teething (Preparations to facilitate —)	D 0092	050116
10	T 0125	Teething rings	A 0560	100018
19	T 0126	Telegraph posts, not of metal	P 0892	190155
06	T 0127	Telegraph posts of metal	P 0891	060222
09	T 0128	Telegraph wires	F 0244	090469
09	T 0129	Telegraphs [apparatus]	T 0156	090467
09	T 0130	Telemeters	T 0161	090195
09	T 0131	Telephone apparatus	T 0166	090423
19	T 0132	Telephone booths, not of metal	C 0010	190041
06	T 0133	Telephone booths of metal	C 0009	060422
19	T 0134	Telephone boxes, not of metal	C 0010	190041
06	T 0135	Telephone boxes of metal	C 0009	060422
09	T 0136	Telephone receivers	E 0121	090207
09	T 0137	Telephone transmitters	T 0170	090473
09	T 0138	Telephone wires	F 0245	090572
09	T 0139	Telephones (Portable —)	T 0164	090661
09	T 0140	Teleprinters	T 0174	090464
09	T 0141	Teleprompters	T 0171	090472
09	T 0142	Telerupters	T 0172	090474
09	T 0143	Telescopes	T 0173	090476
09	T 0144	Telescopes for firearms (Sighting —)	L 0390	090509
09	T 0145	Teletypewriters	T 0174	090464
09	T 0146	Television apparatus	T 0176	090468
09	T 0147	Teller machines (Automated —) [ATM]	G 0368	090686
01	T 0148	Tellurium	T 0178	010517
06	T 0149	Telpher cables	C 0029	060057
12	T 0150	Telpher railways [cable cars]	T 0162	120190
09	T 0151	Temperature indicators	I 0072	090477

Cl.	SERIAL No. (E)	INDICATION OF GOODS	SERIAL No. (F)	BASIC No.
01	T 0152	Tempering preparations (Metal —)	M 0321	010393
28	T 0153	Tennis ball throwing apparatus	B 0114	280173
28	T 0154	Tennis nets	T 0189	280065
01	T 0155	Tensio-active agents	T 0190	010518
06	T 0156	Tension links	T 0192	060249
20	T 0157	Tent pegs, not of metal	P 0525	200168
06	T 0158	Tent pegs of metal	P 0524	060208
22	T 0159	Tents	T 0195	220071
01	T 0160	Terbium	T 0198	010519
09	T 0161	Terminals [electricity]	B 0654	090089
03	T 0162	Terpenes [essential oils]	T 0204	030159
19	T 0163	Terra cotta	T 0210	190172
21	T 0164	Terrariums (Indoor —) [plant cultivation]	T 0205	210305
21	T 0165	Terrariums (Indoor —) [vivariums]	T 0206	210338
16	T 0166	Terrestrial globes	G 0232	160165
01	T 0167	Test paper, chemical	P 0088	010278
09	T 0168	Test tubes	E 0409	090236
10	T 0169	Testing apparatus for medical purposes	A 0488	100180
09	T 0170	Testing apparatus not for medical purposes	A 0489	090249
01	T 0171	Tetrachlorides	T 0222	010529
22	T 0172	Textile fibers [fibres]	F 0164	220076
04	T 0173	Textile oil	H 0165	040080
22	T 0174	Textile (Raw fibrous —)	T 0225	220010
27	T 0175	Textile wallpaper	P 0130	270018
01	T 0176	Textile-brightening chemicals	T 0227	010091
01	T 0177	Textile-impregnating chemicals	T 0228	010363
05	T 0178	Textiles (Deodorants for clothing and —)	D 0133	050400
01	T 0179	Textile-waterproofing chemicals	I 0017	010362
01	T 0180	Thallium	T 0229	010532
28	T 0181	Theatrical masks	M 0185	280089
09	T 0182	Theft prevention installations, electric	V 0305	090497
09	T 0183	Theodolites	T 0242	090479
10	T 0184	Thermal packs for first aid purposes	C 1442	100209
05	T 0185	Thermal water	E 0064	050131
21	T 0186	Thermally insulated containers for food	A 0346	210007
07	T 0187	Thermic lances [machines]	L 0124	070229
09	T 0188	Thermionic tubes	T 0567	090060
09	T 0189	Thermionic valves	T 0567	090060
10	T 0190	Thermo-electric compresses [surgery]	C 1114	100059
10	T 0191	Thermometers for medical purposes	T 0248	100198
09	T 0192	Thermometers, not for medical purposes	T 0249	090429
11	T 0193	Thermostatic valves [parts of heating installations]	V 0022	110319
09	T 0194	Thermostats	T 0251	090238
09	T 0195	Thermostats for vehicles	T 0252	090481
02	T 0196	Thickeners for paints	E 0379	020055
30	T 0197	Thickening agents for cooking foodstuffs	E 0380	300050

Cl.	SERIAL No. (E)	INDICATION OF GOODS	SERIAL No. (F)	BASIC No.
06	T 0198	Thimbles (Rope —) of metal	C 1337	060058
26	T 0199	Thimbles (Sewing —)	D 0114	260050
02	T 0200	Thinners for lacquers	D 0218	020054
02	T 0201	Thinners for paints	D 0219	020053
01	T 0202	Thiocarbanilide	T 0253	010533
08	T 0203	Thistle extirpators [hand tools]	E 0082	080096
01	T 0204	Thorium	T 0255	010535
23	T 0205	Thread *	F 0214	230001
09	T 0206	Thread counters	C 1120	090136
18	T 0207	Thread (Leather —)	C 1601	180040
22	T 0208	Thread, not of metal, for wrapping or binding	F 0216	220079
23	T 0209	Thread of metal for embroidery	C 0180	230032
06	T 0210	Thread of metal for tying-up purposes	F 0215	060286
10	T 0211	Thread, surgical	F 0222	100056
08	T 0212	Threaders	E 0321	080004
01	T 0213	Threading (Compositions for —)	F 0188	010295
07	T 0214	Threading machines	F 0189	070062
09	T 0215	Threads (Identification —) for electric wires	F 0229	090293
17	T 0216	Threads of plastic for soldering	S 0426	170047
23	T 0217	Threads of plastic materials for textile use	F 0236	230020
17	T 0218	Threads of plastic materials, not for textile use	F 0237	170105
14	T 0219	Threads of precious metal [jewellery, jewelry (Am.)]	F 0226	140040
17	T 0220	Threads of rubber, not for use in textiles	F 0221	170095
07	T 0221	Threshing machines	B 0269	070043
01	T 0222	Thulium	T 0256	010534
16	T 0223	Thumbtacks	P 1042	160048
05	T 0224	Thymol for pharmaceutical purposes	T 0257	050284
24	T 0225	Tick [linen]	C 1462	240031
09	T 0226	Ticket dispensers	D 0254	090086
16	T 0227	Tickets	B 0436	160038
08	T 0228	Tickets (Instruments for punching —)	B 0434	080212
24	T 0229	Ticks [mattress covers]	T 0320	240074
14	T 0230	Tie clips	F 0280	140033
14	T 0231	Tie pins	E 0394	140151
06	T 0232	Tie plates	A 0494	060020
21	T 0233	Tie presses	C 1509	210094
19	T 0234	Ties, not of metal (Railroad —)	T 0489	190176
06	T 0235	Ties of metal (Railroad —)	T 0488	060245
25	T 0236	Tights	C 1023	250051
19	T 0237	Tile floorings, not of metal	C 0277	190214
06	T 0238	Tile floorings of metal	C 0276	060322
20	T 0239	Tiles (Mirror —)	M 0413	200261
19	T 0240	Tiles, not of metal	T 0572	190151
19	T 0241	Tiles, not of metal, for building	C 0275	190213
06	T 0242	Tiles of metal	T 0571	060213
06	T 0243	Tiles of metal for building	C 0274	060321
01	T 0244	Tiles (Preservatives for —), except paints and oils	T 0573	010540
07	T 0245	Tilt hammers	M 0178	070250
12	T 0246	Tilt trucks	C 0534	120265
12	T 0247	Tilting-carts	T 0379	120183
19	T 0248	Timber (Building —)	B 0530	190027
19	T 0249	Timber (Manufactured —)	B 0541	190029
19	T 0250	Timber (Sawn —)	B 0535	190031
31	T 0251	Timber (Undressed —)	B 0538	310019
31	T 0252	Timber (Unsawn —)	B 0520	310017
12	T 0253	Timbers [frames] for ships	C 1402	120082
09	T 0254	Time clocks [time recording devices]	P 0717	090649
09	T 0255	Time recording apparatus	T 0180	090478
09	T 0256	Time switches, automatic	M 0406	090353
16	T 0257	Timetables (Printed —)	H 0083	160172
06	T 0258	Tin	E 0478	060373
06	T 0259	Tin cans	B 0599	060093
07	T 0260	Tin openers, electric	O 0155	070287
08	T 0261	Tin openers, non-electric	O 0156	080169
05	T 0262	Tincture of iodine	I 0119	050179
05	T 0263	Tinctures for medical purposes	T 0150	050208
04	T 0264	Tinder	A 0401	040108
06	T 0265	Tinfoil	F 0130	060375
06	T 0266	Tinplate	F 0061	060374
06	T 0267	Tinplate packings	E 0238	060119
26	T 0268	Tinsels [trimmings for clothing]	C 0949	260075
12	T 0269	Tipping apparatus, parts of trucks and waggons	C 1645	120201
12	T 0270	Tipping bodies for lorries [trucks]	B 0306	120042
28	T 0271	Tips (Billiard cue —)	P 0976	280122
34	T 0272	Tips (Cigarette —)	B 0772	340005
10	T 0273	Tips for crutches for invalids	E 0248	100126
25	T 0274	Tips for footwear	B 0771	250016
34	T 0275	Tips of yellow amber for cigar and cigarette holders	A 0419	340002
01	T 0276	Tire repairing compositions	P 0676	010465
09	T 0277	Tires (Automatic indicators of low pressure in vehicle —)	A 0864	090069
12	T 0278	Tires (Flanges of railway wheel —)	B 0691	120033
12	T 0279	Tires for bicycles, cycles	B 0378	120084
12	T 0280	Tires for vehicle wheels	B 0131	120031
01	T 0281	Tires (Mastic for —)	M 0209	010193
12	T 0282	Tires (Non-skid devices for vehicle —)	A 0579	120013
12	T 0283	Tires, solid, for vehicle wheels	P 0684	120157
03	T 0284	Tissues impregnated with cosmetic lotions	S 0271	030197
05	T 0285	Tissues impregnated with pharmaceutical lotions	S 0272	050374
16	T 0286	Tissues of paper for removing make-up	S 0260	160294
24	T 0287	Tissues of textile for removing make-up	S 0259	240101
05	T 0288	Tissues (Surgical —)	T 0299	050078
01	T 0289	Titanite	T 0313	010537
06	T 0290	Titanium	T 0310	060251
01	T 0291	Titanium dioxide for industrial purposes	A 0505	010536
02	T 0292	Titanium dioxide [pigment]	A 0506	020106
06	T 0293	Titanium iron	F 0088	060138
29	T 0294	Toasted laver	V 0033	290159

Cl.	SERIAL No. (E)	INDICATION OF GOODS	SERIAL No. (F)	BASIC No.
11	T 0295	Toasters	G 0348	110171
34	T 0296	Tobacco	T 0001	340003
11	T 0297	Tobacco (Cooling installations for —)	T 0004	110227
05	T 0298	Tobacco extracts [insecticides]	T 0003	050186
34	T 0299	Tobacco jars	P 0899	340032
34	T 0300	Tobacco pipes	P 0517	340009
34	T 0301	Tobacco pouches	B 0461	340004
07	T 0302	Tobacco processing machines	T 0005	070255
11	T 0303	Tobacco roasters	T 0008	110228
01	T 0304	Tobacco (Sauce for preparing —)	S 0097	010471
05	T 0305	Tobacco-free cigarettes for medical purposes	C 0844	050081
29	T 0306	Tofu	T 0316	290140
25	T 0307	Togas	T 0317	250117
11	T 0308	Toilet bowls	C 1676	110235
21	T 0309	Toilet brushes	T 0337	210051
21	T 0310	Toilet cases	N 0036	210115
16	T 0311	Toilet paper	P 0098	160094
21	T 0312	Toilet paper dispensers	D 0257	210116
21	T 0313	Toilet paper holders	P 0830	210335
11	T 0314	Toilet seats	S 0297	110236
21	T 0315	Toilet sponges	E 0402	210123
21	T 0316	Toilet utensils	T 0351	210225
03	T 0317	Toilet water	E 0050	030092
03	T 0318	Toiletries	T 0345	030125
11	T 0319	Toilets, portable	C 0013	110064
11	T 0320	Toilets [water-closets]	T 0353	110105
14	T 0321	Tokens (Copper —)	J 0027	140049
01	T 0322	Toluene	T 0371	010538
01	T 0323	Toluol	T 0371	010538
32	T 0324	Tomato juice [beverage]	T 0374	320030
29	T 0325	Tomato juice for cooking	T 0375	290110
29	T 0326	Tomato purée	P 1047	290101
30	T 0327	Tomato sauce	S 0098	300171
19	T 0328	Tomb or grave enclosures, not of metal	E 0282	190081
06	T 0329	Tombac	T 0377	060253
06	T 0330	Tombs (Enclosures of metal for —)	E 0281	060367
19	T 0331	Tombs [monuments], not of metal	F 0496	190225
06	T 0332	Tombs (Monuments of bronze for —)	B 0858	060055
06	T 0333	Tombs (Monuments of metal for —)	F 0495	060386
19	T 0334	Tombs, not of metal	T 0383	190174
06	T 0335	Tombs of metal	T 0382	060254
19	T 0336	Tombstone plaques, not of metal	P 0608	190088
06	T 0337	Tombstone plaques of metal	P 0607	060387
19	T 0338	Tombstone stelae, not of metal	S 0528	190226
06	T 0339	Tombstone stelae of metal	S 0527	060388
19	T 0340	Tombstones	P 0466	190144
06	T 0341	Tombstones of metal	F 0493	060385
15	T 0342	Tom-toms	T 0096	150068
09	T 0343	Tone arms for record players	B 0794	090095
02	T 0344	Toner cartridges, filled, for printers and photocopiers	E 0297	020123
02	T 0345	Toners [ink] for photocopiers	E 0304	020121
08	T 0346	Tongs	P 0512	080207
10	T 0347	Tongue scrapers	C 1667	100070
05	T 0348	Tonics [medicines]	R 0155	050262
01	T 0349	Toning baths [photography]	B 0081	010099
01	T 0350	Toning salts [photography]	S 0207	010548
18	T 0351	Tool bags of leather, empty	S 0021	180047
08	T 0352	Tool belts [holders]	C 0364	080247
06	T 0353	Tool boxes of metal, empty	B 0604	060423
06	T 0354	Tool chests of metal, empty	C 0995	060424
20	T 0355	Tool handles, not of metal	M 0083	200142
06	T 0356	Tool handles of metal	M 0082	060171
28	T 0357	Tools (Divot repair —) [golf accessories]	O 0148	280179
07	T 0358	Tools (Hand-held —), other than hand-operated	O 0154	070284
07	T 0359	Tools (Holding devices for machine —)	P 0826	070286
07	T 0360	Tools [parts of machines]	O 0152	070285
21	T 0361	Toothbrushes	B 0865	210250
21	T 0362	Toothbrushes, electric	B 0866	210276
21	T 0363	Toothpick holders	P 0811	210275
21	T 0364	Toothpicks	C 1665	210105
25	T 0365	Top hats	H 0047	250076
25	T 0366	Topcoats	P 0150	250115
26	T 0367	Top-knots [pompoms]	P 0782	260083
28	T 0368	Tops (Spinning —) [toys]	T 0414	280112
11	T 0369	Torches for lighting	T 0403	110202
11	T 0370	Torches (Pocket —), electric	L 0098	110051
13	T 0371	Torpedos	T 0407	130076
12	T 0372	Torque converters for land vehicles	C 1232	120227
07	T 0373	Torque converters other than for land vehicles	C 1231	070426
12	T 0374	Torsion bars for vehicles	B 0205	120034
30	T 0375	Tortillas	T 0409	300185
20	T 0376	Tortoiseshell	E 0071	200089
20	T 0377	Tortoiseshell imitation	E 0072	200045
09	T 0378	Totalizators	T 0410	090484
26	T 0379	Toupees	T 0413	260089
22	T 0380	Tow	E 0515	220014
20	T 0381	Towel closets [furniture]	P 0860	200276
20	T 0382	Towel dispensers, fixed, not of metal	D 0262	200084
06	T 0383	Towel dispensers, fixed, of metal	D 0261	060358
21	T 0384	Towel rails and rings	B 0206	210334
16	T 0385	Towels of paper	E 0462	160306
24	T 0386	Towels of textile	E 0461	240072
05	T 0387	Towels (Sanitary —)	S 0270	050234
01	T 0388	Toxic gas neutralizers	N 0061	010403
28	T 0389	Toy masks	M 0182	280090
28	T 0390	Toy pistols	P 0538	280058
28	T 0391	Toy vehicles	V 0084	280163
28	T 0392	Toys	J 0054	280024
28	T 0393	Toys for domestic pets	J 0056	280004

Cl.	SERIAL No. (E)	INDICATION OF GOODS	SERIAL No. (F)	BASIC No.
05	T 0394	Trace elements (Preparations of—) for human and animal use	O 0046	050375
01	T 0395	Trace elements (Preparations of—) for plants	O 0047	010637
24	T 0396	Traced cloths for embroidery	T 0309	240049
18	T 0397	Traces [harness]	T 0456	180057
16	T 0398	Tracing cloth	T 0319	160063
16	T 0399	Tracing needles for drawing purposes	P 0713	160184
16	T 0400	Tracing paper	P 0086	160062
16	T 0401	Tracing patterns	C 0142	160061
10	T 0402	Traction apparatus for medical purposes	E 0562	100215
12	T 0403	Traction engines	L 0359	120137
12	T 0404	Tractors	T 0444	120075
16	T 0405	Trading cards other than for games	C 0286	160354
09	T 0406	Traffic accidents (Reflecting discs, for wear, for the prevention of—)	D 0241	090003
09	T 0407	Traffic-light apparatus [signalling devices]	F 0143	090687
01	T 0408	Tragacanth gum for use in manufactures	A 0122	010024
12	T 0409	Trailer hitches for vehicles	A 0816	120017
12	T 0410	Trailers [vehicles]	R 0219	120057
12	T 0411	Tramcars	T 0459	120187
28	T 0412	Trampolines	T 0458	280209
05	T 0413	Tranquillizers	C 0134	050268
16	T 0414	Transfers [decalcomanias]	D 0015	160119
03	T 0415	Transfers (Decorative—) for cosmetic purposes	D 0036	030181
09	T 0416	Transformers [electricity]	T 0466	090049
17	T 0417	Transformers (Insulating oil for—)	T 0467	170051
09	T 0418	Transistors [electronic]	T 0468	090624
12	T 0419	Transmission chains for land vehicles	C 0436	120226
07	T 0420	Transmission chains other than for land vehicles	C 0435	070427
01	T 0421	Transmission fluid	F 0319	010644
07	T 0422	Transmission shafts (Bearings for—)	P 0044	070290
12	T 0423	Transmission shafts for land vehicles	A 0662	120246
07	T 0424	Transmission shafts, other than for land vehicles	A 0661	070022
12	T 0425	Transmissions, for land vehicles	T 0473	120142
07	T 0426	Transmissions for machines	T 0475	070369
07	T 0427	Transmissions, other than for land vehicles	T 0472	070253
09	T 0428	Transmitters of electronic signals	E 0261	090227
09	T 0429	Transmitters [telecommunication]	T 0469	090488
09	T 0430	Transmitting sets [telecommunication]	E 0262	090228
09	T 0431	Transparencies [photography]	D 0196	090185
16	T 0432	Transparencies [stationery]	T 0476	160262
09	T 0433	Transparency projection apparatus	D 0198	090186
09	T 0434	Transponders	T 0479	090693
12	T 0435	Transport apparatus and installations (Cable—)	T 0480	120188
20	T 0436	Transport pallets, not of metal	P 0037	200145
06	T 0437	Transport pallets of metal	P 0036	060176
07	T 0438	Transporters (Pneumatic—)	P 0680	070304
28	T 0439	Traps (Clay pigeon—)	T 0287	280080
06	T 0440	Traps for wild animals *	P 0444	060025
21	T 0441	Traps (Insect—)	P 0445	210150
20	T 0442	Traps of plastic (Drain—) [valves]	C 0921	200231
21	T 0443	Traps (Rat—)	R 0095	210198
07	T 0444	Traps (Steam—)	P 1049	070320
21	T 0445	Trash cans	P 0905	210194
07	T 0446	Trash compacting machines	C 1094	070418
18	T 0447	Travelling bags	S 0037	180078
24	T 0448	Travelling rugs [lap robes]	C 1482	240034
18	T 0449	Travelling sets [leatherware]	T 0545	180084
18	T 0450	Travelling trunks	C 0996	180029
21	T 0451	Trays for domestic purposes	P 0627	210267
21	T 0452	Trays for domestic purposes, of paper	P 0628	210180
16	T 0453	Trays for sorting and counting money	P 0633	160059
21	T 0454	Trays (Litter—) for pets	B 0008	210306
20	T 0455	Trays, not of metal *	C 1254	200072
12	T 0456	Treads for retreading tires [tyres]	B 0155	120156
12	T 0457	Treads for vehicles [roller belts]	C 0708	120074
12	T 0458	Treads for vehicles [tractor type]	C 0708	120074
01	T 0459	Tree cavity fillers [forestry]	M 0201	010080
06	T 0460	Tree protectors of metal	P 1008	060028
08	T 0461	Tree pruners	E 0177	080100
01	T 0462	Tree-banding (Glutinous preparations for—)	A 0649	010079
01	T 0463	Tree-grafting (Glutinous preparations for—)	A 0649	010079
31	T 0464	Trees	A 0666	310008
31	T 0465	Trees (Trunks of—)	T 0534	310010
24	T 0466	Trellis [cloth]	T 0495	240016
06	T 0467	Trellis of metal	T 0493	060256
19	T 0468	Trellises, not of metal	T 0494	190177
26	T 0469	Tresses of hair	T 0506	260044
20	T 0470	Trestles [furniture]	T 0508	200196
15	T 0471	Triangles [musical instruments]	T 0513	150055
12	T 0472	Tricycles	T 0522	120191
12	T 0473	Tricycles (Carrier—)	T 0529	120162
13	T 0474	Trigger guards for guns and rifles	S 0470	130040
07	T 0475	Trimming machines	D 0311	070159
26	T 0476	Trimmings for clothing	G 0375	260064
18	T 0477	Trimmings of leather for furniture	G 0073	180041
14	T 0478	Trinkets [jewellery, jewelry (Am.)]	B 0803	140018
09	T 0479	Triodes	T 0526	090705
29	T 0480	Tripe	T 0527	290112

Cl.	SERIAL No. (E)	INDICATION OF GOODS	SERIAL No. (F)	BASIC No.
09	T 0481	Tripods for cameras	T 0501	090577
03	T 0482	Tripoli stone for polishing	T 0528	030164
21	T 0483	Trivets [table utensils]	D 0155	210270
10	T 0484	Trocars	T 0530	100151
12	T 0485	Trolleys *	D 0303	120106
20	T 0486	Trolleys for computers [furniture]	D 0139	200266
20	T 0487	Trolleys [furniture]	C 0541	200254
15	T 0488	Trombones	T 0531	150070
20	T 0489	Troughs, not of metal, for mixing mortar	A 0826	200206
06	T 0490	Troughs of metal for mixing mortar	A 0825	060279
26	T 0491	Trouser clips for cyclists	P 0509	260119
21	T 0492	Trouser presses	P 0958	210171
25	T 0493	Trouser straps	S 0472	250083
25	T 0494	Trousers	P 0069	250064
08	T 0495	Trowels	T 0547	080087
08	T 0496	Trowels [gardening]	D 0103	080086
07	T 0497	Truck lifts	M 0460	070271
12	T 0498	Trucks	C 0147	120022
12	T 0499	Trucks (Luggage —)	D 0182	120050
07	T 0500	Trueing machines	R 0157	070326
31	T 0501	Truffles, fresh	T 0549	310121
29	T 0502	Truffles, preserved	T 0548	290113
15	T 0503	Trumpets	T 0532	150072
08	T 0504	Truncheons	M 0230	080130
25	T 0505	Trunks (Bathing —)	C 0125	250125
18	T 0506	Trunks [luggage]	M 0057	180092
31	T 0507	Trunks of trees	T 0534	310010
13	T 0508	Trunnions for heavy weapons	T 0420	130056
10	T 0509	Trusses	B 0802	100039
07	T 0510	Trussing apparatus for hay	B 0660	070058
16	T 0511	T-squares (Drawing —)	T 0218	160298
06	T 0512	Tubbing of metal	C 1672	060111
07	T 0513	Tube conveyors, pneumatic	T 0481	070370
08	T 0514	Tube cutters [hand tools]	C 1398	080075
08	T 0515	Tube cutting instruments	T 0605	080198
12	T 0516	Tubeless tires [tyres] for bicycles, cycles	B 0777	120234
07	T 0517	Tubes (Boiler —) [parts of machines]	T 0561	070471
16	T 0518	Tubes (Cardboard —)	T 0563	160078
11	T 0519	Tubes (Discharge —), electric, for lighting	T 0556	110111
10	T 0520	Tubes (Drainage —) for medical purposes	D 0302	100081
09	T 0521	Tubes (Electric discharge —), other than for lighting	T 0555	090559
17	T 0522	Tubes (Flexible —), not of metal	T 0604	170022
11	T 0523	Tubes (Luminous —) for lighting	T 0565	110189
06	T 0524	Tubes of metal	T 0608	060127
19	T 0525	Tufa	T 0570	190145
24	T 0526	Tulle	T 0574	240089
29	T 0527	Tuna fish	T 0254	290109
06	T 0528	Tungsten	T 0577	060257
06	T 0529	Tungsten iron	F 0089	060139
01	T 0530	Tungstic acid	T 0578	010541
15	T 0531	Tuning forks	D 0193	150033
15	T 0532	Tuning hammers	A 0024	150002
25	T 0533	Turbans	T 0579	250156
12	T 0534	Turbines for land vehicles	T 0581	120192
07	T 0535	Turbines (Hydraulic —)	H 0191	070215
07	T 0536	Turbines other than for land vehicles	T 0580	070375
07	T 0537	Turbocompressors	T 0582	070114
27	T 0538	Turf (Artificial —)	G 0142	270003
31	T 0539	Turf, natural	G 0143	310063
07	T 0540	Turf removing ploughs	D 0051	070148
11	T 0541	Turkish bath cabinets, portable	C 0011	110036
02	T 0542	Turmeric [colorant]	C 1664	020060
30	T 0543	Turmeric for food	C 1663	300051
12	T 0544	Turn signals for vehicles	I 0066	120228
15	T 0545	Turning apparatus for sheet music	M 0577	150053
06	T 0546	Turnstiles	T 0434	060255
06	T 0547	Turntables [railways]	P 0614	060212
03	T 0548	Turpentine, for degreasing	T 0201	030157
05	T 0549	Turpentine for pharmaceutical purposes	T 0199	050282
02	T 0550	Turpentine [thinner for paints]	T 0200	020124
08	T 0551	Tweezers	B 0881	080042
22	T 0552	Twine for nets	F 0223	220039
22	T 0553	Twine made of paper	P 0097	220038
28	T 0554	Twirling batons	C 0175	280164
12	T 0555	Two-wheeled trolleys	D 0182	120050
07	T 0556	Tympans [parts of printing presses]	T 0613	070377
16	T 0557	Type [numerals and letters]	C 0224	160097
07	T 0558	Typecasting machines	C 0225	070120
07	T 0559	Type-setting machines [photocomposition]	P 0387	070112
07	T 0560	Type-setting machines [printing]	C 1106	070076
16	T 0561	Typewriter keys	T 0411	160257
16	T 0562	Typewriter ribbons	R 0443	160245
16	T 0563	Typewriters, electric or non-electric	M 0007	160132
20	T 0564	Typing desks	T 0048	200095
07	T 0565	Typographic machines	T 0615	070378
07	T 0566	Typographic presses	P 0959	070303
01	T 0567	Tyre repairing compositions	P 0676	010465
09	T 0568	Tyres (Automatic indicators of low pressure in vehicle —)	A 0864	090069
12	T 0569	Tyres (Flanges of railway wheel —)	B 0691	120033
12	T 0570	Tyres for bicycles, cycles	B 0378	120084
12	T 0571	Tyres for vehicle wheels	B 0131	120031
01	T 0572	Tyres (Mastic for —)	M 0209	010193
12	T 0573	Tyres (Non-skid devices for vehicle —)	A 0579	120013
17	T 0574	Tyres (Rubber material for recapping —)	R 0133	170109
12	T 0575	Tyres, solid, for vehicle wheels	P 0684	120157

Cl.	SERIAL No. (E)	INDICATION OF GOODS	SERIAL No. (F)	BASIC No.
10	U 0001	Ultraviolet ray lamps for medical purposes	R 0112	100105
11	U 0002	Ultraviolet ray lamps, not for medical purposes	R 0113	110180
10	U 0003	Ultraviolet rays for medical purposes (Filters for —)	F 0270	100181
10	U 0004	Umbilical belts	O 0054	100121
18	U 0005	Umbrella covers	F 0400	180051
18	U 0006	Umbrella handles	P 0700	180068
18	U 0007	Umbrella or parasol ribs	B 0106	180007
18	U 0008	Umbrella rings	A 0563	180003
20	U 0009	Umbrella stands	P 0827	200164
18	U 0010	Umbrella sticks	C 0176	180014
18	U 0011	Umbrellas	P 0138	180043
03	U 0012	Unblocking drain pipes (Preparations for —)	D 0012	030195
12	U 0013	Undercarriages for vehicles	T 0451	120185
25	U 0014	Underclothing	L 0300	250026
25	U 0015	Underclothing (Anti-sweat —)	S 0475	250054
02	U 0016	Undercoating for vehicle chassis	R 0297	020040
25	U 0017	Underpants	S 0352	250112
02	U 0018	Undersealing for vehicle chassis	R 0297	020040
25	U 0019	Underwear	L 0300	250026
25	U 0020	Underwear (Anti-sweat —)	S 0475	250054
31	U 0021	Undressed timber	B 0538	310019
01	U 0022	Ungluing agents [chemical preparations for liquifying starch]	A 0444	010056
01	U 0023	Ungluing preparations	D 0031	010232
25	U 0024	Uniforms	U 0005	250119
07	U 0025	Universal joints [Cardan joints]	J 0048	070479
30	U 0026	Unleavened bread	A 0891	300013
31	U 0027	Unsawn timber	B 0520	310017
01	U 0028	Unsticking and separating preparations	D 0031	010232
22	U 0029	Upholstering (Grasses for —)	H 0067	220044
24	U 0030	Upholstery fabrics	M 0339	240004
22	U 0031	Upholstery (Feathers for stuffing —)	P 0670	220064
12	U 0032	Upholstery for vehicles	G 0090	120195
22	U 0033	Upholstery (Straw for stuffing —)	P 0008	220062
22	U 0034	Upholstery wool [stuffing]	L 0029	220033
25	U 0035	Uppers (Footwear —)	E 0266	250061
01	U 0036	Uranium	U 0010	010542
01	U 0037	Uranium oxide	U 0008	010543
10	U 0038	Urethral probes	U 0012	100153
10	U 0039	Urethral syringes	U 0011	100154
11	U 0040	Urinals [sanitary fixtures]	U 0014	110301
10	U 0041	Urinals [vessels]	U 0013	100110
09	U 0042	Urinometers	U 0018	090492
21	U 0043	Urns*	U 0015	210226
20	U 0044	Urns (Funerary —)	U 0016	200267
10	U 0045	Urological apparatus and instruments	U 0017	100102
09	U 0046	USB flash drives	C 0940	090700
21	U 0047	Utensils for household purposes	U 0022	210159
10	U 0048	Uterine syringes	U 0023	100142

Cl.	SERIAL No. (E)	INDICATION OF GOODS	SERIAL No. (F)	BASIC No.
05	V 0001	Vaccines	V 0001	050107
21	V 0002	Vacuum bottles	B 0752	210046
07	V 0003	Vacuum cleaner attachments for disseminating perfumes and disinfectants	A 0792	070506
07	V 0004	Vacuum cleaner bags	S 0049	070521
07	V 0005	Vacuum cleaner hoses	T 0588	070507
07	V 0006	Vacuum cleaners	A 0791	070508
09	V 0007	Vacuum gauges	V 0002	090302
07	V 0008	Vacuum pumps [machines]	P 0772	070312
09	V 0009	Vacuum tubes [radio]	T 0568	090491
10	V 0010	Vaginal syringes	V 0004	100143
05	V 0011	Vaginal washes	B 0087	050393
18	V 0012	Valises	V 0008	180085
07	V 0013	Valves (Clack—) [parts of machines]	C 0920	070108
10	V 0014	Valves (Feeding bottle—)	F 0072	100169
15	V 0015	Valves for musical instruments	V 0013	150073
12	V 0016	Valves for vehicle tires [tyres]	V 0010	120032
11	V 0017	Valves (Level controlling—) in tanks	S 0459	110194
20	V 0018	Valves, not of metal, other than parts of machines	S 0457	200186
17	V 0019	Valves of india-rubber or vulcanized fiber [fibre]	V 0011	170082
18	V 0020	Valves of leather	V 0012	180087
06	V 0021	Valves of metal, other than parts of machines	S 0456	060243
20	V 0022	Valves of plastic (Water-pipe—)	C 0917	200236
07	V 0023	Valves [parts of machines]	S 0458	070019
09	V 0024	Valves (Solenoid—) [electromagnetic switches]	V 0014	090675
11	V 0025	Valves (Thermostatic—) [parts of heating installations]	V 0022	110319
06	V 0026	Vanadium	V 0015	060259
06	V 0027	Vanes of metal (Weather- or wind-—)	G 0198	060148
30	V 0028	Vanilla [flavoring] [flavouring]	V 0016	300130
30	V 0029	Vanillin [vanilla substitute]	V 0017	300131
21	V 0030	Vanity cases (Fitted—)	N 0036	210115
18	V 0031	Vanity cases, not fitted	C 1004	180093
12	V 0032	Vans [vehicles]	F 0385	120125
04	V 0033	Vaporized fuel mixtures	C 0249	040020
10	V 0034	Vaporizers for medical purposes	V 0030	100109
08	V 0035	Vaporizers (Insecticide—) [hand tools]	P 1041	080144
09	V 0036	Variometers	V 0038	090493
17	V 0037	Varnish (Insulating—)	V 0132	170057
03	V 0038	Varnish (Nail—)	L 0142	030032
02	V 0039	Varnishes *	V 0130	020003
01	V 0040	Varnishes (Solvents for—)	D 0247	010606
03	V 0041	Varnish-removing preparations	V 0133	030088
21	V 0042	Vases	V 0039	210190
20	V 0043	Vats, not of metal	C 1674	200081
06	V 0044	Vats of metal	C 1673	060354
19	V 0045	Vaults, not of metal [burial]	C 0350	190215
06	V 0046	Vaults of metal [burial]	C 0349	060323
08	V 0047	Vegetable choppers	H 0007	080136
21	V 0048	Vegetable dishes	L 0194	210154
32	V 0049	Vegetable juices [beverages]	J 0071	320022
29	V 0050	Vegetable juices for cooking	J 0072	290067
08	V 0051	Vegetable knives	C 1389	080073
29	V 0052	Vegetable salads	S 0061	290102
08	V 0053	Vegetable shredders	C 1389	080073
08	V 0054	Vegetable slicers	C 1389	080073
29	V 0055	Vegetable soup preparations	J 0063	290066
29	V 0056	Vegetables, cooked	L 0187	290030
29	V 0057	Vegetables, dried	L 0193	290031
31	V 0058	Vegetables, fresh	L 0189	310042
29	V 0059	Vegetables, preserved	L 0185	290029
29	V 0060	Vegetables, tinned [canned (Am.)]	C 1196	290152
30	V 0061	Vegetal preparations for use as coffee substitutes	C 0081	300028
09	V 0062	Vehicle breakdown warning triangles	T 0512	090446
12	V 0063	Vehicle bumpers	P 0154	120077
12	V 0064	Vehicle chassis	C 0573	120069
02	V 0065	Vehicle chassis (Undercoating for—)	R 0297	020040
02	V 0066	Vehicle chassis (Undersealing for—)	R 0297	020040
22	V 0067	Vehicle covers, not fitted	V 0057	220075
12	V 0068	Vehicle covers [shaped]	H 0112	120224
01	V 0069	Vehicle engines (Coolants for—)	R 0177	010647
11	V 0070	Vehicle headlights	P 0370	110200
12	V 0071	Vehicle petrol [gas] tanks (Caps for—)	B 0683	120241
17	V 0072	Vehicle radiators (Connecting hose for—)	T 0595	170074
09	V 0073	Vehicle radios	R 0026	090417
11	V 0074	Vehicle reflectors	R 0165	110212
12	V 0075	Vehicle running boards	M 0142	120141
12	V 0076	Vehicle seats	S 0298	120177
12	V 0077	Vehicle suspension springs	R 0278	120171
07	V 0078	Vehicle washing installations	L 0155	070235
12	V 0079	Vehicle wheel rims	J 0012	120174
12	V 0080	Vehicle wheel spokes	R 0107	120168
12	V 0081	Vehicle wheel tires [tyres]	V 0090	120158
12	V 0082	Vehicle wheels	R 0383	120053
12	V 0083	Vehicle wheels (Hubs for—)	M 0562	120060
11	V 0084	Vehicles (Air conditioners for—)	C 0947	110079
12	V 0085	Vehicles (Air cushion—)	A 0134	120237
11	V 0086	Vehicles (Anti-dazzle devices for—) [lamp fittings]	A 0587	110249
12	V 0087	Vehicles (Anti-glare devices for—) *	A 0586	120204
12	V 0088	Vehicles (Connecting rods for land—), other than parts of motors and engines	B 0401	120242
11	V 0089	Vehicles (Defrosters for—)	D 0052	110112
12	V 0090	Vehicles (Electric—)	V 0072	120110
12	V 0091	Vehicles for locomotion by land, air, water or rail	V 0047	120193
12	V 0092	Vehicles for transport (Military—)	V 0085	120144
11	V 0093	Vehicles (Heating apparatus for defrosting windows of—)	V 0071	110250

Cl.	SERIAL No. (E)	INDICATION OF GOODS	SERIAL No. (F)	BASIC No.
11	V 0094	Vehicles (Lighting apparatus for —)	E 0098	110229
11	V 0095	Vehicles (Lights for —)	F 0144	110027
09	V 0096	Vehicles (Navigation apparatus for —) [on-board computers]	V 0051	090659
28	V 0097	Vehicles (Radio-controlled toy —)	V 0103	280185
12	V 0098	Vehicles (Refrigerated —)	V 0077	120128
12	V 0099	Vehicles (Remote control —), other than toys	V 0102	120257
28	V 0100	Vehicles (Scale model —)	M 0435	280091
12	V 0101	Vehicles (Space —)	V 0101	120117
25	V 0102	Veils [clothing]	V 0296	250123
24	V 0103	Velvet	V 0114	240026
07	V 0104	Vending machines	D 0253	070537
19	V 0105	Veneer wood	B 0534	190034
19	V 0106	Veneers	P 0551	190033
06	V 0107	Ventilating and air conditioning installations (Ducts of metal for —)	C 1162	060415
11	V 0108	Ventilation [air-conditioning] installations and apparatus	V 0119	110233
11	V 0109	Ventilation [air-conditioning] installations for vehicles	V 0120	110234
11	V 0110	Ventilation hoods	H 0095	110006
11	V 0111	Ventilation hoods for laboratories	H 0096	110244
30	V 0112	Vermicelli [noodles]	V 0126	300132
30	V 0113	Vermicelli (Ribbon —)	N 0104	300103
05	V 0114	Vermifuges	V 0127	050154
05	V 0115	Vermin destroying preparations	V 0128	050289
09	V 0116	Verniers	V 0129	090494
05	V 0117	Vesicants	V 0184	050290
21	V 0118	Vessels of metal for making ices and iced drinks	S 0405	210211
25	V 0119	Vests	G 0190	250082
09	V 0120	Vests (Am.) (Bullet-proof —)	G 0193	090582
25	V 0121	Vests (Fishing —)	V 0186	250159
10	V 0122	Veterinary apparatus and instruments	V 0215	100156
05	V 0123	Veterinary preparations	V 0216	050287
07	V 0124	Vibrators [machines] for industrial use	V 0230	070509
10	V 0125	Vibromassage apparatus	V 0232	100158
20	V 0126	Vice benches, not of metal	E 0491	200209
06	V 0127	Vice benches of metal	E 0490	060283
06	V 0128	Vice claws of metal	M 0473	060191
08	V 0129	Vices	E 0489	080244
09	V 0130	Video cassettes	C 0337	090650
09	V 0131	Video game cartridges	C 0314	090651
28	V 0132	Video game machines	M 0012	280214
09	V 0133	Video recorders	M 0030	090536
09	V 0134	Video screens	E 0135	090652
09	V 0135	Video telephones	V 0268	090653
09	V 0136	Videotapes	B 0173	090495
09	V 0137	Viewfinders, photographic	V 0265	090392
16	V 0138	Vignetting apparatus	V 0240	160263
01	V 0139	Vine disease preventing chemicals	V 0238	010546
05	V 0140	Vine disease treating chemicals	V 0239	050288
31	V 0141	Vine plants	V 0237	310104
30	V 0142	Vinegar	V 0246	300081
01	V 0143	Vinegar (Wood —) [pyroligneous acid]	V 0244	010133
22	V 0144	Vines (Strips for tying-up —)	B 0144	220003
01	V 0145	Vinic alcohol	V 0248	010547
27	V 0146	Vinyl floor coverings	R 0300	270016
19	V 0147	Vinyl siding	R 0056	190238
15	V 0148	Violas	V 0250	150074
15	V 0149	Violins	V 0251	150075
01	V 0150	Viscose	V 0259	010157
16	V 0151	Viscose sheets for wrapping	V 0261	160310
17	V 0152	Viscose sheets, other than for packing	V 0260	170083
17	V 0153	Viscose sheets, other than for wrapping	V 0260	170083
09	V 0154	Viscosimeters	V 0262	090496
25	V 0155	Visors [hatmaking]	V 0267	250030
05	V 0156	Vitamin preparations	V 0269	050090
22	V 0157	Vitreous silica fibers [fibres] for textile use	F 0153	220037
21	V 0158	Vitreous silica fibers [fibres], not for textile use	F 0154	210283
01	V 0159	Vitriol	V 0288	010225
33	V 0160	Vodka	V 0289	330034
03	V 0161	Volatile alkali [ammonia] [detergent]	A 0458	030167
01	V 0162	Volatile alkali [ammonia] for industrial purposes	A 0279	010558
03	V 0163	Volcanic ash for cleaning	C 0387	030038
09	V 0164	Voltage regulators for vehicles	R 0194	090498
09	V 0165	Voltage surge protectors	R 0189	090676
09	V 0166	Voltmeters	V 0325	090500
09	V 0167	Voting machines	V 0326	090499
01	V 0168	Vulcanisation accelerators	A 0018	010005
07	V 0169	Vulcanisation apparatus	V 0334	070384
01	V 0170	Vulcanising preparations	V 0335	010549
17	V 0171	Vulcanite [ebonite]	C 0194	170036
17	V 0172	Vulcanite [ebonite] molds [moulds]	M 0527	170100
17	V 0173	Vulcanized fiber [fibre]	F 0149	170046
05	V 0174	Vulnerary sponges	E 0404	050136

Cl.	SERIAL No. (E)	INDICATION OF GOODS	SERIAL No. (F)	BASIC No.
22	W 0001	Wadding for filtering	O 0136	220060
05	W 0002	Wadding for medical purposes	O 0138	050072
22	W 0003	Wadding for padding and stuffing upholstery	O 0139	220061
09	W 0004	Wafers [silicon slices]	P 0617	090584
11	W 0005	Waffle irons, electric	G 0102	110258
21	W 0006	Waffle irons, non-electric	G 0103	210309
30	W 0007	Waffles	G 0100	300022
07	W 0008	Waggon lifts	M 0460	070271
12	W 0009	Waggons	W 0002	120076
12	W 0010	Waggons (Refrigerated —) [railroad vehicles]	W 0007	120129
20	W 0011	Wagons (Dinner —) [furniture]	B 0895	200222
12	W 0012	Wagons (Refrigerated —) [railroad vehicles]	W 0007	120129
19	W 0013	Wainscotting, not of metal	L 0069	190189
06	W 0014	Wainscotting of metal	L 0068	060274
25	W 0015	Waistcoats	G 0190	250082
09	W 0016	Waistcoats (Bullet-proof —)	G 0193	090582
09	W 0017	Waling glasses	C 1120	090136
20	W 0018	Walkers (Infant —)	T 0535	200258
09	W 0019	Walkie-talkies	T 0070	090677
11	W 0020	Walk-in refrigerators	C 0465	110156
18	W 0021	Walking cane handles	P 0699	180060
18	W 0022	Walking stick handles	P 0699	180060
18	W 0023	Walking stick seats	C 0179	180016
18	W 0024	Walking sticks	C 0171	180015
06	W 0025	Walking sticks (Ferrules of metal for —)	E 0249	060064
19	W 0026	Wall claddings, not of metal, for building	M 0570	190130
06	W 0027	Wall claddings of metal [building]	M 0569	060192
27	W 0028	Wall hangings, not of textile	T 0125	270013
24	W 0029	Wall hangings of textile	T 0196	240103
06	W 0030	Wall hooks of metal for pipes	C 1040	060312
19	W 0031	Wall linings, not of metal, for building	P 0167	190138
06	W 0032	Wall linings of metal [building]	P 0166	060201
20	W 0033	Wall plugs, not of metal	T 0089	200232
06	W 0034	Wall plugs of metal	T 0088	060087
01	W 0035	Wall tiles (Adhesives for —)	A 0107	010573
19	W 0036	Wall tiles, not of metal, for building	C 0275	190213
18	W 0037	Wallets (Pocket —)	P 0814	180069
20	W 0038	Wall-mounted diaper [napkin] changing platforms	T 0032	200278
27	W 0039	Wallpaper	P 0126	270007
01	W 0040	Wallpaper (Adhesives for —)	C 1036	010203
03	W 0041	Wallpaper cleaning preparations	P 0128	030138
01	W 0042	Wallpaper removing preparations	P 0129	010653
11	W 0043	Warming pans	B 0228	110306
12	W 0044	Warning systems (Audible —) for cycles	S 0402	120098
09	W 0045	Warning triangles (Vehicle breakdown —)	T 0512	090446
05	W 0046	Wart pencils	C 1515	050033
02	W 0047	Wash (Lime —)	L 0052	020042

Cl.	SERIAL No. (E)	INDICATION OF GOODS	SERIAL No. (F)	BASIC No.
11	W 0048	Washers for water taps	R 0359	110219
06	W 0049	Washers of metal	R 0361	060037
17	W 0050	Washers of rubber or vulcanized fiber [fibre]	R 0360	170076
11	W 0051	Wash-hand basins [parts of sanitary installations]	L 0151	110186
11	W 0052	Wash-hand bowls [parts of sanitary installations]	L 0151	110186
07	W 0053	Washing apparatus	L 0153	070233
21	W 0054	Washing boards	P 0567	210006
11	W 0055	Washing coppers	C 0581	110063
21	W 0056	Washing floors (Cloth for —)	S 0242	210303
07	W 0057	Washing installations for vehicles	L 0155	070235
07	W 0058	Washing machines	L 0165	070232
07	W 0059	Washing machines (Coin-operated —)	L 0166	070236
07	W 0060	Washing machines [laundry]	L 0294	070234
24	W 0061	Washing mitts	G 0055	240055
03	W 0062	Washing preparations	L 0205	030124
03	W 0063	Washing soda, for cleaning	C 1564	030072
09	W 0064	Washing trays [photography]	B 0009	090390
11	W 0065	Washrooms (Hand drying apparatus for —)	S 0161	110223
20	W 0066	Washstands [furniture]	T 0039	200137
21	W 0067	Washtubs	C 1677	210106
07	W 0068	Waste compacting machines	C 1094	070418
10	W 0069	Waste (Containers especially made for medical —)	R 0154	100216
07	W 0070	Waste disposals	B 0877	070414
07	W 0071	Waste disposers [machines]	B 0877	070414
31	W 0072	Waste (Distillery —) for animal consumption	R 0257	310048
22	W 0073	Waste [flock] (Cotton —) for padding and stuffing	D 0022	220090
21	W 0074	Waste paper baskets	C 1251	210340
14	W 0075	Watch bands	B 0782	140017
14	W 0076	Watch cases	B 0630	140144
14	W 0077	Watch chains	C 0431	140025
14	W 0078	Watch crystals	V 0175	140059
14	W 0079	Watch glasses	V 0175	140059
14	W 0080	Watch springs	R 0277	140058
14	W 0081	Watch straps	B 0782	140017
14	W 0082	Watches	M 0461	140057
01	W 0083	Water (Acidulated —) for recharging accumulators	E 0002	010251
21	W 0084	Water apparatus for cleaning teeth and gums	D 0291	210262
10	W 0085	Water bags for medical purposes	E 0037	100082
10	W 0086	Water beds for medical purposes	L 0347	100096
20	W 0087	Water beds, not for medical purposes	L 0348	200230
11	W 0088	Water closets	T 0353	110105
11	W 0089	Water conduits installations	C 1150	110104
01	W 0090	Water (Distilled —)	E 0027	010247
11	W 0091	Water distribution installations	D 0266	110096
11	W 0092	Water filtering apparatus	E 0003	110124
11	W 0093	Water flushing installations	C 0562	110272

Cl.	SERIAL No. (E)	INDICATION OF GOODS	SERIAL No. (F)	BASIC No.
01	W 0094	Water glass [soluble glass]	V 0162	010544
11	W 0095	Water heaters	C 0612	110052
11	W 0096	Water heaters [apparatus]	R 0138	110211
07	W 0097	Water heaters [parts of machines]	R 0139	070165
01	W 0098	Water (Heavy —)	E 0035	010253
11	W 0099	Water intake apparatus	P 0972	110276
09	W 0100	Water level indicators	I 0067	090204
32	W 0101	Water (Lithia —)	E 0056	320014
11	W 0102	Water or gas apparatus and pipes (Regulating accessories for —)	R 0181	110216
11	W 0103	Water or gas apparatus and pipes (Safety accessories for —)	S 0601	110217
11	W 0104	Water purification installations	E 0031	110123
11	W 0105	Water purifying apparatus and machines	P 1054	110206
01	W 0106	Water purifying chemicals	P 1055	010608
30	W 0107	Water (Sea —) for cooking	E 0025	300169
01	W 0108	Water (Sea —) for industrial purposes	E 0022	010636
05	W 0109	Water (Sea —) for medicinal bathing	E 0024	050044
32	W 0110	Water (Seltzer —)	E 0026	320017
07	W 0111	Water separators	E 0044	070439
11	W 0112	Water softening apparatus and installations	A 0120	110243
11	W 0113	Water sterilizers	E 0046	110128
11	W 0114	Water supply installations	E 0032	110252
12	W 0115	Water vehicles	N 0019	120149
28	W 0116	Water wings	F 0313	280211
16	W 0117	Watercolor saucers (Artists' —)	G 0257	160166
02	W 0118	Watercolors (Fixatives for —)	A 0632	020011
16	W 0119	Watercolors [paintings]	A 0633	160020
16	W 0120	Watercolour saucers (Artists' —)	G 0257	160166
02	W 0121	Watercolours (Fixatives for —)	A 0632	020011
16	W 0122	Watercolours [paintings]	A 0633	160020
21	W 0123	Watering cans	A 0765	210016
21	W 0124	Watering devices	A 0760	210013
17	W 0125	Watering hose	T 0586	170006
11	W 0126	Watering installations, automatic	A 0013	110001
11	W 0127	Watering machines for agricultural purposes	I 0131	110327
19	W 0128	Water-pipe valves, not of metal or plastic	C 0919	190077
06	W 0129	Water-pipe valves of metal	C 0918	060359
20	W 0130	Water-pipe valves of plastic	C 0917	200236
11	W 0131	Water-pipes for sanitary installations	C 1164	110103
19	W 0132	Water-pipes, not of metal	C 1152	190076
06	W 0133	Water-pipes of metal	C 1151	060091
25	W 0134	Waterproof clothing	I 0020	250087
17	W 0135	Waterproof packings	G 0087	170011
01	W 0136	Waterproofing chemicals (Cement- —), except paints	C 0860	010195
01	W 0137	Waterproofing chemicals (Leather- —)	C 1608	010364

Cl.	SERIAL No. (E)	INDICATION OF GOODS	SERIAL No. (F)	BASIC No.
01	W 0138	Waterproofing chemicals (Textile- —)	I 0017	010362
32	W 0139	Waters [beverages]	E 0047	320012
05	W 0140	Waters (Mineral —) for medical purposes	E 0057	050129
32	W 0141	Waters (Table —)	E 0049	320018
28	W 0142	Waterskis	S 0348	280152
01	W 0143	Water-softening preparations	A 0118	010023
17	W 0144	Water-tight rings	B 0032	170009
09	W 0145	Wavemeters	O 0057	090369
03	W 0146	Waving preparations for the hair	C 0734	030041
03	W 0147	Wax (Cobblers' —)	P 0735	030050
03	W 0148	Wax (Depilatory —)	C 0878	030097
22	W 0149	Wax ends	L 0258	220055
20	W 0150	Wax figures	C 0885	200060
03	W 0151	Wax for floors (Non-slipping —)	C 0884	030207
28	W 0152	Wax for skis	F 0022	280063
01	W 0153	Wax (Grafting —) for trees	C 0879	010198
03	W 0154	Wax (Laundry —)	C 0889	030051
03	W 0155	Wax (Moustache —)	C 0880	030052
03	W 0156	Wax (Parquet floor —)	C 0881	030053
03	W 0157	Wax (Polishing —)	C 0883	030054
04	W 0158	Wax [raw material]	C 0897	040027
16	W 0159	Wax (Sealing —)	C 0877	160055
03	W 0160	Wax (Tailors' —)	C 0891	030055
01	W 0161	Wax-bleaching chemicals	C 0898	010128
20	W 0162	Waxcomb for beehives	C 0886	200039
16	W 0163	Waxed paper	P 0107	160339
03	W 0164	Waxes for leather	C 1541	030074
21	W 0165	Wax-polishing (Apparatus for —), non-electric	C 0900	210080
21	W 0166	Wax-polishing appliances, non-electric, for shoes	C 0902	210264
07	W 0167	Wax-polishing (Machines and apparatus for —), electric	E 0286	070510
28	W 0168	Weapons (Fencing —)	A 0738	280130
06	W 0169	Weather vanes of metal	G 0198	060148
17	W 0170	Weatherstripping	B 0734	170013
17	W 0171	Weatherstripping compositions	C 0128	170015
07	W 0172	Weaving loom (Bobbins for —)	B 0502	070054
29	W 0173	Weed extracts for food	A 0323	290002
08	W 0174	Weeding forks [hand tools]	H 0100	080184
07	W 0175	Weeding machines	S 0088	070344
05	W 0176	Weedkillers	H 0069	050204
30	W 0177	Weeds [condiment]	A 0321	300002
31	W 0178	Weeds for human or animal consumption	A 0325	310003
09	W 0179	Weighbridges	B 0223	090081
09	W 0180	Weighing apparatus and instruments	P 0346	090388
09	W 0181	Weighing machines	P 0347	090080
28	W 0182	Weight lifting belts [sports articles]	C 0357	280176
09	W 0183	Weights	P 0697	090403
12	W 0184	Weights (Balance —) for vehicle wheels	P 0652	120116
07	W 0185	Welding apparatus (Electric —)	S 0433	070526
07	W 0186	Welding apparatus (Electric arc —)	A 0668	070530

Cl.	SERIAL No. (E)	INDICATION OF GOODS	SERIAL No. (F)	BASIC No.
07	W 0187	Welding apparatus, gas-operated	S 0420	070503
01	W 0188	Welding chemicals	S 0412	010487
07	W 0189	Welding machines, electric	S 0429	070349
01	W 0190	Welding (Protective gases for —)	G 0125	010326
06	W 0191	Welding (Rods of metal for —)	S 0409	060304
25	W 0192	Welts for footwear	T 0502	250118
25	W 0193	Wet suits for water-skiing	C 1065	250052
01	W 0194	Wetting preparations for use in bleaching	M 0519	010127
01	W 0195	Wetting preparations for use in dyeing	M 0521	010398
01	W 0196	Wetting preparations for use in the textile industry	M 0520	010530
20	W 0197	Whalebone, unworked or semi-worked	B 0104	200018
26	W 0198	Whalebones for corsets	B 0105	260012
31	W 0199	Wheat	B 0487	310061
01	W 0200	Wheat blight [smut] (Chemical preparations for protection against —)	N 0069	010404
05	W 0201	Wheat blight [smut] (Chemical preparations to treat —)	N 0070	050222
30	W 0202	Wheat flour	F 0289	300063
05	W 0203	Wheat germ dietary supplements	G 0179	050423
31	W 0204	Wheat germ for animal consumption	G 0180	310152
30	W 0205	Wheat germ for human consumption	G 0181	300213
01	W 0206	Wheat smut (Chemical preparations to prevent —)	N 0069	010404
05	W 0207	Wheat smut (Chemical preparations to treat —)	N 0070	050222
06	W 0208	Wheel clamps [boots]	S 0009	060426
12	W 0209	Wheel hubs (Bands for —)	F 0433	120127
12	W 0210	Wheel hubs (Vehicle —)	M 0562	120060
12	W 0211	Wheel tires [tyres] (Vehicle —)	V 0090	120158
12	W 0212	Wheelbarrows	B 0874	120218
12	W 0213	Wheelchairs	F 0029	120062
18	W 0214	Wheeled shopping bags	S 0028	180070
12	W 0215	Wheels for bicycles, cycles	C 1702	120095
07	W 0216	Wheels (Machine —)	R 0382	070336
08	W 0217	Wheels (Sharpening —) [hand tools]	M 0356	080201
07	W 0218	Wheels (Spinning —)	R 0390	070191
12	W 0219	Wheels (Spoke clips for —)	T 0186	120169
12	W 0220	Wheels (Vehicle —)	R 0383	120053
07	W 0221	Wheelwork (Machine —)	R 0378	070335
08	W 0222	Whetstone holders	C 0990	080068
08	W 0223	Whetstones	P 0457	080115
29	W 0224	Whey	P 0357	290073
32	W 0225	Whey beverages	B 0564	320007
22	W 0226	Whipcord	C 1263	220022
29	W 0227	Whipped cream	C 1533	290141
30	W 0228	Whipped cream (Preparations for stiffening —)	C 1534	300045
18	W 0229	Whips	F 0373	180049
11	W 0230	Whirlpool-jet apparatus	R 0220	110320
07	W 0231	Whisks, electric, for household purposes	F 0375	070459
21	W 0232	Whisks, non-electric, for household purposes	F 0377	210134
33	W 0233	Whisky	W 0010	330023
09	W 0234	Whistle alarms	A 0862	090013
02	W 0235	White lead	C 0422	020038
06	W 0236	White metal	B 0468	060046
29	W 0237	White of eggs	B 0467	290012
03	W 0238	Whitening the skin (Cream for —)	P 0235	030023
02	W 0239	Whites [colorants or paints]	B 0486	020109
02	W 0240	Whitewash	B 0465	020110
07	W 0241	Whitewashing machines	B 0022	070030
03	W 0242	Whiting	B 0466	030022
08	W 0243	Wick trimmers [scissors]	M 0514	080164
20	W 0244	Wickerwork	V 0018	200199
04	W 0245	Wicks for candles	M 0244	040046
04	W 0246	Wicks (Lamp —)	L 0108	040061
26	W 0247	Wigs	P 0342	260079
25	W 0248	Wimples	G 0376	250084
07	W 0249	Winches	T 0510	070373
20	W 0250	Wind chimes [decoration]	M 0424	200268
15	W 0251	Wind pipes for organs	P 0862	150058
09	W 0252	Wind socks for indicating wind direction	M 0074	090678
07	W 0253	Wind turbines	E 0376	070523
06	W 0254	Wind vanes of metal	G 0198	060148
06	W 0255	Wind-driven bird-repelling devices made of metal	O 0040	060432
20	W 0256	Winding spools, not of metal, non-mechanical, for flexible hoses	E 0343	200104
06	W 0257	Winding spools of metal, non-mechanical, for flexible hoses	E 0342	060369
06	W 0258	Window casement bolts	C 1543	060104
06	W 0259	Window fasteners of metal	E 0434	060125
20	W 0260	Window fittings, not of metal	G 0075	200123
19	W 0261	Window frames, not of metal	C 0567	190208
06	W 0262	Window frames of metal	C 0566	060315
19	W 0263	Window glass, except glass for vehicle windows	V 0156	190181
19	W 0264	Window glass, for building	V 0282	190183
06	W 0265	Window pulleys	G 0019	060075
06	W 0266	Window stops of metal	A 0756	060035
21	W 0267	Window-boxes	B 0004	210341
17	W 0268	Windows (Anti-dazzle films for —) [tinted films]	F 0127	170115
01	W 0269	Windows (Anti-tarnishing chemicals for —)	V 0281	010523
06	W 0270	Windows (Fittings of metal for —)	G 0074	060130
12	W 0271	Windows for vehicles	V 0279	120198
19	W 0272	Windows, not of metal	F 0052	190068
06	W 0273	Windows of metal	F 0051	060346
19	W 0274	Windows (Stained-glass —)	V 0278	190182
03	W 0275	Windscreen cleaning liquids	G 0217	030126
12	W 0276	Windscreen wipers	E 0459	120121
12	W 0277	Windscreens	P 0153	120154
03	W 0278	Windshield cleaning liquids	G 0217	030126

Cl.	SERIAL No. (E)	INDICATION OF GOODS	SERIAL No. (F)	BASIC No.
12	W 0279	Windshield wipers	E 0459	120121
12	W 0280	Windshields	P 0153	120154
33	W 0281	Wine	V 0249	330013
20	W 0282	Wine (Casks of wood for decanting —)	F 0529	200017
01	W 0283	Wine (Chemicals used in fermenting —)	B 0012	010096
01	W 0284	Wine finings	C 1024	010205
07	W 0285	Wine presses	P 0968	070102
21	W 0286	Wine tasters [siphons]	T 0142	210178
07	W 0287	Winnowers	V 0023	070379
06	W 0288	Wire cloth	T 0307	060184
09	W 0289	Wire connectors [electricity]	S 0245	090442
06	W 0290	Wire gauze	T 0307	060184
06	W 0291	Wire of common metal	F 0239	060108
06	W 0292	Wire of common metal alloys, except fuse wire	F 0235	060268
14	W 0293	Wire of precious metal [jewellery, jewelry (Am.)]	F 0226	140040
06	W 0294	Wire rope	F 0204	060427
08	W 0295	Wire stretchers [hand tools]	T 0184	080160
06	W 0296	Wire stretchers [tension links]	T 0185	060230
08	W 0297	Wire strippers [hand tools]	P 0502	080259
09	W 0298	Wireless aerials (Masts for —)	P 1060	090471
09	W 0299	Wires, electric	F 0232	090255
09	W 0300	Wires of metal alloys [fuse wire]	A 0356	090505
09	W 0301	Wires (Telephone —)	F 0245	090572
01	W 0302	Witherite	W 0011	010550
01	W 0303	Wood alcohol	E 0437	010131
01	W 0304	Wood alcohol (Preparations of the distillation of —)	E 0438	010582
04	W 0305	Wood briquettes	B 0828	040018
31	W 0306	Wood chips for the manufacture of wood pulp	C 1237	310018
02	W 0307	Wood coatings [paints]	B 0539	020026
02	W 0308	Wood (Coloring [colouring] —)	B 0524	020111
02	W 0309	Wood (Dye- —)	B 0524	020111
19	W 0310	Wood for making household utensils	B 0551	190030
02	W 0311	Wood mordants	B 0546	020027
02	W 0312	Wood (Oils for the preservation of —)	H 0159	020082
19	W 0313	Wood panelling	B 0559	190035
19	W 0314	Wood paving	B 0550	190032
02	W 0315	Wood (Preservative oils for —)	H 0159	020082
02	W 0316	Wood preservatives	B 0553	020049
01	W 0317	Wood pulp	P 0192	010132
19	W 0318	Wood pulp board, for building	C 0302	190201
16	W 0319	Wood pulp board [stationery]	C 0303	160278
16	W 0320	Wood pulp paper	B 0548	160279
20	W 0321	Wood ribbon	R 0430	200027
19	W 0322	Wood, semi-worked	B 0545	190026
22	W 0323	Wood shavings	C 1236	220004
04	W 0324	Wood spills for lighting	C 1238	040006
02	W 0325	Wood stains	B 0557	020028
01	W 0326	Wood (Tan —)	B 0518	010130
19	W 0327	Wood veneers	P 0551	190033
01	W 0328	Wood vinegar [pyroligneous acid]	V 0244	010133

Cl.	SERIAL No. (E)	INDICATION OF GOODS	SERIAL No. (F)	BASIC No.
22	W 0329	Wood wool	L 0027	220005
25	W 0330	Wooden shoes	S 0007	250110
07	W 0331	Woodworking machines	B 0544	070055
22	W 0332	Wool (Carded —)	L 0025	220051
22	W 0333	Wool (Combed —)	L 0038	220052
26	W 0334	Wool combing machines (Needles for —)	A 0207	260005
22	W 0335	Wool flock	F 0306	220041
17	W 0336	Wool (Glass —) for insulation	L 0031	170063
04	W 0337	Wool grease	S 0576	040074
17	W 0338	Wool (Mineral —) [insulator]	L 0037	170062
22	W 0339	Wool (Raw or treated —)	L 0024	220050
22	W 0340	Wool (Shorn —)	T 0402	220073
17	W 0341	Wool (Slag —) [insulator]	L 0028	170061
23	W 0342	Wool (Spun —)	L 0034	230012
21	W 0343	Wool (Steel —) for cleaning	P 0004	210005
22	W 0344	Wool (Upholstery —) [stuffing]	L 0029	220033
21	W 0345	Wool waste for cleaning	D 0023	210163
22	W 0346	Wool (Wood —)	L 0027	220005
24	W 0347	Woollen cloth	L 0033	240064
24	W 0348	Woollen fabric	L 0033	240064
26	W 0349	Woollen laces	L 0026	260067
23	W 0350	Woollen thread and yarn	L 0035	230004
09	W 0351	Word processors	M 0013	090541
20	W 0352	Work benches	E 0474	200106
09	W 0353	Workmen's protective face-shields	E 0131	090210
06	W 0354	Works of art of common metal	A 0771	060278
21	W 0355	Works of art, of porcelain, terra-cotta or glass	A 0774	210234
14	W 0356	Works of art of precious metal	A 0772	140109
19	W 0357	Works of art of stone, concrete or marble	A 0773	190193
20	W 0358	Works of art, of wood, wax, plaster or plastic	A 0770	200205
23	W 0359	Worsted	L 0034	230012
20	W 0360	Woven timber blinds [furniture]	S 0546	200269
16	W 0361	Wrappers [stationery]	C 1485	160108
06	W 0362	Wrapping and packaging (Foils of metal for —)	F 0134	060416
07	W 0363	Wrapping machines	E 0358	070177
22	W 0364	Wrapping or binding bands, not of metal	L 0244	220063
06	W 0365	Wrapping or binding bands of metal	B 0146	060285
16	W 0366	Wrapping paper	E 0231	160130
26	W 0367	Wreaths of artificial flowers	C 1415	260099
31	W 0368	Wreaths of natural flowers	C 1416	310044
08	W 0369	Wrenches [hand tools]	T 0422	080063
07	W 0370	Wringing machines for laundry	L 0295	070239
09	W 0371	Wrist rests for use with computers	R 0236	090664
25	W 0372	Wristbands [clothing]	M 0086	250095
16	W 0373	Wristbands for the retention of writing instruments	B 0787	160045
14	W 0374	Wristwatches	M 0467	140016
16	W 0375	Writing board erasers	E 0170	160348
16	W 0376	Writing brushes	B 0873	160342
16	W 0377	Writing cases [sets]	N 0038	160302

Cl.	SERIAL No. (E)	INDICATION OF GOODS	SERIAL No. (F)	BASIC No.
16	W 0378	Writing cases [stationery]	P 0074	160300
16	W 0379	Writing chalk	C 1496	160109
20	W 0380	Writing desks	S 0168	200180
16	W 0381	Writing instruments	E 0154	160343
16	W 0382	Writing materials	E 0153	160136
16	W 0383	Writing or drawing books	C 0091	160058
16	W 0384	Writing pads	S 0471	160255
16	W 0385	Writing paper	L 0212	160182
16	W 0386	Writing slates	A 0685	160023
16	W 0387	Writing tablets	S 0471	160255

Cl.	SERIAL No. (E)	INDICATION OF GOODS	SERIAL No. (F)	BASIC No.

Cl.	SERIAL No. (E)	INDICATION OF GOODS	SERIAL No. (F)	BASIC No.
01	X 0001	Xenon	X 0001	010551
10	X 0002	X-ray apparatus for medical purposes	R 0114	100024
09	X 0003	X-ray apparatus not for medical purposes	R 0115	090425
09	X 0004	X-ray films, exposed	F 0211	090573
01	X 0005	X-ray films, sensitized but not exposed	R 0035	010464
10	X 0006	X-ray photographs for medical purposes	R 0032	100132
09	X 0007	X-ray photographs, other than for medical purposes	R 0033	090625
10	X 0008	X-ray tubes for medical purposes	R 0120	100136
09	X 0009	X-ray tubes not for medical purposes	R 0121	090421
10	X 0010	X-rays (Apparatus and installations for the production of—), for medical purposes	R 0116	100131
09	X 0011	X-rays producing apparatus and installations, not for medical purposes	R 0117	090420
10	X 0012	X-rays (Protection devices against—), for medical purposes	R 0118	100137
09	X 0013	X-rays (Protection devices against—), not for medical purposes	R 0119	090422
16	X 0014	Xuan paper for Chinese painting and calligraphy	P 0120	160347
04	X 0015	Xylene	X 0002	040078
04	X 0016	Xylol	X 0003	040077
19	X 0017	Xylolith	X 0004	190186
15	X 0018	Xylophones	X 0005	150076

Cl.	SERIAL No. (E)	INDICATION OF GOODS	SERIAL No. (F)	BASIC No.
12	Y 0001	Yachts	Y 0001	120202
23	Y 0002	Yarn *	F 0214	230001
17	Y 0003	Yarns (Elastic—), not for use in textiles	F 0231	170038
30	Y 0004	Yeast *	L 0222	300087
05	Y 0005	Yeast dietary supplements	L 0224	050424
31	Y 0006	Yeast for animal consumption	L 0225	310077
05	Y 0007	Yeast for pharmaceutical purposes	L 0223	050194
20	Y 0008	Yellow amber	A 0418	200005
34	Y 0009	Yellow amber (Tips of—) for cigar and cigarette holders	A 0419	340002
02	Y 0010	Yellowwood [colorant]	F 0523	020074
29	Y 0011	Yoghurt	Y 0002	290065
30	Y 0012	Yoghurt (Frozen—) [confectionery ices]	Y 0003	300181
29	Y 0013	Yogurt	Y 0002	290065
11	Y 0014	Yogurt (Electric appliances for making—)	Y 0004	110312
30	Y 0015	Yogurt (Frozen—) [confectionery ices]	Y 0003	300181
25	Y 0016	Yokes (Shirt—)	E 0267	250072
29	Y 0017	Yolk of eggs	J 0021	290064
01	Y 0018	Ytterbium	Y 0006	010552
01	Y 0019	Yttrium	Y 0007	010553

Cl.	SERIAL No. (E)	INDICATION OF GOODS	SERIAL No. (F)	BASIC No.
24	Z 0001	Zephyr [cloth]	Z 0001	240094
06	Z 0002	Zinc	Z 0003	060223
02	Z 0003	Zinc oxide [pigment]	G 0357	020081
26	Z 0004	Zip fasteners	F 0071	260053
26	Z 0005	Zippers	F 0071	260053
01	Z 0006	Zirconia	Z 0004	010556
06	Z 0007	Zirconium	Z 0005	060264
15	Z 0008	Zithers	C 0910	150022

ALPHABETICAL LIST OF SERVICES

Cl.	SERIAL No. (E)	INDICATION OF SERVICES	SERIAL No. (F)	BASIC No.
40	A 0001	Abrasion	A 0005	400001
41	A 0002	Academies [education]	A 0006	410002
38	A 0003	Access time to global computer networks (Rental of —)	L 0083	380041
36	A 0004	Accident insurance underwriting	A 0008	360001
36	A 0005	Accommodation bureaux [apartments]	A 0045	360045
43	A 0006	Accommodation bureaux [hotels, boarding houses]	A 0044	430004
43	A 0007	Accommodation (Rental of temporary —)	L 0062	430028
43	A 0008	Accommodation reservations (Temporary —)	R 0067	430162
35	A 0009	Accounting	C 0087	350015
35	A 0010	Accounts (Drawing up of statements of —)	R 0046	350016
36	A 0011	Actuarial services	A 0016	360003
35	A 0012	Administration (Commercial —) of the licensing of the goods and services of others	A 0018	350096
35	A 0013	Administrative processing of purchase orders	T 0060	350095
45	A 0014	Adoption agency services	A 0041	450193
35	A 0015	Advertising	P 0136	350039
35	A 0016	Advertising agencies	A 0047	350047
35	A 0017	Advertising by mail order	P 0138	350077
35	A 0018	Advertising material (Updating of —)	M 0051	350027
35	A 0019	Advertising matter (Dissemination of —)	D 0036	350008
35	A 0020	Advertising space (Rental of —)	L 0098	350070
35	A 0021	Advice for consumers (Commercial information and —) [consumer advice shop]	I 0034	350093
44	A 0022	Aerial and surface spreading of fertilizers and other agricultural chemicals	E 0055	440115
37	A 0023	Air conditioning apparatus installation and repair	C 0092	370028
40	A 0024	Air conditioning apparatus (Rental of —)	L 0028	400118
40	A 0025	Air deodorising	D 0024	400081
40	A 0026	Air freshening	R 0011	400082
40	A 0027	Air purification	P 0144	400003
39	A 0028	Air transport	A 0019	390004
39	A 0029	Aircraft rental	L 0025	390102
37	A 0030	Airplane maintenance and repair	A 0122	370008
40	A 0031	Alteration (Clothing —)	R 0080	400098
45	A 0032	Alternative dispute resolution services	R 0072	450214
39	A 0033	Ambulance transport	T 0087	390006
41	A 0034	Amusement arcade services (Providing —)	E 0100	410084
41	A 0035	Amusement parks	P 0010	410003
41	A 0036	Amusements	D 0058	410004
35	A 0037	Analysis (Cost price —)	A 0072	350007
36	A 0038	Analysis (Financial —)	A 0073	360046
42	A 0039	Analysis for oil-field exploitation	A 0074	420008

Cl.	SERIAL No. (E)	INDICATION OF SERVICES	SERIAL No. (F)	BASIC No.
44	A 0040	Animal breeding	E 0018	440009
44	A 0041	Animal grooming	P 0004	440131
41	A 0042	Animal training	D 0066	410005
43	A 0043	Animals (Boarding for —)	P 0024	430134
40	A 0044	Animals (Slaughtering of —)	A 0001	400094
35	A 0045	Answering (Telephone —) for unavailable subscribers	R 0061	350074
36	A 0046	Antique appraisal	E 0063	360051
37	A 0047	Anti-rust treatment for vehicles	T 0070	370082
36	A 0048	Apartment house management	G 0015	360033
36	A 0049	Apartments (Renting of —)	L 0034	360035
40	A 0050	Applying finishes to textiles	A 0090	400005
36	A 0051	Appraisal (Antique —)	E 0063	360051
36	A 0052	Appraisal (Art —)	E 0066	360052
36	A 0053	Appraisal (Jewellery [jewelry (Am.)] —)	E 0064	360061
36	A 0054	Appraisal (Numismatic —)	E 0070	360062
36	A 0055	Appraisal (Real estate —)	E 0074	360014
36	A 0056	Appraisal (Stamp —)	E 0065	360064
35	A 0057	Appraisals (Business —)	E 0067	350032
44	A 0058	Aquaculture services	A 0093	440207
45	A 0059	Arbitration services	A 0094	450205
42	A 0060	Architectural consultation	C 0100	420036
42	A 0061	Architecture	A 0096	420011
39	A 0062	Armored-car transport	T 0086	390062
44	A 0063	Aromatherapy services	A 0099	440193
41	A 0064	Arranging and conducting of colloquiums	O 0038	410044
41	A 0065	Arranging and conducting of concerts	O 0039	410185
41	A 0066	Arranging and conducting of conferences	O 0040	410045
41	A 0067	Arranging and conducting of congresses	O 0041	410046
41	A 0068	Arranging and conducting of seminars	O 0042	410070
41	A 0069	Arranging and conducting of symposiums	O 0043	410072
41	A 0070	Arranging and conducting of workshops [training]	O 0037	410076
35	A 0071	Arranging newspaper subscriptions for others	A 0003	350076
41	A 0072	Arranging of beauty contests	O 0027	410077
39	A 0073	Arranging of cruises	O 0029	390024
39	A 0074	Arranging of tours	O 0032	390050
35	A 0075	Arranging subscriptions to telecommunication services for others	A 0004	350094
36	A 0076	Art appraisal	E 0066	360052
44	A 0077	Artificial insemination services	I 0041	440194
37	A 0078	Artificial snow-making services	E 0034	370123
35	A 0079	Artists (Business management of performing —)	D 0045	350079
37	A 0080	Asphalting	A 0107	370005
40	A 0081	Assembling of materials (Custom —) for others	A 0108	400083
35	A 0082	Assistance (Business management —)	A 0058	350001
35	A 0083	Auctioneering	V 0016	350030
35	A 0084	Auditing	V 0018	350017

Cl.	SERIAL No. (E)	INDICATION OF SERVICES	SERIAL No. (F)	BASIC No.
42	A 0085	Authenticating works of art	A 0115	420132

Cl.	SERIAL No. (E)	INDICATION OF SERVICES	SERIAL No. (F)	BASIC No.

Cl.	SERIAL No. (E)	INDICATION OF SERVICES	SERIAL No. (F)	BASIC No.
45	B 0001	Baby sitting	G 0006	450195
42	B 0002	Bacteriological research	R 0022	420017
45	B 0003	Baggage inspection for security purposes	I 0042	450196
36	B 0004	Bail-bonding	C 0022	360018
36	B 0005	Banking	A 0024	360013
36	B 0006	Banking (Home —)	B 0010	360072
43	B 0007	Bar services	B 0012	430138
39	B 0008	Barge transport	C 0024	390103
44	B 0009	Baths for hygiene purposes (Public —)	B 0003	440018
44	B 0010	Baths (Turkish —)	B 0004	440019
41	B 0011	Beauty contests (Arranging of —)	O 0027	410077
44	B 0012	Beauty salons	S 0002	440020
35	B 0013	Bill-posting	A 0037	350003
42	B 0014	Biological research	R 0019	420190
40	B 0015	Blacksmithing	F 0031	400029
40	B 0016	Bleaching (Fabric —)	B 0028	400008
44	B 0017	Blood bank services	B 0011	440133
43	B 0018	Boarding for animals	P 0024	430134
43	B 0019	Boarding house bookings	R 0068	430104
43	B 0020	Boarding houses	P 0023	430066
41	B 0021	Boarding schools	P 0022	410075
39	B 0022	Boat rental	L 0040	390012
39	B 0023	Boat storage	E 0045	390071
39	B 0024	Boat transport	T 0088	390049
45	B 0025	Body guarding (Personal —)	P 0122	450001
37	B 0026	Boiler cleaning and repair	C 0030	370011
40	B 0027	Boiler-making	C 0031	400099
40	B 0028	Bookbinding	R 0047	400049
41	B 0029	Booking of seats for shows	R 0069	410078
39	B 0030	Booking of seats for travel	R 0070	390056
35	B 0031	Book-keeping	C 0087	350015
41	B 0032	Bookmobile services	B 0020	410041
41	B 0033	Books (Publication of —)	P 0125	410024
39	B 0034	Bottling services	M 0052	390100
37	B 0035	Bricklaying	P 0084	370101
38	B 0036	Broadcasting (Cable television —)	T 0031	380021
38	B 0037	Broadcasting (Radio —)	R 0005	380003
38	B 0038	Broadcasting (Television —)	D 0038	380005
36	B 0039	Brokerage *	C 0146	360005
39	B 0040	Brokerage (Freight —)	C 0148	390072
36	B 0041	Brokerage of carbon credits	C 0147	360104
39	B 0042	Brokerage (Transport —)	C 0149	390073
37	B 0043	Building construction supervision	S 0052	370031
37	B 0044	Building insulating	I 0054	370054
37	B 0045	Building of fair stalls and shops	C 0109	370115
37	B 0046	Building sealing	E 0078	370042
37	B 0047	Buildings (Cleaning of —) [exterior surface]	N 0014	370112
37	B 0048	Buildings (Cleaning of —) [interior]	N 0008	370009
43	B 0049	Buildings (Rental of transportable —) *	L 0049	430160
37	B 0050	Bulldozers (Rental of —)	L 0041	370013
37	B 0051	Burglar alarm installation and repair	V 0036	370016
37	B 0052	Burner maintenance and repair	B 0044	370012
40	B 0053	Burnishing by abrasion	P 0073	400048
39	B 0054	Bus transport	A 0116	390010
35	B 0055	Business appraisals	E 0067	350032
35	B 0056	Business consultancy (Professional —)	C 0124	350062
35	B 0057	Business information	I 0021	350065
35	B 0058	Business inquiries	R 0056	350002
35	B 0059	Business investigations	I 0050	350033
36	B 0060	Business liquidation services, financial	L 0017	360073
35	B 0061	Business management and organization consultancy	C 0103	350018
35	B 0062	Business management assistance	A 0058	350001
35	B 0063	Business management consultancy	C 0122	350020
35	B 0064	Business management of hotels	G 0012	350078
35	B 0065	Business management of performing artists	D 0045	350079
35	B 0066	Business management of sports people	G 0016	350105
35	B 0067	Business organization consultancy	O 0033	350036
35	B 0068	Business research	R 0030	350041
35	B 0069	Businesses (Relocation services for —)	R 0048	350069

Cl.	SERIAL No. (E)	INDICATION OF SERVICES	SERIAL No. (F)	BASIC No.
37	C 0001	Cabinet making [repair]	E 0004	370092
38	C 0002	Cable television broadcasting	T 0031	380021
40	C 0003	Cadmium plating	P 0057	400013
43	C 0004	Cafés	C 0002	430024
43	C 0005	Cafeterias	C 0003	430025
42	C 0006	Calibration [measuring]	E 0076	420136
41	C 0007	Calligraphy services	C 0006	410186
41	C 0008	Camp services (Holiday—) [entertainment]	C 0009	410055
43	C 0009	Camp services (Holiday—) [lodging]	C 0010	430145
41	C 0010	Camp services (Sport—)	C 0011	410071
43	C 0011	Campground facilities (Providing—)	M 0048	430026
39	C 0012	Canal locks (Operating—)	E 0007	390032
43	C 0013	Canteens	C 0012	430027
36	C 0014	Capital investments	P 0059	360017
39	C 0015	Car parking	P 0011	390033
39	C 0016	Car rental	L 0036	390008
39	C 0017	Car transport	A 0117	390009
37	C 0018	Car wash	L 0006	370007
37	C 0019	Carpentry services	C 0028	370132
39	C 0020	Carting	C 0029	390017
41	C 0021	Casino facilities [gambling] (Providing—)	C 0021	410042
43	C 0022	Catering (Food and drink—)	T 0071	430010
38	C 0023	Cellular telephone communication	R 0009	380022
45	C 0024	Chaperoning	A 0010	450002
36	C 0025	Charitable fund raising	C 0070	360015
38	C 0026	Chatrooms (Providing internet—)	F 0039	380043
39	C 0027	Chauffeur services	C 0034	390074
36	C 0028	Check [cheque] verification	V 0019	360053
42	C 0029	Chemical analysis	A 0069	420007
42	C 0030	Chemical research	R 0023	420031
42	C 0031	Chemistry services	C 0043	420030
37	C 0032	Chimney sweeping	R 0012	370026
44	C 0033	Chiropractics	C 0045	440032
40	C 0034	Chromium plating	C 0048	400017
41	C 0035	Cine-films (Rental of—)	L 0055	410019
41	C 0036	Cinema presentations	P 0110	410057
40	C 0037	Cinematographic films (Processing of—)	T 0068	400002
41	C 0038	Circuses	C 0055	410009
37	C 0039	Cleaning (Diaper—)	N 0009	370102
37	C 0040	Cleaning (Dry—)	N 0007	370103
37	C 0041	Cleaning machines (Rental of—)	L 0064	370090
37	C 0042	Cleaning of buildings [exterior surface]	N 0014	370112
37	C 0043	Cleaning of buildings [interior]	N 0008	370009
37	C 0044	Cleaning of clothing	N 0015	370050
37	C 0045	Cleaning (Vehicle—)	N 0012	370087
36	C 0046	Clearing, financial	C 0083	360021
36	C 0047	Clearing-houses, financial	C 0083	360021
44	C 0048	Clinic (Medical—) services	C 0058	440021
37	C 0049	Clock and watch repair	H 0006	370051
40	C 0050	Cloth cutting	D 0010	400021
40	C 0051	Cloth dyeing	T 0009	400060
40	C 0052	Cloth edging	B 0037	400010
40	C 0053	Cloth fireproofing	I 0001	400037
40	C 0054	Cloth pre-shrinking	R 0083	400069
40	C 0055	Cloth treating	T 0043	400058
40	C 0056	Cloth waterproofing	I 0008	400036
40	C 0057	Clothing alteration	R 0080	400098
37	C 0058	Clothing (Cleaning of—)	N 0015	370050
45	C 0059	Clothing rental	L 0089	450081
37	C 0060	Clothing repair	C 0137	370032
42	C 0061	Cloud seeding	E 0042	420202
41	C 0062	Club services [entertainment or education]	C 0062	410043
39	C 0063	Coach (Motor—) rental	L 0035	390104
39	C 0064	Coach (Railway—) rental	L 0091	390045
41	C 0065	Coaching [training]	C 0063	410189
36	C 0066	Collection (Rent—)	R 0033	360063
36	C 0067	Collections (Organization of—)	C 0069	360023
41	C 0068	Colloquiums (Arranging and conducting of—)	O 0038	410044
40	C 0069	Colour separation services	T 0065	400107
35	C 0070	Commercial administration of the licensing of the goods and services of others	A 0018	350096
35	C 0071	Commercial information agencies	A 0051	350006
35	C 0072	Commercial information and advice for consumers [consumer advice shop]	I 0034	350093
35	C 0073	Commercial or industrial management assistance	D 0041	350025
35	C 0074	Communication media (Presentation of goods on—), for retail purposes	P 0088	350092
38	C 0075	Communications by computer terminals	C 0077	380023
38	C 0076	Communications by fiber [fibre] optic networks	C 0076	380030
38	C 0077	Communications by telegrams	C 0079	380008
38	C 0078	Communications by telephone	C 0080	380010
35	C 0079	Comparison services (Price—)	C 0082	350091
41	C 0080	Competitions (Organization of—) [education or entertainment]	O 0028	410010
41	C 0081	Competitions (Organization of sports—)	O 0026	410059
35	C 0082	Compilation of information into computer databases	R 0036	350080
35	C 0083	Compilation of statistics	E 0075	350100
38	C 0084	Computer aided transmission of messages and images	T 0080	380024
35	C 0085	Computer databases (Compilation of information into—)	R 0036	350080
35	C 0086	Computer databases (Systemization of information into—)	S 0058	350081
42	C 0087	Computer hardware (Consultancy in the design and development of—)	C 0117	420141

Cl.	SERIAL No. (E)	INDICATION OF SERVICES	SERIAL No. (F)	BASIC No.
37	C 0088	Computer hardware (Installation, maintenance and repair of—)	O 0019	370116
42	C 0089	Computer programming	P 0104	420090
42	C 0090	Computer programs (Duplication of—)	D 0068	420197
42	C 0091	Computer rental	L 0104	420083
42	C 0092	Computer software consultancy	C 0118	420204
42	C 0093	Computer software design	E 0014	420139
42	C 0094	Computer software (Installation of—)	I 0044	420201
45	C 0095	Computer software (Licensing of—) [legal services]	C 0090	450212
42	C 0096	Computer software (Maintenance of—)	M 0005	420176
42	C 0097	Computer software (Updating of—)	L 0114	420140
42	C 0098	Computer system analysis	A 0070	420177
42	C 0099	Computer system design	C 0089	420194
38	C 0100	Computer terminals (Communications by—)	C 0077	380023
42	C 0101	Computer virus protection services	P 0120	420206
41	C 0102	Conducting fitness classes	C 0144	410194
41	C 0103	Conducting of concerts (Arranging and—)	O 0039	410185
41	C 0104	Conferences (Arranging and conducting of—)	O 0040	410045
41	C 0105	Congresses (Arranging and conducting of—)	O 0041	410046
37	C 0106	Construction *	C 0108	370029
37	C 0107	Construction consultation	C 0101	370131
42	C 0108	Construction drafting	C 0110	420038
37	C 0109	Construction equipment (Rental of—)	L 0066	370020
37	C 0110	Construction information	I 0024	370104
42	C 0111	Consultancy (Computer software—)	C 0118	420204
36	C 0112	Consultancy (Financial—)	C 0121	360054
42	C 0113	Consultancy in the design and development of computer hardware	C 0117	420141
42	C 0114	Consultancy in the field of energy-saving	C 0102	420207
36	C 0115	Consultancy (Insurance—)	C 0116	360055
45	C 0116	Consultancy (Intellectual property—)	C 0104	450206
35	C 0117	Consultancy (Professional business—)	C 0124	350062
45	C 0118	Consultancy (Security—)	C 0120	450117
35	C 0119	Consumers (Commercial information and advice for—) [consumer advice shop]	I 0034	350093
44	C 0120	Convalescent homes	M 0007	440043
42	C 0121	Conversion of data or documents from physical to electronic media	C 0132	420198
43	C 0122	Cooking apparatus (Rental of—)	L 0029	430190
40	C 0123	Coppersmithing	C 0031	400099
45	C 0124	Copyright management	G 0014	450207
41	C 0125	Correspondence courses	E 0040	410011
42	C 0126	Cosmetic research	R 0024	420045
35	C 0127	Cost price analysis	A 0072	350007
39	C 0128	Courier services [messages or merchandise]	M 0030	390075
40	C 0129	Crease-resistant treatment for clothing	I 0039	400038
42	C 0130	Creating and maintaining web sites for others	C 0157	420199
36	C 0131	Credit bureaux	A 0042	360006
36	C 0132	Credit card services	C 0017	360056
36	C 0133	Credit cards (Issuance of—)	E 0022	360068
45	C 0134	Crematorium services	C 0161	450047
39	C 0135	Cruises (Arranging of—)	O 0029	390024
40	C 0136	Cryopreservation services	C 0163	400121
40	C 0137	Custom assembling of materials for others	A 0108	400083
40	C 0138	Custom fashioning of fur	F 0001	400028
36	C 0139	Customs brokerage	A 0053	360011
40	C 0140	Cutting (Cloth—)	D 0010	400021

Cl.	SERIAL No. (E)	INDICATION OF SERVICES	SERIAL No. (F)	BASIC No.
37	D 0001	Damp-proofing [building]	E 0078	370042
42	D 0002	Data conversion of computer programs and data [not physical conversion]	C 0131	420203
35	D 0003	Data search in computer files for others	R 0021	350086
45	D 0004	Dating services	C 0060	450005
43	D 0005	Day-nurseries [crèches]	C 0158	430098
36	D 0006	Debit card services	C 0018	360057
36	D 0007	Debt collection agencies	A 0048	360009
40	D 0008	Decontamination of hazardous materials	D 0006	400109
42	D 0009	Decor (Design of interior—)	D 0008	420048
39	D 0010	Delivery (Flower—)	L 0019	390096
39	D 0011	Delivery (Message—)	D 0056	390087
39	D 0012	Delivery of goods	L 0020	390027
39	D 0013	Delivery of goods by mail order	L 0021	390089
39	D 0014	Delivery of newspapers	D 0051	390088
37	D 0015	Demolition of buildings	D 0014	370036
35	D 0016	Demonstration of goods	D 0015	350023
40	D 0017	Dental technician (Services of a—)	M 0025	400102
44	D 0018	Dentistry	A 0101	440113
36	D 0019	Deposits of valuables	D 0019	360066
42	D 0020	Design (Computer system—)	C 0089	420194
42	D 0021	Design (Industrial—)	D 0025	420049
44	D 0022	Design (Landscape—)	C 0088	440199
42	D 0023	Design of interior decor	D 0008	420048
42	D 0024	Design services (Packaging—)	D 0028	420050
42	D 0025	Designing (Dress—)	D 0027	420142
42	D 0026	Designing (Graphic arts—)	D 0026	420144
40	D 0027	Destruction of waste and trash	D 0033	400105
45	D 0028	Detective agencies	A 0043	450003
40	D 0029	Development (Photographic film—)	D 0035	400023
37	D 0030	Diaper cleaning	N 0009	370102
42	D 0031	Digitization of documents [scanning]	N 0018	420210
35	D 0032	Direct mail advertising	D 0053	350024
41	D 0033	Disc jockey services	D 0046	410191
41	D 0034	Discotheque services	D 0047	410047
37	D 0035	Disinfecting	D 0022	370038
35	D 0036	Dissemination of advertising matter	D 0036	350008
39	D 0037	Distribution of energy	D 0054	390090
35	D 0038	Distribution of samples	D 0039	350028
39	D 0039	Diving bells (Rental of—)	L 0046	390078
41	D 0040	Diving equipment (Rental of skin—)	L 0096	410065
39	D 0041	Diving suits (Rental of—)	L 0078	390079
35	D 0042	Document reproduction	R 0066	350026
45	D 0043	Domain names (Registration of—) [legal services]	E 0036	450213
37	D 0044	Doors and windows (Installation of—)	I 0045	370128
42	D 0045	Drafting (Construction—)	C 0110	420038
42	D 0046	Dress designing	D 0027	420142
40	D 0047	Dressmaking	C 0155	400012
37	D 0048	Drilling of deep oil or gas-wells	F 0030	370133
37	D 0049	Drilling of wells	F 0029	370114
37	D 0050	Dry cleaning	N 0007	370103
41	D 0051	Dubbing	P 0086	410079
42	D 0052	Duplication of computer programs	D 0068	420197
40	D 0053	Dyeing (Cloth—)	T 0009	400060
40	D 0054	Dyeing (Fur—)	T 0008	400072
40	D 0055	Dyeing services	T 0011	400056
40	D 0056	Dyeing (Textile—)	T 0007	400057

Cl.	SERIAL No. (E)	INDICATION OF SERVICES	SERIAL No. (F)	BASIC No.
35	E 0001	Economic forecasting	P 0094	350063
40	E 0002	Edging (Cloth —)	B 0037	400010
41	E 0003	Editing (Videotape —)	M 0062	410090
41	E 0004	Education information	I 0032	410048
41	E 0005	Education (Religious —)	E 0013	410080
41	E 0006	Educational examination	E 0057	410049
41	E 0007	Educational services	E 0011	410017
35	E 0008	Efficiency experts	E 0095	350029
37	E 0009	Electric appliance installation and repair	E 0016	370003
39	E 0010	Electricity distribution	D 0052	390031
38	E 0011	Electronic bulletin board services [telecommunications services]	A 0038	380036
41	E 0012	Electronic desktop publishing	M 0044	410092
38	E 0013	Electronic mail	M 0031	380025
40	E 0014	Electroplating	R 0085	400026
37	E 0015	Elevator installation and repair	A 0106	370004
40	E 0016	Embroidery	B 0043	400063
35	E 0017	Employment agencies	B 0047	350012
39	E 0018	Energy (Distribution of —)	D 0054	390090
40	E 0019	Energy (Production of —)	P 0101	400103
42	E 0020	Energy-saving (Consultancy in the field of —)	C 0102	420207
42	E 0021	Engineering	I 0040	420064
40	E 0022	Engraving	G 0024	400035
41	E 0023	Entertainer services	A 0104	410007
41	E 0024	Entertainment	D 0058	410004
41	E 0025	Entertainment information	I 0025	410050
42	E 0026	Environmental protection (Research in the field of —)	R 0025	420208
45	E 0027	Escorting in society [chaperoning]	A 0010	450002
39	E 0028	Escorting of travellers	A 0009	390002
36	E 0029	Estate agencies (Real —)	A 0054	360007
36	E 0030	Estate management (Real —)	G 0013	360032
36	E 0031	Evaluation (Financial —) [insurance, banking, real estate]	E 0071	360026
36	E 0032	Evaluation of standing timber (Financial —)	E 0068	360105
42	E 0033	Evaluation of standing timber (Quality —)	E 0089	420213
36	E 0034	Evaluation of wool (Financial —)	E 0069	360107
42	E 0035	Evaluation of wool (Quality —)	E 0090	420214
36	E 0036	Evaluation (Repair costs —) [financial appraisal]	E 0072	360103
45	E 0037	Evening dress rental	L 0086	450046
37	E 0038	Excavators (Rental of —)	L 0099	370044
36	E 0039	Exchanging money	O 0009	360019
35	E 0040	Exhibitions (Organization of —) for commercial or advertising purposes	O 0035	350064
41	E 0041	Exhibitions (Organization of —) for cultural or educational purposes	O 0036	410051
42	E 0042	Exploration (Underwater —)	E 0103	420167
44	E 0043	Exterminating (Vermin —) for agriculture, horticulture and forestry	D 0031	440168
37	E 0044	Exterminating (Vermin —), other than for agriculture	D 0030	370091
37	E 0045	Extraction (Mining —)	E 0109	370107

Cl.	SERIAL No. (E)	INDICATION OF SERVICES	SERIAL No. (F)	BASIC No.
40	F 0001	Fabric bleaching	B 0028	400008
40	F 0002	Fabric fireproofing	I 0001	400037
40	F 0003	Fabric waterproofing	I 0008	400036
38	F 0004	Facsimile transmission	T 0082	380026
36	F 0005	Factoring	A 0021	360027
37	F 0006	Factory construction	U 0001	370052
44	F 0007	Farming equipment rental	L 0070	440084
41	F 0008	Fashion shows for entertainment purposes (Organization of —)	D 0011	410188
35	F 0009	Fashion shows for promotional purposes (Organization of —)	D 0012	350103
39	F 0010	Ferry-boat transport	N 0004	390036
44	F 0011	Fertilizers and other agricultural chemicals (Aerial and surface spreading of —)	E 0055	440115
36	F 0012	Fiduciary	F 0009	360028
35	F 0013	File management (Computerized —)	G 0017	350061
41	F 0014	Film production, other than advertising films	P 0098	410020
37	F 0015	Film projector repair and maintenance	P 0109	370046
36	F 0016	Financial consultancy	C 0121	360054
36	F 0017	Financial evaluation [insurance, banking, real estate]	E 0071	360026
36	F 0018	Financial information	I 0036	360059
36	F 0019	Financial management	G 0018	360030
36	F 0020	Financial sponsorship	P 0012	360071
36	F 0021	Financing services	F 0014	360029
37	F 0022	Fire alarm installation and repair	I 0016	370015
45	F 0023	Fire alarms (Rental of —)	L 0037	450203
45	F 0024	Fire extinguishers (Rental of —)	L 0101	450204
36	F 0025	Fire insurance underwriting	I 0015	360034
45	F 0026	Fire-fighting	E 0108	450179
40	F 0027	Fireproofing (Cloth —)	I 0001	400037
40	F 0028	Firing pottery	C 0023	400015
36	F 0029	Fiscal assessments	E 0096	360025
40	F 0030	Flour milling	M 0043	400044
44	F 0031	Flower arranging	C 0085	440143
39	F 0032	Flower delivery	L 0019	390096
40	F 0033	Food and drink preservation	C 0105	400066
40	F 0034	Food smoking	F 0052	400033
40	F 0035	Foods (Freezing of —)	C 0097	400117
35	F 0036	Forecasting (Economic —)	P 0094	350063
42	F 0037	Forecasting (Weather —)	I 0037	420076
40	F 0038	Framing of works of art	E 0028	400084
39	F 0039	Franking of mail	A 0039	390097
37	F 0040	Freezing equipment installation and repair	R 0044	370078
40	F 0041	Freezing of foods	C 0097	400117
39	F 0042	Freight brokerage [forwarding (Am.)]	C 0148	390072
39	F 0043	Freight forwarding	E 0093	390060
39	F 0044	Freight [shipping of goods]	F 0050	390038
39	F 0045	Freighting	A 0040	390039
39	F 0046	Frozen-food locker rental	L 0076	390043
40	F 0047	Fruit crushing	P 0091	400032
40	F 0048	Fulling of cloth	F 0034	400120
36	F 0049	Fund investments	P 0059	360017
36	F 0050	Fund raising (Charitable —)	C 0070	360015
36	F 0051	Funds transfer (Electronic —)	T 0075	360058
45	F 0052	Funerals	E 0043	450056
37	F 0053	Fur care, cleaning and repair	F 0041	370048
40	F 0054	Fur conditioning	F 0047	400020
40	F 0055	Fur (Custom fashioning of —)	F 0001	400028
40	F 0056	Fur dyeing	T 0008	400072
40	F 0057	Fur glossing	L 0119	400070
40	F 0058	Fur mothproofing	T 0062	400030
40	F 0059	Fur satining	S 0007	400071
37	F 0060	Furnace installation and repair	F 0035	370047
37	F 0061	Furniture maintenance	M 0056	370001
37	F 0062	Furniture restoration	R 0075	370060
39	F 0063	Furniture (Transporting —)	M 0041	390047

Cl.	SERIAL No. (E)	INDICATION OF SERVICES	SERIAL No. (F)	BASIC No.
40	G 0001	Galvanization	G 0003	400034
41	G 0002	Gambling	J 0006	410052
41	G 0003	Game services provided on-line from a computer network	J 0005	410094
41	G 0004	Games equipment rental	L 0069	410198
39	G 0005	Garage rental	L 0058	390040
44	G 0006	Gardening	J 0001	440077
44	G 0007	Gardening (Landscape —)	J 0002	440012
45	G 0008	Genealogical research	R 0027	450216
42	G 0009	Geological prospecting	P 0118	420118
42	G 0010	Geological research	R 0028	420119
42	G 0011	Geological surveys	E 0097	420062
40	G 0012	Gilding	D 0064	400024
40	G 0013	Glass-blowing	S 0031	400062
40	G 0014	Glossing (Fur —)	L 0119	400070
40	G 0015	Gold-plating	P 0055	400085
41	G 0016	Golf facilities (Providing —)	M 0046	410053
39	G 0017	Goods (Delivery of —)	L 0020	390027
39	G 0018	Goods (Storage of —)	D 0018	390028
42	G 0019	Graphic arts designing	D 0026	420144
37	G 0020	Greasing (Vehicle —)	G 0022	370049
38	G 0021	Greeting cards online (Transmission of —)	T 0077	380046
40	G 0022	Grinding	M 0042	400041
40	G 0023	Grinding (Optical glass —)	P 0075	400088
44	G 0024	Grooming (Animal —)	P 0004	440131
44	G 0025	Grooming (Pet —)	T 0055	440173
36	G 0026	Guarantees	C 0022	360018
39	G 0027	Guarded transport of valuables	T 0086	390062
45	G 0028	Guards	P 0119	450099
45	G 0029	Guards (Night —)	A 0049	450006
41	G 0030	Guidance (Vocational —) [education or training advice]	O 0044	410102
41	G 0031	Gymnastic instruction	G 0025	410021

Cl.	SERIAL No. (E)	INDICATION OF SERVICES	SERIAL No. (F)	BASIC No.

Cl.	SERIAL No. (E)	INDICATION OF SERVICES	SERIAL No. (F)	BASIC No.
44	H 0001	Hair implantation	I 0009	440180
44	H 0002	Hairdressing salons	S 0003	440034
42	H 0003	Handwriting analysis [graphology]	G 0023	420211
37	H 0004	Harbour construction	P 0083	370074
39	H 0005	Hauling	C 0007	390014
44	H 0006	Health care	S 0005	440060
44	H 0007	Health centers	D 0048	440209
44	H 0008	Health centres	D 0048	440209
41	H 0009	Health club services [health and fitness training]	C 0061	410054
36	H 0010	Health insurance underwriting	M 0011	360038
44	H 0011	Health spa services	S 0044	440202
40	H 0012	Heating apparatus (Rental of space —)	L 0027	400119
37	H 0013	Heating equipment installation and repair	C 0033	370024
36	H 0014	Hire-purchase financing	C 0160	360042
41	H 0015	Holiday camp services [entertainment]	C 0009	410055
43	H 0016	Holiday camp services [lodging]	C 0010	430145
36	H 0017	Home banking	B 0010	360072
44	H 0018	Homes (Convalescent —)	M 0007	440043
44	H 0019	Homes (Nursing —)	M 0010	440114
43	H 0020	Homes (Retirement —)	M 0008	430013
43	H 0021	Homes (Tourist —)	M 0009	430071
45	H 0022	Horoscope casting	H 0007	450146
39	H 0023	Horse rental	L 0045	390019
44	H 0024	Horticulture	H 0008	440072
44	H 0025	Hospices	H 0009	440147
44	H 0026	Hospitals	H 0010	440059
42	H 0027	Hosting computer sites [web sites]	H 0004	420200
43	H 0028	Hotel reservations	R 0071	430105
43	H 0029	Hotels	H 0011	430073
35	H 0030	Hotels (Business management of —)	G 0012	350078
45	H 0031	House sitting	O 0002	450197
43	H 0032	Houses (Boarding —)	P 0023	430066
36	H 0033	Housing agents	C 0151	360008

Cl.	SERIAL No. (E)	INDICATION OF SERVICES	SERIAL No. (F)	BASIC No.

Cl.	SERIAL No. (E)	INDICATION OF SERVICES	SERIAL No. (F)	BASIC No.
39	I 0001	Ice-breaking	B 0042	390013
35	I 0002	Import-export agencies	A 0050	350005
44	I 0003	In vitro fertilization services	F 0003	440196
40	I 0004	Incineration of waste and trash	I 0017	400106
42	I 0005	Industrial design	D 0025	420049
35	I 0006	Industrial management assistance (Commercial or—)	D 0041	350025
38	I 0007	Information about telecommunication	I 0028	380027
35	I 0008	Information agencies (Commercial—)	A 0051	350006
35	I 0009	Information (Business—)	I 0021	350065
37	I 0010	Information (Construction—)	I 0024	370104
41	I 0011	Information (Education—)	I 0032	410048
41	I 0012	Information (Entertainment—)	I 0025	410050
36	I 0013	Information (Financial—)	I 0036	360059
36	I 0014	Information (Insurance—)	I 0023	360060
40	I 0015	Information (Material treatment—)	I 0030	400087
41	I 0016	Information (Recreation—)	I 0026	410064
37	I 0017	Information (Repair—)	I 0027	370105
39	I 0018	Information (Transportation—)	I 0031	390077
35	I 0019	Inquiries (Business—)	R 0056	350002
45	I 0020	Inspection (Baggage—) for security purposes	I 0042	450196
45	I 0021	Inspection of factories for safety purposes	I 0043	450202
42	I 0022	Installation of computer software	I 0044	420201
37	I 0023	Installation of doors and windows	I 0045	370128
36	I 0024	Instalment loans	P 0001	360002
41	I 0025	Instruction services	E 0011	410017
37	I 0026	Insulating (Building—)	I 0054	370054
36	I 0027	Insurance brokerage	C 0150	360010
36	I 0028	Insurance consultancy	C 0116	360055
36	I 0029	Insurance information	I 0023	360060
36	I 0030	Insurance underwriting	A 0110	360012
45	I 0031	Intellectual property consultancy	C 0104	450206
45	I 0032	Intellectual property (Licensing of—)	L 0014	450208
45	I 0033	Intellectual property watching services	S 0056	450209
37	I 0034	Interference suppression in electrical apparatus	D 0017	370117
41	I 0035	Interpretation (Sign language—)	I 0048	410105
35	I 0036	Investigations (Business—)	I 0050	350033
45	I 0037	Investigations (Missing person—)	E 0035	450053
45	I 0038	Investigations (Personal background—)	I 0051	450199
36	I 0039	Investment (Capital—)	P 0059	360017
35	I 0040	Invoicing	F 0002	350098
37	I 0041	Ironing (Linen—)	R 0060	370079
37	I 0042	Irrigation devices installation and repair	I 0053	370053
36	I 0043	Issuance of credit cards	E 0022	360068
36	I 0044	Issue of tokens of value	E 0021	360065
36	I 0045	Issuing of travellers' checks [cheques]	E 0023	360020

Cl.	SERIAL No. (E)	INDICATION OF SERVICES	SERIAL No. (F)	BASIC No.
36	J 0001	Jewellery appraisal	E 0064	360061
36	J 0002	Jewelry appraisal	E 0064	360061

Cl.	SERIAL No. (E)	INDICATION OF SERVICES	SERIAL No. (F)	BASIC No.

Cl.	SERIAL No. (E)	INDICATION OF SERVICES	SERIAL No. (F)	BASIC No.
40	K 0001	Key cutting	C 0133	400108
37	K 0002	Kitchen equipment installation	E 0058	370035
37	K 0003	Knife sharpening	A 0060	370106
40	K 0004	Knitting machine rental	L 0065	400112

Cl.	SERIAL No. (E)	INDICATION OF SERVICES	SERIAL No. (F)	BASIC No.

Cl.	SERIAL No. (E)	INDICATION OF SERVICES	SERIAL No. (F)	BASIC No.
42	L 0001	Laboratory (Scientific—) services	L 0001	420217
40	L 0002	Laminating	L 0003	400040
42	L 0003	Land surveying	L 0010	420079
44	L 0004	Landscape design	C 0088	440199
44	L 0005	Landscape gardening	J 0002	440012
41	L 0006	Language interpreter services	I 0049	410192
40	L 0007	Laser scribing	T 0057	400086
39	L 0008	Launching of satellites for others	L 0004	390095
37	L 0009	Laundering	B 0029	370010
44	L 0010	Lawn care	E 0053	440148
35	L 0011	Layout services for advertising purposes	M 0053	350101
41	L 0012	Layout services, other than for advertising purposes	M 0054	410187
36	L 0013	Lease-purchase financing	C 0160	360042
36	L 0014	Leasing of farms	L 0100	360036
36	L 0015	Leasing of real estate	A 0036	360004
37	L 0016	Leather care, cleaning and repair	C 0164	370034
40	L 0017	Leather staining	T 0010	400019
40	L 0018	Leather working	C 0166	400064
45	L 0019	Legal research	R 0029	450210
36	L 0020	Lending against security	N 0001	360108
41	L 0021	Lending libraries	P 0092	410023
41	L 0022	Libraries (Lending—)	P 0092	410023
41	L 0023	Library services (Mobile—)	B 0020	410041
45	L 0024	Licensing of computer software [legal services]	C 0090	450212
45	L 0025	Licensing of intellectual property	L 0014	450208
35	L 0026	Licensing of the goods and services of others (Commercial administration of the—)	A 0018	350096
36	L 0027	Life insurance underwriting	V 0028	360044
37	L 0028	Lift installation and repair	A 0106	370004
39	L 0029	Lighterage services	A 0015	390016
37	L 0030	Linen ironing	R 0060	370079
40	L 0031	Lithographic printing	I 0013	400110
45	L 0032	Litigation services	C 0126	450211
41	L 0033	Live performances (Presentation of—)	S 0039	410056
36	L 0034	Loans [financing]	P 0093	360024
45	L 0035	Locks (Opening of security—)	O 0046	450033
37	L 0036	Locks (Repair of security—)	R 0057	370125
45	L 0037	Lost property return	R 0082	450200
41	L 0038	Lotteries (Operating—)	L 0117	410081
37	L 0039	Lubrication (Vehicle—)	G 0022	370049

Cl.	SERIAL No. (E)	INDICATION OF SERVICES	SERIAL No. (F)	BASIC No.
37	M 0001	Machinery installation, maintenance and repair	M 0001	370058
40	M 0002	Magnetization	M 0003	400004
38	M 0003	Mail (Electronic —)	M 0031	380025
42	M 0004	Maintaining (Creating and —) web sites for others	C 0157	420199
42	M 0005	Maintenance of computer software	M 0005	420176
37	M 0006	Maintenance (Vehicle —)	V 0008	370085
35	M 0007	Management (Advisory services for business —)	D 0044	350048
35	M 0008	Management assistance (Commercial or industrial —)	D 0041	350025
35	M 0009	Management (Computerized file —)	G 0017	350061
35	M 0010	Management consultancy (Personnel —)	C 0123	350019
45	M 0011	Management (Copyright —)	G 0014	450207
36	M 0012	Management (Financial —)	G 0018	360030
44	M 0013	Manicuring	M 0014	440151
36	M 0014	Marine insurance underwriting	M 0017	360039
39	M 0015	Marine transport	M 0019	390061
35	M 0016	Marketing	M 0020	350106
35	M 0017	Marketing research	R 0016	350051
35	M 0018	Marketing studies	E 0087	350031
45	M 0019	Marriage agencies	A 0055	450112
37	M 0020	Masonry	M 0002	370059
44	M 0021	Massage	M 0021	440086
42	M 0022	Material testing	E 0061	420058
40	M 0023	Material treatment information	I 0030	400087
42	M 0024	Mechanical research	R 0026	420101
45	M 0025	Mediation	M 0027	450201
44	M 0026	Medical assistance	A 0109	440087
44	M 0027	Medical clinic services	C 0058	440021
44	M 0028	Medical equipment rental	E 0059	440208
37	M 0029	Mending clothing	R 0002	370075
39	M 0030	Message delivery	D 0056	390087
38	M 0031	Message sending	T 0079	380004
40	M 0032	Metal casting	C 0140	400100
40	M 0033	Metal plating	R 0084	400018
40	M 0034	Metal tempering	T 0095	400043
40	M 0035	Metal treating	M 0037	400042
42	M 0036	Meteorological information	I 0037	420076
41	M 0037	Microfilming	M 0045	410182
44	M 0038	Midwife services	A 0059	440152
40	M 0039	Milling (Flour —)	M 0043	400044
40	M 0040	Millworking	F 0048	400031
37	M 0041	Mining extraction	E 0109	370107
45	M 0042	Missing person investigations	E 0035	450053
41	M 0043	Mobile library services	B 0020	410041
35	M 0044	Modelling for advertising or sales promotion	M 0013	350049
41	M 0045	Modelling for artists	M 0059	410036
36	M 0046	Money (Exchanging —)	O 0009	360019
45	M 0047	Monitoring of burglar and security alarms	S 0054	450194
42	M 0048	Monitoring of computer systems by remote access	T 0025	420215
36	M 0049	Mortgage banking	O 0008	360040
43	M 0050	Motels	M 0065	430183
40	M 0051	Mothproofing (Fur —)	T 0062	400030
40	M 0052	Mothproofing (Textile —)	T 0061	400059
41	M 0053	Motion pictures (Rental of —)	L 0055	410019
37	M 0054	Motor vehicle maintenance and repair	A 0118	370006
37	M 0055	Motor vehicle wash	L 0006	370007
41	M 0056	Movie projectors and accessories (Rental of —)	L 0032	410006
41	M 0057	Movie studios	S 0049	410008
41	M 0058	Movie theatre presentations	P 0110	410057
41	M 0059	Museum facilities (Providing —) [presentation, exhibitions]	M 0067	410062
41	M 0060	Music composition services	C 0086	410097
37	M 0061	Musical instruments (Restoration of —)	R 0076	370127
41	M 0062	Music-halls	M 0068	410027
36	M 0063	Mutual funds	F 0026	360016

Cl.	SERIAL No. (E)	INDICATION OF SERVICES	SERIAL No. (F)	BASIC No.
38	N 0001	News agencies	A 0046	380012
35	N 0002	News clipping services	R 0087	350088
41	N 0003	News reporters services	R 0063	410103
39	N 0004	Newspaper delivery	D 0051	390088
35	N 0005	Newspaper subscriptions (Arranging —) for others	A 0003	350076
40	N 0006	Nickel plating	N 0016	400045
41	N 0007	Night clubs	B 0035	410098
45	N 0008	Night guards	A 0049	450006
36	N 0009	Numismatic appraisal	E 0070	360062
41	N 0010	Nursery schools	E 0008	410058
44	N 0011	Nursing homes	M 0010	440114
44	N 0012	Nursing, medical	G 0007	440153

Cl.	SERIAL No. (E)	INDICATION OF SERVICES	SERIAL No. (F)	BASIC No.
37	O 0001	Office machines and equipment installation, maintenance and repair	B 0045	370014
35	O 0002	Office machines and equipment rental *	L 0067	350013
40	O 0003	Offset printing	I 0012	400113
40	O 0004	Oil (Processing of—)	T 0069	400091
42	O 0005	Oil prospecting	P 0117	420095
42	O 0006	Oil-field exploitation (Analysis for—)	A 0074	420008
42	O 0007	Oil-field surveys	E 0094	420063
42	O 0008	Oil-well testing	C 0127	420042
35	O 0009	On-line advertising on a computer network	P 0137	350084
45	O 0010	Opening of security locks	O 0046	450033
39	O 0011	Operating canal locks	E 0007	390032
41	O 0012	Operating lotteries	L 0117	410081
35	O 0013	Opinion polling	S 0029	350066
40	O 0014	Optical glass grinding	P 0075	400088
44	O 0015	Opticians' services	O 0013	440092
41	O 0016	Orchestra services	O 0015	410028
41	O 0017	Organization of balls	O 0025	410082
36	O 0018	Organization of collections	C 0069	360023
41	O 0019	Organization of competitions [education or entertainment]	O 0028	410010
35	O 0020	Organization of exhibitions for commercial or advertising purposes	O 0035	350064
41	O 0021	Organization of exhibitions for cultural or educational purposes	O 0036	410051
45	O 0022	Organization of religious meetings	O 0030	450184
41	O 0023	Organization of shows [impresario services]	O 0031	410083
41	O 0024	Organization of sports competitions	O 0026	410059
35	O 0025	Organization of trade fairs for commercial or advertising purposes	F 0025	350082
35	O 0026	Outdoor advertising	A 0037	350003
35	O 0027	Outsourcing services [business assistance]	S 0035	350097

Cl.	SERIAL No. (E)	INDICATION OF SERVICES	SERIAL No. (F)	BASIC No.
42	P 0001	Packaging design	D 0028	420050
39	P 0002	Packaging of goods	E 0019	390022
38	P 0003	Paging services [radio, telephone or other means of electronic communication]	A 0089	380028
37	P 0004	Painting, interior and exterior	P 0019	370068
40	P 0005	Paper finishing	A 0091	400006
37	P 0006	Paper hanging	P 0085	370064
40	P 0007	Paper treating	P 0006	400061
37	P 0008	Parasol repair	P 0009	370066
39	P 0009	Parcel delivery	D 0050	390020
39	P 0010	Parking place rental	L 0074	390042
41	P 0011	Parks (Amusement—)	P 0010	410003
41	P 0012	Party planning [entertainment]	P 0063	410060
39	P 0013	Passenger transport	P 0014	390051
40	P 0014	Pattern printing	I 0011	400022
37	P 0015	Paving (Road—)	R 0086	370109
36	P 0016	Pawnbrokerage	G 0001	360031
35	P 0017	Payroll preparation	P 0015	350067
41	P 0018	Performances (Presentation of live—)	S 0039	410056
40	P 0019	Permanent-press treatment of fabrics	C 0005	400014
45	P 0020	Personal background investigations	I 0051	450199
45	P 0021	Personal body guarding	P 0122	450001
41	P 0022	Personal trainer services [fitness training]	P 0087	410193
35	P 0023	Personnel management consultancy	C 0123	350019
35	P 0024	Personnel recruitment	R 0035	350068
44	P 0025	Pet grooming	T 0055	440173
45	P 0026	Pet sitting	G 0008	450198
44	P 0027	Pharmacists' services to make up prescriptions	P 0039	440204
44	P 0028	Pharmacy advice	C 0119	440154
40	P 0029	Photocomposing services	P 0040	400114
35	P 0030	Photocopying services	P 0041	350009
37	P 0031	Photographic apparatus repair	P 0045	370002
40	P 0032	Photographic film development	D 0035	400023
40	P 0033	Photographic printing	T 0048	400089
41	P 0034	Photographic reporting	R 0062	410100
41	P 0035	Photography	P 0042	410101
40	P 0036	Photogravure	P 0047	400090
41	P 0037	Physical education	C 0169	410012
44	P 0038	Physical therapy	P 0048	440097
42	P 0039	Physics [research]	P 0050	420096
44	P 0040	Physiotherapy	P 0048	440097
37	P 0041	Pier breakwater building	M 0060	370061
39	P 0042	Piloting	P 0051	390052
37	P 0043	Pipeline construction and maintenance	O 0006	370063
39	P 0044	Pipeline (Transport by—)	O 0007	390041
40	P 0045	Planing [saw mill]	R 0001	400050
45	P 0046	Planning and arranging of wedding ceremonies	P 0065	450217
41	P 0047	Planning (Party—) [entertainment]	P 0063	410060
44	P 0048	Plant nurseries	P 0026	440094
37	P 0049	Plastering	P 0068	370070

Cl.	SERIAL No. (E)	INDICATION OF SERVICES	SERIAL No. (F)	BASIC No.
44	P 0050	Plastic surgery	C 0047	440156
40	P 0051	Plating (Metal—)	R 0084	400018
39	P 0052	Pleasure boat transport	B 0014	390011
37	P 0053	Plumbing	P 0069	370071
37	P 0054	Polishing (Vehicle—)	P 0074	370072
35	P 0055	Polling (Opinion—)	S 0029	350066
39	P 0056	Porterage	P 0080	390021
40	P 0057	Pottery firing	C 0023	400015
41	P 0058	Practical training [demonstration]	F 0032	410061
35	P 0059	Presentation of goods on communication media, for retail purposes	P 0088	350092
40	P 0060	Pre-shrinking (Cloth—)	R 0083	400069
37	P 0061	Pressing of clothing	P 0089	370062
35	P 0062	Price comparison services	C 0082	350091
40	P 0063	Printing	I 0014	400111
40	P 0064	Printing (Lithographic—)	I 0013	400110
40	P 0065	Printing (Offset—)	I 0012	400113
40	P 0066	Printing (Photographic—)	T 0048	400089
35	P 0067	Processing (Administrative—) of purchase orders	T 0060	350095
40	P 0068	Processing of oil	T 0069	400091
35	P 0069	Processing (Word—)	T 0066	350075
35	P 0070	Procurement services for others [purchasing goods and services for other businesses]	A 0092	350085
35	P 0071	Production of advertising films	P 0099	350104
40	P 0072	Production of energy	P 0101	400103
41	P 0073	Production of music	P 0102	410196
41	P 0074	Production of radio and television programmes	M 0063	410026
41	P 0075	Production of shows	S 0038	410030
41	P 0076	Production (Videotape film—)	P 0100	410074
42	P 0077	Project studies (Technical—)	E 0088	420061
42	P 0078	Prospecting (Geological—)	P 0118	420118
42	P 0079	Prospecting (Oil—)	P 0117	420095
42	P 0080	Protection services (Computer virus—)	P 0120	420206
36	P 0081	Provident fund services	P 0095	360109
38	P 0082	Providing access to databases	F 0036	380044
41	P 0083	Providing amusement arcade services	E 0100	410084
43	P 0084	Providing campground facilities	M 0048	430026
38	P 0085	Providing internet chatrooms	F 0039	380043
41	P 0086	Providing karaoke services	M 0049	410095
41	P 0087	Providing on-line electronic publications, not downloadable	M 0047	410099
42	P 0088	Providing search engines for the internet	F 0040	420209
41	P 0089	Providing sports facilities	M 0050	410035
38	P 0090	Providing telecommunication channels for teleshopping services	F 0038	380042
38	P 0091	Providing telecommunications connections to a global computer network	R 0003	380037
38	P 0092	Providing user access to global computer networks	F 0037	380040

Cl.	SERIAL No. (E)	INDICATION OF SERVICES	SERIAL No. (F)	BASIC No.
42	P 0093	Provision of scientific information, advice and consultancy in relation to carbon offsetting	I 0035	420212
35	P 0094	Psychological testing for the selection of personnel	S 0018	350090
44	P 0095	Psychologist (Services of a—)	P 0123	440185
44	P 0096	Public baths for hygiene purposes	B 0003	440018
35	P 0097	Public relations	R 0045	350042
41	P 0098	Publication of books	P 0125	410024
41	P 0099	Publication of electronic books and journals on-line	P 0128	410091
35	P 0100	Publication of publicity texts	P 0127	350038
41	P 0101	Publication of texts, other than publicity texts	P 0126	410016
35	P 0102	Publicity	P 0136	350039
35	P 0103	Publicity agencies	A 0047	350047
35	P 0104	Publicity columns preparation	C 0143	350021
35	P 0105	Publicity material rental	L 0071	350035
35	P 0106	Publicity texts (Publication of—)	P 0127	350038
35	P 0107	Publicity texts (Writing of—)	R 0042	350099
37	P 0108	Pumicing	P 0078	370069
37	P 0109	Pump repair	P 0077	370073
35	P 0110	Purchase orders (Administrative processing of—)	T 0060	350095

Cl.	SERIAL No. (E)	INDICATION OF SERVICES	SERIAL No. (F)	BASIC No.
42	Q 0001	Quality control	C 0128	420157
37	Q 0002	Quarrying services	E 0099	370108
40	Q 0003	Quilting	S 0053	400092

Cl.	SERIAL No. (E)	INDICATION OF SERVICES	SERIAL No. (F)	BASIC No.
35	R 0001	Radio advertising	P 0139	350040
41	R 0002	Radio and television programmes (Production of—)	M 0063	410026
41	R 0003	Radio and television sets (Rental of—)	L 0075	410025
38	R 0004	Radio broadcasting	R 0005	380003
35	R 0005	Radio commercials	P 0139	350040
41	R 0006	Radio entertainment	D 0060	410015
39	R 0007	Railway transport	T 0089	390018
37	R 0008	Rat exterminating	D 0021	370076
36	R 0009	Real estate agencies	A 0054	360007
36	R 0010	Real estate appraisal	E 0074	360014
36	R 0011	Real estate brokers	C 0151	360008
36	R 0012	Real estate (Leasing of—)	A 0036	360004
36	R 0013	Real estate management	G 0013	360032
37	R 0014	Rebuilding engines that have been worn or partially destroyed	R 0051	370118
37	R 0015	Rebuilding machines that have been worn or partially destroyed	R 0050	370119
41	R 0016	Recorders (Rental of video cassette—)	L 0068	410068
41	R 0017	Recording studio services	S 0050	410063
42	R 0018	Recovery of computer data	R 0037	420175
41	R 0019	Recreation facilities (Providing—)	L 0116	410014
41	R 0020	Recreation information	I 0026	410064
35	R 0021	Recruitment (Personnel—)	R 0035	350068
40	R 0022	Recycling of waste and trash	R 0038	400068
37	R 0023	Refilling of toner cartridges	R 0015	370130
40	R 0024	Refining services	R 0010	400093
39	R 0025	Refloating of ships	R 0054	390055
39	R 0026	Refrigerator rental	L 0076	390043
45	R 0027	Registration of domain names [legal services]	E 0036	450213
44	R 0028	Rehabilitation for substance abuse patients	D 0023	440195
41	R 0029	Religious education	E 0013	410080
35	R 0030	Relocation services for businesses	R 0048	350069
39	R 0031	Removal services	D 0013	390065
37	R 0032	Renovation of clothing	R 0055	370022
36	R 0033	Rent collection	R 0033	360063
42	R 0034	Rental (Computer—)	L 0104	420083
38	R 0035	Rental of access time to global computer networks	L 0083	380041
35	R 0036	Rental of advertising space	L 0098	350070
35	R 0037	Rental of advertising time on communication media	L 0084	350087
40	R 0038	Rental of air conditioning apparatus	L 0028	400118
41	R 0039	Rental of audio equipment	L 0026	410085
37	R 0040	Rental of bulldozers	L 0041	370013
41	R 0041	Rental of camcorders	L 0043	410088
43	R 0042	Rental of chairs, tables, table linen, glassware	L 0044	430186
41	R 0043	Rental of cine-films	L 0055	410019
42	R 0044	Rental of computer software	L 0063	420159
37	R 0045	Rental of construction equipment	L 0066	370020
43	R 0046	Rental of cooking apparatus	L 0029	430190
37	R 0047	Rental of cranes [construction equipment]	L 0060	370120
39	R 0048	Rental of diving bells	L 0046	390078
39	R 0049	Rental of diving suits	L 0078	390079
43	R 0050	Rental of drinking water dispensers	L 0056	430191
37	R 0051	Rental of excavators	L 0099	370044
38	R 0052	Rental of facsimile apparatus	L 0081	380031
45	R 0053	Rental of fire alarms	L 0037	450203
45	R 0054	Rental of fire extinguishers	L 0101	450204
39	R 0055	Rental of freezers	L 0048	390099
40	R 0056	Rental of generators	L 0059	400104
41	R 0057	Rental of lighting apparatus for theatrical sets or television studios	L 0031	410086
43	R 0058	Rental of meeting rooms	L 0077	430187
38	R 0059	Rental of message sending apparatus	L 0033	380029
38	R 0060	Rental of modems	L 0072	380032
41	R 0061	Rental of motion pictures	L 0055	410019
39	R 0062	Rental of motor racing cars	L 0090	390091
41	R 0063	Rental of movie projectors and accessories	L 0032	410006
36	R 0064	Rental of offices [real estate]	L 0042	360069
35	R 0065	Rental of photocopying machines	L 0073	350083
41	R 0066	Rental of radio and television sets	L 0075	410025
37	R 0067	Rental of road sweeping machines	L 0038	370121
45	R 0068	Rental of safes	L 0047	450215
44	R 0069	Rental of sanitation facilities	L 0103	440188
41	R 0070	Rental of show scenery	L 0052	410013
41	R 0071	Rental of skin diving equipment	L 0096	410065
41	R 0072	Rental of sound recordings	L 0093	410018
40	R 0073	Rental of space heating apparatus	L 0027	400119
41	R 0074	Rental of sports equipment, except vehicles	L 0095	410066
41	R 0075	Rental of sports grounds	L 0087	410190
41	R 0076	Rental of stadium facilities	L 0080	410067
41	R 0077	Rental of stage scenery	T 0045	410032
39	R 0078	Rental of storage containers	L 0050	390080
38	R 0079	Rental of telecommunication equipment	L 0030	380033
38	R 0080	Rental of telephones	L 0082	380034
43	R 0081	Rental of temporary accommodation	L 0062	430028
41	R 0082	Rental of tennis courts	L 0051	410087
43	R 0083	Rental of tents	L 0085	430189
43	R 0084	Rental of transportable buildings *	L 0049	430160
39	R 0085	Rental of vehicle roof racks	L 0057	390081
35	R 0086	Rental of vending machines	L 0053	350089
41	R 0087	Rental of video cameras	L 0043	410088
41	R 0088	Rental of video cassette recorders	L 0068	410068

Cl.	SERIAL No. (E)	INDICATION OF SERVICES	SERIAL No. (F)	BASIC No.
41	R 0089	Rental of videotapes	L 0039	410069
39	R 0090	Rental of warehouses	L 0094	390035
42	R 0091	Rental of web servers	L 0079	420205
39	R 0092	Rental of wheelchairs	L 0054	390092
35	R 0093	Rental (Office machines and equipment —) *	L 0067	350013
35	R 0094	Rental (Publicity material —)	L 0071	350035
36	R 0095	Renting of apartments	L 0034	360035
36	R 0096	Renting of flats	L 0034	360035
36	R 0097	Repair costs evaluation [financial appraisal]	E 0072	360103
37	R 0098	Repair information	I 0027	370105
37	R 0099	Repair of security locks	R 0057	370125
37	R 0100	Repair (Underwater —)	R 0059	370111
41	R 0101	Reporters services (News —)	R 0063	410103
35	R 0102	Reproduction (Document —)	R 0066	350026
39	R 0103	Rescue operations [transport]	S 0014	390082
42	R 0104	Research and development for others	R 0018	420161
42	R 0105	Research (Biological —)	R 0019	420190
35	R 0106	Research (Business —)	R 0030	350041
42	R 0107	Research (Geological —)	R 0028	420119
42	R 0108	Research in the field of environmental protection	R 0025	420208
39	R 0109	Reservation (Transport —)	T 0093	390083
39	R 0110	Reservation (Travel —)	V 0039	390084
43	R 0111	Reservations (Temporary accommodation —)	R 0067	430162
44	R 0112	Rest homes	M 0007	440043
43	R 0113	Restaurants	R 0078	430102
43	R 0114	Restaurants (Self-service —)	R 0074	430107
37	R 0115	Restoration (Furniture —)	R 0075	370060
37	R 0116	Restoration of musical instruments	R 0076	370127
37	R 0117	Restoration of works of art	R 0077	370126
35	R 0118	Retail purposes (Presentation of goods on communication media, for —)	P 0088	350092
37	R 0119	Re-tinning	R 0079	370080
43	R 0120	Retirement homes	M 0008	430013
36	R 0121	Retirement payment services	C 0004	360070
37	R 0122	Retreading of tires [tyres]	R 0014	370077
39	R 0123	River transport	T 0091	390037
37	R 0124	Riveting	R 0088	370081
37	R 0125	Road paving	R 0086	370109
39	R 0126	Roof racks (Rental of vehicle —)	L 0057	390081
37	R 0127	Roofing services	T 0094	370122
37	R 0128	Rustproofing	T 0063	370037

Cl.	SERIAL No. (E)	INDICATION OF SERVICES	SERIAL No. (F)	BASIC No.

Cl.	SERIAL No. (E)	INDICATION OF SERVICES	SERIAL No. (F)	BASIC No.
40	S 0001	Saddlery working	S 0019	400051
36	S 0002	Safe deposit services	D 0020	360022
37	S 0003	Safe maintenance and repair	C 0065	370027
45	S 0004	Safes (Rental of—)	L 0047	450215
45	S 0005	Safety (Inspection of factories for—) purposes	I 0043	450202
35	S 0006	Sales promotion for others	P 0113	350071
44	S 0007	Salons (Beauty—)	S 0002	440020
44	S 0008	Salons (Hairdressing—)	S 0003	440034
39	S 0009	Salvage of ships	S 0009	390015
39	S 0010	Salvage (Underwater—)	S 0011	390085
39	S 0011	Salvaging	S 0010	390057
35	S 0012	Samples (Distribution of—)	D 0039	350028
44	S 0013	Sanatoriums	S 0004	440106
40	S 0014	Sandblasting services	S 0001	400122
37	S 0015	Sanding	P 0079	370110
38	S 0016	Satellite transmission	T 0084	380035
40	S 0017	Satining (Fur—)	S 0007	400071
44	S 0018	Sauna services	S 0008	440200
36	S 0019	Savings bank services	E 0056	360041
40	S 0020	Sawing [saw mill]	S 0013	400052
37	S 0021	Scaffolding	M 0064	370093
41	S 0022	Schools (Boarding—)	P 0022	410075
41	S 0023	Schools (Nursery—)	E 0008	410058
40	S 0024	Scribing (Laser—)	T 0057	400086
41	S 0025	Scriptwriting services	R 0040	410089
37	S 0026	Sealing (Building—)	E 0078	370042
42	S 0027	Search engines (Providing—) for the internet	F 0040	420209
35	S 0028	Secretarial services	S 0015	350072
36	S 0029	Securities brokerage	C 0152	360043
45	S 0030	Security consultancy	C 0120	450117
43	S 0031	Self-service restaurants	R 0074	430107
41	S 0032	Seminars (Arranging and conducting of—)	O 0042	410070
38	S 0033	Sending apparatus (Rental of message—)	L 0033	380029
42	S 0034	Servers (Rental of Web—)	L 0079	420205
37	S 0035	Service stations (Vehicle—) [refuelling and maintenance]	S 0045	370083
37	S 0036	Sharpening (Knife—)	A 0060	370106
39	S 0037	Shipbrokerage	C 0153	390023
37	S 0038	Shipbuilding	C 0112	370021
39	S 0039	Ships (Refloating of—)	R 0054	390055
37	S 0040	Shoe repair	C 0134	370025
40	S 0041	Shoe staining	C 0036	400016
35	S 0042	Shop window dressing	D 0007	350046
35	S 0043	Shorthand	S 0047	350043
41	S 0044	Show scenery (Rental of—)	L 0052	410013
41	S 0045	Shows (Production of—)	S 0038	410030
39	S 0046	Sightseeing [tourism]	V 0031	390025
41	S 0047	Sign language interpretation	I 0048	410105
37	S 0048	Signs (Painting or repair of—)	E 0041	370040
40	S 0049	Silkscreen printing	S 0021	400115
40	S 0050	Silver-plating	A 0098	400007
40	S 0051	Skin dressing	P 0018	400047
40	S 0052	Slaughtering of animals	A 0001	400094
43	S 0053	Snack-bars	R 0073	430108
37	S 0054	Snow-making services (Artificial—)	E 0034	370123
42	S 0055	Software design (Computer—)	E 0014	420139
42	S 0056	Software (Rental of computer—)	L 0063	420159
42	S 0057	Software (Updating of computer—)	L 0114	420140
44	S 0058	Solarium services	S 0028	440201
40	S 0059	Soldering	S 0030	400011
40	S 0060	Sorting of waste and recyclable material [transformation]	T 0096	400116
41	S 0061	Sound recordings (Rental of—)	L 0093	410018
36	S 0062	Sponsorship (Financial—)	P 0012	360071
35	S 0063	Sponsorship search	R 0017	350102
41	S 0064	Sport camp services	C 0011	410071
41	S 0065	Sports equipment (Rental of—), except vehicles	L 0095	410066
41	S 0066	Sports events (Timing of—)	C 0049	410073
41	S 0067	Stadium facilities (Rental of—)	L 0080	410067
41	S 0068	Stage scenery (Rental of—)	T 0045	410032
36	S 0069	Stamp appraisal	E 0065	360064
35	S 0070	Statements of accounts (Drawing up of—)	R 0046	350016
35	S 0071	Statistics (Compilation of—)	E 0075	350100
39	S 0072	Stevedoring	A 0014	390093
36	S 0073	Stock exchange quotations	C 0138	360067
36	S 0074	Stocks and bonds brokerage	C 0152	360043
39	S 0075	Storage	E 0044	390034
39	S 0076	Storage (Boat—)	E 0045	390071
39	S 0077	Storage containers (Rental of—)	L 0050	390080
39	S 0078	Storage information	I 0033	390076
39	S 0079	Storage of goods	D 0018	390028
39	S 0080	Storage (Physical—) of electronically-stored data or documents	E 0046	390094
37	S 0081	Street cleaning	N 0011	370124
39	S 0082	Streetcar transport	T 0072	390059
40	S 0083	Stripping finishes	D 0002	400095
37	S 0084	Strong-room maintenance and repair	C 0025	370018
42	S 0085	Studies (Technical project—)	E 0088	420061
41	S 0086	Studios (Movie—)	S 0049	410008
42	S 0087	Styling [industrial design]	S 0051	420165
35	S 0088	Subscriptions (Arranging—) to telecommunication services for others	A 0004	350094
35	S 0089	Subscriptions (Arranging newspaper—) for others	A 0003	350076
41	S 0090	Subtitling	S 0034	410093
37	S 0091	Supervision (Building construction—)	S 0052	370031
36	S 0092	Surety services	C 0022	360018
44	S 0093	Surgery (Plastic—)	C 0047	440156
44	S 0094	Surgery (Tree—)	C 0046	440166
42	S 0095	Surveying	E 0098	420193
42	S 0096	Surveys (Geological—)	E 0097	420062
42	S 0097	Surveys (Land—)	L 0010	420079
42	S 0098	Surveys (Oil-field—)	E 0094	420063
37	S 0099	Swimming-pool maintenance	E 0054	370129

Cl.	SERIAL No. (E)	INDICATION OF SERVICES	SERIAL No. (F)	BASIC No.
41	S 0100	Symposiums (Arranging and conducting of—)	O 0043	410072
35	S 0101	Systemization of information into computer databases	S 0058	350081

Cl.	SERIAL No. (E)	INDICATION OF SERVICES	SERIAL No. (F)	BASIC No.

Cl.	SERIAL No. (E)	INDICATION OF SERVICES	SERIAL No. (F)	BASIC No.
40	T 0001	Tailoring	T 0001	400053
40	T 0002	Tanning	T 0002	400054
44	T 0003	Tattooing	T 0004	440197
35	T 0004	Tax preparation	D 0005	350073
39	T 0005	Taxi transport	T 0006	390058
40	T 0006	Taxidermy	T 0005	400055
41	T 0007	Teaching	E 0011	410017
42	T 0008	Technical research	R 0031	420040
38	T 0009	Telecommunication channels (Providing —) for teleshopping services	F 0038	380042
38	T 0010	Telecommunication (Information about —)	I 0028	380027
35	T 0011	Telecommunication services (Arranging subscriptions to —) for others	A 0004	350094
38	T 0012	Telecommunications routing and junction services	A 0012	380038
38	T 0013	Teleconferencing services	T 0016	380039
38	T 0014	Telegrams (Communications by —)	C 0079	380008
38	T 0015	Telegrams (Transmission of —)	T 0083	380006
38	T 0016	Telegraph services	T 0020	380007
35	T 0017	Telemarketing services	S 0026	350107
44	T 0018	Telemedicine services	T 0021	440198
35	T 0019	Telephone answering for unavailable subscribers	R 0061	350074
38	T 0020	Telephone (Communications by —)	C 0080	380010
37	T 0021	Telephone installation and repair	T 0022	370084
38	T 0022	Telephone services	T 0024	380009
38	T 0023	Teleshopping services (Providing telecommunication channels for —)	F 0038	380042
35	T 0024	Television advertising	P 0140	350044
38	T 0025	Television broadcasting	D 0038	380005
35	T 0026	Television commercials	P 0140	350044
41	T 0027	Television entertainment	D 0061	410031
41	T 0028	Television programmes (Production of radio and —)	M 0063	410026
41	T 0029	Television sets (Rental of radio and —)	L 0075	410025
38	T 0030	Telex services	T 0032	380011
40	T 0031	Tempering (Metal —)	T 0095	400043
42	T 0032	Testing (Material —)	E 0061	420058
35	T 0033	Testing (Psychological —) for the selection of personnel	S 0018	350090
40	T 0034	Textile fireproofing	I 0001	400037
40	T 0035	Textile mothproofing	T 0061	400059
42	T 0036	Textile testing	T 0040	420109
40	T 0037	Textile treating	T 0043	400058
40	T 0038	Textiles (Applying finishes to —)	A 0090	400005
41	T 0039	Texts (Publication of —), other than publicity texts	P 0126	410016
41	T 0040	Texts (Writing of —), other than publicity texts	R 0041	410184
35	T 0041	Texts (Writing of publicity —)	R 0042	350099
41	T 0042	Theatre productions	R 0065	410029
44	T 0043	Therapy services	T 0046	440205
41	T 0044	Ticket agency services [entertainment]	B 0027	410183
40	T 0045	Timber felling and processing	A 0002	400067
36	T 0046	Timber (Financial evaluation of standing —)	E 0068	360105
42	T 0047	Timber (Quality evaluation of standing —)	E 0089	420213
41	T 0048	Timing of sports events	C 0049	410073
40	T 0049	Tin-plating	E 0077	400027
37	T 0050	Tires (Retreading of —)	R 0014	370077
37	T 0051	Tires (Vulcanization of —) [repair]	V 0042	370113
36	T 0052	Tokens of value (Issue of —)	E 0021	360065
37	T 0053	Toner cartridges (Refilling of —)	R 0015	370130
43	T 0054	Tourist homes	M 0009	430071
39	T 0055	Tours (Arranging of —)	O 0032	390050
39	T 0056	Towing	R 0052	390054
41	T 0057	Toy rental	L 0061	410197
35	T 0058	Trade fairs (Organization of-) for commercial or advertising purposes	F 0025	350082
39	T 0059	Traffic information	I 0029	390098
41	T 0060	Training (Animal —)	D 0066	410005
41	T 0061	Training (Practical —) [demonstration]	F 0032	410061
39	T 0062	Tram transport	T 0072	390059
35	T 0063	Transcription	T 0074	350045
36	T 0064	Transfer (Electronic funds —)	T 0075	360058
41	T 0065	Translation	T 0058	410104
38	T 0066	Transmission (Facsimile —)	T 0082	380026
38	T 0067	Transmission of digital files	T 0078	380047
38	T 0068	Transmission of greeting cards online	T 0077	380046
38	T 0069	Transmission of messages and images (Computer aided —)	T 0080	380024
38	T 0070	Transmission of telegrams	T 0083	380006
39	T 0071	Transport	N 0003	390048
39	T 0072	Transport and storage of trash	T 0090	390064
39	T 0073	Transport and storage of waste	T 0090	390064
39	T 0074	Transport brokerage	C 0149	390073
39	T 0075	Transport by pipeline	O 0007	390041
39	T 0076	Transport of travellers	V 0041	390063
39	T 0077	Transport reservation	T 0093	390083
39	T 0078	Transportation information	I 0031	390077
39	T 0079	Transportation logistics	L 0115	390101
39	T 0080	Transporting furniture	M 0041	390047
39	T 0081	Travel reservation	V 0039	390084
36	T 0082	Travellers' checks [cheques] (Issuing of —)	E 0023	360020
39	T 0083	Travellers (Escorting of —)	A 0009	390002
39	T 0084	Travellers (Transport of —)	V 0041	390063
44	T 0085	Tree planting for carbon offsetting purposes	P 0067	440206
44	T 0086	Tree surgery	C 0046	440166
39	T 0087	Truck (Railway —) rental	L 0092	390046
36	T 0088	Trusteeship	F 0009	360028
41	T 0089	Tuition	E 0011	410017
44	T 0090	Turkish baths	B 0004	440019
35	T 0091	Typing	D 0001	350022
37	T 0092	Tyres (Retreading of —)	R 0014	370077

Cl.	SERIAL No. (E)	INDICATION OF SERVICES	SERIAL No. (F)	BASIC No.
37	T 0093	Tyres (Vulcanization of—) [repair]	V 0042	370113

Cl.	SERIAL No. (E)	INDICATION OF SERVICES	SERIAL No. (F)	BASIC No.

Cl.	SERIAL No. (E)	INDICATION OF SERVICES	SERIAL No. (F)	BASIC No.
37	U 0001	Umbrella repair	P 0008	370065
45	U 0002	Undertaking	P 0076	450057
37	U 0003	Underwater construction	S 0032	370030
42	U 0004	Underwater exploration	E 0103	420167
37	U 0005	Underwater repair	R 0059	370111
39	U 0006	Underwater salvage	S 0011	390085
39	U 0007	Unloading cargo	D 0003	390026
35	U 0008	Updating of advertising material	M 0051	350027
37	U 0009	Upholstering	R 0049	370067
37	U 0010	Upholstery repair	C 0015	370017
42	U 0011	Urban planning	P 0064	420192

Cl.	SERIAL No. (E)	INDICATION OF SERVICES	SERIAL No. (F)	BASIC No.

Cl.	SERIAL No. (E)	INDICATION OF SERVICES	SERIAL No. (F)	BASIC No.
36	V 0001	Valuables (Deposits of—)	D 0019	360066
39	V 0002	Valuables (Guarded transport of—)	T 0086	390062
36	V 0003	Valuation of standing timber (Financial—)	E 0068	360105
42	V 0004	Valuation of standing timber (Quality—)	E 0089	420213
36	V 0005	Valuations (Fiscal—)	E 0096	360025
37	V 0006	Varnishing	V 0020	370086
37	V 0007	Vehicle breakdown assistance [repair]	V 0007	370089
39	V 0008	Vehicle breakdown assistance [towing]	V 0006	390007
37	V 0009	Vehicle cleaning	N 0012	370087
37	V 0010	Vehicle lubrication [greasing]	G 0022	370049
37	V 0011	Vehicle maintenance	V 0008	370085
37	V 0012	Vehicle polishing	P 0074	370072
39	V 0013	Vehicle rental	L 0088	390044
42	V 0014	Vehicle roadworthiness testing	C 0129	420195
37	V 0015	Vehicle service stations [refuelling and maintenance]	S 0045	370083
37	V 0016	Vehicle wash	L 0007	370055
35	V 0017	Vending machines (Rental of—)	L 0053	350089
36	V 0018	Verification (Check [cheque]—)	V 0019	360053
44	V 0019	Vermin exterminating for agriculture, horticulture and forestry	D 0031	440168
37	V 0020	Vermin exterminating, other than for agriculture	D 0030	370091
44	V 0021	Veterinary assistance	A 0103	440111
41	V 0022	Videotape editing	M 0062	410090
41	V 0023	Videotape film production	P 0100	410074
41	V 0024	Videotapes (Rental of—)	L 0039	410069
41	V 0025	Videotaping	E 0037	410106
44	V 0026	Visagists' services	V 0030	440203
41	V 0027	Vocational guidance [education or training advice]	O 0044	410102
41	V 0028	Vocational retraining	R 0039	410195
38	V 0029	Voice mail services	M 0032	380045
40	V 0030	Vulcanization [material treatment]	V 0043	400101
37	V 0031	Vulcanization of tires [tyres] [repair]	V 0042	370113

Cl.	SERIAL No. (E)	INDICATION OF SERVICES	SERIAL No. (F)	BASIC No.

Cl.	SERIAL No. (E)	INDICATION OF SERVICES	SERIAL No. (F)	BASIC No.
37	W 0001	Wallpapering	P 0085	370064
37	W 0002	Warehouse construction and repair	E 0048	370041
39	W 0003	Warehouses (Rental of—)	L 0094	390035
39	W 0004	Warehousing	E 0044	390034
40	W 0005	Warping [looms]	O 0045	400046
37	W 0006	Wash (Vehicle—)	L 0007	370055
37	W 0007	Washing	L 0009	370057
37	W 0008	Washing of linen	L 0008	370056
40	W 0009	Waste and trash (Destruction of—)	D 0033	400105
40	W 0010	Waste and trash (Incineration of—)	I 0017	400106
40	W 0011	Waste and trash (Recycling of—)	R 0038	400068
40	W 0012	Waste treatment [transformation]	T 0067	400097
37	W 0013	Watch repair (Clock and—)	H 0006	370051
42	W 0014	Water analysis	A 0071	420216
39	W 0015	Water distribution	D 0055	390030
39	W 0016	Water supplying	A 0017	390003
40	W 0017	Water treating	E 0002	400025
40	W 0018	Waterproofing (Cloth—)	I 0008	400036
42	W 0019	Weather forecasting	I 0037	420076
44	W 0020	Weed killing	D 0032	440171
37	W 0021	Wells (Drilling of—)	F 0029	370114
37	W 0022	Window cleaning	N 0010	370045
40	W 0023	Window tinting treatment, being surface coating	C 0072	400065
37	W 0024	Windows (Installation of doors and—)	I 0045	370128
38	W 0025	Wire service	A 0046	380012
38	W 0026	Wireless broadcasting	D 0040	380048
40	W 0027	Woodworking	B 0034	400009
40	W 0028	Wool treating	L 0002	400039
35	W 0029	Word processing	T 0066	350075
42	W 0030	Works of art (Authenticating—)	A 0115	420132
40	W 0031	Works of art (Framing of—)	E 0028	400084
41	W 0032	Workshops (Arranging and conducting of—) [training]	O 0037	410076
39	W 0033	Wrapping of goods	E 0027	390086
44	W 0034	Wreath making	C 0095	440037
35	W 0035	Writing of publicity texts	R 0042	350099
41	W 0036	Writing of texts, other than publicity texts	R 0041	410184

Cl.	SERIAL No. (E)	INDICATION OF SERVICES	SERIAL No. (F)	BASIC No.
41	Z 0001	Zoological garden services	J 0004	410033

Cl.	SERIAL No. (E)	INDICATION OF SERVICES	SERIAL No. (F)	BASIC No.